MIND AND IMAGINATION

IN ARISTOTLE

MICHAEL V. WEDIN

MIND AND IMAGINATION

IN ARISTOTLE

YALE UNIVERSITY PRESS

NEW HAVEN AND LONDON

Designed by Jo Aerne and set in Bembo type by Brevis
Press, Bethany, Connecticut. Printed in the United States
of America by Vail-Ballou Press, Binghamton, New York.

Library of Congress Cataloging-in-Publication Data
Wedin, Michael V. (Michael Vernon) 1943–
Mind and imagination in Aristotle / Michael V. Wedin.
    p. cm. Bibliography: p. Includes index.
ISBN 0–300–04231–0 (alk. paper)
    1. Aristotle—Contributions in philosophy of psychol-
ogy. 1. Aristotle—Contributions in philosophy of
imagination. 3. Psychology—History. 4. Imagination
(Philosophy)—History.
I. Title.
B491.P8W33 1988   128'.2'0924—dc19   88–11092
                                        CIP

The paper in this book meets the guidelines for perma-
nence and durability of the Committee on Production
Guidelines for Book Longevity of the Council on Library
Resources.

10 9 8 7 6 5 4 3 1

TO J. K.

CONTENTS

PREFACE

The past two decades or so have witnessed a renewal of interest in Aristotle's philosophy of mind. It is no accident that this same period has also seen a resurgence of activity in the philosophy of mind itself. The increase of sophistication in theory and the wealth of problems addressed by philosophers of mind have contributed greatly to our growing appreciation of the subtlety of Aristotle's program in such works as *De Anima* and *Parva Naturalia*. The literature is rich in analyses that are informed by contemporary materialist, physicalist, and functionalist stances.

On the whole, the effect of this attention has been salubrious—even where the glove has failed to fit, we have learned something of the shape of the hand. This is not to deny disagreement its place; on the contrary, it recommends even closer scrutiny of contemporary work as a source of insight. Thus, my differences with contending interpretations are at once an acknowledgment of their role in the development of my own views. To some extent, these, in turn, have also been shaped by contemporary discussion, in particular, by what might be called the cognitivist program in psychology and the philosophy of mind. I do not wish to claim that cognitive science fell full-born from Aristotle's hand, but in the course of working through Aristotle's views on psychology, I have persuaded myself that the *form* of explanation he recommends for psychology is arguably cognitivistic, even if its appearance remains outwardly ancient. It is this thesis that I shall be developing and defending in what follows.

Such an account faces at least two problems. One is the danger of making Aristotle younger than he is. I know of no way to deal with the threat of anachronism in advance. One simply has to look at a given account, this one included, and determine how well it tracks the text. There is, however, more than a single way of regarding this. At one extreme there is what might be called "narrow textualism" with its insistence on unwavering allegiance to the literal message: "If Aristotle didn't actually say it, he can't

ix

have meant it." At the opposite pole are what might be called the "wide intentionalists." In their hands the text amounts to an open invitation to interpretation, subject at most to the constraint of consistency. It is, of course, unlikely that there are many pure examples of either of these admittedly ideal types, at least none worth pausing over. The text is neither as radically underdetermined as the wide intentionalist requires nor as determinate as the narrow textualist assumes. Indeed, because virtually no one thinks that text determines doctrine independently of *any* interpretive context, narrow textualists tend to be strict historicists as well. Thus, interpretation is to be constrained by the use of historically close categories only—ideas that were alive in Greek culture of the day, problems that were set by Aristotle's predecessors, and so on.

Although its virtues are apparent, reliance on the historical constraint alone leaves untouched the question of the *kind* or *logical form* of the theory that is being proposed. This is especially crucial in Greek philosophical writing that makes no attempt to hide its preoccupation with theory. Still, it would be rash at best to venture interpretations of Thales, Heraclitus, and even Plato apart from historical and cultural context. Simply reflect on the intricacies involved in fathoming Plato's cosmology. So why, as it seems to me, is Aristotle less demanding on this score? Part of the answer lies in the historical fact that Aristotle authored a philosophical agenda that extends, to some degree, even down to the present day. But, primarily, it concerns the very notion of a theory. With Aristotle we get, for the first time, theories of sufficient complexity and completeness to bear scrutiny on their own. This is particularly true of his "scientific" theories. So it is this feature that allows us to investigate the shared theoretical basis, if any, between ancient and contemporary psychological theories. There is no way to determine a priori a set of adequacy conditions for accounts of this sort— no way, for example, to say in advance when we have changed, rather than explained, the subject matter. Nonetheless, one can make quite good judgments about the plausibility of *proposed* interpretations. This is, perhaps, enough for present purposes, especially if one bears in mind that I am pursuing only one of several complementary strategies for interpretation.

The second problem is a studied skepticism about finding a single account that does justice to the variety of texts that are at our disposal. Some, for example, argue that what Aristotle says about the mind [νοῦς], especially productive mind [νοῦς ποιητικός], resists incorporation into the central theory of *De Anima* and *Parva Naturalia*. And while most commentators have despaired of fitting imagination [φαντασία] into the general account of the soul, some have gone so far as to urge that Aristotle does not even offer us a consistent set of remarks on the subject. As a consequence, most recent work has tended to focus on selected parts of the picture. Although there has been a good deal of progress here, the power and generality of Aristotle's theory has, it seems to me, been underappreciated. I would hope that what follows might go some distance toward remedying this.

Apart from the treatment of particular arguments and passages, some of which stands on its own, the book has two broad aims. One is to offer a defense and exploration of the thesis that Aristotle's account of the mind can profitably be viewed as an early exercise in functionalist or, more exactly, cognitivist explanation. The second is to provide an interpretation of Aristotle's views on imagination and thinking that is consistent with this and that shows why imagination is not, for Aristotle, a standard faculty at all and why thinking is not, in any serious sense, divine. I am interested, frankly, in seeing how far a certain line of interpretation can be pursued. Some who are sympathetic to the first aim would simply assert that Aristotle invented functionalism, and so, of course, the thesis not only is true but requires no argument. Unsurprisingly, however, this is not a settled matter. Indeed, precisely the opposite has been argued by more than one of Aristotle's contemporary expositors. Thus, although the cognitivist reading will ultimately turn on its explanatory usefulness in the book as a whole, I devote some time in the first chapter to defusing at least one recent argument against the very possibility of such an account. In the main, however, chapter 1 focuses on the general shape of Aristotle's psychology and its place among the theoretical sciences. This will, of course, give us only a partial view of Aristotle's theory. One factor that seems crucial to the full picture is the global role played by imagination [φαντασία].

Chapter 2 expounds Aristotle's official theory of imagination, what I am calling the "canonical theory of imagination." This theory, which is introduced in De Anima III.3, fits nicely with a functionalist reading. In particular, I argue that imagination is not a faculty in its own right but rather subserves the operation of full-fledged faculties in the sense that images [φαντάσματα] are required as the means by which such a faculty is able to represent its object in complete intentional acts. Aristotle's theory then takes on a distinctly cognitivist flavor when we add the fact that, besides representations, the language of the theory appears to countenance internal structures that interpret them.

The view of imagination I am proposing diverges from that of almost all recent writers on the topic and carries with it considerable interpretive demands. In finding in De Anima III.3 a canonical theory of imagination, I am not only isolating the account that admittedly best suits a cognitivist theory of mind but also giving it an importance over other things Aristotle says, or appears to say, about φαντασία. And it is well known that Aristotle does have other things to say on the topic, some of which seems, prima facie at least, incompatible with the canonical theory. So chapter 3 collects and deals with problems of divergence and shows that what Aristotle says generally about imagination can be interpreted in light of the canonical theory.

Chapter 4 explores, on this basis, the relation between thought and imagination. Φαντασία has a role in thought because it has a role in all cognitive or quasi-cognitive operations, but it cannot be the same as thought because it is not a faculty at all. Here the representational role of images provides the link. It also turns out that language may play a crucial role, particularly in accounting for acquisition of the materials for thinking, namely, τὰ νοήματα (thoughts or concepts).

Providing Aristotle with a thoroughly naturalistic account of the soul's operations is recommended by his characterization of psychology as a part of physics. It is also a desideratum in its own right—at least, for those of us with a lingering fondness for desert landscapes. Thus, chapter 5 addresses an especially vexed issue: the status of De Anima III.5's νοῦς ποιητικός (productive mind). I argue that the mind of De Anima III.4 and 5 fits the cognitivist account in the sense that it must have a functional organization that explains the fact that from a ready stock of concepts persons are able to produce thoughts autonomously and spontaneously. If the first falls to receptive mind (the mind that becomes each thing), it is to productive mind (the mind that produces each thing) that autonomy and spontaneity is assigned. Rather than two distinct intellects, these are the sort of lower-level entities or structures familiar from recent psychological theory.

Chapter 6 relates these considerations to questions bearing on the divine mind. In particular, I am concerned to counter the increasingly popular view, dubbed superrationalism in one of its recent guises, that human and divine thought, the thought of Metaphysica XII.9's unmoved mover, are the same in kind. I argue against this partly for the reason that the arguments for the view fail but mainly for the reason that human, but not divine, thought is representational, and so necessarily involves images. In a sense, then, it is imagination, or φαντασία, that holds the key to a unitary account of the soul's cognitive operations.

It will be obvious to anyone familiar with recent literature that much of what I argue runs against contemporary received opinion. Thus, I devote a good deal of attention to major contenders to my view. By the same token I am, of course, indebted to the stimulation I have received from this impressive body of work. The project's first cause, however, can be traced to a seminar on Aristotle's *Ethica Nicomachea* at the University of California, Davis, in the spring of 1978. For better or for worse, I decided that what Aristotle meant by εὐδαιμονία (happiness) and by activity generally could be made clear by a quick look at his theory of mental activity. That was nearly a decade ago and I have been involved, intermittently, in the details of the theory ever since.

Along the way I have, happily, incurred many debts, not the least of which is to the students who listened to and puzzled over my interpretations of Aristotle. A first, and now ancient, draft was read with care by Deborah Modrak some eight years ago, and I have received encouragement and assistance throughout from a number of my colleagues at Davis, particularly John Malcolm and Neal Gilbert. Some of the ideas in chapter 5 were aired at a West Coast Aristotelian Society meeting at Berkeley in the spring of 1983 and have appeared, somewhat differently shaped, under the title "Tracking Aristotle's ΝΟΥΣ," in Donagan, Perovich, and Wedin (1986). A section of chapter 6 was read to the fourth annual Classics-Philosophy Colloquium in Ancient Philosophy at the University of California, Berkeley, in 1985, and a mix of different material from chapters 5 and 6 was tried out on a receptive audience at Stanford University in late spring of 1986. In all these forums I have received helpful and sympathetic criticism. Perhaps even more important has been the happy circumstance of finding myself in the midst of a genuine community of scholars on the West Coast whose tolerance for the exegesis of Aristotelian texts is exceeded only by their good humor and unfailing spirit of cooperation. I can hardly mention them all, but Alan Code, Julius Moravcsik, Anthony Long, John Driscoll, David Glidden, Richard McKirahan, Michael Wigodsky, Henry Mendell, Bruce Rosenstock, Jim Bogen, Timothy Roche, Charles Young, and, as a visitor, Mary Louise Gill, have all, in one way or another, left their marks on my argument—certainly for the better even where disagreement remains.

There are a number of less local, but no less important, debts. Three in particular bear mention. Over the years I have benefited from the friendship and critical counsel of Michael Frede and Ian Mueller. In different ways their influence has shaped what is best in the book. Its excesses, which they will be quick to spot, remain, I fear, entirely mine. And, finally, it is only fitting to register long overdue thanks to Charles Drekmeier of Stanford University, whose inspiration at the start has left its mark, even where its outward form has changed.

At Davis thanks are due to my research assistants, Kyle Turner, Shona Kelly, and Ms. Melinda Campbell, as well as to Mrs. Jacqui Levy, Ms.

Karen Ward, and, especially, Ms. Lesley Byrns of the Department of Philosophy, who mastered the ways of international mail and the mysteries of the UCD Computer Center while I was shipping in material from sabbatical perches in Europe. Their help has been invaluable.

MIND AND IMAGINATION

IN ARISTOTLE

I

ARISTOTLE ON THE
SCIENCE OF THE SOUL

It is a commonplace that Aristotle invented logic—not that he invented logical inference, nor even that he was the first to treat inferences in explicitly logical terms, but rather that he gave us the first virtually complete system of certain kinds of logical inference. It is for this reason that we rank him as the inventor of the *science* of logic. As with logic, so with the soul. From his predecessors Aristotle inherited a wealth of insight and speculation on the nature of the soul, but it was left to him to invent its science. In a series of related works, we are given for the first time a surprisingly systematic account of the nature and interconnection of a wide variety of psychological capacities, processes, and activities. The centerpiece is unquestionably *De Anima*. It contains what might be called Aristotle's general theory of the soul because, while he is cautious about calling it a definition, *De Anima* does attempt a fully general formulation of the soul and an equally broad account of the nature and number of its principal faculties and operations. Subsequent works, principally those that have been collected as the *Parva Naturalia*, apply the general theory to a broad array of psychological phenomena from memory and recollection to dreaming, sleeping, and waking.[1]

The systematic nature of his account, however, is not the only reason that Aristotle qualifies as the founder of psychology. Another concerns its style. It will be instructive to approach this from a more contemporary standpoint—in order to illuminate, not assimilate, the ancient account. Nowadays, it is fairly common to require of a psychological theory that it relate the ordinary commonsense behavior of a person to underlying phys-

---

1. The lead essay of the *Parva Naturalia, De Sensu,* deals with perception and so should perhaps be seen less as an application of the theory of *De Anima* than as an extension of its remarks on perception.

iological states and processes.[2] Typically, we think of persons as things that, for example, possess beliefs and desires, experience pains and pleasures, and initiate actions. This is part of our commonsense notion of a person. Although arguably the most deeply imbedded, it is still only one way of describing the person. In effect, we are describing a system of a certain kind, namely, a system with beliefs, desires, and a host of other intentional attitudes. It has, thus, become standard to speak of such descriptions as capturing the person at the intentional level and so of regarding the person as an *intentional system*.[3] I shall sometimes adopt that idiom here. But the person can also be regarded in strictly physiological terms. Thus, we can speak of descriptions at the physiological or physical level or, alternatively, we can regard the person as a *physical system*. From this perspective the task of a psychological theory will be to relate descriptions at the intentional level to descriptions at the physiological level or, more dramatically, to explain how one and the same thing can be both an intentional and a physical system.[4]

According to one view, favored by physiologically minded psychologists, a successful theory will provide more or less direct correlations between types of intentional-level behavior and types of processes or states at the physiological level. Here there is no intervening level of explanation. For cognitively minded psychologists, on the other hand, there is an explanatory gap between the intentional and the physiological levels. Between public behavior and physical process there is room for the question of how an entity is to be organized or designed in order to recognize faces, prove geometric theorems, play chess, and so on. The explanation is said to be cognitivistic because the target ability or performance is explained by appeal to various internal capacities and operations that are themselves cognitively endowed. An explanatory circle is avoided because the intentional-level performance, say, recognizing a face, is broken down into a number of simpler performances, none of which by itself counts as face recognition but all of which together manage the operation. We are to think of these performances as subroutines that go on at a lower level of the system. Each of these can, in turn, be further decomposed until, ideally, we reach a system description capable of direct realization in some kind of hardware.

2. This oversimplifies. Behaviorists, for example, would claim that psychology has available only empirically derived correlations between behavior and external circumstances. Behaviorists, thus, reject the possibility that much can be said about how internal states play a causal role in behavior. But this is not a view that Aristotle has much sympathy for, so we shall merely mention it here.

3. See, for example, Dennett (1978a). I give references by author's name and date. Full citations are in the References.

4. Psychologists are, of course, interested in organisms other than persons. In the interests of simplicity and because the case of persons is the one that is relevant here, I shall, for the most part, treat the notion of a psychological system as coextensive with that of a person.

For the cognitivist what is crucial is explaining how a system is designed or organized to accomplish tasks of a given sort, and this is usually held to be independent of whatever material realizes the design—be it gray matter or silicon and chips. I shall have relatively little to say here concerning Aristotle's opinion on the latitude permitted the material realization of a given form. Although he is certainly sensitive to the question—he says, for example, that saws must be of relatively inert material and that the eye need only be realized in matter that subserves and so preserves the function (*De Sensu* 438b6–9)—there simply is no clear way to decide how far he would be willing to go in the direction of alternative realizations. Whatever his attitude here, it is, I think, at least clear that Aristotle shares with the cognitivist the view that what is essential to the soul is its design or organization and that this is to be characterized at a fairly abstract level.

If we take the psychological works as a whole, *De Sensu*'s distinctly physiological emphasis suggests that the difference between *De Anima* and the *Parva Naturalia* consists in the fact that the former shows little interest in physiological details. It would, however, be misleading to see the two works simply as offering introductory and detailed treatments, respectively. What needs to be appreciated is the fact that the theory of *De Anima* is formulated at a surprisingly abstract level. Although it discusses the relation of the soul and its parts to physical structures, it does so in terms that are entirely general and that display scant interest in the specific nature of these structures. In short, the question of what sort of material the soul is realized in does not appear to play a central role in *De Anima*. What does play such a role, I will argue, is the notion of the soul as a functional or cognitive system. Certainly, this turns out to be the case for that part of the soul in virtue of which the person thinks.

On the interpretation I shall be exploring, a governing assumption of Aristotle's psychology is that there is an important explanatory gap between the intentional and physiological levels. This is already evident in Aristotle's discussion of psychology as a branch of physics. That discussion also makes clear that Aristotle has doubts about closing the gap simply by explaining psychological phenomena in strictly physical terms and that one task of the psychological works is to show how to close it in a satisfactory manner. Thus, he appears to eschew explanatory reductionism and to leave room for cognitive structures to play a role in psychological explanation.

I. PSYCHOLOGY AS A BRANCH OF PHYSICS

So let us begin with some remarks on Aristotle's classification of the sciences. In *Metaphysica* VI.1 Aristotle identifies three theoretical sciences and individuates them in terms of three kinds of objects. Theology studies what is separate and changeless, physics what is separate but not changeless, and mathematics what is changeless but not separate. Since by "separate" Aristotle here means what can exist on its own, not what can exist apart from matter, both physics and theology study substances, the one sensible substances such as plants and animals, the other insensible substances such as the unmoved mover. Mathematics, on the other hand, does not study either kind of substance, at least not in any straightforward way, but rather focuses on certain properties of sensible substances, for example, straightness, triangularity, or oddness. Such properties neither exist separately nor are in fact changeless, for an object's shape or volume may change or vary and there may be no actual straight lines. The mathematician simply eliminates such unwanted features of actual objects and so regards them as perfectly exemplifying the properties he is investigating. In effect, he treats them *as if* they were changeless and separate [ἦ ἀκίνητα καὶ ἦ χωριστά at 1026a9–10] with respect to the property of interest. He does this by separating them in thought or, as some prefer to say, by abstracting from change and matter.[5] From Aristotle's point of view this procedure is entirely legitimate because, although surfaces, volumes, lines, and points are always found in physical substances, the mathematician does not study them as the limits *of* the physical bodies they characterize. Such ontological facts do not affect the correctness or scope of his explanations. The account of straightness, concavity, and so on, proceeds smoothly precisely because it does not require mention of matter.

When we turn to physics, on the other hand, the situation is rather different. Unlike theology its objects are subject to change and, hence, they

---

5. One must be careful here. The separation is connected with Aristotle's notion of abstraction, but historically this has been given more than one reading. On the one hand, it has been seen as abstracting from or eliminating matter, on the other hand, as simply eliminating those of an object's properties that are irrelevant to its role as a mathematical object. The first view, favored by Philoponus (1887) and Simplicius (1882a), promotes the opinion that Aristotle's mathematical objects are properties such as diagonality and triangularity. The second, and more pleasing, view treats them as physical objects regarded in a certain way, namely, as exemplifying specific mathematical properties. (For more on this, see the helpful account in Mueller [1970]).

It is, further, a matter of some discussion whether, as Mueller (1970) and Annas (1976) urge, Aristotle denies that physical objects perfectly instantiate mathematical properties. (See, for instance, Lear's (1982) countervailing argument.) For our purposes the issue need not be decided. Indeed, the mathematician need not concern himself with the question at all, for in either case he may regard objects as perfect exemplars and this is sufficient for his mathematics. It is an additional question whether his abstraction agrees with reality or is an operation on it. It is worth noting, in this connection, that Aristotle stresses that the separation is separation *from change,* and, hence, separation from matter appears to enter only as a consequence of this. Thus, his singling out change as the focus of abstraction may be directed mainly at the fact that mathematical knowledge consists of *eternal* truths.

must be material. Aristotle is not just insisting on the ontological point that what falls under an account suitable for physics *be* something that is material. The same could be said for objects of mathematics. Yet here, as Aristotle says at *Physica* II.2, 193b34–35, "it makes no difference nor does any falsity result" if the objects are separated in thought from change [χωριστὰ τῇ νοήσει κινήσεως] or, we may presume, from matter. Not so in the case of physics, however, because the material nature of what the student of physics investigates is somehow essential to the adequacy of his account. So mathematics and physics agree on an ontological point but diverge on a point about what counts as an adequate explanation. From the ontological perspective—that is, from the perspective of separateness from matter—the objects of mathematics are no more separate than those of physics. Nonetheless, the mathematician, but not the physicist, can separate his objects in thought. Since Aristotle has just insisted that such objects are not actually separate, separability in thought concerns explanatory adequacy. For the case of mathematics, then, Aristotle can be seen as giving us ontological reduction without explanatory reduction. Explanations in mathematics are autonomous with respect to the objects that instantiate mathematical properties, yet, unlike the case in Platonism, this does not require the existence of separate mathematical objects.[6]

Why exactly is the physicist barred from abstracting his objects, and, in particular, does this mean that the physicist is free to provide reductionist explanations? We can approach these points by recalling that Aristotle is fond of reminding his reader that the physicist must investigate his objects as one would investigate the essence of snubness. What stands behind this rather curious recommendation is not simply the recognition that the physicist studies the world qua material object. The connection is more intimate, and Aristotle stresses this by invoking what is almost a semantic point to make a point about worldly objects. To understand "snub" or "snubness" is ipso facto to understand that one is talking about noses. But the term applies to a nose not because the nose has the determinate property of snubness but because it has the property of concavity. For snubness *is* concavity in a nose or, to use the more explanatory idiom, snubness is a characteristic of noses that develop in a concave fashion.[7] Concavity itself, on

6. This is admittedly a simplification of what is only one kind of interpretation of Aristotle's views on mathematics. See, for more, Mueller (1970) and Annas (1976) and, for a different account, Lear (1982).

7. Because *snub* is defined as concave nose, talk of a snub nose would, strictly speaking, be talk of a concave nose nose. Aristotle adds (the text is *Metaphysica* VII.5, 1030b28–1031a1) that if one then also holds that snub nose = concave nose, it follows that concave nose nose = snub nose nose and with that an infinite regress ensues. For, by the definition of *snub*, snub nose nose = concave nose nose nose. Thus, snubness cannot apply to a nose as a

the other hand, is not an essentially realized property or, in Aristotle's terms, an essentially realized form. Virtually anything can be or become concave. This reflects the fact that the definition of concavity places no constraints on what material the property can be realized in. So concavity, as opposed to snubness, can be separated in thought and, hence, is suited for study by the mathematician. Not so snubness. Thus, it parades as a clear model of how the objects and properties of physics are to be studied.

Like the snub, the very accounts of natural objects essentially involve reference to matter. One cannot say, at least not scientifically, what a given natural object is without saying something about its material structure. In *Physica* II.1–2 the point is expressed in the canonical idiom of form and matter. What the physicist studies, primarily, are the principles and causes of natural things, that is, the principles and causes of their changing into and remaining what they essentially are. Although "nature" itself has two chief senses, form and matter, the physicist focuses on the form because it is a thing's form that governs and explains its natural behavior. Form is primary in the sense that the identity of a natural process depends on specifying its end and this requires mention of form. Suppose, for example, that φ is the process that takes an acorn into an oak. Aristotle's point appears to be that one cannot say what kind of a process φ is without mentioning oakhood, the form that is realized at the final stage of the process. But explaining how form governs a natural process or constitutes the essence of a natural object requires saying what kind of matter this is, or could be, realized in. Every natural process or object has certain material conditions and these are determined by the form. Hence, mention of matter can be omitted only at the cost of explanatory adequacy.

We might, then, say that the physicist is interested in forms that are *essentially realized* in some matter or other. This holds even when the object under investigation is the soul. As *Metaphysica* VI.1 goes on to say, "it is clear also that it falls to the student of physics [φυσικός] to investigate a certain sort of soul, namely, whatever is not without matter [ὄση μὴ ἄνευ τῆς ὕλης]" (1026a5–6). This passage leaves the point without comment, but it is clear how it is to be developed. When Aristotle introduces us to his official view of the soul in *De Anima* II, it appears as the form of a natural body with the potentiality for life. Since definitions are always accounts of a thing's form, to define the soul is to give a certain kind of account of one kind of essentially realized form—on the assumption, of course, that psychology is a part of physics. This assumption, which remains tacit in the

determinate property in the way that concavity applies. (I reserve comment on the argument's cogency.)

Metaphysica passage, is explicitly endorsed in *De Anima* I.1 where it plays a major role in shaping the overall strategy of the book. And, of course, it is *De Anima* that is of principal interest to us. So let us move to that work.

De Anima opens by advertising the value of its investigations not just to truth generally but especially to the understanding of nature. The discussion that immediately concerns us begins at 403a2–4 where Aristotle asks whether all properties of the soul [πάθη τῆς ψυχῆς] are common also to the body or whether some of them are peculiar [ἴδιον] to the soul? A property will be peculiar to the soul if, and only if, it applies to the soul and to the soul only. If at least one property is peculiar, then it is possible for the soul to be separated. Let us defer for the moment full discussion of this notion of separation.[8] The only point we need to understand now is that were a part of the soul separable, presumably from matter, it would not fall within the study of physics. The best candidate, says Aristotle, would seem to be thinking [νοεῖν], although even it will depend on the body should it turn out to involve imagination. So the question is whether there are any essentially mental or nonphysical predicates, that is, predicates whose subjects neither are nor depend on entities, states, or processes that themselves take physical predicates.

Although discussion of thought is deferred until the third book of *De Anima*, Aristotle continues in *De Anima* I.1 by immediately entertaining the proposition that all affections of the soul involve the body [τὰ τῆς ψυχῆς πάθη πάντα εἶναι μετὰ σώματος] and, thus, that "it is clear that the affections are principles involving matter [λόγοι ἔνυλοι]. Hence, their definitions are like: Anger is a particular movement of a body of such and such a kind [κίνησίς τις τοῦ τοιουδὶ σώματος], or a part or potentiality of it, resulting from this thing and for the sake of that" (403a25–27). We have here one paradigm governing the relation between mental or psychological properties and the body. If the example is to be generalized, a definition of a given affection of the soul must mention at least three things: a physical process, a cause, and an end. The student of nature is said to define anger in terms of its physiological manifestation, say, the boiling of blood around the heart. For the dialectician, on the other hand, anger is desire for retaliation on account of an unjustifiable harm. Here both end and cause are mentioned. Whereas the first gives only the matter, the dialectician gives only the form and principle [τὸ εἶδος καὶ τὸν λόγον]. But this student of nature, mentioned at 403a31–b1, is presumably untutored in light of Aristotle's final view at the end of the chapter where he is charged with knowing both form and matter. For an account to be complete both are needed because

8. This is discussed further in chapters 5 and 6.

in order for something to serve as a principle of this sort it must be in a certain sort of matter [ἐν ὕλῃ τοιᾳδί at 403b3].⁹

The forms that figure in psychological explanations are, then, essentially realized forms, and thus psychology falls under the science of physics: "the physicist is concerned with everything that is a function or affection of a certain sort of body or a certain sort of matter [ὁ φυσικὸς περὶ ἅπανθ᾽ ὅσα τοῦ τοιουδὶ σώματος καὶ τῆς τοιαύτης ὕλης ἔργα καὶ πάθη]" (403b11–12). As *De Anima*'s first chapter closes, then, we are left with the distinct possibility that all properties and functions of the soul fall within the purview of physics—unless, of course, there are some that are peculiar [ἴδιον] to the soul. At this stage of the investigation, however, this caveat may simply reflect Aristotle's unusual prudence. In any case, when he finally turns to thinking [νοεῖν], the most likely candidate, what we get are a series of chapters (III.4–8) that sketch, or attempt to sketch, a naturalistic account of thinking.¹⁰

Although the physicist may be concerned with the same form as the dialectician, at least for certain cases such as anger, he is not concerned with the form in the same way nor for the same reasons. After all, his domain is still the material world. Thus, at the end of *Physica* II.2 Aristotle asks to what extent the physicist must know the form or essence. The doctor, says Aristotle at 194b9–11, needs to know the form in order to understand the purpose of the physical processes he is investigating. Thus, suppose for a given subject of investigation, say S₁, that we have a physical process, P₁, and a correlated form, F₁. The physicist wants to tell us what goes on at the physical level when S₁ occurs. The objection to omitting mention of F₁ is not just that it leaves the physicist's account incomplete. Rather, it leaves the physicist with no account at all because the identity of P₁ depends on F₁. Without mention of the form there is no way of determining or significantly individuating physical processes, no way of even picking out a proper subject of inquiry.¹¹

---

9. Thus, *Metaphysica* VIII.4, 1044b15ff., urges, in the case of sleep, inclusion of the process [πάσχειν] with the formula. To say that sleep is immobility but not to say with respect to what processes the immobility is occasioned, is to fall short in point of explanatory adequacy. So, as 1044b12–13 suggests, we could have a formal definition [τὸ ὡς εἶδος ὁ λόγος] and yet leave matters unclear [ἄδηλος] if we fail to indicate the (presumably, efficient) cause along with the formula [ἐὰν μὴ μετὰ τῆς αἰτίας ἢ ὁ λόγος]. As *Metaphysica* VII.10–13 makes abundantly clear, it is a difficult question whether the efficient cause supplements or is part of the formal definition.

10. This, at least, is what I argue in later chapters, especially 5 and 6.

11. The text, *Physica* II.2, 194b10–13, says that knowing the purpose of certain physical structures requires that the physicist be concerned with things insofar as they are in matter but separable in form [μέχρι τοῦ τίνος ἕνεκα ἕκαστον, καὶ περὶ ταῦτα ἃ ἔστι χωριστὰ μὲν εἴδει, ἐν ὕλῃ δέ]. This is obscured by Hardie and Gaye's Oxford translation which reads "the

As Aristotle puts the point in *Physica* II.2, while accounts of physical phenomena cannot omit matter, neither can they proceed simply in terms of matter [ὥστε οὔτ' ἄνευ ὕλης τὰ τοιαῦτα οὔτε κατὰ τὴν ὕλην at 194a14–15]. We can take the first to warn against the dangers of separating the objects of physics even in thought. We can also read this as asserting a version of reductionism. For it would amount to claiming only that, as far as physics is concerned, what really exist are material objects and processes involving material objects. It does not follow from this, however, that explanations can be reduced to descriptions of material bodies, their properties, positions, and the like. In short, explanatory reduction fails. Thus, even if embracing one sort of reductionism for physics, it appears that Aristotle will reject another.[12] We shall return to the topic of reductionism later. For the moment, however, there is still some scene setting to be done.

2. FORM AND FUNCTION IN THE ARISTOTELIAN SOUL

Aristotle's classification of psychology under physics reflects more than the fact that psychological phenomena cannot exist apart from matter. Part of the point is that explanations of psychological activities and processes must mention matter. Consequently, we ought to expect Aristotle to deploy principles and techniques proper to physics in his explanations of the soul's characteristics and capacities. This, in fact, turns out to be the case, and we shall encounter a number of such instances in the course of this investigation. But psychological explanation does not simply amount to application of principles of Aristotelian physics in a new domain. Because they need to explain, for example, a system's ability to represent objects, psychological explanations are a distinctively cognitivist brand of naturalist explanation. To better see this we need to take a somewhat wider approach

---

physicist is concerned only with things whose forms are separable indeed, but [which] do not exist apart from matter." This is an odd reading of the Greek and, in any case, fails to give us a distinction between the physicist and the mathematician—the announced point of the entire chapter.

12. The account in *Physica* III.1–3 and V.1–4 of a process or κίνησις is itself reductionist to the extent that it denies that processes are part of the world's ultimate ontological furniture. Rather, as the actualization or actuality (to reflect the two lines of interpretation on the issue) of the potential qua potential, a process is analyzed in terms of "more basic" ontological categories such as substance and potentiality. Because the potentiality in question will be the potentiality of a thing to be something else, that is, something actual, the end of a process is essential to its specification and so this reduction will not give us an account that is κατὰ τὴν ὕλην or purely material.

to the issue by looking at the general framework within which Aristotle locates the soul and its operations.

Book I of *De Anima* retails and criticizes a number of views of Aristotle's predecessors. The practice is familiar to his readers. But the book also contains a number of remarks, principally methodological, that he appears to endorse. These contain the first indications of Aristotle's attitude toward psychological theory. At the outset he announces that we should first determine the nature [φύσις] and essence [οὐσία] of the soul and then turn to consider its properties [ὅσα συμβέβηκε περὶ αὐτήν]. Of the latter some might be thought to be peculiar to the soul [τὰ ἴδια πάθη], whereas others belong also to the body. For the moment let us put aside this last distinction and concentrate on that between the essence of the soul and its properties. By the first Aristotle points to the definition of the soul as the form of a body with the potentiality for life. This is the definition that inaugurates his own positive account of the soul in *De Anima* II.1–3. The balance of *De Anima* amounts to an investigation of the various properties of the soul. To get an idea of what this is supposed to look like we can begin with 403a3ff.'s examples of such properties [τὰ πάθη τῆς ψυχῆς]: being angry, wanting, perceiving, and thinking. These are immediately glossed in slightly more exact terms as functions or affections of the soul [τὰ τῆς ψυχῆς ἔργα ἢ παθήματα]. Thus, for simplicity, we may adopt this terminology and speak, intuitively, of the soul as the form of systems that function in certain ways.

If the system is a person, then it is tempting to speak of the soul as performing the various functions that are characteristic of persons. Thus, we might say that the soul is grieved, or rejoices, or perceives, or thinks. But there is a danger here. To say this, says Aristotle, would be like saying that the soul weaves or builds. Rather,

> it is surely better to say not that the soul pities or learns or thinks but rather that the person does so in virtue of the soul [τῇ ψυχῇ] and (one should say this) not because the movement takes place in the soul but because sometimes the movement reaches as far as the soul and sometimes starts from it. Thus, perception starts from particular objects [ἀπὸ τωνδί] while recollection starts from it [ἐκείνης = the soul] and extends to movements or states in the sense organs [ἐπὶ τὰς ἐν τοῖς αἰσθητηρίοις κινήσεις ἢ μονάς].
> (408b13–18)

Several things about this passage merit comment. If we think of the person as a psychological system consisting of a soul and certain physical structures, then Aristotle is recommending that a function or property of the system as a whole be explained in terms of one of its parts or subsystems. Aristotle's admonition against saying that the soul perceives is not a plea for linguistic reform. The idiom is natural enough but will not do when speaking strictly. The point, rather, is that attributing to a part of the system what is properly a function or property of the system as a whole involves mixing of levels.[13] This is true even when the part in question is the one in virtue of which the system as a whole manages the function in question. This is because it is not required that the property or function occur in that part or subsystem (what Aristotle means in requiring that the movement does not take place in the soul) but only that the part figure in a causal explanation of how the system as a whole perceives or recollects, to take the cases at hand. We are urged, in effect, to see the soul as part of the causal structure of the system as a whole.

If we put the matter this way, we can see the connection with Aristotle's doctrine of causes [αἰτίαι]. It is common now to speak of Aristotelian αἰτίαι less as causes than as "becauses," that is, as the proper factors to be mentioned in genuine scientific explanations. Thus, Moravcsik (1975) reads the so-called efficient cause as the source, the material cause as the constituent, the formal cause as the structure, and the end, or final cause as the function. In any given system or phenomenon one or more of these factors may play a role and a fully adequate explanation will be that giving the complete set of causes for the case at hand. Mathematics, for instance, has no place for the source as an explanatory factor, whereas all would figure in explaining what a person is and does. Of these four factors the form or structure is central in the sense that it specifies the essential nature of the system or entity under scrutiny. The function, or end cause specifies what the system does. Thus, to explain what a person is will involve spelling out how it operates (its form) in order to accomplish what it does (its function, or end). And, of course, for Aristotle this involves appeal to the soul as the form of the person's body. Thus, we can think of the soul as what explains how a person is able to exercise a wide variety of intentional functions. And, as we have seen, this amounts to treating the soul as a certain kind of causal structure.[14]

To explain function by form is, so far as we have gone, tantamount to treating the soul as a "black box." If, that is, we simply say that Ortcutt, for example, sees in virtue of his soul, the soul is left as an unanalyzed, internal capacity. There may be nothing wrong with this but it leaves us

13. See Dennett (1978a) for more on this from a contemporary point of view. I have noted that Woodger (1952, 290ff.) contains an elegant warning against the mistake.

14. See Cartwright and Mendell (1984) for some excellent remarks on formal causes and explanatory structure.

without a satisfactory explanation of seeing because the same explanation will be given for hearing, wanting, thinking, and the rest. So Aristotle moves to a new level of analysis. Just as the person, as a system, was decomposed, cognitively speaking, into soul and physical structure so now the soul itself is broken down into finer cognitive units—into the so-called δυνάμεις, or faculties of the soul. To explain, in other words, how the soul manages thinking involves, in this model, appeal to some part of the soul in virtue of which it does this. Or, paralleling the remarks two paragraphs back, rather than saying that the soul thinks, we ought to say that it thinks in virtue of one of its parts, namely the νοητικόν, or that which thinks. But since we know that it is the system as a whole that thinks, the correct thing to say is that the person thinks *in virtue of* the faculty of thought. This is because the soul is a complex of related capacities and not something additional. From this point of view one might think of *De Anima* as a whole as pursuing a top-down strategy familiar to cognitivists: Book II.1–3 simultaneously introduces us to and cautions us against a general definition of the soul. The following chapters then consider more narrowly defined capacities such as touch, seeing, hearing, thinking, desiring, and acting.[15]

Two passages, in particular, support this line of interpretation. The first occurs at 402b9–16, as one of the methodological guidelines of the work. After remarking that there are not many souls but only parts of the soul, Aristotle says that it is difficult to decide which of them are really different from each other [χαλεπὸν δὲ καὶ τούτων διορίσαι ποῖα πέφυκεν ἕτερα ἀλλήλων]. He links this to the methodological question of whether the parts [τὰ μόρια] are to be investigated first or rather their functions [τὰ ἔργα]. And this in turn is linked to the question of whether one should first in-

---

15. Because the definitions of these capabilities will be of the form ". . . is such and such capacity of the soul," they appear to qualify as per se attributes [καθ' αὑτὰ συμβεβηκότα] of the soul. For *Analytica Posteriora* I.4 defines two different per se relations, the second of which applies to the case at hand: (a) A belongs per se$_1$ to B ≡ A occurs in the definition of B; (b) A belongs per se$_2$ to B ≡ B occurs in the definition of A. (For more on this, see Wedin, 1973.) These are also the sort of attributes that figure in demonstrative science (see Tiles, 1983). So when, as we saw three paragraphs back, Aristotle promises that *De Anima* will investigate the essence and the properties [συμβεβηκότα] of the soul, he clearly means to include the soul's per se attributes. It is interesting to note, further, that this is entirely in line with his recommendation to investigate natural objects as one would investigate the snub. For, while *De Anima* understandably stresses the ontological point that the forms physics investigates are essentially realized, elsewhere the snub is used to illustrate the logical point made in *Analytica Posteriora* I.4. In *Metaphysica* VII.5, for example, snub is coupled with odd, which is the star case of a per se$_2$ item in the *Analytica Posteriora* passage. They occur as examples of things that must be defined "by addition" [ἐκ προσθέσεως], namely, snub nose and odd number. Their definitions are definitions "by addition" because they are expressions in which the same thing is said twice (1031a4–5). "Snub" already contains, as it were, "nose" and, hence, to say "snub nose" is tantamount to saying "nose" twice over.

vestigate the corresponding objects of the function [τὰ ἀντικείμενα]. Should one, for example, investigate the object of perception before that which can perceive [τὸ αἰσθητὸν τοῦ αἰσθητικοῦ], and the object of thought before the mind [τὸ νοητὸν τοῦ νοῦ]?

Now it might appear that Aristotle is raising nothing more than a methodological question concerning the best way to do psychology. But in raising the problem of deciding which parts of the soul are different Aristotle is raising a point about the identity or individuation of the various parts or faculties of the soul. This is quite clear from the parallel passage at the beginning of *De Anima* II.4:

> If we are to say what each of them is [τί ἕκαστον αὐτῶν = each of the faculties], i.e., what that which thinks is or that which perceives or that which nourishes, we must first say what thinking [νοεῖν] and perceiving [αἰσθάνεσθαι] are; for activities [ἐνέργειαι] and actions [πράξεις] are prior in definition [κατὰ τὸν λόγον] to faculties [δυνάμεων]. And, if this is so and if yet prior to them their correlate objects should have been investigated, then for the same reason [διὰ τὴν αὐτὴν αἰτίαν] we must first make a determination about these [περὶ ἐκείνων]. (415a16–22)

This is more than a mere methodological recommendation. In order to say *what* each faculty is we need to specify its function and this in turn requires saying toward what objects the function is directed. So this passage makes it clear that faculties are to be *individuated and identified* in terms of functions and, ultimately, objects.[16] I shall call this condition the FFO (faculty/function/object) condition. It is important to bear in mind that the FFO condition is not extensional. An object thought of may be desired as well and what is now remembered was once perceived. What counts as an object of thought, desire, and so on, thus, depends on how the object is described. In effect, FFO proposes that we determine a function by providing a description such that any object satisfying the description counts as an object of the corresponding faculty. So FFO imposes something like a formal object requirement on faculties.[17] The general picture here is that a faculty of the soul is a capacity to (cognitively) receive objects. The exercise or functioning of the faculty is simply the receiving of the object. So it is hardly surprising

---

16. The point appears to be echoed at *Categoriae* 7b23ff., where the object of knowledge [ἐπιστητόν] is said to be prior to knowledge [ἐπιστήμη] and the object of perception [αἰσθητόν] to perception [αἴσθησις].

17. The notion of a formal object is quite tricky. Here I am content to follow Kenny's characterization (1963, 189ff.).

that Aristotle requires that faculties be individuated in terms of their objects. As he says, they are prior to both faculty and function.[18]

If 402b9–16 couches the FFO condition in the more neutral language of a *part* of the soul, 415a16–22 employs the canonical idiom of a capacity or potentiality [δύναμις]. But the picture of a faculty as a capacity is too simple.[19] Already in *De Anima* II.1, at the outset of his positive account, Aristotle had distinguished two kinds of actuality or actualization [ἐντελέχεια], likening one to knowledge [ὡς ἐπιστήμη] and the other to contemplation [ὡς τὸ θεωρεῖν]. The soul is an actuality of the first sort and, thus, is defined as the first actuality of a natural body with the capacity for life [ἡ ψυχή ἐστιν ἐντελέχεια ἡ πρώτη σώματος φυσικοῦ δυνάμει ζωὴν ἔχοντος]. But this account is by its nature introductory. In *De Anima* II.5, Aristotle moves to deepen the account.

The passage of immediate interest,[20] 417a21–b16, I call the Framework Passage because it contains a model of a faculty and its function that provides a framework for a good deal of the psychology. Here is what (part of) the passage says:

> We must make some distinctions concerning potentiality and actuality [περὶ δυνάμεως καὶ ἐντελεχείας], for currently we are speaking of them without qualification [ἁπλῶς]. For, in the first place, something is a knower [ἐπιστῆμόν τι] in the sense that we say a man is a knower because man is one of the things that is a knower and has knowledge; in the second place, something is a knower in the sense that we say that someone who already has knowledge of grammar is a knower. (Each of these is a potential knower [δυνατός] albeit not in the same sense—rather the first is a potential knower because his matter and kind is of this sort [τὸ γένος τοιοῦτον καὶ ἡ ὕλη], the other because he can contemplate, if he wishes [ὁ βουληθεὶς δυνατὸς θεωρεῖν], so long as nothing external prevents him.) In the third place, there is the man who is already contemplating [ὁ ἤδη θεωρῶν], who is actually and in the strongest sense [ἐντελεχείᾳ καὶ κυρίως] knowing this A [τόδε τὸ A].

18. In *Categoriae* 7 Aristotle puts the point by saying that although faculty and object are relatives [τὰ πρός τι], they are not simultaneous by nature [ἅμα τῇ φύσει]. Rather, as he says, the existence of the object of knowledge and perception is independent, respectively, of knowledge and perception themselves.

19. At least for cognitive abilities. Perhaps the nutritive part of the soul satisfies a simpler account.

20. Other parts of *De Anima* II.5 will figure prominently in later chapters. We shall also have occasion to make further use of the present passage.

The announced aim of this passage is to distinguish, in some detail, different sorts of potentiality and actuality, and it proposes to accomplish this by distinguishing three grades of knower:

K1. S is a knower$_1$ $\longleftrightarrow$ S is the sort of thing that is capable$_1$ of developing into a knower$_2$
(S belongs to the appropriate species, and so on);

K2. S is a knower$_2$ $\longleftrightarrow$ S is capable$_2$ of knowing$_3$
(S has actualized$_1$ its capability$_1$ to know$_2$);

K3. S is a knower$_3$ $\longleftrightarrow$ S is contemplating a particular object of thought
(S has actualized$_2$ its capacity$_2$ to know$_3$ or S is exercising its knowledge$_2$).

In *De Anima* II.1 Aristotle merely asserted what he here explains, namely, that the soul is actuality in the way that knowledge is. By K2 this would mean that the soul is a capacity to *do* something. The trouble with this, as we have already seen, is that there is no one thing that counts as the soul's operation. Rather, what the soul does is a function of what its various faculties do. The faculties themselves may be described as actualizations of certain initially given capacities or as developed capacities for seeing, thinking, and the like. The latter, as the soul's proper activity, are a higher sort of actualization of the soul (an actualization$_2$). But this does not constitute the soul's essence; otherwise the sleeping man would cease to be a man. Thus, for Aristotle, a faculty is a certain kind of actualization$_1$ or a capacity$_2$ to perform certain (cognitive) functions and the soul is to be regarded as a complex of such actual capacities. As what is here true for the soul as a whole is true for its various faculties so also what is true for a faculty generally is true for its various employments. Thus, in *De Anima* II.5 the accomplished mathematician has actualized$_1$ his mathematical capacity$_1$ and this is to say that he has acquired a new capacity—the capacity$_2$ to exercise or actualize$_2$ various bits of his knowledge.

Notice that the Framework Passage heeds the FFO condition. For a knower$_2$ is defined in terms of the knower$_3$ and so, ultimately, in terms of the notion of an object of knowledge.[21] Notice, also, that the notions of potentiality and actuality cannot, at least not here, be simply assimilated to the matter-form distinction. For at 412a9–11 Aristotle remarks that "matter is potentiality but form [εἶδος] is actuality and this in two ways, on the one hand, as knowledge is and, on the other hand, as contemplation is." Matter does not figure centrally in FFO and the Framework Passage. Thus,

---

21. For that matter, so is the knower$_1$.

room is left open for a somewhat abstract notion of form insofar as they call for characterizations of psychological entities that need not mention matter. The idea would be that while we can, perhaps, say *what* a given faculty is, we cannot explain *how* it does what it does without bringing matter into the account.[22] There is, in short, more to psychological explanation than definition and this is pretty much the message of the Framework Passage. Something like this may also be at work in *Metaphysica* VII.11, 1036b1ff.'s remark that the material parts in which the form of man is realized are not, properly speaking, parts of the form and the formula.[23] So the essentially realized nature of psychological forms does not, then, conflict with the fact that Aristotle's faculties are conceived of as quite abstract structures.[24] Thus, so far from being material, the soul or, better, its faculties are the *forms of* certain material structures and this in an appropriately abstract manner.

In the Framework Passage form and function are brought very close together. This is unsurprising if the form of a system is defined in terms of its function. We can put the point in a slightly more Aristotelian setting with the help of the following diagram:

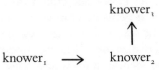

The transition, represented by the horizontal arrow, between a knower₁ and a knower₂ concerns development over time of the faculty in virtue of which S thinks, knows, or whatever.[25] The vertical arrow marks the exercise of

22. The provisional account of *De Anima* I.1, 403a25–27, mentioned above, should be read in light of this point.

23. *De Anima* II.1–2, on the other hand, appears to draw matter into the definition. But this may simply be reflected in Aristotle's uncertainty about calling the result a definition.

24. Indeed, to take Aristotle's favorite case, because a nose is itself a functionally characterized entity, the dependence on it of snub already operates at a first level of abstraction from matter.

25. The horizontal arrow should not be taken to suggest that one could develop into a knower₂ without performing actual noetic acts. It simply represents the transition to such a state, a transition that is different in kind from that represented by the vertical arrow but one whose fine structure will doubtless include performances of noetic acts. This appears to mean either that such performances are not genuine exercises of a faculty or that they somehow coincide with the acquisition of certain kinds of knowledge₂. The first alternative harks back to *Ethica Nicomachea* II.4's distinction between acting in accordance with virtue and acting virtuously because only the second entails that one has acquired virtue. If this makes perfectly good sense where one is considering acquisition of the very faculty itself, the second alternative would appear to cover the acquisition of particular bits of knowledge, and the like, by an already able knower₂.

the developed faculty. So it is in the switch from knower₂ to knower₃ that the intimacy of form and function is located. The knower₃ is, says Aristotle, "the man who is actually and in the strongest sense knowing this particular A [ἐντελεχείᾳ ὢν καὶ κυρίως ἐπιστάμενος τόδε τὸ Α]" (417a28–29), and the transition to this state is rather different from the developmental process required for moving from knower₁ to knower₂ because, in moving to knower₃, a knower₂ simply "passes from having arithmetical or grammatical knowledge but not exercising it to its exercise [μὴ ἐνεργεῖν δέ, εἰς τὸ ἐνεργεῖν], in a different way" (417a32–b1), "for what has knowledge comes to contemplate [θεωροῦν γὰρ γίγνεται τὸ ἔχον τὴν ἐπιστήμην]" (417b5–6). However, the switch is "into itself and into actuality [εἰς αὑτὸ γὰρ ἡ ἐπίδοσις καὶ εἰς ἐντελέχειαν]" (417b6–7) because "the person who reasons is not altered whenever he reasons [διὸ οὐ καλῶς ἔχει λέγειν τὸ φρονοῦν, ὅταν φρονῇ, ἀλλοιοῦσθαι] nor the builder when he builds" (417b8–9).

Form and function enjoy an especially close relation precisely because the actual functioning of a system is the highest manifestation of what it is equipped to do—that is, of its essence or form. It is, to use the Aristotelian idiom, the system's end. This much is clear from the model contained in the Framework Passage. What we do not get there is an account of the causal factors that are involved in a system's changing from actualization₁ to actualization₂. There are two kinds of factors to consider. One is what causes the transition to the actual₂ state and the other is how the system is able to accomplish what is demanded by a given actual₂ state.[26] The first requires that we place the faculty in question in a causal context involving the object of the faculty's function. Sometimes the object will be external, as in the case of perception, sometimes internal, as in the case of thought. But in all cases it appears that what causes the faculty's actual functioning is the object of the function. We shall have more to say about this later. The second factor concerns what internal structure we need to attribute to the system in order to explain how it can accomplish perceiving, remembering, thinking, and the like. For Aristotle, central to this is the question of how the system can [re]present[27] the objects of its various intentional acts. It is here that the cognitivist side of Aristotle's psychology emerges and in the course of this investigation we shall be primarily concerned with this feature of the theory. In particular, it is the [re]presentational role of images [φαν-

26. I do not mean to imply that Aristotle has or here employs a technical notion of a system state (see Penner, 1970, who argues that Aristotle does not have any such notion). At this point I am using the word rather loosely, allowing it to cover functions, activities, or almost anything involved, internally, in explaining what a system actually *does*.

27. I apologize for the somewhat clumsy use of brackets here. Its point is to alert the reader to the fact that I am not foisting on Aristotle the view that we do not actually perceive objects but only make inferences to them from Hume-like images.

τάσματα] that gives the account its cognitivist flavor. In the next chapter we turn to imagination [φαντασία] proper and its role in [re]presentation. First, however, something more needs to be said about attribution of cognitivism to Aristotle.

3. ON COGNITIVISM IN THE ARISTOTELIAN SOUL

The thesis that there are cognitivist strains in Aristotle's thought is intended as a modest proposal. It would, for example, be implausible to hold out for the "essential identity" of the theory of *De Anima* with one or another modern version of cognitivism. Nonetheless, some commentators (Wilkes [1978] is a case in point)[28] have courageously argued as much for the case of functionalism. But essential identity is a strong notion. Although Wilkes does not characterize it in precise terms, presumably something like the following is involved. T_1 and T_2 are essentially identical if, and only if, T_1 and T_2 are isomorphic with respect to their essential features. The trouble lies in deciding just what counts as an essential feature. If, for example, a rigorous notion of computability is deemed essential to functionalism, then it is implausible to insist on its essential identity with Aristotle's theory. If, on the other hand, what is essential is that some kind of internal interpretation be countenanced, then, on this point at least, the isomorphism might hold up. But it would be incautious to insist that *this* supports the essential identity of the ancient and modern theories.

A less ambitious strategy is called for. Thus, let T_1 be Aristotle's theory and T_2 a modern, perhaps, functionalist theory. Suppose that we also have a more general theory $T^\star$ that is gotten by abstraction from T_1 or, perhaps, from T_1 and T_2. The idea is that both of the specific theories satisfy the constraints of the higher level theory $T^\star$ and, thus, that they *are* identical *at that level*. Notice that even were $T^\star$ gotten from T_1 alone, the effect of the procedure, at least in the case at hand, is to strip Aristotle's theory of doctrines that no longer ring true to the contemporary ear. These, however, are precisely what makes T_1 *Aristotle's* theory. Still, it will be replied, the fact that $T^\star$ can be abstracted from T_1 tells us something about Aristotle's theory and, hence, about the shared basis with the contemporary theory T_2. In the immediate case, this appears to be an impressive result because it promises us grounds for asserting the essential identity of some part of the specific theoretical bases of the ancient and modern functionalist theories. But in this case appearances promise too much. The trouble is that a

28. See, especially, chapter 7, "Mind Undermined."

host of other, unintended, theories may satisfy $T^\star$ equally well. So far as we know, nothing guarantees that $T^\star$ does not have a dizzying array of unintended models, some of which will bear little, if any, intuitive similarity to Aristotle's theory. Thus, it is premature to begin interpretation by imposing such an apparatus of abstraction.[29]

So if we are interested in the form of *Aristotle*'s theory, there is no substitute for deliberate and detailed attention to what he says. This does not exclude, but it does constrain the use of, contemporary frameworks. They best serve as methodological guideposts by delineating a clear picture of what the theory might look like. Actual degree of fit will depend on a detailed showing of what the ancient text can accommodate. It is in this spirit that I deploy contemporary idioms. In particular, I am interested only in exploring the extent to which Aristotle's views on imagination and thought embody two general cognitivist constraints on psychological explanation: (1) psychological systems have internal systems of [re]presentation that explain how the system's internal states (beliefs, desires, and so on) can be about the world and, thus, play a causal role in explaining the system's behavior; and (2) psychological systems have parts or subsystems that interpret these [re]presentations.

But before moving, finally, to the details of Aristotle's account, we should address a recently raised objection to the very possibility of an interpretation along the lines we are proposing. Ironically, it comes from a recent and, perhaps, overly enthusiastic use of what I have called the apparatus of abstraction. Satisfied that Aristotle is essentially a functionalist in the modern sense of the term, Wilkes (1978) is forced to deny [re]presentation any role at all in Aristotle's psychology. In short, she asserts

W1. Functionalism implies that no internal [re]presentational devices are relevant to the formal account of cognitive activity.

and attributes it to Aristotle because "Aristotle seems to have been immune to either temptation, (i.e.) never reifying mental events nor talking of *acts* or occasions of thinking or remembering" (1978, 123).

But what is Wilkes's evidence for Aristotle's immunity on this score? It amounts to asserting or, better, borrowing an assertion to the effect that Aristotle never countenances entities such as sense data or sense impressions and then extending this point to strictly intentional modalities such as

29. This seems to me to be the procedure followed by Wilkes (1978, chap. 7), and by David Charles when he urges (1984, chap. 1) that Aristotle's theory of action is a worthy alternative to contemporary theories. For the latter is asserted only for Aristotle's theory construed at an abstract level.

thought and desire. The assertion, recently used by Rorty to the same effect (1979, 47ff.), looks like this:

> The difficulty is in finding a Greek equivalent for "sensation" in the sense philosophers make it bear. It is true that in translation of *De Anima* one finds "sensation" and "perception" used freely where Aristotle has *aisthesis*. But this is seldom right. *Aisthesis* means "sense" ("the five senses"), or "sensing" (a generic term for cases of seeing, hearing, etc., individually or collectively taken . . .).
>   . . . the comparatively rare formation *aisthema*, "that which is the consequence of the activity in *aisthesis*," occurs in Aristotle's writings some ten times, and in three of these cases it is natural and perhaps inevitable to translate it by "sensation," "sense impression," or even "sense datum." All of them, though, occur in the treatise *On Dreams* (460b2, 461a19, 461b22), and the spooky context, the need for a word to designate a floating image not ascribable to sense perception, explains the usage. (Matson, 1966, 101)

Wilkes immediately extends Matson's point as folows:

> Nor does Aristotle want to discuss occasions of thinking or de-siring, or of individual memory-episodes—we no more find an ontology of the propositional attitudes than we do of sensations. Always the primary concern is with the ability to think, to desire, or to remember, rather than with specific instances of such abil-ities being exercised; hence, he has no reason to reify any such instances into "mental events." (1978, 124)

I shall comment first on Wilkes's use of Matson's claim and then on her extension of it. Notice that the passage says, in effect, that Aristotle refers to *aisthemata* [αἰσθήματα] at least ten times and that on three occasions he *must* be understood to refer to something like sense data or sensory impres-sions. To my mind this is granting the war before the battle has begun. In fact, however, the three occurrences in question do not *demand* a nonphys-icalist reading, what I take to be the upshot of a sense data–based theory, simply because Aristotle does not say in any of the cited passages that the *aisthema* itself is the free-floating image Matson refers to. Rather, as a certain activity remaining in the perceptual system, it is part of the explanation of such images in cases of deception or in dream phenomena. Whether the activity continues in the absence of the object or αἰσθητόν that caused it, as at 460b2, or whether it comes about by a nonstandard cause, as at

461a19, there is no reason here to award αἰσθήματα, or perceptual states, nonphysical status. Deception ensues not because the αἰσθήματα are non-physical, but because the process, presumably physical, in which they figure occurs in a nonstandard context.[30]

It is important to notice that this suggests only that Aristotle does not operate with two different kinds of αἰσθήματα. It does not suggest that αἰσθήματα are nothing but physical or functional states of the subject. So far, then, it remains an open question, particularly when construed as a question about the need for [re]presentational devices. To keep the question open, for the moment at least, we need to look at Wilkes's extension of Matson's claim. For if Aristotle is interested only in one's ability to perceive, think, and so on, then he may be committed to a dispositional analysis that leaves little room for the whole notion of [re]presentational devices. So if, as Wilkes urges, Aristotle simply has no interest in episodes of thinking, the cognitivist interpretation may be wrongheaded from the start.

For a number of reasons this conclusion should be resisted. First, Wilkes appears to endorse the principle that a theory can address episodes or occasions of thought, desire, and the like only by countenancing an ontology of propositional attitudes. This is anything but obvious. For although such a theory will, of course, invoke mechanisms involved in episodes of thought and although this will involve reflection on structure and functional organization, it need not involve an ontology of propositional attitudes. Second, although Aristotle is primarily concerned, as Wilkes indicates, with the ability to think, this concern *must* take account of the actual exercise of the ability. After all, to define a faculty as a capacity$_2$ is to define it as a capacity to actually$_2$ have an object in a certain way. But these havings just are episodes of thought, desire, and the like. So it is misleading in the extreme to suggest that Aristotle does not need to attend to episodes of thought. This is precisely what his faculty is a faculty for. Third, it is simply false to say that he never talks of occasions of thinking. Indeed, as we shall see in later chapters, a central thesis in his account of thought is the thesis that the mind *in activity* is the same as the object of thought. This is clearly a thesis about episodes of thinking. Indeed, it is part of the explanation of how persons can grasp distinct objects in acts of thought. Analogous forms of the thesis hold for perceptual faculties, so it appears that to drop occasions or episodes from Aristotle's theory of the soul is to drop a general and crucial feature of the theory.

The considerations raised in the past two paragraphs suggest, then, that

30. For more on the topic of this paragraph, see the next chapter.

Aristotle does not hold W1 as Wilkes would urge. To the extent that she
agrees with commentators such as Robinson (1978) on the centrality of W1
to anything that goes by the name of functionalism, her attempt to make
Aristotle a functionalist of modern stripe threatens to defeat itself. So far
as I can tell the only way to avoid this situation without descending into
dualist or sense-data talk in the manner of Robinson (1978) is to view
Aristotle as committed to internal [re]presentations.

We can best appreciate this point by recalling that Aristotelian faculties
are capacities that explain how a system is able to grasp or receive something as the object of an intentional act.[31] This appears to commit Aristotle
to some version of what is sometimes called "Brentano's problem." This
is the problem of giving an adequate, yet materialistically faithful, account
of belief, desire, thought, and the other intentional attitudes. From the point
of view of psychology as physics we can assume that Aristotle is a materialist of some description. We also take it that Aristotle held that persons
do exhibit beliefs, desires, thoughts, and the like. Together these two
propositions imply that Brentano's problem can be solved. But how?
Again, a recent suggestion will prove instructive. Field (1978) has argued
that the solution to Brentano's problem requires a system of internal
[re]presentations that enables a person to have desires, beliefs, and thoughts
about objects and situations in the world. Although Field thinks that something like sentence tokens are called for, Aristotle, we shall see, appears to
opt for a rather different style of [re]presentation. But, even if it ultimately
tells against Aristotle's theory, this difference is slight in comparison to the
shared vision. For Aristotle, too, sees exactly that [re]presentations are
required to explain how a physical system is capable of actual$_2$ operations
of an intentional sort. This, at any rate, is what I intend to argue in the
following chapters.

A key part of this will be providing him with a general theory of
[re]presentational devices that play an essential role in the account of cognitive faculties and intentional acts.[32] In the next chapter I propose that
imagination [φαντασία] plays the central role by arguing that, rather than
a standard or complete faculty in its own right, imagination is best thought
of as a quite general [re]presentational capability that subserves the operations of standard faculties.

31. Although Aristotle usually employs the idiom of function and affection, in *De Partibus
Animalium* I.5 he talks freely of practices as well. So talk of intentional *acts* is not entirely out
of place.

32. Field also argues that a system of internal [re]presentation can be made part of psychological theory without cost to the theory's functionalist credentials. If so, then Robinson
(1978) (and, perhaps, Wilkes, 1978) cannot be correct to hold that functionalism is *incompatible*
with the notion of internal [re]presentations.

II

THE CANONICAL THEORY
OF IMAGINATION

Imagination figures centrally in a number of Aristotle's theories. His accounts of action, memory, dreaming, and perception, as well as thought, make essential use of the notion. But only in *De Anima* III.3 do we get a systematic account of imagination proper. So here, if anywhere, one might expect to find his official or, as I shall say, canonical theory of imagination.[1] Strictly speaking, only 428b10–429a10, what I call the "C" section of the chapter, is devoted to presentation of the canonical theory. The A section, 427a17–b16, distinguishes thought and perception and the B section, 427b16–428b10, shows how imagination differs from other activities and operations of the soul. What one finds in C is indeed a theory of imagination but hardly one that scholars have found unproblematic. First, the canonical theory has seemed to specify a kind of imagination that is too narrow to cover the broad and diverse use Aristotle elsewhere makes of the notion. Second, *De Anima* III.3 may itself be inconsistent if, as some allege, several considerations advanced in B employ a notion of imagination that is incompatible with the technical notion marked out in C. Third, it is commonly held that the *kind* of theory Aristotle offers in C is, at best, uninteresting and, at worst, incoherent.

The tendency, particularly among recent scholars, to downgrade or restrict the role accorded imagination in Aristotle's psychology and even to dismiss as inconsistent the account itself stems, at least in part, from failure to appreciate the subtlety of much that Aristotle says. Perhaps chief among

---

1. Throughout I follow the tradition and translate "φαντασία" as imagination in full cognizance of the fact that the English usage does not fit Aristotle's notion. Although Beare's "the faculty of presentation" is a close approximation, it has the disadvantage of suggesting that φαντασία is a faculty. In any case, so long as we keep Aristotle's account at the forefront the question of translation is not crucial.

these is the still popular practice of simply assimilating Aristotle's φαντασία into classical empiricist theories of imagination. The restrictive impulse is evident even in some of the more interesting contemporary accounts. Thus, for example, Schofield (1978, passim) limits the canonical theory to perceptually deviant states and Nussbaum (1978) argues that Aristotle's fundamental use of imagination, to account for the seeing-as aspect of perception, simply cannot be brought within the scope of the canonical theory. I shall argue, on the other hand, that Aristotle's notion is better seen as a creature of theory, in particular that it plays a technical role in a general account of the possibility of object awareness. For persons it yields a surprisingly sophisticated theory of [re]presentational structures within an essentially functionalist framework. Although its general shape may be familiar and even uncontroversial, the details of my account are not. I argue, for example, that imagination is not a standard faculty at all and suggest, rather, that in its [re]presentational role imagination subserves full faculties in the sense that images are the devices by which such faculties [re]present the objects toward which they are directed.

I begin in this chapter with a detailed account of the canonical theory, reserving for the next the issue of consistency. So I shall, for the moment, focus mainly on the C section of *De Anima* III.3. Parts of the theory of perception will, of course, also prove relevant. It turns out that certain passages from *Parva Naturalia* are also very helpful, particularly in *De Memoria* and *De Insomniis* where Aristotle puts the canonical theory to work. Some commentators might balk at this use of the *Parva Naturalia,* but this is due largely to specific views about *De Anima*'s imagination.[2] It is for this reason that I begin, rather austerely, with the technical statement of the canonical theory in the C section.

I. THE CANONICAL TEXT

The core of the canonical theory of φαντασία is given at 428b10–17.

> But since (1) it is possible that when one thing is moved a different thing is moved by it [. . . κινηθέντος τουδὶ κινεῖσθαι ἕτερον ὑπὸ τούτου] and since (1a) imagination [φαντασία] is thought to be a sort of movement [κίνησίς τις] and (1b) [is thought] not to occur [γίγνεσθαι] apart from perception [οὐκ ἄνευ αἰσθήσεως] but (1c) only in perceiving things [αἰσθανομένοις] and (1d) in relation

2. Schofield (1978, 104–05), for example.

to that of which there is perception [ὧν αἴσθησις ἔστιν] and since
(2) it is possible for movement [κίνησιν] to occur as a result of
actual perception [ὑπὸ τῆς ἐνεργείας τῆς αἰσθήσεως] and since
(2a) this [movement] is necessarily like the perception [ταύτην
ὁμοίαν ἀνάγκη εἶναι τῇ αἰσθήσει], (2b) this movement [αὕτη ἡ
κίνησις] cannot exist apart from perception [οὔτε ἄνευ αἰσθήσεως]
or (2c) in things that are not perceiving things [οὔτε μὴ αἰσθανο-
μένοις]. And (2d) the possessor [of the movement] may do and
be affected by many things in respect of it [πολλὰ κατ᾽ αὐτὴν καὶ
ποιεῖν καὶ πάσχειν τὸ ἔχον]; and (2e) it may be true and false.

For convenience, I shall sometimes refer to this text as the canonical text,
or "CT."

Most commentators follow Aquinas (1951, 396) in taking CT to contain
the central thesis of the canonical theory, namely, that imagination is identical with a movement resulting from sense perception. In fact, however,
this thesis is not asserted until 428b30–429a1 where imagination [φαντασία]
is finally identified as a movement [κίνησις] resulting from the activity of
perception. Failure to see this requires treating the latter passage as mere
reiteration of the reasoning in CT. But, as we shall see, Aristotle's strategy
is subtler than this.

It is at least clear that the canonical text is meant to give support for the
central thesis announced later—but not deductive support. For CT *entails*
something weaker, only, say, the thesis that imagination is a movement
coextensive with a movement resulting from sense perception. Rather than
a deductive argument, Aristotle offers something like an argument from
the best explanation. What does the explaining is the central thesis identifying imagination with a certain sort of perception-induced movement and
what is to be explained is the correlation between two sorts of facts: facts
involved in imagination and certain facts involved in perception. Once these
are clearly laid out the central thesis can be adopted on the strength of its
explanatory power.

The relevant features of imagination are retailed in 1a–1d: imagination
is a certain kind of movement (1a), it presupposes perception (1b), and it
occurs in perceiving things only (1c), and in connection with what can be
perceived (1d). We may also add that it can be true and false (1e), since this
has already been mentioned at 428a18 as a chief characteristic of imagination. The relevant features of perception are given in 2a–2e. What I want
to suggest is that the correlation between these features is what makes it
plausible to assert the central thesis of the canonical theory. The theory that
he begins in 2 clearly depends on 1. For we know from *De Anima* II.5 that

in actual perception a certain kind of movement or being affected takes place. So if it is possible for movement to result from actual perception, it must be possible for movement in one thing to result from a different thing's being moved or affected. Thus, failing 1, 2 would be impossible.

Of course, the above consideration makes possible only theories having the general form of the canonical theory. To get the canonical theory itself we must match features of the explanatory account with the salient features of imagination. Can we do this? Corresponding rather neatly to 1b and 1c are 2b and 2c, respectively; 1a can be matched with at least part of 2a or even with 2. It is less clear, however, what to do with the notion of likeness introduced in 2a. I shall suggest that it is meant to be paired with 1d. According to 1d, imagination occurs only in connection with what can be perceived [ὧν αἰσθήσ᾽ς]. The genitive "ὧν" restricts φαντασία to objects that are or, possibly, can be objects of perception. Notice first that 1d does not say just what 1c says. From the fact that imagination or φαντασία occurs only in what is capable of perception, it does not follow that φαντασία occurs only relative to what is an object of perception. So 1d adds a new restriction on φαντασία. On the other hand, Aristotle is not imposing the severe requirement that whatever is an object of the imagination must also be an object of perception. Indeed, he is not even talking about *objects of* the imagination but only about its occurrence *relative to* objects of perception. So far as 1d is concerned it is unclear whether there are, strictly speaking, any objects at all proper to φαντασία. Later I shall argue that this is Aristotle's view. It is also worth mentioning that Aristotle's language allows for the occurrence not just of φαντασία whose content is relative to objects that can be perceived but also of φαντασία the parts of whose content is relative to such objects. The latter might be needed in order to accommodate the sort of φαντασία that figures in dreams and hallucinations.[3] At any rate we can see how 2a constitutes something of a match for 1d: because perception-induced movement is necessarily like what is perceived, such movement can only occur relative to what can be perceived [ὧν αἴσθησις.] Hence, to anticipate, the central thesis that imagination is such a movement would account for another received fact of imagination.

What about 2d? The lines, 428b16–17, are difficult in their own right apart from the question of what feature of imagination they are meant to explain. Hicks's translation reads "in virtue of this motion it is possible for its possessor to do and experience many things," but in his commentary on the lines, "κατ᾽ αὐτήν" (with respect to it) is taken to mean "κατὰ τὴν φαντασίαν" (with respect to imagination) rather than "κατὰ τὴν κίνησιν"

---

3. We deal later with the question of squaring 1d with imagination's role in thinking.

(with respect to the movement). Thus, Hicks fails to appreciate that 2d is part of an *explanation of* imagination as opposed to mere presentation of doctrine. Besides this, his construal of the context, "κατά...," possessively is nonstandard and requires the line to be read "it is possible for the possessor of the movement to do and be affected by many things in virtue of possessing the movement." This makes the line curiously uninformative. Giving "κατά..." a more familiar sense, we get "it is possible for the possessor of the movement to do and be affected by many things in accordance with (or, perhaps, with respect to) the movement." We now get a very plausible reading of the line, namely, that the movement induced by perception is such that it can play an essential *causal* role in a wide variety of intentional or quasi-intentional operations or activities. Thus, 2d is designed to cover the received fact that imagination is involved in action, memory, dreams, and so on, as well as thought.

We come, finally, to 2e. On the interpretation I am offering 2e asserts that the perception-induced *movement* may be true or false. Some commentators, notably Hicks, take 2e to assert that *imagination* may be true or false. While this may not be false, strictly speaking, the remark would make little sense, if, as I am arguing, 2e is part of an explanation of imagination. Besides this, it is hard to see how the subject of "εἶναι" (is) at 428b17 (the "it" of 2e) can be anything but the "αὕτη ἡ κίνησις" (the movement itself) at 428b15 (the movement of 2b). The reading is also difficult in light of 428b17–30 which claims to explain 2e, for what gets explained, strictly speaking, is not how imagination or φαντασία can be true and false but rather how the movement that results from perception can be true and false.

The development of 2e is straightforward in strategy. First, following *De Anima* II.6, three kinds of perception are introduced: perception of proper objects of sense [τῶν ἰδίων], perception of objects incidentally [κατὰ συμβεβηκός] and perception of common objects [τῶν κοινῶν]. Then Aristotle says:

> The movement [κίνησις] which comes about as a result of the activity of perception will differ depending on which of the three types of perception it results from. The first [movement from perception] is true so long as perception is present [παρούσης], while the others may be false whether perception is present or absent, and especially when the object perceived is far away. (428b25–30)

What this passage gives us is a crisp explanation of how perception-induced movement may be true or false. Notice that there is no explicit mention of φαντασία. Indeed, were such mention made we would no longer have an independent account of the facts in question. So 2e asserts a fact about perception that will ultimately explain the received fact that imagination is thought to be true and false (1e).

Aristotle's account of imagination, at least the canonical theory of *De Anima* III.3, is, then, not merely a set of related dicta but consists rather in a theory of two parts—an explanatory part and a domain of facts to be explained. Thus, his procedure, if not his theory, is considerably subtler than is usually recognized. It also gives the account a rather contemporary shape, for the thesis that φαντασία is perception-induced movement is argued for strictly on the grounds that this provides the best explanation of the facts to be explained. So the canonical theory may be likened to a scientific theory whose main tenets are acceptable because of the theory's explanatory power.

This is surely an unusual, if not unprecedented, modus operandi for Aristotle. Nonetheless, that it is in fact Aristotle's procedure is confirmed by 428b30–429a2 which asserts (finally) that φαντασία is a certain kind of κίνησις:

> If, then, (*a*) imagination has no other features than those mentioned and if (*b*) this is what was accounted for, then (*c*) imagination will be a movement which results from the activity of perception.

Unfortunately, the manuscripts disagree substantially. I follow Hicks in adopting E, probably the best manuscript, which is:

> εἰ (*a*) οὖν μηθὲν μὲν ἄλλο ἔχοι ἢ τὰ εἰρημένα ἡ φαντασία, (*b*) τοῦτο δ᾽ ἐστὶ τὸ λεχθέν, (*c*) ἡ φαντασία ἂν εἴη κίνησις ὑπὸ τῆς αἰσθήσεως τῆς κατ᾽ ἐνέργειαν γιγνομένη.

Ross and Hamlyn, on the other hand, follow the manuscripts that have "ἤ" rather than "ἡ" before "φαντασία" in *a*. Hamlyn, for instance, translates: "If, then, nothing else has the stated characteristics except imagination, and this is what was said, . . . " There are difficulties with this. For, as has been shown, "this" ["τοῦτο" in *b*] cannot refer to the whole of *a* because no such statement has been made regarding φαντασία. Neither can "this" refer to the stated characteristics [τὰ εἰρήμενα] for grammatical reasons as well as for the reason that *b* is then pleonastic. Finally, grammar rules against supplying "φαντασία" (or, for that matter, "κίνησις" [movement]) as the antecedent for "this."

Most renderings of E also encounter difficulties in dealing with *b*. Hicks reads *b* in light of 428b11 (my 1a) and suggests that it means "and if this (namely, φαντασία) is what some have described it as being." This fails for two reasons. First, "this" [τοῦτο] is still made to refer to φαντασία and this is grammatically difficult. Second, it gives *b* a vague role at best in the passage, for the passage now says that if imagination has no other features than those mentioned and if imagination has the mentioned features, then imagination will be a certain kind of movement. Since *a* already implies that imagination has the mentioned features, it is unclear what *b* is supposed to add.

The correct solution is, I submit, the following. Given that the canonical theory is a two-part theory and that the parts have so far not been explicitly related, we can plausibly expect this to occur at this juncture in the presentation of the theory. Accordingly, the τὰ εἰρήμενα, or mentioned features of *a* are just those features of imagination that are to be accounted for by the explanatory part of the theory, namely, 2–2e. Then *b* can be taken as saying "and this (namely, the mentioned features being all the salient features of imagination) is what was accounted for (in the explanatory part of the theory)." If *a* and *b* are so construed, not only do we have a grammatically acceptable reference for "this" [τοῦτο] but also we get a clear picture of how *c* results from *a* and *b*: since the explanatory part of the theory adequately accounts for all the salient features of φαντασία, we are justified in adopting the central thesis that imagination, or φαντασία, is a movement that results from the activity of perception.[4]

Of course, CT does not, by itself, completely determine the canonical theory. In the hands of clever interpreters it might be made to accommodate different sets of "facts" about imagination; facts about the so-called creative imagination come to mind, depending on what weight is given to imagination itself. And, thus, the point itself of the canonical theory might appear indeterminate as well. Happily, Aristotle himself removes a good deal of the potential for variant interpretations by spelling out a canonical notion of imagination at 428a1–2. It is this that is the target of the canonical theory. In a moment we shall have a good deal more to say about this canonical imagination, but at this point three observations will suffice. First, it is defined as that in virtue of which images [φαντάσματα] came about in us. Thus, the canonical theory is, in effect, a theory about images. Second, by inclusion of 2a the canonical theory appears to cast images in a [re]presentational role, and 2d suggests that this is conceived of as a causal as well as a global role. This recalls the functionalist's fondness for defining psychological states in terms of their causal role in the system. Third, CT

---

4. Contrast this with Aquinas who finds the thesis given much earlier. He is followed here by Tricot (1947).

gives us a *theory* about images; it does not report observational results. This suggests that images, in the technical sense of the canonical theory, are countenanced on the grounds that they occur in a successful explanatory theory. Contrast Ross, who finds it difficult to maintain his unusual generosity, claiming that Aristotle "concludes rather lamely that φαντασία is a process caused by an actual perception" (1955, 33). Thus, it may turn out to be more appropriate to liken them to entities of scientific psychological theory rather than to creatures of folk psychology. This would, of course, be congenial to our cognitivist leanings. But it also appears to be quite congenial to Aristotle's leanings.

2. PERCEPTION AND ITS INGREDIENTS

In the canonical theory, imagination is movement resulting from the activity of perception. Because the considerations offered in CT do not explain this central thesis but rather are to be explained by it, we still need an account of *how* the movement that is imagination results from the activity of perception. Otherwise, the central thesis little more than nominally explains the facts in question. What is needed, at least, is a detailed account of the causal relation between imagination and perception. I shall develop such an account by first laying out the essential features of actual episodes of perception and then relating these to imagination.

We may begin with a list of the terms of Aristotle's discussion of perception: (1) αἴσθησις (perception), (2) αἰσθητικόν (that by which perception occurs), (3) αἴσθημα (perceptual state), (4) αἰσθητόν (perceived thing), (5) αἰσθητήριον (perceptual organ), and (6) αἰσθάνεσθαι (perceiving). Number 1 is a generic notion and covers actual perceivings as well as the capacity for such perceivings. Number 6, typically at least, is reserved for episodes of perception and numbers 2–5 give the ingredients of such episodes. It is numbers 2–5 that are of immediate concern since it is from the *activity* of perception that imagination is held to result.

How, then, does Aristotle conceive of what occurs in an episode of perception? Roughly, as follows: When an object, say O, impinges, via an appropriate medium, on the surface of a sensory organ [αἰσθητήριον] at t_1, sensory input is transmitted through the organ until, if unimpeded, it reaches what Aristotle calls the starting point of perception [ἀρχὴ τῆς αἰσθήσεως] at t_2. At that point the subject, say S, becomes an actual perceiver, at least with respect to O, and O, the αἰσθητόν, becomes an actually perceived thing. So S's perceiving O at t_2 amounts, in terms of De Anima

II. 5's Framework Passage, to S's undergoing a change at t_2 from a potential$_2$ to an actual$_2$ perceiver.

The change from potential to actual perceiverhood appears to be an instantaneous or durationless change. In his physics generally Aristotle certainly makes room for changes of this sort. *De Caelo* I.2, 280b25ff. entertains the possibility of something's at one time existing and at another time not without undergoing corruption [τὸ ἄνευ φθορᾶς ὁτὲ μὲν ὂν ὁτὲ δὲ μὴ ὂν at 280b26–27] and offers as an example things that occur by contact [τὰς ἁφάς]. To the extent that Socrates' change at t_2 from a potential to an actual perceiver is like this—and I suggest that it is—that change is in all relevant respects like the case Aristotle uses. *De Sensu* VI also countenances durationless changes, of a slightly different sort, for light and vision. Generally, says Aristotle, alteration [ἀλλοίωσις] and local movement [φορᾶς] are to be treated differently, the latter always counting as a movement [κίνησις], as something that occurs over time. But changes of state can occur at once [ἀθρόον]. Something like this would happen were water to freeze all at once and it does occur in the case of light. For although light is due to the existence of something, namely, the operation of a causal factor on the transparent, it is not a movement[5] (unlike sound which is a certain movement of something that is in motion). Thus, the transparent changes all at once. This also explains why vision, unlike the other senses, is immediate: the medium between sense organ and object is affected as a whole and not progressively, part by part. Although this accounts for the causal relation between external object and sense *organ,* it does show that Aristotle would be comfortable with talk of Socrates changing his state at t_2 from a potential to an actual perceiver and of his doing so all at once and as a whole (that is, as Socrates).

Together, the *De Caelo* and *De Sensu* passages show that, from the point of view of physics, Aristotle would have no qualms about making room for durationless changes in the account of perception [αἴσθησις]. As it turns out they are, in fact, accorded a role in psychology. *De Sensu* VI, 446b3–6, makes quite clear that durationless changes are essential to the causal explanation of perception: "always one hears and has heard, at the same moment, and so in general one perceives and has perceived; and there is no coming into being of these [μή ἐστι γένεσις αὐτῶν] but nonetheless they occur without coming to be [ἀλλ᾽ εἰσὶν ἄνευ τοῦ γίγνεσθαι]." Moreover, in view of the Framework Passage (chap. 1, sec. 2), durationless changes

5. *De Sensu* VI, 446b27–28: τῷ εἶναι γάρ τι τὸ φῶς ἐστίν, ἀλλ᾽ οὐ κίνησίς τις. Pace Ross (1955), I see no particular reason to follow P which has ἐνεῖναι in place of εἶναι. The point is just that though light is subject to a causal account and causal accounts typically feature movements, it is, nonetheless, not a movement itself.

would seem to be a feature of psychological systems generally. For there the change from knower$_2$ to knower$_3$ did not occur over time but at a moment and the knower$_2$ was paraded simply as an example, even if an especially good one, of a system with a developed capacity$_2$. Thus, durationless changes will be required to explain the actual$_2$ operation of any faculty.

This durationless change cannot, however, be the movement that yields imagination. For the durationless change is not, as the canonical theory requires, a movement resulting from the activity of perception; rather it is the cause of, or at least the switch to, this activity. Indeed, durationless changes do not easily fit the standard κίνησις–ἐνέργεια dichotomy at all. That dichotomy divides actions into movements [κινήσεις] and activities [ἐνέργειαι] on the basis of two tests: the tense test and the quickly/slowly test. Where "φing" ranges over actions, the tense test asks whether "x is φing" implies "x has φed" and the quickly/slowly test asks whether "x is φing" implies "x can φ quickly or slowly." If, for a given action, the result of applying the first test is negative and the result of applying the second test is positive, then we have a movement. If the reverse, then we have an activity.[6] The standard dichotomy thus pertains to what I shall call durational movements because anything that can be done quickly or slowly is something that occurs in time. They are also incomplete actions in the sense that, with the trivial exception of the terminating moment, at no moment in their careers are such actions complete. Since durationless movements fail the quickly/slowly test (my coming at t to perceive something is nothing I can do more or less quickly) and the tense text (my coming at t to perceive something simply resists expression in the continuous tense), they do not seem to be standard movements. And although Aristotle denies that they are activities, he does not provide a criterion separating durationless movements from activities. The following might do, however. In principle an activity can occur over time without threat to its completeness at any given moment of time. But a durationless movement cannot occur over time at all. This is an attractive suggestion and merely requires that we restrict the standard dichotomy to actions that can go on for a period of time. Surely there is nothing exceptionable in this. In any case, the durationless movement involved in perception is neither the perceptual activity that produces imagination nor the result of such activity. We must look elsewhere.

6. The so-called standard dichotomy is, of course, rather more tricky than here indicated. For a good discussion of its various nuances, see Penner (1970).

Besides the durationless change occurring at t_2 there is, of course, the change occurring between t_1 and t_2.[7] At *De Insomniis* 459b24 Aristotle says that perception happens quickly and he means the causal process occurring in the αἰσθητήριον between t_1 and t_2. So the t_1–t_2 interval may be fleeting but it is an interval. Otherwise the account of perception would conflict with his account of dreaming. For the causal process could not, as required for dreaming, be impeded from reaching the starting point of perception were that process not a temporal affair. So the causal process is, in our earlier idiom, a durational movement. Suppose we call this sort of causal process an internal operating process of the system.

Now it is clear from *De Anima* II.5 that Aristotle confesses considerable reluctance to label the durationless change at t_2 an alteration [ἀλλοίωσις] and he may well extend this to the internal operating process as well. At 417b32, in explaining his hesitation, he remarks that there is no name for the difference between the change from child to general and adult to general. By the first he clearly has in mind an actualization₁, the durational process of developing the talents and capacities₂ requisite for generalship. This involves, as Aristotle says at 417b2–3, the destruction of something by its contrary and so counts as a genuine case of alteration: ignorance or ineptitude at strategy is replaced by cleverness and skill.[8] The second case is ambiguous, if not somewhat awkward. One could, after all, embark at a mature age on the project of becoming a general and this seems to be simply another actualization₁ and so a straightforward case of alteration. But it is unclear how this would exemplify, as it must, the case of perception. So Aristotle probably has in mind the adult, already an actual₁ general, who exercises his generalship as occasions of state demand. And this does parallel the sort of change needed for the match with perception, or for that matter, thought. When Socrates contemplates or perceives something at t_2, he is not developing away from a privative state but rather exercising a state he already has developed. He switches, to invoke the idiom of the Framework Passage, into himself and his actualization [εἰς αὐτό... ἡ ἐπίδοσις καὶ εἰς ἐντελέχειαν], and this is either not an alteration at all or a different kind of alteration.[9] Thus, actual exercises of faculties are said to involve πάσχειν (being affected) or ἀλλοιοῦσθαι (being altered) by courtesy only (418a1–3).

7. There is, on the model proposed, an obvious connection between these changes, namely, that the durationless change at t_2 is caused by the t_1–t_2 durational change.

8. Thus, only if the t_1–t_2 operating process can be thought of as involving the destruction of something by its contrary would Aristotle count it as a case of alteration.

9. The hesitation is explicit at *Physica* 244b10–11 [ἀλλοιοῦνται γάρ πως καὶ αἱ αἰσθήσεις] and implicit at *De Anima* 429a14–15.

It should, perhaps, be mentioned that "ἐπίδοσις" is sometimes translated as development and, thus, is taken to suggest that the change from, say, knower₂ or builder₂ to knower₃ or builder₃ is not simply a switch to activity but may involve a further development of what one already is. On this view, a builder may further develop *as a builder* and, hence, this cannot be said to involve the destruction of his capacity₂ to build. But "ἐπίδοσις" need not be so translated. It has, rather, the sense of giving way or going over to something (see Liddell, Scott, 631b), in this case, activity. This is probably to be recommended in light of *De Sensu* 446b3–6's point, quoted four paragraphs back, that actual perception occurs without any process of becoming and the Framework Passage's characterization of the switch from knower₂ to knower₃ as passing from the having of arithmetical or grammatical knowledge without exercising it to its exercise. There is no suggestion here that the *transition* amounts to any sort of further development of the knower₂'s knowledge. In fact, "ἐπιδόσις" and "preservation" cannot *mean* development of a thing if the sentences in which they occur espouse general principles. For, surely, one case these principles are intended to cover is that whereby the knower₂ merely exercises previously acquired knowledge, that is, where no development can be supposed to occur. It is, of course, entirely consistent with this that the builder is involved in two different kinds of alteration once he begins to exercise his craft. One, the process of constructing the house, is irrelevant to our present concerns. The other involves a process affecting him qua builder, namely, the further development of his knowledge and skill. But this is no part of the transition at t₂ to actual building; rather it concerns what happens once building is underway. Indeed, *if* his acquisition of new skill can be classified as local destruction, that is, as the destruction of ignorance about a certain technique, then perhaps it is an alteration after all.

These remarks are important to point out because the building example often misleads commentators. The point of the passage, after all, is to give an account of the operation of the soul's faculties, in particular, of the perceptual faculties. The builder (and knower) is introduced as a plain man's case of what it means to exercise a certain kind of capacity. On the reading in question, however, it is no longer able to discharge this responsibility. Finally, from the point of view of the person, there is no additional act that effects the transition to active knowing. That is, there are not two acts— the switch at t₂ to active knowing and, on the other hand, the active knowing itself that ensues at t₂. Rather, the transition occurs simply by virtue of the active exercise of the faculty.

Although Aristotle locates the causal process in the circulatory system and heart, his account applies mutatis mutandis to the nervous system and brain. What is important is that it is a sufficient condition of S's perceiving O that the causal process reach the starting point, whatever the starting point turns out to be. This is so because at that point S either (i) has an αἴσθημα (is in a perceptual state) that is the result of the causal process or (ii) has such an αἴσθημα and *in addition* is aware of it. If i is correct, then Aristotle would be holding that occurrence of an αἴσθημα, or perceptual state, involves neither more nor less than completion of the causal process and that awareness of an external object involves no additional, presumably mental, act of being aware of the αἴσθημα as part of being aware of the αἰσθητόν, or object of perception.

If ii is correct, then it would be possible to have an αἴσθημα without being aware of it. On this alternative an αἴσθημα will not be an exclusively mental item, for how could one be unaware of such a thing? Rather ii recommends construing an αἴσθημα as a certain state of a certain αἰσθητήριον, or perceptual organ. Hence, to be aware of an αἴσθημα is to be aware of a certain state of a sensory organ or at least to be aware of something causally resulting from such a state. Against ii, which I favor, it might be objected that, Aristotle could simply hold unnoticed αἰσθήματα (perceptual states) to be items that have resulted from the causal process reaching the starting point but that go unnoticed because competing αἰσθήματα block them out. After the suppressed αἰσθήματα pass away, goes the objection, there remains an associated movement and it is the subsequent awareness of this movement that makes dreaming, for example, possible. Attractive though this suggestion may appear, it does not fit Aristotle's account. By 461a30–31 in ordinary cases of perception a sufficient condition of being aware of something is that the causal process [κίνησις] beginning in the sense organ has reached the starting point: "for it is in virtue of the movement extending from there [the αἰσθητήριον] to the starting point [πρὸς τὴν ἀρχήν] that one who is awake also believes that he sees, hears, and perceives."

Now it is certainly true that the passage can be seen as supporting i, for it appears to count perceptual awareness as the result of *nothing but* a completed physical process. And, indeed, this suggestion appears to gain further support in *Physica* VII.2's idiom, "for actual perception is a motion through the body" [ἡ γὰρ αἴσθησις ἡ κατ' ἐνέργειαν κίνησίς ἐστι διὰ σώματος at 244b11–12]. Such an account would remain sparsely physicalist, leaving little room for internal cognitive structures. There is, however, reason to think that more is involved. First, when Aristotle speaks more precisely, the above formula turns out to be glossed in terms of the *soul*'s being moved via the body: "what is called perception, as an actual thing, is a kind of movement of the soul via the body" [ἡ δὲ λεγομένη αἴσθησις, ὡς ἐνέργεια, κίνησίς τις διὰ τοῦ σώματος τῆς ψυχῆς ἐστί at 454a9–11]. Of course, one could still insist that the soul's being moved comes to nothing more than the causal process reaching the ἀρχή, or starting point, of perception.

But *De Insomniis* suggests something more interesting. At 461b3–5 we find Aristotle saying the following: "Generally, the starting point [ἀρχή] affirms [φησιν] what results from each sense unless something else more authoritative [ἑτέρα κυριωτέρα] opposes it." Presumably, it is νοῦς that can override, since here it would be overriding the ἀρχή of perception. But that is secondary to our main point of interest in the passage, namely, the fact that something like a *judgment* is made by the ἀρχή. This is a very interesting remark for several reasons. First, the judgment is a routine and standard part of the causal process. Second, what does the judging is, from the point of view of the process, an internal item that is a component of the system as a whole. Because it can be overridden, as when seasoned desert explorers resist giving chase after mirages, the ἀρχή cannot be the system as a whole. So far from being a separate unitary entity, such as a Cartesian self, this looks like the sort of entity that cognitively minded functionalists are fond of.

Since what the ἀρχή of 461b3–5 affirms is presumably the movement of the αἰσθήματα (perceptual states) mentioned at 460b29, αἰσθήματα have an obvious role to play in this picture. They are precisely what are affirmed by the ἀρχή. It would, however, be mistaken to suppose that the αἴσθημα enters the story only when the causal process has reached the starting point. The context of the remark makes this clear. The chapter begins by stating a crucial condition on dreaming, namely, that movement can arise from perceptual states that are caused by something external as well as from those that are brought about by something within the body [αἱ κινήσεις αἱ ἀπὸ τῶν αἰσθημάτων γινόμεναι τῶν τε θύραθεν καὶ τῶν ἐκ τοῦ σώματος ἐνυπαρχουσῶν] (460b28–30). Wha: happens at night, Aristotle goes on to say, is that these movements reach the starting point of perception [ἐπὶ τὴν ἀρχὴν τῆς αἰσθήσεως καταφέρονται] and become evident [καὶ γίνονται φανεραί]. Since the subject of καταφέρονται can be only the κίνησις of 460b28 and since this is clearly durational, the lines imply that we are aware of something at t₂ that is the causal result of a perceptual state or states occurrent at an earlier time t₁. Although there may well be cases when we are aware at t₁ of the αἴσθημα as well as its later causal product, perhaps the case of afterimages, dreaming will not be one. To have an αἴσθημα is not ipso facto to have an awareness of something and so αἰσθήματα cannot be exclusively mental items.

Some commentators seem to favor the view that perceptual states [αἰσθήματα] are not essential items in the account of perception but figure only in so-called nonstandard contexts. Matson's "spooky context" suggests as much and he is apparently followed by Wilkes and Rorty. It has also been suggested that an αἴσθημα is best construed as an object of perception but without the connotation of externality carried by the term "αἰσθητόν." Although my main thesis can absorb such downgrading of αἰσθήματα, they would simply not figure as genuine ingredients of the perceptual process. I am nonetheless inclined to retain them in the account. First, they play a causal role in explaining what we *do* as perceptual systems. Indeed, so far from importing an exclusively mental sense, "αἴσθημα" means rather something like "that which is the causal result of the action of an αἰσθητόν" (object of perception).[10] In fact, this suggests that we might explain internal awareness of αἰσθήματα in terms of their (causal) role in ordinary perceptual awareness. Thus, my leaping out of the path of an onrushing cement truck is explained, in part, by the fact there is some sort of internal state, an αἴσθημα, that is causally related to the αἰσθητόν or perceived object in question, namely, the truck. On a cognitivist account this is just the sort of item we want to countenance.[11] Ordinarily, *I* am not aware of the perceptual state, or αἴσθημα, but only of the truck. When I do seem to be aware of the αἴσθημα itself, it is when there no longer exists a standard causal relation to an ordinary object of perception. It is, thus, not surprising that they enjoy a higher profile in nonstandard or "spooky" perceptual contexts.

A second reason for retaining perceptual states [αἰσθήματα] is that Aristotle himself seems ready to grant them a general role. Witness 459a24–28: "the perceived objects corresponding to each sense organ [τὰ αἰσθητὰ καθ᾽ ἕκαστον αἰσθητήριον] produce perception [αἴσθησιν] in us and the affection [πάθος] produced by them inheres [ἐνυπάρχει] in the sense organs not only when episodes of perceiving occur [ἐνεργουσῶν τῶν αἰσθήσεων] but also when they have gone." This passage clearly suggests that as a matter of course perception [αἴσθησις] involves production of an affection [πάθος]. It is also clear, from context, that the passage is supposed to tell us something about the difference between perceiving and dreaming. Thus, we have Aristotle saying that in cases of straightforward perception the perceived object produces an affection concurrent with the actual episode of perceiving. Notice that this is a very general condition, for the notion of a πάθος is sufficiently broad to be used in a variety of ways. Thoughts, beliefs, desires, and, perhaps, even images count as παθήματα of the soul. That Aristotle here has perceptual states [αἰσθήματα] in mind is, however, clear from the course of his argument in chapters II and III of *De Insomniis*.

10. Here I agree with Matson (1966, 101).
11. Although, as we shall shortly see, the exact nature of the causal role is rather complex.

The passage just introduced opens chapter II. From there until 460a32, some seventy-four lines of Bekker text, we get a discussion of how the principle functions in cases of actual perception. This discussion serves two purposes. First, it provides an inductive ground for the principle, and, second, it articulates features of actual perceptual experience that will have parallels for the case of dreaming. It should be clear from this that he intends to explain dreaming by general principles of his psychology, in particular, principles governing the mechanics of perception. In the course of this discussion we get, at 459b3–7, another principle:

> so in the case of perceiving [ἐν ᾧ τὸ αἰσθάνεσθαι], because actual perception [ἡ κατ' ἐνέργειαν αἴσθησις] is a sort of change of state [ἀλλοίωσίς τις],[12] this must also hold. Consequently, the affection [πάθος] is in the sense organs, on the surface as well as down deep, when they are in the process of perceiving as well as when they have ceased this.

The "this" at 459b5 refers to the diminishing aftereffects of causation, such as the eddies that recede only gradually after the surface of the pond has been struck. If the first principle, introduced at 459a24–28, simply followed from the facts about dreaming, 459b3–7 appears to give us a general causal principle that goes some distance toward explaining the first one.

At 460a32 Aristotle returns to the original topic, saying, "from what has been said it is apparent that perceptual states remain perceptible [ἐμμένει τά αἰσθήματα αἰσθητὰ ὄντα] even when the object perceived [τὸ αἰσθητόν] is gone" (460b1–3). This passage deserves several comments. Notice, first, that Aristotle says that αἰσθήματα, or perceptual states, themselves are, at least sometimes, items of awareness. Since this can occur when the object of perception [αἰσθητόν] is gone, Aristotle can't be read as counting perceptual states as themselves objects of perception. Without the definite article, "αἰσθητὰ ὄντα" need not carry commitment to objects but only bear the sense that we are somehow aware of perceptual states without their being standard objects of perception.[13] In light of the fact that "αἰσθητόν" and its ilk connote causal force[14] I am inclined to take the "αἰσθητὰ ὄντα" phrase as indicating that αἰσθήματα play a causal role in awareness. Second, the perceptual states are said to *remain* in the sense organs. Not only, then, can they hardly be exclusively mental items, but also Aristotle has them in

12. Note the "τὶς," meant to caution us against taking perception as an alteration in the primary sense of that term. Clearly, the writer of these lines has *De Anima* II.5's caveat in mind.

13. So the thrust of our discussion three paragraphs back.

14. For more on the causal force in question, see chap. 5, sec. 2.

the sensory organs even while the perceived object is present. This, at any rate, is what he implies. So the passage supports the interesting claim that, for Aristotle, αἰσθήματα do figure as ingredients in episodes of perception and that they are nonmental items that play a role in the story of perceptual awareness.[15]

The general role granted αἰσθήματα, or perceptual states, in 460b1–3 is hardly a slip. For it is introduced as a consequence of the earlier discussion. Since this clearly includes the principles introduced at 459a24–28 and 459b3–7, Aristotle is, in effect, suggesting that the affection [πάθος] there mentioned turns out to be the αἴσθημα. Thus, the evidence of De Insomniis indicates a general role for perceptual states [αἰσθήματα] in the theory of perception.

In closing discussion of αἰσθήματα we should return, finally, to the objection that the spooky context of De Insomniis contaminates evidence wrung from it. For several reasons this is unpersuasive. First, an account of phenomena that are spooky need not itself be spooky. We do not, for example, find Aristotle adducing meddlesome gods or occult presences in an explanatory role. In fact his attitude in De Divinatione, the sequel to De Insomniis, is precisely the opposite. Gods, prophetic forces, and the like are dismissed as devoid of explanatory power. Second, the account he in fact provides in De Insomniis not only is consistent with the canonical theory but also squares with De Anima generally: its opening lines are reminiscent of De Anima II.5's distinction of the proper objects of sense, and dreaming is explained as a feature, if somewhat peripheral, of a perceptual-psychological system that is recognizably that of De Anima. If anything, there is positive gain in taking a serious look at De Insomniis and De Memoria, for these accounts force Aristotle to use more of the explanatory repertoire of his psychological theory.

3. ACQUISITION OF [RE]PRESENTATIONAL STRUCTURES

We are now in a position to say something more about the sort of movement imagination is said to be. Again De Insomniis is helpful. Thus, consider

15. One might object to Aristotle's account that one simply can't make sense of nonmental items' playing this role in perceptual awareness. But, even were one to talk of direct awareness of αἰσθήματα, this just shows that it is misleading to characterize perceptual states in terms of a mental–physical dichotomy at all. This is unsurprising if they enter the discussion via the functionalist role they play, for sometimes this will call for "physicalist" and sometimes for "awareness" talk.

460b28–29 and 462a8–9 in light of 1 and 2 of the canonical theory. The first, 460b28–29, tells us that certain movements [κινήσεις] result from perceptual states [αἰσθημάτων], and 462a8–9 refers to certain of these as *imaginal movements* in the sensory organs [κινήσεις φανταστικαὶ ἐν τοῖς αἰσθητηρίοις]. Now 1 and 2 of the canonical theory imply that whatever produces the movement that is φαντασία is something that is itself a movement and a movement involved in perception. The perception-induced movement cannot be the causal process spanning the t₁–t₂ interval, at least not directly, for it is this process that induces the movement in question. Neither can the movement be the durationless movement occurring at t₂ when the subject becomes an actual perceiver. The two passages cited from *De Insomniis* suggest that the αἴσθημα, or perceptual state of the sensory organ, is itself a movement and indeed the very movement that yields the movement that is φαντασία. So the definition of imagination as a movement resulting from the activity of perception can be read: imagination is a movement resulting from an αἴσθημα which is one sort of movement involved in the activity of perception.

This result has considerable utility, for it accommodates two requirements that fall to imagination in our interpretation. In its general [re]presentational role, imagination will be involved in any intentional act that requires [re]presentation of an object. The discussion of dreaming already suggests this because the apparent appearance of something in a dream (the φαίνεται without τὸ φαινόμενον of 461b5–6) is explained in terms of the production, in sleep, of an image from the movement of a perceptual state [τὸ φάντασμα τὸ ἀπὸ τῆς κινήσεως τῶν αἰσθημάτων at 462a29–31]. And the discussion at 428b25–30 in C (see section 2 of this chapter) hardly makes sense if we deny φαντασία an episodic role, for it concerns how images may be true and false in actual episodes of perceiving. We shall have a good deal more to say about this role later. For the moment, however, let us defer that discussion and turn to the second requirement. If imagination is to play a general [re]presentational role in cognitive activity, then it will have to be the sort of movement that explains how [re]presentational structures are acquired in the first place. We may come to the perceptual scene endowed with a good deal of potential, but we do not come armed with innate [re]presentational structures. There are no innate ideas in Aristotle's universe but only the innate capacity to develop into a system that has ideas, and this requires that we be innately able to develop or acquire structures for [re]presenting a wide array of objects in a wide array of acts. Imagination enables us to do this.

Let us approach this by making somewhat clearer what Aristotle might mean by holding that perceptual states [αἰσθήματα] are movements. We need, first, to emphasize that the t₁–t₂ causal process is not a one-shot affair but an ongoing process. Since this process is occurring in a given sensory organ and since a perceptual state [αἴσθημα] is just a certain state of such a sensory organ, the αἴσθημα will be a certain state of a process in the sensory organ. In typical cases of perception the stimulatory input exhibits a relatively stable pattern and the causal process transfers this feature to the subject's perceptual states [αἰσθήματα].[16] Thus, despite continual renewal of input, the subject enjoys a relatively invariant perception of the external object. The point to stress is that Aristotle thinks of the perceptual state [αἴσθημα] simply as the pattern or form in which transitory input is given.[17]

Entities capable of perceptual states [αἰσθήματα] are not automatically entities capable of images [φαντάσματα]. Certain animals seem capable of nothing more than registration of immediate objects, which causally induce perceptual states. Once the object is removed there remains no awareness of it. From Aristotle's examples of such creatures (ants, bees, and grubs),[18] minimal-level perceivers are animals for which perception involves no cognitive features and that fail to exhibit even the slightest intentional or quasi-intentional behavior. For these entities perceptual movement simply cannot induce further movement or at least none that might count as imagination.

These appear to be the imperfect animals mentioned at 433b31–434a5, those capable of touch only. Apparently ready to grant them pains and pleasures and, thus, perhaps even wants [ἐπιθυμίαν],[19] Aristotle hesitates over imagination. Perhaps, he suggests, they have no imagination but are moved only indeterminately [κινεῖται ἀορίστως] or have pains, pleasures, and wants only indeterminately.[20] There is no doubt that the case perplexes Aristotle some, but he is clear at least on the point that *were* they to have imagination, they would be capable of determinate action. So although such creatures may register pleasure or pain upon actual contact with various objects encountered in the course of their indeterminate wanderings, they

16. This is a general point about cognitive states. At 461a26ff. it is the persistence of *stable* movement from perceptual states [σωζομένη τῶν αἰσθημάτων ἀφ' ἑκάστου τῶν αἰσθητηρίων ἐρρωμένα] that causes dreams [ποιεῖ τὰ ἐνύπνια], something's appearing [φαίνεσθαί τι], and a subject to believe that he hears or sees such and such.

17. This is suggested by *De Anima*'s idiom of that which can perceive becoming like the perceived object as well as, to give one context, 461b16ff. It also explains, incidentally, how perception is at once a movement [κίνησις] and an activity [ἐνέργεια]. (On this, see Gosling and White, 1982).

18. *De Anima* 428a9–11. See also 415a10–11. In light of Aristotle's high regard elsewhere for the first of these, we are probably wise to follow Torstrik (1970), in restricting the point to grubs with the emendation μύρμηκι μὲν ἢ μελίτῃ, σκώληκι δ' οὔ.

19. As he also does in *De Somno et Vigilia* 454b29–31.

20. Notice that Aristotle carefully avoids saying they have desire [ὄρεξις]. In that case, as 433b27–29 asserts, they would have imagination and be capable of action.

cannot be said to be aware of anything as the object of such movement because, it seems clear, they cannot even [re]present objects.[21] Then at 434b18–29 animals capable of perceiving at a distance are said to need senses other than touch. They must, in short, be capable of perceiving objects through a medium. Together these passages suggest that animals capable of perception at a distance need imagination in order to survive as the sort of animals they are. The obvious explanation is that they need ways to [re]present objects of actions that are essential to their survival.

For most animals, then, more needs to be said. In particular we need an account of how certain entities are capable of perceptual behavior of a cognitive or quasi-cognitive sort. At a minimum we need to add, following *Analytica Posteriora* II.19, that the perceptual equipment of certain animals allows for the persistence of the perceptual state [μονὴ τοῦ αἰσθήματος] or, given the result several paragraphs back, for the persistence of the pattern or form in which perceptual input is given. Where this does not happen, as in minimal perceivers, cognition [γνῶσις] is either absent or equivalent to something like registration of immediate objects. At 99b37–39 Aristotle aptly characterizes such animals as bereft of any cognition beyond the actual act of perceiving [ἔξω τοῦ αἰσθάνεσθαι]. In certain nonminimal perceivers, on the other hand, repeated persistence of perceptual states of a given kind somehow generates what Aristotle calls a logos [λόγον ἐκ τῆς τῶν τοιούτων μονῆς at 100a2–3]. The "somehow" is immediately explained in terms of perception generating memory [μνήμη] and memory in turn generating experience. So nonminimal perceivers appear to come in two varieties, those capable of memory only and those capable of experience as well. Since it is clear that imagination is required for memory, *Analytica Posteriora* II.19's minimal perceivers seem to be *De Anima*'s imperfect animals. Ac-

---

21. Contrast this with Nussbaum's attempt (1978, 233–37) to establish the claim that all animals enjoy imagination. She takes this as equivalent to the claim that "the same physiological apparatus sufficient for perception is sufficient for imagination." But this, of course, is ambiguous and may mean either (i) that, in creatures with imagination, the same apparatus is sufficient for both or (ii) that, in any creature, the physiological apparatus sufficient for perception is also sufficient for imagination. There is no reason to think Aristotle opts for the second. It doesn't follow from his point that the αἰσθητικόν (that which perceives) and φανταστικόν (that whereby imagination occurs) are extensionally the same but differ intensionally (in their essence), for this may be explained in terms of i. And although the "δοκεῖ δ' οὔ" (it seems not to be the case) at 428a10 may, as Nussbaum says, express uncertainty, it is hardly, we have seen, uncertainty that is resolved in *De Anima* III.11 "in favor of granting it [imagination] to all self-movers." Pace Nussbaum, 433b31–434a5, remains uncommitted on the point and the uncertainty is rather due to the fact that the behavioral repertoire of the grub is too impoverished to enable *attribution* of imagination. It is an empirical-scientific remark, not to be overturned by a priori classifications. See now Labarrière (1984, 23–24) for further criticism of Nussbaum's view.

cordingly, imagination seems to be the minimal structure required for an entity to be capable of acts involving [re]presentation of objects.[22]

Notice that acquisition of a logos is glossed simply as acquisition of experience. It amounts to a whole universal coming to rest in the soul (100a5–6 with the explicative gloss a6–7: ἐκ δ' ἐμπειρίας ἢ ἐκ παντὸς ἠρεμήσαντος τοῦ καθόλου ἐν τῇ ψυχῇ). Whatever else one says about it, the occurrence of "λόγον" in this context is noteworthy. It cannot be read proportionally, as Aristotle frequently allows; nor can it be read propositionally, as Aristotle sometimes requires. Rather, the point here is that a certain relatively invariant pattern exhibited in a number of persisting perceptual states gradually produces an item whose existence in the soul is then independent of occurrences of particular perceptual states or particular persistings of perceptual states of the associated kind. However else one might characterize this item, it need only be formally identical with the perceptual states.[23] Hence, "λόγον" at 100a2 is best read as "form."[24]

Production of the form is a durational process, for it takes repeated episodes of the right kind of persistence (not just perception) to generate the form.[25] Consequently, if that which, in Analytica Posteriora II.19, results from the persisting of perceptual states [αἰσθήματα] is the same as the image [φαντάσματα] of the canonical theory, then imagination will be the κίνησις, or process involved in their formation and, thus, in the formation of forms as well. In the idiom of De Memoria 450a31–b3 the change in the soul produced by perception amounts to something like imprinting a sort of pattern of the perceptual state [ἐνσημαίνεται οἷον τύπον τινὰ τοῦ αἰσθήματος]. These items are, of course, not analogues to Platonic forms; nor, I will later urge, are they concepts. In terms of the canonical theory, φαν-

22. Memory and imagination are also explicitly linked at Metaphysica 980b25–26 in a text closely paralleling Analytica Posteriora II.19. But Metaphysica I.1 countenances a somewhat wider notion of experience [ἐμπειρία]. The passage at 981a7–9 seems to require it for singular judgments, while acquisition of universals appears to wait upon the capacity for universal judgments characteristic of art [τέχνη] and science [ἐπιστήμη]. This merely calls for a shift in the point at which a logos is said to be acquired and so has little bearing on my thesis concerning the role of imagination in the story. In any case, Aristotle seems to be indicating how we are to close the gap at 100a16–18 where he claims that, while the object of perception is particular, perception is of the universal (more on this in chap. 4, sec. 7).

23. This becomes clearer in chapter 4 in the discussion of the relation between perceptual states, images, and thoughts.

24. Notice, to anticipate a later argument, that Analytica Posteriora II.19 is not obviously of a piece with the decaying sense interpretation of imagination. For even if persisting perceptions are construed as decaying sense perceptions, imagination will be a process that requires, but is not identical with, such decaying sense perceptions. So at best decaying sense perceptions are a necessary condition for imagination.

25. The process will be durational, even if, as I suspect some would urge, repeated episodes aren't required or, at least, not always.

τάσματα are simply devices or structures in the soul (nowadays we might say brain) that enable objects to be [re]presented to a subject such that the subject can do more than merely register or react to a causally impinging item. Certain operations, such as memory and dreaming, do not require presence of the object at all but only of an appropriately related image. Other operations, such as perception, do require presence of the object. But if the perception is to be more than mere registration of an impinging object (if, for example, one can say what one is perceiving), then images are required. Otherwise, as *De Memoria* suggests, one could never remember what one has earlier perceived.

So far, then, we have focused on one way to explain the thesis that imagination is a movement resulting from the activity of perception. On this explanation the durational movement we have isolated is not analogous to the durational movement occurring in actual episodes of perception—what I have called the t_1–t_2 movement. Rather, appropriate to its genetic or acquisitional role, it is analogous to what Aristotle in *De Anima* II.5 calls "a kind of destruction of something by its contrary." This sort of movement occurs, for instance, when a child acquires knowledge. Children are potential knowers not in the sense that they are capable of producing actual pieces of knowledge but only in the sense that they are capable of becoming actual producers of knowledge. They do this by acquiring certain structures that enable them, for example, to give a geometric proof on demand. Acquiring a structure of this sort amounts to a partial structuring of the soul itself and so amounts also to destruction of a previous state of it. In the idiom of chapter 1 we may call a child a potential$_1$ knower. A potential$_2$ knower is, then, someone, say S, who can produce a certain piece of knowledge. Thus, a potential$_2$ knower could be said to know a geometric proof even while asleep or reflecting on other matters. A potential$_2$ knower is also an actual knower, what we have called an actual$_1$ knower. Finally, we said that S is an actual$_2$ knower if, and only if, S is contemplating (to use Aristotle's *De Anima* II.5 term) or exercising a piece of actual$_1$ knowledge. Indeed, what S actually$_1$ knows depends for Aristotle on what S can actually$_2$ know.[26] The movement from potential$_1$ to potential$_2$ is analogous to the durational movement that accounts for acquisition of φαντάσματα or [re]presentational devices. But the analogy is imperfect for, as the balance of the chapter argues, what one acquires when one acquires such devices is

26. This is implicit from the discussion in *De Anima* 417a21–b2 and is explicitly stated at 415a19–20: γὰρ εἰσι τῶν δυνάμεων αἱ ἐνέργειαι καὶ αἱ πράξεις κατὰ τὸν λόγον (for activities and actions are prior in definition to their potentialities).

not obviously a faculty or at least not a faculty that has anything like an actual₂ employment. So although imagination has an episodic or occurrent role, it turns out to be strikingly different from that of standard faculties.

4. THE FUNCTIONAL INCOMPLETENESS OF IMAGINATION

It is widely agreed that there is something problematic about Aristotle's treatment of imagination. Hamlyn, for example, is sounding a common chord when he remarks, "imagination has an unsatisfactory halfway status between perception and the intellect and its exact position is never made clear" (1968, xiv). Unlike most commentators, I do not see that Aristotle shows much uncertainty at all about imagination itself. The canonical theory shows too steady a hand and is used too often with too much confidence. And his worry about imagination's range is that of a sensible and empirically grounded scientist. Who wouldn't puzzle over attribution of cognitive powers to grubs? But while hesitation over the troublesome imperfect creatures admittedly, and unsurprisingly, fosters hesitation about an entailment from perception to imagination, it leaves imagination itself untouched. The mixed verdict on Aristotle's discussion of imagination is due to the fact that most commentators have assumed that imagination must be a faculty. Hamlyn implicitly adopts the assumption by putting imagination on a par with perception and thought, and it leads Ross to the uncharacteristically harsh appraisal that Aristotle "regards it [imagination] not as a valuable faculty but as a disability, and that is why it never figures, in the *De Anima,* among the main faculties of soul" (1961, 39). It is this assumption I wish to challenge in the balance of the chapter.

Since faculties are certain potentialites₂ and since, as we saw above, such potentialities must be capable of actual₂ use, imagination can hardly be a genuine faculty if it has no actual₂ use. In the remainder of the chapter I shall argue just this. I should reiterate at the outset, however, that I am not thereby claiming that the only role for imagination is genetic or acquisitional. For it is clear, or will become clear, that for Aristotle images [φαντάσματα] occur in a variety of actual₂ operations of the soul and that imagination [φαντασία] is operative in such occurrences. Rather, I shall argue that it is a mistake to suppose that imagination *itself* is actually₂ exercised, that it has an actual₂ function.

Let me begin with some rather broad considerations concerning the structure and context of *De Anima* III.3. They provide the first hint that imagination has a different role. Aristotle has just concluded, so he says at

427a15–16, discussion of the principle [ἀρχή]²⁷ in virtue of which we say an animal is a perceiver. This suggests that he will proceed to another principle, and true to form, he begins De Anima III.4 by staking out as his target that part of the soul in virtue of which it knows and understands. Between comes the discussion of imagination. But it is a different style of discussion, one that follows a difficult and circuitous route. No similar announcement starts us on the topic; indeed, imagination is not even mentioned in the first twenty-eight lines of text, what I have called the A section of the chapter. And the B section, 427b16–428b10, would appear to be more interested in what imagination is not. So it is not until the canonical theory begins at 428b10, more than two-thirds of the way into the chapter, that Aristotle has anything positive to say about imagination.

What, it may be fairly asked, is going on here? It is unlikely that Aristotle is simply muddled about imagination, for when he finally turns to it in C, his account is straightforward and canonical. The suggestion I wish to explore is this. If imagination is not a standard faculty, then it cannot be investigated in the manner recommended by FFO at De Anima II.4:

> If we are to say what each of them is [τί ἕκαστον αὐτῶν = each of the faculties], i.e., what that which thinks is or that which perceives or that which nourishes, we must first say what thinking [νοεῖν] and perceiving [αἰσθάνεσθαι] are; for activities [ἐνέργειαι] and actions [πράξεις] are prior in definition [κατὰ τὸν λόγον] to faculties [δυνάμεων]. And, if this is so and if yet prior to them their correlate objects should have been investigated, then for the same reason [διὰ τὴν αὐτὴν αἰτίαν] we must first make a determination about them [περὶ ἐκείνων]. (415a16–22)

This does not mean imagination will have no account but only a different sort of account. In particular, if imagination, itself not a full faculty, is nonetheless a cognitive capability that is involved in the operation of cognitive capabilities that are full faculties, then we should expect Aristotle first to distinguish it from such faculties and then to provide a theory broad enough to accommodate its role in relation to them. On this suggestion, the canonical theory does the latter and B the former.

If the general context and structure of De Anima III.3 offer support for our thesis, it is short of conclusive support. So let us narrow the scope some. At 428a1–5 Aristotle stipulates, as we have seen, what sort of imagination is relevant to psychological theory and then proposes a strategy that

---

27. Hamlyn (1968) has "*first* principle" but without textual warrant.

governs the argument until the canonical theory of section C. Here is what he says.

> If then [εἰ δή] imagination is that in virtue of which we say an image [φάντασμά τι] comes about in us [ἡμῖν γίγνεσθαι][28] and is not spoken of metaphorically [μή τι κατὰ μεταφορὰν λέγεται], is it one of those, a faculty or disposition [δύναμις ἢ ἕξις], in virtue of which [καθ' ἥν] we discriminate [κρίνομεν] and are true and false? Such [τοιαῦται] are perception [αἴσθησις], belief [δόξα], knowledge [ἐπιστήμη], and mind [νοῦς].

The passage, which we shall return to in the next chapter, implies that if the canonical imagination is a discriminative faculty, then it will be one of perception, belief, knowledge, or mind. Immediately, and for the balance of the B section, Aristotle argues against *all* four identifications as well as *any* combination of belief and perception.

One might, of course, resist this conclusion by appealing to the interrogative context or by claiming that perhaps imagination is yet another discriminative faculty. But 428b8–10 concludes the B section by stating that it has been proven that imagination is none of these nor any combination of them. So much for the first line of resistance. And *De Anima* III.9 makes the second unlikely. The chapter begins by distinguishing two kinds of animal potentialities or faculties [δυνάμεις]: that in virtue of which discrimination occurs [τῷ κριτικῷ at 432a16] and that in virtue of which local movement is produced. The first includes perception [αἴσθησις] and mind [νοῦς] and these, Aristotle says, have been dealt with. The remainder of *De Anima* is devoted to movement and action. The point I wish to emphasize is just that *Aristotle* has said all he has to say about the discriminative part of the soul and no new discriminative faculties have emerged besides our original perception, belief, knowledge, and mind.

Although I have followed Ross's emendation "ἆρα" at 428a3,[29] my arguments apply equally to 428a1–5 read as a statement.[30] For we may now

---

28. Reading, with most editors, against sᴛᴠx which have "γενέσθαι."

29. The emendation is at least as old as Smith's Oxford translation. In any case, it is not clear to me (contrast now Watson, 1982, n. 10) that the sentence cannot be read interrogatively even without the emendation.

30. See also Watson (1982, 107) who sees Aristotle returning to the C section to "demonstrate that it must have its place among the capacities in virtue of which we are enabled to judge and arrive at truth or falsity, even though it is not an actual judgement, in any of the forms of judgement, about truth or falsity, and is not ἐπιστήμη or νοῦς." The claim about demonstration strikes me as rather strong but the cautionary tone about what is demonstrated is appropriate. This, however, seems to put Aristotle in the perplexing position of arguing that imagination is a faculty on a par with the mentioned four and yet providing a theory adequate only to something less. Better to reject the claim to full facultyhood. In fact, Watson

simply read Aristotle as mounting a *modus tollens* argument against the antecedent. Thus, Hicks's comment, "Imagination is then shown, 428a5–b9, to be identical with no one of them, but it ranks with them as a separate faculty (δύναμις)" (1965, 461), follows neither from 428a1–5 nor from the canonical theory. Indeed, the canonical theory contains no occurrence of "δύναμις" or a like-minded expression, does not proceed in the manner suggested for investigating a faculty, and concludes finally that imagination is a movement [κίνησις], certainly an unlikely way to characterize a faculty. So it does appear that Aristotle means to argue that imagination is not a discriminative faculty.

And in *Ethica Nicomachea* VI.3 he lists as that in virtue of which the soul is true in affirmation and denial, art [τέχνη], knowledge [ἐπιστήμη], practical reason [φρόνησις], wisdom [σοφία], and mind [νοῦς], omitting supposition [ὑπόληψις] and belief [δόξα] because they can be false as well. In VI.9, he mentions skill in conjecture [εὐστοχία], mental agility [ἀγχίνοια], and discursive reason [διάνοια], and in VI.10–11 adds understanding [σύνεσις] and judgment [γνώμη]. Nowhere in this list of discriminative faculties do we find imagination [φαντασία]. Nor will it do to suggest that imagination is a nondiscriminative faculty. Although it figures in action, *De Anima* has discussed it in connection with the discriminative faculties and that seems its proper home. Two points bear mention here. The first is that a capability can be primarily associated with one faculty and incidentally with another. *De Memoria* says this about memory (450a13–14) and imagination (450a22–25; see below) with respect to that which perceives [τὸ αἰσθητικόν] and that which thinks [τὸ νοητικόν], and there is no reason to suppose the same does not hold for imagination with respect to discrimination and action. But, and this is the second point, that imagination is required for discriminative behavior by no means implies that it is a discriminative *faculty* any more than its role in action implies that it is a faculty of local movement. What, if anything, is implied is just that imagination subserves such faculties.

The context and structure of argumentation of *De Anima* III.3 do, then, lend support to the thesis that imagination is not a full faculty. But more needs to be said, for one might still object that, the above considerations notwithstanding, imagination just is a discriminative faculty in its own right. Perhaps it might even be insisted that this explains why it can't be identified with perception, belief, knowledge, or mind. What attraction this suggestion may enjoy is diminished by the observation that "τοιαῦται" at

---

(1982, n. 10) comes close to this in saying that imagination merely provides the materials on which the mind builds judgments. Unfortunately, the point is left unappreciated.

428a4 suggests less that perception and the like are mere examples than that they are the discriminative faculties.[31] Nor is there anything in the language of the canonical theory that threatens our reading of the conclusion of the section. While these observations are friendly, they more preserve than enhance the support for our thesis. So we need to look directly at the crucial contention that imagination has no actual₂ employment.

The very language in which the canonical imagination is introduced is itself suggestive. Perception and thought are introduced by the expressions "the principle in virtue of which we say that an animal is capable of receiving" [ἡ ἀρχὴ ᾗ φαμὲν αἰσθητικὸν εἶναι τὸ ζῷον] at 427a15–16 and "the part of the soul in virtue of which the soul knows" [τὸ μόριον τῆς ψυχῆς ᾧ γινώσκει] at 429a10, whose logical form is "the X in virtue of which Y φs." As a rule X and Y will not be the same: perception is that part of the soul whereby the *soul* or the whole system, say Socrates, perceives. The canonical imagination, on the other hand, is said to be "that in virtue of which we say that an image occurs in us" [καθ᾽ ἣν λέγομεν φάντασμά τι ἡμῖν γίγνεσθαι] at 428a1–2. Apart from the fact that it is not said to be a part or principle at all, the designating expression is of a rather different form: "the X in virtue of which some Z occurs in Y." Together these forms suggest, that whereas perception and thought are faculties of a thing in virtue of which it *does* something, imagination is not. Even 428b16–17, 2b of the canonical text, suggests only that animals do much *in accordance with* it [κατ᾽ αὐτήν].

The case need not rest on this point, however. For even where something is said to do something in virtue of φαντασία, it is still the case that imagination is not the faculty responsible for the doing. Thus, when *De Anima* III.10, 433a20–21, the best counterexample I know, remarks "whenever imagination produces [κινῇ] movement, it does not do so without desire," it is making an entirely concessive point. First, interpretation is governed by 433a10ff.'s notion that imagination produces movement just in the sense that animals sometimes *follow* it. It is the animal that is doing the acting and that in virtue of which it so does is not imagination at all. Second, the 433a21–22 remark *entails* (the force of "δή" at 433a21) that only one thing produces movement, the object of desire [ὀρεκτόν],[32] and,

---

31. In this "specifying" use "τοιαυτός" functions much like the "such that" idiom familiar from quantificational techniques. *Ethica Eudemia* 1222a6–7 provides a parallel: "Virtue has been taken to be such a state [ἡ τοιαύτη ἕξις] as (a) makes people do the best and (b) in virtue of which they are best disposed in regard to the best." There is simply no suggestion here that (a) and (b) are mere examples of the state that virtue is. Rather, they specify it.

32. Reading with the manuscripts and against Torstrik's (1970) emendation, "τὸ ὀρεκτικόν." Despite its popularity (Hicks, Hamlyn, Rodier, and Ross adopt it), the manuscripts give a perfectly good sense to the passage. Because there is a determinate object of desire, the

therefore,[33] ὄρεξις is the faculty that does the moving. Imagination is involved, after the fashion of the canonical theory, simply as that which produces an image. This hardly calls for an actual$_2$ employment. Indeed, since it is absurd to suppose that the image is the object of desire, the image must figure in a secondary role as a device for [re]presenting the true pretender.

There are other indications that imagination has no actual$_2$ employment even where its role is most salient. *De Memoria,* for example, opens with the global question: to which part of the soul does this affection (τοῦτο τὸ πάθος at 449b5 = the memory) belong? The affection is officially glossed as the possession, in a certain way, of course, of an image, taken as a likeness of that of which it is an image [φαντάσματος, ὡς εἰκόνος οὗ φάντασμα, ἕξις at 451a15–16].[34] So although imagination is rung in to explain memory, the object of memory is not the image. These occur only in the *explanation* of episodes of remembering and here their role is transparently [re]presentational. Even where the theory appears to require awareness of the image, at 450b18 and 28, for example, it is the verb αἰσθάνεσθαι (perceiving) that is pressed into service. *De Insomniis* follows the same pattern, opening with the question whether dreams appear, in the first instance, to what thinks [τὸ νοητικόν] or to what perceives [τὸ αἰσθητικόν], these being the sole means by which we grasp things. If we assume that what is here grasped is the dream [τὸ ἐνύπνιον], then what is grasped is a certain image occurring in sleep [φάντασμα τι καὶ ἐν ὕπνῳ at 462a16]. Aristotle is very careful to point out that, although we are aware of dreams neither by perception [οὐκ τῇ αἰσθήσει] nor by belief [οὐδὲ τῇ δόξῃ], we nonetheless are somehow aware of them [αἰσθανόμεθα at 458b9] and belief sometimes is impeded and wrongly assents to an image [ἀκολουθεῖ at 459a6–7]. So if these cases are typical, as they appear to be, even in contexts where a faculty is active with respect to an image, the faculty does not appear to be imagination. And, as we have already seen, these will be nonstandard contexts in any case.

None of the above entails that imagination has no occurrent or episodic

---

ὀρεκτόν, there is a complete actual$_2$ function and so a single faculty whose exercise the function is. The fact that 433b19–21 indicates that the function is common to soul and body [ἐν τοῖς κοινοῖς σώματος καὶ ψυχῆς ἔργοις] means only that a faculty may be common to both as well.

33. Emphasis is to call attention to the fact that desire [ὄρεξις] is the faculty involved in action because the object of the action is to be described as an "ὀρεκτόν." This squares with our account of faculty individuation (FFO) and anticipates our later argument that imagination has no proper object at all.

34. ἕξις lends itself rather nicely to both an episodic and a dispositional sense of memory. See the discussion in *Metaphysica* V.22.

employment but only that it will not be the actual₂ employment of a *full faculty*. If I am correct in reading imagination as a general [re]presentational capability subserving other faculties, then it will at least be the case that it occurs in the course of another faculty's operation. We need to say more about this.

Suppose we begin with the claim, issued at *De Insomniis* 459a15–28 and elsewhere, that the φανταστικόν (that by which imagination occurs) and the αἰσθητικόν (that by which perception occurs) are extensionally the same but intentionally different. This I take to be the force of Aristotle's idiom that the being of the one is different from the being of the other [τὸ δ' εἶναι φανταστικῷ καὶ αἰσθητικῷ ἕτερον]. By extensional sameness we need understand nothing stronger than the requirement that the thing that perceives is also the thing that has φαντάσματα. What the alternative means is slightly less clear. To apply being-the-same but not same-in-being to two things is not, here at least, to contrast incidental with essential unity. For there is no evidence to suggest that Aristotle countenances the possibility that the φανταστικόν and the αἰσθητικόν are only incidentally connected. The first clearly depends on the second. Nor is he making the weak claim, more appropriately expressed with the relative "ᾗ," that the same thing can be regarded in two ways. The point of the contrast best emerges by taking seriously the possibility that Aristotle thinks of αἴσθησις and φαντασία in strictly functionalist terms. For if imagination and perception are functions, they may be functions of one and the same thing (even characteristic or essential functions) and yet be essentially different in their own right. Subject to certain modifications, we may say that different functions are specified by the conditions that must be satisfied by actualizations of the functions. But in order to guarantee unity of the experiencing subject, the conditions, for imagination and perception respectively, that there be something in virtue of which imagination occurs and something in virtue of which perception occurs must involve quantification over the *same* thing.

This, roughly, is the thrust of what might be called the principle of the discernibility of identicals:

PDI. $(\exists \Phi)\ (\exists \Phi')\ (\exists x)\ (\exists y)\ (\Phi$ is a faculty $\&\ \Phi'$ is faculty $\&\ \Phi \neq \Phi'$
$\&\ \Phi$ is realized in $x\ \&\ \Phi'$ realized in $y\ \&\ x = y)$.

Thus, the φανταστικόν and the αἰσθητικόν are distinguished only by differences in the functional specifications for φαντασία and αἴσθησις. Central to this, of course, is FFO with its requirement that functions be identified in terms of their formal objects. From a functionalist point of view the difference is couched in especially suggestive language. For Aristotle does not merely signal a functional difference but immediately adds a second point of distinction, namely, that imagination is movement that comes about because of actual perception [ἡ ὑπὸ τῆς κατ' ἐνέργειαν αἰσθήσεως γινομένη κίνησις at 459a17–18]. There is here at least the hint of a levels difference, especially if "ὑπό . . ." retains some of its locative force. For then the point might be that occurrences of imagination come about by way of subserving exercises of perception. It would follow from this, given *De Partibus Animalium* I. 5, 645b28–33's insistence that dependence relations between actual functions be paralleled by dependence relations between what exercises the functions, that imagination is a more general capacity than perception and one that subserves it.

Where two functions are essentially the same, neither can occur without the other occurring. If they are essentially different, it does not follow that both functions cannot co-occur. Nevertheless, certain functions seem by their nature to be incompatible with each other. Thus, remembering is incompatible with perceiving not in the sense that what does the first is necessarily different from what does the second but rather in the sense that the same thing cannot satisfy at the same time the conditions for perceiving and remembering the same thing (*De Memoria* 449b16). Wishing and believing might also exhibit incompatibility. Certain functions, however, can and some must involve other functions. Thus, the same thing can believe and perceive and anything that knows must also believe.

The crucial point is that Aristotle must hold that imagination and perception are co-occurrent in the sense that perception typically involves imagination. Indeed, he may hold the stronger thesis that if perception can involve imagination for things of a certain kind, then it always involves imagination for such things. At this point it is unclear in what, if any, sense Aristotle holds the converse. It may turn out that actual operations of imagination do not involve actual functionings of perception, but that because of the canonical theory whatever has the first must have the second. This much said, it does appear that Aristotle holds that, for all but the lowest level of perception, if S perceives A, then S has an A-related image [φάντασμα]. *De Anima* III.3 clearly implies that this thesis holds for Aristotle's three varieties of perception: perception of a proper object of sense, perception of an object incidentally, and perception of an object common to the senses. In each case an image is present *while* perception occurs.[35] Where

35. It should be clear that it is misleading to call φαντασία decaying sense perception because, as we have seen, Aristotle wants his images [φαντάσματα] to occur in actual sense perception. The temptation to regard an Aristotelian image [φάντασμα] as a decaying sense perception is, I suspect, traceable to works that deal with images that could not occur in the context of an episode of sense perception, namely, those involved in dreams and memories. These passages can be explained equally well by construing φαντάσματα as something like the form of sense perceptions. This notion, suggested by Aristotle's language in *De Anima* III.8, certainly fits nicely with the discussion of perception and is preferable.

the three varieties of perception differ is in their varying susceptibility to error. And this is due not to intrinsic qualitative features of the attendant imagination [φαντασία] but rather to the relation between this and the object apparently [re]presented by the imagination.

The point I wish to emphasize is that not only is imagination co-occurrent with perceptions in the sense indicated but also it is co-occurrent with dreaming, remembering, desiring, thinking, and the like.[36] And in each context φαντασία has the same functional value: it is what enables something to occur as the object of an episode of thinking, dreaming, remembering, and so on. De Memoria 450a1–2 reports, for example, that the same affection [τὸ αὐτὸ πάθος] occurs in thinking and constructing a diagram. This is an explicit gloss on the preceding line's reiteration of De Anima's thesis that there is no thinking without an image [νοεῖν οὐκ ἔστιν ἄνευ φαντάσματος]. So the same image is involved in contemplating a triangle and in drawing one. And an image involved in, say, remembering has no feature that, on introspection, tags it as a memory or memory-related image. This is part of the point of De Memoria 450b12–451a3's discussion to the effect that there is no intrinsic feature of an image or affection that indicates it is about another thing and so is occurring in an episode of remembering. At 450b24–26 Aristotle says that one must regard [ὑπολαβεῖν] the image in us [τὸ ἐν ἡμῖν φάντασμα] both as a thing contemplated in its own right [αὐτὸ καθ᾽ ἑαυτὸ εἶναι θεώρημα] and as an image of another thing [ἄλλου φάντασμα]. It is obvious from this passage that nothing about

36. This may be in play at De Anima III.9 where Aristotle carefully avoids associating imagination with standard faculties. The passage at 432a22–b7 raises a problem concerning the number of parts of the soul, mentioning, on the one hand, a calculative [λογιστικόν], emotive [θυμικόν], and desiderative [ἐπιθυμητικόν] division and, on the other hand, a rational [λόγον] and irrational [ἄλογον] division. Then he says: "And then there is that by which imagination occurs [τὸ φανταστικόν], on the one hand, it is different in being [τῷ εἶναι ἕτερον] from all of these and, on the other hand, it is extremely difficult to say whether it is the same [ταὐτόν] or different from any of them, if one is to suppose that the parts of the soul are separate" (432a31–b3). Since we already know that the φανταστικόν (that whereby an image occurs) and αἰσθητικόν (that whereby perception occurs) are extensionally the same [ταὐτόν] but intentionally different, what is the problem here? Apparently, it is that one cannot hold both that two different faculties are separate and that imagination is the same as one of them. This is a problem only on the assumption that imagination is involved in all faculties in just the way indicated by the case of αἴσθησις. That is, for any faculty φ, the φανταστικόν is the same as that which φs but the being of that which φs is different from the being of the φανταστικόν. At least two points emerge from this. First, Aristotle is unimpressed with talk of different parts of the soul, except in the weak sense of different functions of the soul. (See also Ethica Eudemia II.1, 1219b32–36, for an especially strong statement of the point.) How one divides the soul will depend on what functions one is interested in. Second, imagination is necessarily co-occurrent with other faculties and so is free to play a general role in accounting for how genuine faculties are directed toward objects. (Contrast Nussbaum's account, 1978, 225.)

the image itself marks it as a memory image as opposed to an image in thought.[37] Less obvious, but more important, is that the passage also makes it difficult to see how images can occur independently of some complete mental act. For if there is no intrinsic feature of an affection or image that tags it as a copy of something (and so a memory image) and if images can occur independently of functionally complete acts, then it would have to be possible for the mind to operate on an affection or image in such a way as to render it a copy. But by what mechanism is the mind supposedly able to endow an image *I* but not *I**, which differs in no relevant way, with a memory-related feature? It is not enough that the mind bring certain beliefs to bear on the image; indeed, it is unclear to me what this would even mean. Rather, the case demands that the mind supply an image with the *causal* property of being-a-copy (of something). And this is an operation the *mind* plainly cannot perform.

Fortunately, Aristotle is not committed to this rather difficult view. The point rather is that in each case the image occurs in a different cognitive context. As 452b23–29 makes clear, when one remembers something at least two things are involved. First, one is aware of or has a [re]presentation of a fact or thing, and, second, one simultaneously has an awareness of temporal distance in virtue of some present state that is causally related to what is remembered. If the causal link is absent, one can do no better than *think* (incorrectly) that one is remembering something. Aristotle puts this by saying that the change connected with the thing and the change connected with time [ἣ τοῦ πράγματος γίνηται κίνησις καὶ ἡ τοῦ χρόνου] must occur together for an episode of memory to take place. The details of Aristotle's account are not transparent, but it is clear at least that he is requiring, quite reasonably, that the soul must be capable of acquiring certain structures for [re]presenting temporal distance. Given this, it is hardly plausible to attribute to Aristotle the view that images occur independently, for that would require us to suppose that memory is an act that consists of two other acts—say, the noticing of an image and the noticing of temporal distance. How, one wonders, are these brought together in actual cases of remembering? Certainly not by noticing that the initial noticings go together. We may avoid such awkward questions by taking remembering as the basic act. Then the distinction between images as contemplated items (involved in thought) and images as copies (involved in memory) is simply part of an account of the necessary conditions for performing an act of remembering. And a necessary condition for performance

---

37. Although images and thoughts are here brought close together, *De Anima* III.8 makes clear that they are not identical. In chapter 4 I discuss this as well as the *De Memoria* account of images and thought.

of a complete act need not in turn be a performable act. Indeed, if the act is basic as well as functionally complete, then its necessary conditions could not be performable acts.

Thus construed, Aristotle's remarks on memory support the thesis that imagination is not a genuine faculty in the sense that there is no complete act that counts as imagining something. This means that imagination is functionally incomplete insofar as it has no actual₂ exercise but occurs only in the context of actual₂ exercises of functionally complete faculties.[38] Here it may be instructive to draw a partial analogy between imagination as a functionally incomplete faculty and Searle's notion of a propositional speech act. A propositional speech act such as referring can occur only as part of an illocutionary speech act. I cannot refer to Jones apart from uttering some sentence about Jones. Referring simply cannot be done on its own. An analogous point holds, I am suggesting, for imagination. One cannot, as it were, simply [re]present something.[39]

Failure to appreciate the functional incompleteness of φαντασία can have serious results. Witness Freudenthal's account (1863) of the sort of movement [κίνησις] imagination is supposed to be. Insensitive to imagination's functional incompleteness, and so to its co-occurrence with perception, Freudenthal interprets imagination as arising from delayed perceptual movement. (See also Cassirer, 1968, 108). On the basis of De Insomniis 459a15–28, he argues for the following general characterization of imagination. When stimulatory input reaches the starting point of perception (the heart or nowadays we might say the brain), the subject is aware of the object of

---

38. See De Somno, 456b11–15, which implies that the same image occurs, now in a faint, now in sleep. A puzzle arises on the assumption that the φάντασμα in each state is tied, causally or otherwise, to the state. Hence, when the state gives way so should the image. But in the case at hand it remains. Thus, again, φαντασία enters as a general [re]presentational capacity underlying other psychological states and functions.

39. It is, in this connection, worth mentioning 460b16–18: αἴτιον δὲ τοῦ συμβαίνειν ταῦτα τὸ μὴ κατὰ τὴν αὐτὴν δύναμιν κρίνειν τὸ κύριον καὶ ᾧ τὰ φαντάσματα γίγνεσθαι, which in Hett's translation, "the reason why this happens is that the controlling sense does not judge these things by the same faculty as that by which sense images occur," might encourage holdouts for full facultyhood. The business of the passage is deception and allied perceptual phenomena, the ταῦτα of the first line, and the explanatory principle it forwards is, in the line immediately following, said to be evident from ordinary cases of perception: the sun appears a foot across, but something else, presumably τὸ κύριον, or the controlling sense, contradicts this. Since the cases are meant to be parallel and since it is by virtue of sight, and so perception, that the sun appears a foot across, it must also be in connection with perception that images arise in the case of deception. So the passage says no more than that which controls does not judge by the same faculty as that in connection with which images come about. Depending on what weight we give to "τὸ κύριον," the first faculty will presumably be belief [δόξα] (see 459a6–7) or mind [νοῦς] and the second perception. Thus, while the passage may mention two faculties, neither is imagination. It turns out to be another passage in which imagination occurs by way of subserving a full faculty.

perception (τὸ αἰσθητόν) in virtue of having a picture (*Bild*) of it. This picture, called a perceptual picture by Freudenthal, is, presumably, the αἴσθημα or perceptual content. So far, wrongly I believe, imagination does not enter into the story. In certain cases, the stimulatory input is impeded and fails to reach the heart (brain); then a *second* picture is produced, namely, the image (φάντασμα). This, Freudenthal claims, is the proper sense of image and the delayed movement here is the proper sense of imagination.

I think we can see that this story is incoherent and how the functional incompleteness doctrine allows us to avoid it. First, we should be careful in drawing general conclusions about imagination from what is arguably, especially for an incompleteness theorist, only one of its contexts. Second, the view faces a dilemma. For the second picture is said to be a picture of the first picture: the image is a picture of the perceptual picture, or *Wahrnehmungsbild*. Now the first picture is either an αἴσθημα or a movement, albeit delayed, in the αἰσθητήριον or sensory organ. It cannot be the first because then the subject would be aware of the object of perception. If it is in the sensory organ, then we must explain how a movement in the sensory organ can be a picture, since in this context pictures seem to be the sort of thing one is aware of. If we can circumvent this difficulty, then it must make sense to distinguish between a picture in the sensory organ and a picture that results when the stimulus reaches the heart (brain) *even in ordinary cases* of perception. So in ordinary cases there will be two rather than one picture, or *Wahrnehmungsbild*.

The way to avoid this bizarre result is to deny that the image, or φάντασμα, occurring in sleep is a picture at all of the alleged first picture (the perceptual or immediate picture of the object). This is unacceptable to Freudenthal because it leaves him with no images at all or with images that are not pictures. Since Aristotle does seem to treat images as pictorially [re]presentational[40] at least some of the time, this is a serious problem. The solution is to apply the causal and incompleteness aspects of the canonical theory with equal force to dreams and to ordinary perception. In the first case there is only one [re]presentational device involved, namely, the image that results from a delayed causal process but a causal process nonetheless. In the second case we hold, as indicated, that in all ordinary cases of perception, imagination is involved as a necessary condition. Of course, the latter point is difficult to grasp if one thinks of imagination not as capability subserving mental acts but as a complete mental act itself.[41]

---

40. See chap. 6, sec. 6, for more on this notion.

41. One of the arguments against identifying perception and imagination may, by itself, exclude imagination's claims to full facultyhood, *if* "τούτων" picks up "δύναμις ἢ ἐνέργεια" in 428a6–7: "While perception is either a potentiality or an activity [δύναμις ἢ ἐνέργεια], for

If, then, imagination is not a full faculty, it is surely involved in the actual₂ use of such faculties. Perception, desire, and thought require it and so do memory and even dreams. Imagination is required because images are required not as the object toward which the faculty is directed but as a means by which a faculty accomplishes this. The draftsman does not draw the image nor the theoretician think it, but nonetheless the image is involved in what they do. So also for desire[42] and memory. One could characterize the situation in the following way. Whenever a subject S performs a cognitive act, S does so in virtue of a faculty and the faculty, in turn, uses images in accomplishing its task. So we have the subject, paradigmatically a person, at the level of the intentional system, a faculty at the subsystem level, and images as general [re]presentational devices that are used by faculty subsystems when the system as a whole performs a given cognitive act (more on this later). Although the language is anachronistic and Aristotle has at best a rudimentary notion of information storage and interpretation, what he does say more than justifies the cognitivist idiom.

5. FUNCTIONAL INCOMPLETENESS AND THE INGREDIENTS OF IMAGINATION

Now it seems to me that the thesis we have been urging is not surprising if we keep the canonical theory at the front. For by restricting itself to that in virtue of which images come about in us, the canonical theory focuses on the production rather than the independent use of images. Hence, its imagination will not be an active faculty let alone the so-called creative imagination. Full cognitive faculties, on the other hand, use images as the devices by which the object of the faculty is [re]presented. Without images there would be no actual₂ exercises of faculties, at least not of typically cognitive faculties. So if imagination simply subserves other faculties, then there will be no role for it as a full faculty. Thus, the canonical theory leads

---

instance sight or seeing, something can appear when neither of these [μηδετέρον τούτων] obtains, for instance what appears in sleep." However, most commentators find, not implausibly, that the passage opposes imagination to potential and actual *perception*.

42. In *De Motu Animalium* Aristotle puts it thus: "affections [τὰ πάθη] suitably prepare the organic parts [τὰ ὀργανικὰ μέρη], desire [ἡ ὄρεξις] prepares the affections, and imagination prepares the desire; and imagination comes about because of [γίνεται διά] thinking [νοήσεως] or perceiving [αἰσθήσεως]" (702a18–19). Since the preparation in question is preparation for action, imagination is again linked with determinateness in action. And since, from our discussion of the canonical theory and *Analytica Posteriora* II.19, we know that "γίνεται διά" cannot here have acquisitional or genetic force, the passage squares with, indeed, appears to imply that imagination operates only in conjunction with the actual exercise of standard faculties.

to the important and striking conclusion that, canonically, imagination has no object at all. It fails, in short, to satisfy a necessary condition of full facultyhood.

The thesis that there are no objects of imagination is displayed dramatically in the tally of φαντασία's ingredients. We may give these as follows: (1′) φαντασία (imagination), (2′) φανταστικόν (that by which imagination occurs), (3′) φάντασμα (image or [re]presentation), (4′) . . . , (5′) . . . , (6′) φαντάζεσθαι (imagining or imaging).

It is instructive to compare 1′–6′ with the ingredients of perception, 1–6, given at the beginning of section 2 of this chapter. Both 1 and 1′ seem to be generic notions with 2–5 providing the ingredients of an episode of perception and 2′–3′ providing the ingredients of an occurrence of imagination. An obvious contrast in the lists is the omission at 5′ of any physical organ for imagination. This, of course, does not imply that φαντασία is not dependent on the body but only that, if it is dependent, it is so nonspecifically. In contrast a given proper faculty of sense is specifically dependent on the body insofar as that faculty, and no other, can be exercised only through the use of a given bodily organ. So the dependence of imagination on the body will be general in the sense that it need not occur in connection with the operation of any given sensory organ. As Aristotle says at De Memoria 450a10–12, "the image is an affection of the common sense [τὸ φάντασμα τῆς κοινῆς αἰσθήσεως πάθος ἐστίν]; so this is clear that awareness of them [τούτων ἡ γνῶσις] is due to the first thing that perceives [τῷ πρώτῳ αἰσθητικῷ]."

The nonspecific dependence of imagination on the body is frequently misunderstood. Ross (1955), for example, construes the De Memoria passage to claim that imagination is especially or properly concerned with the common sensibles. Presumably, this means that the paradigm cases of images are images of objects of the common sense. This is unwarranted. That sometimes we have φαντάσματα of common sensibles is sufficient for associating φαντασία with the common sense rather than just the special senses, but it is hardly sufficient to make its paradigm occurrences those in which a common sensible is [re]presented. Just as perception of a common object of sense is no less perception than perception of a proper object of sense so the φαντασία involved in the first case is no less φαντασία than that involved in the second case.

Indeed, it is not even clear that 450a10–12 intends to assert a general point about images as opposed to images involved in [re]presenting time. But if imagination is said to belong to the common sense, taking "τῆς κοινῆς αἰσθήσεως" (of the common sense) at a10–11 and "τῷ πρώτῳ αἰσθητικῷ" (by the first thing that perceives) at a11–12 as codesignative, it is simply because at least one case requires it, namely, memory. For we must be capable of grasping [γνωρίζειν] time, and this will be done by the same thing that grasps motion and magnitude. Thus, the images involved in such cognition must themselves belong to the common sense. So although it appears that imagination is located more deeply in the psychological system, it does not follow that it is involved any less in the operation of standard faculties. Indeed, if imagination is a general [re]presentational capability, then one would expect to find it located at just such a point in the cognitive model.

For immediate purposes, however, the most striking fact about the primed list is the omission of the φανταστόν or object of imagination at 4'. Were there a significant correlation between 4 and 4', then we might expect that just as there is a domain of objects of perception so also is there a domain of objects of imagination. As what one perceives is an αἰσθητόν so what one imagines would be a φανταστόν. Absence of the φανταστόν means not just that imagination lacks an ingredient enjoyed by perception, for νοῦς too lacks an ingredient; there is no organ of thought, yet none doubt its status as a faculty. Nor does the absence signal simply that objects of imagination, unlike objects of perception, are not external items, for Aristotle countenances objects of thought [τὰ νοητά] despite the fact that they are in some sense internal.[43] The point, rather, is that imagination's missing ingredient appears to be a necessary condition for full facultyhood. It is precisely what is required by FFO.

At least twice, at 402b9–16 and 415a14–22, we have seen Aristotle either assert or imply, in laying down methodological guidelines, that faculties are determined in terms of actual₂ functions and actual₂ functions in terms of objects. One is, he asserts at 402b16, first to examine the object of perception [τὸ αἰσθητὸν] and the object of thought [τὸ νοητὸν], and so on. And De Anima III.10 (see below) counts desire as a faculty because it is triggered by the object of desire [τὸ ὀρεκτόν]. Aristotle is not sparing with the form. Besides "αἰσθητόν" (object of perception), "νοητόν" (object of thought), and "ὀρεκτόν" (object of desire), "μνημονευτόν" (object of memory) occurs in De Memoria at 449b9 and 450a24 (and also in Rhetorica 1367a24 and 1370b1), and "ἐπιστητόν" (object of knowledge), a favored expression in Categoriae VII, occurs unproblematically in De Anima at 430a5, 431b23 and b27.[44] The φανταστόν, on the other hand, makes no uncontested appearance in the corpus.

43. See De Anima II.5 and chapter 5 below.
44. Also at Analytica Priora I.33, with "δοξαστόν" (object of belief) as well. The latter occurs again at Analytica Priora I.39,49b6–7, alongside "ὑποληπτόν" (object of supposition), which corresponds to the very general notion of supposition [ὑπόληψις]. (On the latter, see

The least that is suggested by the omission is that imagination is not to be investigated in the manner of a full faculty. This, of course, squares with what we have already observed about the argumentation of *De Anima* III.3. But 415a14–22 (see beginning of chap. 2, sec. 4) is not merely methodological. Aristotle says that in order to say *what* each faculty is [τί ἕκαστον αὐτῶν] it is necessary to say what its actual₂ function is—what, for instance, thinking is [τί τὸ νοεῖν]. And this in turn requires saying toward what objects [περὶ ἐκείνων] the function is directed (415a21–22's διὰ τὴν αὐτὴν αἰτίαν leans on πράξεις κατὰ τὸν λόγον two lines earlier). So Aristotle appears committed to the stronger point that imagination cannot be *defined* as a faculty at all.

It is important to reiterate that the FFO condition is not extensional. An object touched may be seen as well and what is now remembered was once perceived. Something is an object of thought, desire, and so on, relative to an appropriate description of the object. So FFO's formal object requirement on faculties requires that they be identified in terms of the functions they explain and that the functions be determined by providing descriptions such that any object satisfying the description in question counts as an object of the corresponding faculty.[45] Faculties *are* capacities for having, cognitively, certain kinds of objects. So, of course, the objects are definitionally prior. And since to have a given faculty is to have capability that is caused to act (causally actualized₂) by an object of the appropriate sort objects have a crucial causal role as well.

The canonical theory, on the other hand, is a theory about a capability that has no formal object and so cannot be brought to action in the manner required for faculties. Rather than the φανταστόν causing occurrence of an image, Aristotle needs the more complex account involving a first movement causing a second. From the point of view of Aristotle's psychology, then, φανταστά, or objects of imagination, are irrelevant items. Again our interpretation of CT explains this. If imagination is a general [re]-presentational capability, involved equally in the full range of a person's cognitive repertoire, then it will not have a distinct object range.[46] Hence, it cannot be defined in terms of its proper objects, and so its account must

---

chapter 4.) And at *Metaphysica* 1012a1, 1021a30, and *De Motu Animalium* 700b24 we get "διανοητόν" (object of discursive thought).

45. As already mentioned, the notion of a formal object is anything but straightforward. For convenience, I am following Kenny's characterization (1963, 189ff.).

46. The principle invoked here is not threatened by *De Anima* III.4's remark that νοῦς thinks anything, for, while in a sense true, the remark occurs in a preparative section of the chapter and Aristotle later offers a specific characterization of objects of thought. More on this below.

proceed by locating it within the field of functions it subserves. And this seems to me pretty much what we saw Aristotle do in *De Anima* III.3.

Because FFO is a strong requirement, it cautions that not every use of an intentional verb can be assumed to introduce an actual, function of a full faculty. This will not, for example, be the case with "φαντάξεσθαι" (imagining) at 5'. This is borne out by *De Anima* 433b10–12, where imagination is discussed as a factor in desire: "Hence, that which produces movement will be one in kind, the faculty of desire as such [τὸ ὀρεκτικόν ἦ ὀρεκτικόν] and first of all the object of desire [τὸ ὀρεκτόν], for this produces movement without being moved, by being thought of or imaged [τῷ νοηθῆναι ἦ φαντασθῆναι]." This passage is interesting for several reasons. Notice, first, that just as something counts as an object of a faculty relative to a description so also something counts as a faculty relative to its being determined by such an object. This is the point of the "ἦ ὀρεκτικόν" (as such). Second, the passage shows that absence of the φανταστόν cannot be due to the intransitivity of "φαίνεται" (appears), for Aristotle here shows himself capable of the transitive "φαντάζεσθαι." Third, the form, rare in any event for Aristotle, clearly has passive force at this, its sole occurrence in *De Anima*.[47] Fourth, the object of the verb, τὸ ὀρεκτόν, or the object of desire, is the object of a complete faculty. Thus, the passage is at once in accordance with FFO and in agreement with the functional incompleteness of imagination.[48]

Careful readers will, however, object that at least once, although only once, at 450a24 in one of the very texts cited in defense of our view, Aristotle mentions objects of imagination [φανταστά]. Most editors[49] read the crucial lines, 450a23–25, with manuscript M: "καὶ ἔστι μνημονευτὰ καθ' αὑτὰ μὲν {ὅσα ἐστὶ φανταστά} κατὰ συμβεβηκὸς δὲ ὅσα μὴ ἄνευ φαντασίας," which we can render: "whatever is an object of imagination is an object of memory per se and whatever is not without imagination is an object of memory incidentally." Now *if* Aristotle is going to mention the object of imagination [φανταστόν], then this is the sort of thing we might expect him to say.[50]

47. Indeed, if Schofield is right, "φαντάξεσθαι" has passive force in all of its pre-Hellenic appearances.

48. Our interpretation may alleviate Kenny's (1967) difficulty over ranking φαντασία and αἴσθησις on a par. For imagination may be essential to the faculty of perception without itself being a faculty. Hence, it can be involved in explaining perception without superseding that faculty. In particular, imagination is not, as Beare thought (1908, 292–93), the faculty that causes perceptual error. Error in perception is still perception and the only role for imagination is in accounting for the conditions of such perception.

49. Bekker, Biehl (followed by G. R. T. Ross), Hett, Mugnier, for instance, Sorabji's "objects of imagination" (1972, 49) would appear to put him in this camp.

50. This is exactly the characterization of the φανταστόν attributed to Chrysippus. See below and Appendix A for more on this.

Yet, even here, while the φαντασtά are said to be *objects* of a cognitive act, it is not imagining but remembering. But even if they are not properly objects of *memory*, we still are stuck with a solitary mention of *objects* of imagination—an undesirable largesse from our point of view.

Fortunately, a look at the manuscripts undermines confidence in even this thin gesture toward φαντασtά. For there are, in fact, no less than three distinct readings of the crucial phrase (which I set off in braces): M, as we have seen, has ὅσα ἐστὶ φαντασtά; the manuscripts EY have been taken to read ὅσα μὴ ἐστὶ φαντασtά; LSU have ὧν ἐστὶ φαντασία and are followed by a marginal comment in E. The problem with the received reading is not simply that the text is unusually corrupt; it is rather the nature of the corruption that is striking. From Biehl on there has been general agreement that EMY form one manuscript group and LSU another. Ross (1955, 61–68) regards Y as a transcription of E and finds E and M to be in remarkable agreement. Here he appears to follow Mugnier (1953; see the introduction to his edition) who took E, the oldest of all the manuscripts, to be the true prototype of M and Y. Faced with broad divergence in readings between the two groups, Mugnier recommended an all-or-nothing strategy and opted for EMY.

The immediate case, however, calls for decision and Mugnier opted for M as against EY (presumably, for reasons of interpretation). But this is more than a little awkward, for not only does M contradict EY, but also E, the reading Mugnier rejects, is supposed to be the prototype for the entire group. So if his prototype argument is correct, we seem forced either to stay with E or to adopt LSU's "ὧν ἐστὶ φαντασία" (the things of imagination). Either choice leaves Aristotle's account free of objects of imagination [φαντασtά].[51] Indeed, the first has him rejecting them outright. But the troublesome contradiction would remain, and thus I am inclined to follow Ross (1955)[52] and E's marginal annotator by reading with LSU.[53]

The sense of the passage then becomes: the objects of memory, per se, are the things of imagination and the objects of memory, incidentally, are the things that are not without imagination. From 450a10–14's remark that imagination belongs properly or primarily to perception and incidentally to

51. There is, of course, a third alternative—simply washing one's hands of the whole affair. And this is one case where it might not be too harsh a response.

52. He does, however, talk about objects of imagination (1955, 33, 236).

53. Siwek (1963) also follows LSU but reads the marginal notation in E as "ᾧ ἐστὶ φαντασtά." It is possible that a later, post-Aristotelian use of "φαντασtόν" supported the anomalous transcription of "φαντασtόν" in E. As it turns out there is just such a usage. (See Appendix A.) But however we explain the deviations of M and Y from E, one thing is clear: there simply are no firm grounds for finding in *De Memoria* mention of φαντασtά. Equally, then, we are further supported in our thesis that for Aristotle imagination is not a full faculty.

mind, it is clear that the per se objects of memory are objects of perception [αἰσθητά] and the incidental ones objects of thought [νοητά]. So φαντασtά are required neither by the manuscripts nor by interpretation, and thus the claim that Aristotle nowhere countenances objects of imagination holds up. Either he uses the expression "φανταστά" by way of making an entirely negative point about them or else he avoids it entirely in making a positive point about something else. And the positive point is carefully couched in terms of the genitive pronoun "ὧν," the same idiom used in 1d of the canonical text. There, too, imagination was said to concern itself with the things of perception [ὧν αἴσθησις]. And there, as here, the point would appear to be that imagination's role is [re]presentational, strictly or properly that of [re]presenting objects of perception,[54] even when these are [re]presented in acts of remembering.

54. Below I discuss how this figures in the argument that thought requires images.

III

THE CONSISTENCY OF
THE CANONICAL THEORY

Aristotle's canonical theory occupies approximately one third of *De Anima* III.3. Although it is put to use elsewhere, its claim to be a general theory has been challenged on at least two fronts. For some the unity of Aristotle's notion of φαντασία looks too fragile to yield a coherent theory. Other, less optimistic commentators find that Aristotle has not even managed to provide a consistent set of remarks on the topic—even in *De Anima* III.3 itself. In this chapter I address both concerns and argue that the canonical theory is consistent with the balance of III.3 and that it can be consistently extended to a variety of other texts as well.

1. METAPHORICAL VERSUS
CANONICAL IMAGINATION

Doubts about the internal consistency of *De Anima* III.3 can be traced to the beginning of B where Aristotle imposes the following limitation on his investigation: "If, then, imagination [φαντασία] is that in virtue of which we say an image comes about in us [καθ' ἣν λέγομεν φάντασμά τι ἡμῖν γίγνεσθαι] and is not spoken of metaphorically [μὴ τι κατὰ μεταφορὰν λέγομεν], is it one of those, a faculty or disposition, in virtue of which we discriminate and are true or false?" (428a1–4).[1] Most commentators agree that the nonmetaphorical notion of imagination is just the notion addressed by the canonical theory. But the latter has seemed to be an entirely different

---

1. We have already discussed the general role of this passage in the chapter as a whole. Here the focus is strictly on the disctinction between metaphorical and nonmetaphorical imagination.

notion from the one used in the remainder of B. It appears, then, that B isolates one notion of imagination, whereas section C (428b10–429a10) provides a theory about a completely different notion. This is hardly a model of sound theory construction and we would be well-advised to spare Aristotle its authorship. Reconciling B and C requires getting clear on the exact nature of the alleged inconsistency, and this depends, in part, on what weight one gives the words "κατὰ μεταφορὰν λέγομεν." Here there is considerable divergence.

Hicks held that the metaphorical use "replaces in turn ἐπιστήμη [knowledge], δόξα [belief], αἴσθησις [perception], and νόησις [thought]" and that "in fact, it may be said to mean πᾶν τὸ φαινόμενον [anything that appears] or πάθος ὁτιοῦν τῶν ἐν τῇ ψυχῇ [affection of whatever is in the soul]" (1965, 460–61). The first of these claims cannot be correct, for 428a1–4 precludes that the notion of imagination to be scrutinized in De Anima III.3 is the metaphorical one. So when Aristotle proceeds to inquire whether imagination is identical with knowledge, belief, perception, or thought, he is asking whether imagination, nonmetaphorically taken, is identical with any of these, not whether imagination in the broader, variable sense is. Otherwise he would be asking, absurdly, whether something that is either knowledge, belief, perception, or thought is identical with either knowledge, belief, perception, or thought. So the metaphorical imagination cannot play the role Hicks assigns to it. This also shows, incidentally, that Hicks's two claims do not mean the same thing.

Hamlyn (1968) links the metaphorical sense of imagination with appearing [φαίνεσθαι] and the strict sense with image-producing [φαντάζεσθαι].[2] This is superior to Hicks's reading but threatens to leave Aristotle with an inconsistent mix. For, in Hamlyn's view, 428a1–4 commits Aristotle to discussion of imagination as image-production, yet much of the argumentation in B is relevant to only the wider notion of imagination as appearing. A reading free of this inconsistency would obviously be preferable.

Schofield (1978) turns the distinction between the nonmetaphorical and metaphorical notions of imagination into a contrast between a skeptical or noncommittal notion of appearing and the notion occurring in ordinary perceptual reports or reports of beliefs. The nonmetaphorical φαντασία is not, as with Hamlyn, to be associated with φαντάζεσθαι (image-produc-

---

2. This is muddied some by the fact that Hamlyn (1968, 152) makes the distinction in the final lines of De Anima III.10 between imagination concerned with reasoning [λογιστική] and that concerned with perception [αἰσθητική] equivalent to imagination qua kind of thought and imagination qua perceptual illusion. This is unlikely given the chapter's ultimate sentence which sets both in the context of a discussion of action.

ing) but rather with φαίνεται (appearing). The latter, however, is given skeptical weight. Only two points about Schofield's view need concern us immediately: first, the claim that the arguments in B are without point unless they concern a skeptical notion of imagination and, second, the connected claim that Aristotle's account is consistent after all because the canonical theory of C is an account of nonparadigmatic sensory experience and not an account of sensory experience in general. In particular, it is held to be an account tailored for the skeptical use of φαίνεσθαι (appearing), which Schofield thinks dominates the discussion in B.

I shall presently argue that there is no support for the first of the above claims. Before doing so, however, we should look at two considerations that defeat the second claim. First, restriction of the canonical theory to nonparadigmatic sensory experiences undermines the general strategy of De Anima. Recall only that one of its lead themes is the dependence of mind on body and that this is examined in terms of the dependence of thought on imagination. When the point is pursued in De Anima III.7 and 8, there simply is no role for skeptical imagination. It would be bizarre at best were Aristotle to promote, as his official version, a notion of imagination that was irrelevant to the main concerns in De Anima. Schofield's attempt (1978, 133n24) to deal with this problem strikes me as rather weak. He argues, or at least needs to argue, (i) that the sort of imagination that accompanies thinking is like visualizing and (ii) that this is sufficiently like ordinary perceptual experience to be a nonstandard form of it. Apart from the fact that i appears to give imagination an active role, something we have denied in the last chapter, there simply is no plausible way to give this use of imagination the requisite skeptical weight. Aristotle never suggests that imagination has skeptical force here. So its primary role cannot be a skeptical role because surely its employment in connection with thought counts as a primary employment.[3] Thus, Schofield's suggestion that were one to think about "the accompanying imagery . . . one would certainly wish to report it in terms which make clear that one is not necessarily making a claim about how one sees the world" simply amounts to moving counters about. In any event, as he states the case, we still have no skeptical use—unless he infers from the fact that images need not be true descriptions of what they [re]present that imagination is an essentially skeptical operation. But this would be a simple fallacy.

Second, within C itself there are conclusive grounds for rejecting Schofield's view. The passage 428b17–30, introduced above, implies that images

3. See chap. 4, sec. 1, which argues that the extension of φαντασία to thought requires that it is the same notion of imagination that is being extended.

accompany perceptual experiences that one reports correctly as well as those one reports incorrectly. Moreover, the passage implies that where a proper object of sense is present the image involved is invariably trustworthy. This is part of an account of ordinary sensory experience and its relation to imagination. So the very development of the canonical theory contains a passage that excludes restriction of the theory to the skeptical φαντασία.

Schofield's attempt to deal with this troublesome passage is predictably desperate:

> The account of φαντασία at 428b25–30 . . . does present an embarrassment for my own interpretation. . . . what of the notion that while someone is perceiving a special object, e.g., seeing something white, he may also enjoy an infallible kind of φαντασία of that selfsame object? I have no answer to this puzzle. All I can suggest is that Aristotle has here been overwhelmed by the scholasticism of this attempt to distinguish three sorts of φαντασία corresponding to his three kinds of sense perception, which strikes most readers as a baroque extravagance. That is, he is so intent on constructing parallel subdivisions that he fails to notice that the idea of an infallible type of φαντασία cannot bear scrutiny. (1978, 115)

It is hardly Aristotle who is overwhelmed. First, there is *no* reason to find 428b17–30 distinguishing three kinds of imagination as opposed to three kinds of perception in which imagination occurs. Our objection in the last chapter to Ross's reading of *De Memoria* 450a11–12 applies here as well: imagination is uniformly involved in the special and the common sensibles. Second, the answer to the alleged puzzle is simply that the canonical theory need not be so rudely curtailed because B does not force upon us a skeptical use of φαντασία. But even were some of B's arguments to utilize the so-called skeptical φαντασία, it would not follow that the canonical theory is a theory of nonparadigmatic sensory experiences. For it may be the case that the theory explains both paradigmatic and nonparadigmatic sensory experiences. Indeed, 428b17–30 would seem to suggest how this might work.

Nussbaum (1978, 252–55) preserves the connection between the non-metaphorical imagination [φαντασία] and appearing [φαίνεσθαι] but denies the latter skeptical force. She thus rejects Schofield's interpretation. On the other hand, she also rejects Hamlyn's linkage of the nonmetaphorical imagination with image production. Two reasons are given for this. First, there are no good grounds for supposing that "φάντασμα" must mean pictorial image in 428a1–4 or in any other passage. For certain construals of "pictorial image" this is doubtless true, but, as we have already seen, it is demonstrably false if images [φαντάσματα] are interpreted as forms of a certain kind. Whether, qua forms, images are pictorial images is a matter for later discussion. But it is clear at this point that the canonical imagination is image-producing insofar as images can be interpreted as forms or [re]presentational structures. Second, Nussbaum objects that tying the non-metaphorical imagination to image-production renders it inconsistent with the balance of B. Since I hold that the nonmetaphorical imagination is just the variety dealt with in the canonical theory, I defer discussion of this objection until I turn to my own proposal for reconciling B and C.

Preferring to live with the inconsistency between B and C, Nussbaum counsels that "the best course for the interpreter seems to be not to try to read inconsistencies away, or to try to make everything fit with what seems the most technical passage" (1978, 252). Obviously, this is the best course only if a plausible reconciliation is unavailable. It is also odd advice given that the passage in question is not "merely" technical but shows all the signs of being the preferred notion. It appears, then, what Nussbaum leaves unmentioned, that now the nonmetaphorical φαντασία cannot be the canonical φαντασία of C, for she reads the latter but not the former in terms of a decaying-sense theory of imagination. This is surely a prima facie mark against her interpretation, for it means that Aristotle's announced subject of investigation is not the one developed in the canonical theory. Thus, on Nussbaum's account, there could be no inconsistency between B and C because the chapter is too disjoint even for this.

Nussbaum obviously cannot join Schofield and Hamlyn in taking the metaphorical use of "φαντασία" to signify the notion of appearing in general. Following Freudenthal, she remarks that "φαντασία" can mean "(mere) show, pomp, ostentatiousness" and argues that this is the metaphorical sense meant in 428a1–4.[4] The remark on the point of usage is acceptable, but that 428a2 counts as a case in point is, I submit, mistaken. An initial reservation is that only one passage in Aristotle can be marshaled in support of the Freudenthal reading, namely, *Rhetorica* 1404a11: "But all of these (that is, fine points of diction) are φαντασία and are aimed at the listener." Although this could be made to suggest that certain rhetorical uses of *language* are metaphorical (or, perhaps, imaginative) uses, nothing is said here about a metaphorical use of φαντασία itself. So further argument is needed. Nussbaum offers two additional considerations. First, Aristotle standardly uses "κατὰ μεταφοράν" (metaphorically) to mark the transfer or extension of a term to an area where it does not strictly apply:

4. Now also Watson (1982, 105–9).

"a conscious shift away from the basic ordinary usage" (1978, 253). Second, in the context of 428a1–4, the metaphorical use of "φαντασία" cannot involve or mention images [φαντάσματα], since this is the salient feature of the nonmetaphorical use. Since the basic or ordinary use of φαντασία is said to be that connected with appearing in general and since the canonical (for Nussbaum decaying-sense) notion obviously is excluded from consideration, only the rhetorical imagination seems to remain.

The second additional consideration is correct but, as we shall see, can be satisfied by a rather different interpretation of 428a1–4. The first consideration deserves special scrutiny because it underlies Nussbaum's pessimism about reconciling B, the locus of 428a1–4, with the canonical theory of C. Although it is correct that, literally, "κατὰ μεταφοράν" standardly indicates the transfer or extension of a term, this need not be transfer or extension beyond the term's *ordinary* usage. It is sufficient that the term be used in a transferred or extended sense relative to some fixed sense. This, I submit, is precisely Aristotle's procedure in 428a1–4. Here I follow Simplicius who suggests that Aristotle is distinguishing the sort of imagination that concerns him "from that which we derive *from* it metaphorically, when we use φαντασία for τὸ φαινόμενον (what appears to be the case) in perception and belief" (1882b, 208, lines 7–8). This suggests the following reading of the passage. First, Aristotle specifies a kind of imagination according to which something describable in φαντασία-related language, namely, the image, or φάντασμα, occurs in us. Since the notion of something describable in φαντασία-related language can be extended beyond this strict or proper domain to τὰ φαινόμενα or whatever appears to us to be the case, it is arguably the latter that is being denied systematic consideration in *De Anima* III.3. We should note here, what we later argue, that this restriction does not preclude Aristotle's holding that φαντάσματα (images) are involved in contexts where φαινόμενα (things that appear) are involved.[5] Rather, he is interested in φαντασία simply as part of an account of how the mind [re]presents objects, and this, we have already seen, requires discussion of φαντάσματα but not of φαινόμενα.

The Simplicius-inspired reading of "κατὰ μεταφοράν" agrees rather nicely with the results of chapter 2. For if there are no proper objects of φαντασία, then Aristotle would surely not isolate for investigation a notion of φαντασία that included φαινόμενα, for the latter are indeed objects, namely, whatever objects (however widely construed) appear to us in epi-

5. Incidentally, since such contexts typically involve belief, on our view it is unsurprising that B devotes considerable space to distancing φαντασία from belief and the like.

sodes of perceiving, believing, and the like.[6] On the other hand, if φαντάσματα are nothing more than [re]presentational devices that are necessary
for such episodes, it would, contra Nussbaum, be quite appropriate for
Aristotle at 428a1–4 to restrict the discussion to φαντασία in this technical
role. Besides, if Nussbaum *is* correct about the metaphorical imagination,
then φαίνεται, or appearance, contexts turn out after all to be φαντάσματα,
or image, contexts. At least this will be so if 428a1–4's contrast is drawn
generally, as it surely seems.[7] Thus, it will be essential to argue that "φάντασμα" does not mean anything like "image." And, if the contrast isn't to
be taken generally, then it loses point.[8]

Let me close this section by taking a final look at Schofield's arguments
for a skeptical reading of the nonmetaphorical imagination [ἡ φαντασία καθ'
ἣν λέγομεν φάντασμά τι ἡμῖν γίγνεσθαι]. First, he eschews the "mental
image" reading of "φάντασμα" and takes it "simply [it "does duty"] as
the noun corresponding to the cautious, sceptical, and non-committal φαίνεται" (1978, 199). I am unclear what the last part of this claim means.
Schofield apparently means to deny that images [φαντάσματα] are the sorts
of things to be quantified over, that they are not to figure as items mentioned in the psychological theory of *De Anima* and *Parva Naturalia*. But
this would be hard to square with the fact that "φάντασμα," as "αἴσθημα"
suggests, at a minimum, what results from a process of the relevant kind.
In addition, it would be odd at best for Aristotle to give canonical status
to φαντάσματα that fail to fit his account of action, have no place in his
theory of thinking, and run counter to his explanation of how various kinds
of perception admit of truth and falsity.[9]

Second, Schofield makes much of the "λέγομεν" (we say) at 428a1, arguing that it indicates not that imagination *is* the faculty in virtue of which
φαντάσματα occur to us but only that imagination is the faculty in virtue
of which we *say* that they occur to us. The "λέγομεν" is alleged to import
a linguistic criterion for the nonmetaphorical imagination, for Schofield one
that embodies the skeptical "φαίνεται" (1978, 119–20). The idea, roughly,
is that we make such pronouncements when registering doubt or caution

6. This tells against Hicks's suggestion that the metaphorical use of "φαντασία" means
"πᾶν τὸ φαινόμενα" or "πάθος ὁτιοῦν τῶν ἐν τῇ ψυχῇ."

7. Watson, who sides with Nussbaum on the identity of the metaphorical imagination,
may not be vulnerable to this difficulty because of his openness to a more global role for an
image-producing imagination.

8. Thus, if anything, what gets left out of the story is the so-called rhetorical sense of
"φαντασία." This is what one would expect of a notion that is so distant to the concerns of
De Anima in the first place.

9. Schofield thinks the sun example at *De Anima* 428b2–4 and *De Insomniis* 460b16ff.
clearly support his thesis. In the following section, I give the first a rather different reading
and I have already dealt with the second, if in a slightly different regard, in the above chapter.

about our perceptual experience or that of someone else. Intuitively, it strikes me as straining the Greek unduly to give such doctrinal weight to the occurrence of "λέγομεν" let alone to find in it a criterion. There is further consideration that, by itself, undercuts this support for the view. At the end of the preceding chapter, Aristotle says that he has now completed the account of the principle in virtue of which we say [φαμέν] that the animal is capable of perception. It would be silly to find here even a hint of skepticism, yet the passage parallels 428a1–4. Or does "λέγομεν" but not "φαμέν" carry skeptical force? Simply put, the formula "καθ᾽ ἣν λέγομεν" (in virtue of which we say) lends no support to the skeptical interpretation of φαντασία. And the thesis will have even less support if we can show that the arguments in B do not require a skeptical reading.

2. RECONCILING THEORY AND PRACTICE IN *DE ANIMA* III. 3

Several passages in B have been held to conflict with the canonical theory insofar as they seem to ascribe to imagination certain properties the canonical imagination by its nature cannot have. In this section I consider such passages together with some supposedly kindred passages from other texts. What shall be shown is that the inconsistency is only apparent.

We begin with passages supposedly establishing that imagination is simply a kind of thinking. This would, of course, damage our interpretation by forcing abandonment of functional incompleteness for at least those cases of imagination that are cases of thinking. (Here I assume that anything that counts as thinking is functionally complete.) Two such troublesome passages from *De Anima* III.3 are 427b14–17:

> For imagination is different from both perception and thought [διανοίας] and this [αὕτη = imagination] does not occur without perception nor supposition without it. That imagination is not the same kind of thinking as supposition is clear [ὅτι δ᾽ οὐκ ἔστιν ἡ αὐτὴ νόησις καὶ ὑπόληψις φανερόν].

and 427b27–29:

> As for thought [περὶ τοῦ νοεῖν], since it is different from perceiving and seems to include on the one hand imagination [φαντασία] and on the other supposition [ὑπόληψις], we must determine about imagination before going on to discuss the other.

We can add two passages extrinsic to *De Anima* III.3, namely, 403a8–10:

> But if this [τοῦτο = νοεῖν] too is a form of imagination [φαντασία
> τις] or does not exist apart from imagination, it would not be
> possible even for this [νοεῖν] to exist apart from body.

and 433a9–12:

> It is at any rate clear that these two produce movement, either
> desire [ὄρεξις] or intellect [νοῦς], if we set down the imagination
> as a kind of thought [εἴ τις τὴν φαντασίαν τιθείη ὡς νόησίν τινα];
> for many follow their imaginations against their knowledge, and
> in other animals thought and reasoning do not exist, although
> imagination does.[10]

Freudenthal thought 433a9–10 conclusive evidence that Aristotle regarded imagination as a kind of thought[11] and found in 403a8–10 the view
that thought is sometimes a kind of imagination. Apart from the question
of their compatibility, Freudenthal's interpretations are not demanded by
the texts. The passage 403a8–10, which occurs at the beginning of De
Anima, is intended to introduce the operative question in deciding the relation between mind and body. In context, the passage carries no commitment to either of the mentioned alternatives and only the second even
receives serious consideration. Lines 433a9–10 implicitly eschew that imagination *is* a kind of thought allowing us only to *set it down* as such (note the
optative "τιθείη") in order to assert that desire and intellect are the two
things that govern all movement. The motivation for this is plainly preservation of the thesis that there are two main components in any action.[12]
Were he asserting flatly that animals think, he would hardly have used an
optative. Since he nowhere seems tempted by the latter,[13] the passage as a

10. These four passages follow Hamlyn's translation.
11. Also Wallace (1882, xciii) and Brentano (1977, 209).
12. Watson (1982, 102) appears to agree. Labarrière (1984, 20) now also agrees on the
point but seems to me to go too far in reading "ὡς νόησιν" as *"pensée pratique"* and in
restricting imagination's primary role to action.
13. There are a few passages that associate διάνοια, or discursive thought, with the behavior of certain nonhuman animals. Principally in *Historia Animalium*, the association is
always modified by cautionary language: certain of the longer-lived animals *appear* [φαίνονται]
to have a sort of capacity [τινα δύναμιν] corresponding to deliberative reason [φρόνησις]
(608a13–15); 612a3's remark that many quadrupeds behave cleverly [φρονίμως] is to be understood in terms of 611a15–16's more cautious point that of the wild quadrupeds the hind not
least of all is *thought* to have practical intelligence [οὐχ ἥκιστα δοκεῖ εἶναι φρόνιμον]; surfacing
dolphins hold their breath *as if* they were calculating [ὥσπερ ἀναλογισάμενοι] the distance to
the surface (631a24–27). Finally, 612b18ff. ventures a general remark on such attributions:
"Generally speaking, in lives of the other animals many mimicries [μιμήματα] to human living
may be observed [with the optative θεωρηθείη]." Thus, we are counseled that attributing
φρόνησις and the like to other animals is tantamount to asserting that they *mimic* various
human behaviors. So, at the very most, Aristotle appears tempted by the proposal that animals
may, in more recent idiom, merely simulate intelligent behavior.

whole merely affirms that imagination plays the role in certain action contexts that intellect plays in other action contexts. So neither of the extrinsic passages requires giving up the functional incompleteness of imagination.

By itself 427b27–29 does not, pace Beare (1908, 293), Brentano (1977, 209), and Engmann (1976, 259), succeed in assimilating imagination to thought. If νοεῖν (thinking) is construed generically, then the passage need say no more than that imagination and supposition are involved in any complete mental act. In particular, it need not say that these are two kinds of thought. This agrees perfectly with our interpretation.[14] The less friendly reading would only follow on an equally unfriendly reading of 427b14–17. So let us turn to that passage.

Hamlyn's translation of 427b16–17 is not its literal rendering, namely, "that thinking is not the same as supposal is clear." Following Freudenthal, Hamlyn rejects the literal reading because the passage proceeds to discuss imagination and this requires that νόησις (thinking) be construed to cover imagination. And this, he argues, would be embarrassing in light of 427b14–15, which differentiates between imagination and thinking [διάνοια]. But even assuming "ἡ φαντασία" as the understood subject, the line still implies that imagination is a kind of thought. Hence, Hamlyn is still left with the awkward problem that thought must cover imagination. Besides this we are required to take "ἡ αὐτη νόησις" as predicate and to give "καί" (and) the force of "as." This gives a possible but decidedly strained reading. In view of these difficulties the most promising maneuver is to follow Madvig and Ross[15] and bracket "νόησις." We then get "That it [that is, imagination] is not the same as supposition is clear." This reading ensures that the contrast is between imagination and supposition and so fits the line neatly into the following discussion.[16] It also follows intuitively from the immediately preceding line, 427b16, which has just asserted that supposition does not occur without imagination, and it would be natural to remark that, despite this, they are indeed distinct. So neither of the passages occurring within De Anima III.3 shows that imagination is a kind of thought.[17]

14. Failing to see that both passages have alternative interpretations, Rees (1971, 497–98) finds 427b27–29 to conflict with 403a8–10.

15. W. D. Ross (1961, 285). Rees follows Ross but apparently does not appreciate the significance of doing so.

16. If the fact that in the following discussion belief [δοξάζειν] is substituted for supposition is difficult, it is difficult on any interpretation.

17. This is not an idle result. Hicks, for example, claims that "the free play of the imagination repeatedly occurs as the first and most obvious instance of thought, νόησις, in the wider sense" (1965, 457), citing De Anima 432b30 and De Memoria 450a1–7 as further cases. But unless 427b16 unambiguously establishes that imagination is a kind of thought, the alleged

But if this is the case, we are faced with a further problem. For immediately Aristotle gives a reason for imagination's not being the same as supposition, and most commentators take this to suggest that imagination is something we do at will. This would clash with the canonical theory insofar as it implies that imagination has an active$_2$ employment and so is not functionally incomplete after all. Let us, then, add to the line the reason given at 427b16–21:

> It is clear that imagination is not the same as supposition [ὑπό-ληψις], for (i) the former is something (an affection) that is up to us [τὸ πάθος ἐφ' ἡμῖν] whenever we desire [βουλώμεθα] (for we can produce something before our eyes, as do those who set things down in mnemonic systems and form mental pictures [εἰδωλο-ποιοῦντες]); but (ii) believing [δοξάζειν] is not up to us, for it must [ἀνάγκη γάρ] be either true or false.

Comments on i are obviously in order because its unparenthesized portion might be thought, at least prima facie, to lend support to imagination's claim to an active$_2$ use. But notice, first, that Aristotle says imagination is up to us *whenever we wish*. So it is at least clear that he is here not asserting that imagination is after all the poets' creative imagination. Nor is he using the philosophers' "imagine that." He has that notion, but he will express it by a different verb.[18] It is still the canonical, image-producing variety that interests him. The question for us is just what does he mean? First, just as imagination is involved and images are produced in the desiring or perceiving of something so also may it be engaged in this role somehow at our discretion. Second, when imagination is so engaged Aristotle is careful not to say that we *imagine* something. This is clear from the parenthesized explanation. For producing something before one's eye *mnemonically* involves, first, committing to memory a system of background places, and, second, using this as a means of ordering a second set of items one wants to remember.[19] So there will be images involved in setting up the system of background places and images of the facts or things to be remembered. Which of these Aristotle has in mind is not completely clear but both are produced in the course of remembering or committing to memory something else, a place or thing. Thus, to produce an image at

further cases show only that thought involves images. Contrast my reading with Schneider's rather strained "das sie aber selbst, nicht νόησις und zwar ὑπόληψις ist, ist offenbar" (1827, 447–48).

18. Thus, *Metaphysica* IV.5, 1010b10–11: "At least no one, when he is in Libya and one night has supposed [ὑπολάβῃ] he might be in Athens, sets out for the Odeum."

19. For an introduction to the theory of mnemonic systems, see Sorabji (1972).

will is, in effect, just to remember something one has earlier *committed* to memory. This is what makes the imagination involved in such cases "up to us." So when something (presumably an image) is produced at will before our eyes, what is actively₂ involved is memory and not imagination.[20] And, of course, nothing in our account prohibits images from occurring in episodes of remembering.

It may be possible to get a friendly reading from 427b16 while retaining νόησις (thinking). Thus, let the line read, more or less with Hicks: "That thinking is not the same as supposition is clear." On this reading imagination is no longer said to be up to us and, hence, ceases to even be a candidate for an actual₂ use. There may also be a natural reading of the explanation in parentheses. Suppose we take thinking's being up to us whenever we wish in light of De Anima II.5's contemplating whenever one wishes (417a27–28: βουληθεὶς δυνατὸς θεωρεῖν). Since, we know from De Anima III.8 and De Memoria I, thinking always involves images, thinkers must somehow manage to employ images and, because thinking is done at will, in some sense at their discretion. And if images are produced simply by dint of thinking, then imagination need not be given an actual₂ use.[21] This, however, requires that ὑπόληψις (supposition) be equated with δόξα (belief) or at least that it be restricted to intentional acts whose objects are not, in the idiom of De Anima II.5, "somehow in the soul itself." Thus, the reading would appear to clash with 427b24–25 which counts ἐπιστήμη (knowledge) as a branch of ὑπόληψις (supposition). So the logic would have to run: νόησις (thinking) is not the same as ὑπόληψις (supposition) because one brand of ὑπόληψις, namely, δόξα (belief), is not up to us, whereas another brand, namely, νοῦς (mind) in its epistemic role, is up to us. Even if this is possible, it remains unclear why Aristotle would want, at this point, to distinguish νόησις and ὑπόληψις at all. So the Madvig-Ross emendation may be preferable after all.

Taken together, i and ii pose a further difficulty, for i suggests that imagination is up to us and ii implies that what is up to us is not something that is true or false. It follows that imagination is not something that is true

20. Hicks (1965) rightly directs us to De Insomniis 458b17–25 where Aristotle discusses the apparent use of mnemonic techniques in sleep. Not all images that occur in sleep are dreams. Some, he says, who believe they are arranging items according to a mnemonic rule [κατὰ τὸ μνημονικὸν παράγγελμα] find that they move something into position besides the dream [παρὰ τὸ ἐνύπνιον] in putting an image into a place [τίθεσθαι . . . εἰς τὸν τόπον φάντασμα]. But notice that, so far from resulting from an active use of imagination, these images arise because of "an exercise of the faculty of opinion" (with Beare's Oxford translation): καὶ ὅτι ὃ ἐνοοῦμεν τῇ δόξῃ δοξάζομεν.

21. Pace Hicks (1965, 457–58); see n. 17 above.

or false.[22] This would clash with several passages in B that proclaim imagination's suitability for truth and falsity (for example, 428a11–12, a17–18, and b2) as well as with 2e of the canonical theory (given at the beginning of section 1 of chapter 2) and the theory's discussion at 428b25–30. So there must be some way to defuse the inference drawn from i and ii. Perhaps the following considerations will help. Notice, first, that ii says believing is *always* true or false (the force of ἀνάγκη), so it would still be distinguishable from imagination were the latter sometimes neither. Even this would be ruled out on the skeptical reading. Thus, Schofield's insistence on finding a voluntary activity in the "criteria" (his expression) of 427b16–24 forces him to conjecture that there is in Aristotle the "normal" imagination of the criteria and an "abnormal" imagination for *De Insomniis* and like texts (1978, 121–23). What would be desirable would be to give an account that shows both how imagination plays a role in truth and falsity and how it can be up to us, where this contrasts with the necessity of having truth value.

This can be done by stressing the fact that ii means to underline the logical point that the truth or falsity of something is crucial to whether we believe it in just the sense that if *a* believes *p,* then *a* believes *p* is true. No one believes known falsehoods. It is in just this sense that belief is not something that is entirely up to us.[23] There simply is no analogous condition for imagination and this is all that i and ii need imply. And this is not because imagination is skeptical or artistic but because it is essentially a [re]presentational capability that in its own right asserts nothing about the way things are. It is, however, important to notice that nothing here rules out that an image [φάντασμα] may be true *of* or false *of* something. It is exactly in this latter sense, but this sense only, that truth value attaches to φαντασία.[24]

One advantage of restricting truth and falsity for imagination to an image being true of or false of something is enhanced explanatory power. We are, for example, able to explain two otherwise difficult passages—428a11–12: "Further, (perceptions) are always true [αἱ ἀληθεῖς ἀεί], while episodes of imagination [αἱ φαντασίαι] are for the most part false" and

22. This tells conclusively against the literal rendering of 427b16–17, for Aristotle would never want to suggest that νόησις is not something that is true or false. It is typically true, as 428a16–17 notes.

23. Thus, Hamlyn's implied criticism is not to the point: "It is not absolutely clear that this is correct, since we can at any rate set out to believe things or make ourselves believe things" (1968, 131).

24. Perhaps the difficulty in *De Anima* II.8 of separating images [φαντάσματα] and primary thoughts [πρῶτα νοήματα] is traceable to the fact that both are true of. See below for more on this.

428b2–4: "But something can also appear false [φαίνεται ψευδῆ] at the same time that we have a true supposition about it [περὶ ὧν ἅμα ὑπόληψιν ἀλαθῆ ἔχει]; for example, the sun appears [φαίνεται] a foot across, yet we believe it to be larger than the inhabited world."

The first passage, 428a11–12, is difficult on two scores. It has been thought to conflict, first, with 427b16–21 and, second, with 428b25–30's account of the relation between perception and imagination. The first conflict presupposes that 427b16–21 denies that any notion of truth and falsity is appropriate for imagination. Since that was seen to be false, the conflict does not arise after all. But even were the presupposition true for a propositional sense of truth, the conflict still fails to materialize because we are free to interpret 428a11–12 as mentioning truth in the sense of *true of* only.[25] The second point of conflict is this. The passage at 428b25–30 suggests a parallel between perceptual truth and imaginal truth, more precisely between perceptual activity that is true or false and a related image that is true or false of the perceived thing.[26] Given the general trustworthiness of perceptual reports, how could there be a disparity as great as that demanded by 428a11–12?

The response to the immediately mentioned difficulty involves clarifying how the notion of true of or false of is used in the context in question. Aristotle has just indicated (428b24–25) that perception of common objects is most susceptible to error. He is not asserting that such perception is susceptible to error most of the time. Aristotle is not attracted to skepticism and can hardly be thought to impugn here the general reliability of perceptual reports of common objects, even those distantly perceived. Rather he is saying, more plausibly, that where an object is perceived at an angle or at considerable distance the disparity between the object and the image is greater in the case of common objects (that is, perceiving a square thing in the distance) than in the case of proper objects (that is, perceiving a red thing in the distance).[27] Although the greater disparity would explain the higher incidence of error in perception of common objects, no inclination toward skepticism lurks here despite the fact that in these cases the image

25. This meets Rees's difficulty with the passage (1971, 498).

26. I assume here, in accord with chapter 2, that the κίνησις (movement) mentioned at 428b25 is or involves a φάντασμα.

27. This answers Hamlyn's puzzle as to why perception of common objects is more susceptible to error than perception of incidental objects such as Socrates (1968, 15). Beare's lack of success in pondering this (1908, 286) is due partly to his holding that perception of incidental objects is an inference from perception of proper objects (236) and that the proper objects of common sense are internal αἰσθήματα rather than external αἰσθητά (289). Both points conspire to make all perception save that of proper objects inferential, but both points are false.

is false *of* the perceived object. Indeed, this is typical of even ordinary cases of perception and 428a11–12 says as much.

The result just reached is also implicit in the second "otherwise difficult passage" cited above, 428b2–4. With its parallel at *De Insomniis* 460b18–20,[28] it concerns a straightforward, if infrequent, case of perception. It is clear that the perceptual report is not being challenged despite the fact that, owing to distance, the image had of the sun is not *true* of it. Rather, it is an image that *would* be true of something one foot in diameter. The same sort of point holds for most ordinary episodes of perception. When I perceive a round coin at an oblique angle, the image I have is an image that would be true of an elliptically shaped thing. Error is avoided because of associated beliefs.[29] One senses here Aristotle's appreciation for what Quine has called the objective pull. He is then making a general and significant point about the relation of perception and imagination and not dissecting a special case only. It follows that interpretation of the passage does not, contra Hamlyn, require reference to illusion and cannot, contra Schofield, focus on a skeptical sense of imagination.[30]

Nor is this interpretation subject to Nussbaum's rather curious objection:

> To say the sun appears a foot across is not to claim that when we look at the sun we must have before us a mental picture that is a foot wide—or even a picture that we somehow internally measure and find to be a foot wide. There is no evidence that Aristotle wanted to make such an unilluminating claim. The person's *phantasia* has as its object the sun itself. (1978, 248–49)

Of course, Aristotle makes no such claim. But it doesn't follow from this that he does not countenance our having an image that *would* be true of something a foot wide when we are perceiving the sun. This requires no internal measuring but only that the perceiver have an image that, in relevant aspects, is like the image he typically has, or would have, were he actually

---

28. "The sun appears a foot wide but this φαντασία is usually contradicted by something different."

29. There is no need to introduce here a propositional sense of φαντασία, contra Rees's "the formation of a possible belief which is suggested by the appearance but to which one does not commit oneself" (1971, 499). Nothing like this is alive in either of the passages in question.

30. See Labarrière who links 428a11–12 with what he calls the *expérience faible* of *Metaphysica* I.1, 980b26–27: the more distant one is from nature the greater is the error (1984, 23). But I fail to see how the first passage helps explain why imagination is, for the most part, false. The suggestion that animals without connected experience are without deliberative capabilities and so are unable to correct their "phantasms" is simply too remote from the *De Anima* text. It is, however, the sort of thing that is required if one insists, with Labarrière and Schofield, on the skeptical, non-[re]presentational role of imagination.

perceiving a foot-wide disk. So the false image is simply one that would be true of a foot-wide disk stationed, under standard conditions, in an optimal position vis-à-vis the perceiver. This is fairly straightforward, if we think of an optimal position for perceiving O simply as a position P such that one couldn't be in a better position than P to perceive O. Possibly, the demand for internal measuring is connected with a certain view about the function images would have to have, namely, that of providing information about the world. But on our interpretation they are only necessary for the operation of other faculties that may or may not have this function.[31]

This echoes *De Insomniis* 460b16–20 where the case is explained in terms of control [τὸ κύριον] withholding assent from the involved φαντασία and so refusing to issue the potentially false belief. Since the "φαντασίαν" at 460b19–20 refers to ᾧ τὰ φαντάσματα γίνεται (that in virtue of which images occur) two lines earlier, images are explicitly involved here,[32] and, thus, in 428b2–4 as well. The true belief that τὸ κύριον, or control, does issue will involve, typically, the original image plus certain others. But among the latter we need not count a second image of the sun but simply images involved in the set of associated beliefs that keep control from heading down a false path.[33] So neither 428a11–12 nor 428b2–4 shows that the practice of B is inconsistent either in its own right or with the theory of C.

There is, finally, a more general and perhaps more serious difficulty facing the reconciliation of B and C. Almost all commentators report that B employs at various points a broader and quite different notion of imagination from that figuring in the canonical theory of C. Hamlyn connects the broader notion with appearing, Rees speaks of a propositional sense of imagination, and Nussbaum finds the seeing-as idiom fruitful. Hamlyn and Nussbaum find this broader notion inconsistent with the canonical theory. In Nussbaum's words, "The decaying-sense analysis at the chapter's

31. Incidentally, it is worth noting that, contra Nussbaum, a person's perception [αἴσθησις], and not his imagination [φαντασία], has the sun as its object. This, of course, impugns the plausibility of the seeing-as interpretation of imagination. My view also counters Warnock's claim that "φαντασία" *means* "how the object appears" (1976, 38). Certainly, the canonical imagination *means* no such thing.

32. Nussbaum cites just 460b19–20, omitting the lines that mention images. Only in this way can she claim that the *De Insomniis* passage "though characteristically interpreted with reference to images, is quite comprehensive without them" (1978, 245). Aristotle apparently thought otherwise. The "canonical" nature of the *De Insomniis* passage also makes rather unlikely Schofield's curious gloss on 428b2–4: "it is hard to see any more immediate reason for his taking the sun example to be a case of φαντασία than that he has observed that people say 'The sun looks a foot across,' when they believe it to be very much larger" (1978, 121).

33. See also 459a7–8 which would explain the case in terms of belief's not assenting to the image.

end does not fit the entire discussion" (1978, 252). And although Rees
asserts that sensation provides the essential basis for the propositional sense
of imagination, he explains neither how this works nor whether it is equivalent to holding that images are essentially involved even in propositional
imagination. So we need to look at some of the passages in question and
then consider proposals for reconciliation.

The two star examples of B's interest in the wider notion of imagination
are 428b2–4, quoted earlier, and 428a12–15: "Further, it is not when we
are exercising [a sense?] in a precise way with regard to the perceived object
[ἐνεργῶμεν ἀκριβῶς περὶ τὸ αἰσθητόν] that we say that it appears [φαίνεται
τοῦτο] to us to be a man, but rather when we do not distinctly [μὴ ἐναργῶς]
perceive it; and then it is either true or false." In order for these passages
to threaten the internal *consistency* of De Anima III.3 it must be shown that
the canonical theory is strictly incompatible with at least one of them. If
this cannot be shown, something weaker must be meant, for example, that
it is implausible to have Aristotle apply the canonical theory to the facts in
question. Since we have already shown how to wed the canonical theory
with 428b2–4, we will here address 428a12–15 only.

Notice, first, that the passage deploys the principle that it is logically
odd to issue a weaker statement when a stronger one is in order. Aristotle
need not be asserting that it would be false to say of an object perceived in
a precise way [ἀκριβῶς] that it appears to be a man but only that it would
be odd to say so. Thus, contra Schofield, there is no interest here in a
skeptical imagination. More to the point, however, is whether room is made
for the canonical imagination. The answer is plainly affirmative, for we
need only admit that an image is involved in the perceptual report in a way
that squares with the canonical theory. There are at least two ways this
might proceed. Either we can say simply that one has an image but not a
distinct enough image to support the stronger claim that one is *seeing* a
man, or we can say that one has a distinctly manlike image but believes
oneself to be in circumstances, such as bad lighting, that do not warrant
making the stronger claim. The former is unattractive insofar as it leaves
obscure what grounds there are at all for claiming that a thing appears to
be a man instead of something else. So the latter seems the most plausible
reading of perceiving something imprecisely [μὴ ἀκριβῶς] and gives the
image an essential role in the *conditions* governing the appropriateness of
asserting the weaker claim. And following De Insomniis 460b16ff. and
kindred passages we can fill in the story by adding that belief or "control"
withholds full assent, perhaps because of circumstances in the immediate
environment. So we have images after all. Moreover, the last line of the
passage suggests that, when we do not distinctly perceive something, our

perceptions are sometimes true and sometimes false.[34] This agrees with the canonical theory's account of the relation between images and perception. Although I am not claiming that the canonical theory or anything like it *must* be introduced to account for the cases in question, I am claiming that Aristotle thought so. Consequently, not only are 428b2–4 and 428a12–15 consistent with the canonical theory (contra Hamlyn and Nussbaum) but also the canonical theory can be made to explain them (thus, remedying Rees's omission).

Our claims on behalf of the canonical theory would be enhanced by showing that it fits with the whole of *De Anima* as well as with the balance of *De Anima* III.3. There are two particularly crucial passages here, one at the beginning and the other toward the end of the work. The first of these, 402b22–25, "for when we are able to give an account, in terms of imagination [κατὰ τὴν φαντασίαν], of all or most of the attributes, then we shall be able to speak best about the substance [περὶ τῆς οὐσίας]," is left without comment by Ross and Hamlyn. Rees (1971, 500) doubts that mental images have any place in the passage and Nussbaum (1978, 246) takes the passage as a primary expression of Aristotle's general interest in a notion of appearing that does not import images. While I would urge that Bonitz, and later Hicks, were hasty to find here a kind of φαντασία separate from the canonical imagination, I am puzzled to find Nussbaum in agreement here. For she grants that the canonical theory does not fit with the broader notion of appearing that is her preferred reading of φαντασία. Hence, the two must be different kinds of imagination.

At any rate the crucial point is whether the passage has an interpretation in terms of the canonical theory. A look at the context of the passage suggests that it does. The procedure retailed in our passage is the converse of one just described, at 402b16–22, whereby determination of what a thing is aids in determining the reasons for the attributes of the thing [τὰς αἰτίας τῶν συμβεβηκότων ταῖς οὐσίαις]. Thus, knowing what straight and curved or line and surface are will be of use in seeing how many right angles a triangle equals. By analogy, then, the converse procedure recommends that giving an account of the number of right angles in a triangle will be of some aid in getting clear about what straight, curved, line, and surface are. The recommendation is more global than this, of course, and for a reason. By taking a large number of such cases, cases we may roughly characterize as employing the prior notions of straight, curved, and so on, we tend to isolate those features of the cases that reflect and, presumably, are due to the nature or essence of the prior notions. Thus, we get clearer on exactly

---

34. I do not understand the popularity of bracketing "τότε ἢ ἀληθὴς ἢ ψευδής" at 428a15.

what straightness and the like are. Similarly, in deductive procedure a grasp of instances of kinds of valid inferences might conduce to a clearer idea of validity itself.

But why is the account to be given in terms of imagination? Putting the question in this way connects the notion of being in accordance with imagination [κατὰ τὴν φαντασίαν] with the giving of the account [ἀποδιδόναι] rather than the attributes accounted for [περὶ τῶν συμβεβηκότων]. This differs from the usual, but grammatically less happy, construal which makes the passage discuss *attributes* that appear to us. Even apart from grammatical ease another reason favors my reading, namely, that an account of a per se attribute, no matter how it is grasped or appears to us, must be given in terms of what it is an attribute of. That is, where A is a per se attribute of S, the account of A must mention S.[35] Consequently, because one must already understand what it is to be S, an account of A and its ilk could not be of aid in grasping the nature of S. This is avoided by insisting that what is in accordance with imagination [κατὰ τὴν φαντασίαν] is the account. Aristotle is, then, simply saying that by reflecting on, and perhaps being guided by, relevant cases one can come to a nearer grasp of the fundamental notions presupposed by the cases. And, what is the point for our purposes, nothing here excludes that such reflection may involve images. Indeed, certain passages suggest that this must be so.[36]

The second crucial passage occurs at 434a5–10:

> Imagination connected with perception [ἡ αἰσθητικὴ φαντασία], as was said, is found in other animals also; but that connected with deliberation [ἡ βουλευτικὴ φαντασία] only in those having reason [ἐν τοῖς λογιστικοῖς] (for whether to do this or that is already a task for reason; and one must measure by one standard, for one pursues what is superior; hence, one has the capability to fashion one thing from many images [δύναται ἓν ἐκ πλειόνων φαντασμάτων ποιεῖν]).

Hamlyn (1968, 153) correctly associates this passage with 433b29's remark that all imagination is either connected with reason [ἡ λογιστική] or connected with perception [ἡ αἰσθητική]. The first of these he takes as a kind of thinking and the second he makes responsible for perceptual illusion. The second point is misleading because it suggests that the main role of

---

35. For more on this, see chapter 1, n. 15, and Wedin (1973).

36. For instance, 432a3–9, which receives full attention below, suggests that all objects of thought, including abstract objects, require images. Indeed, as we shall see (chap. 4, sec. 6), the mathematician is said to utilize an image in doing his particular brand of theorizing.

the perceptual imagination is in accounting for illusions. This cannot be the case both for reasons already retailed as well as for the reason that the context of 433b29 tells against the suggestion. Aristotle is discussing animal movement in terms of desire for some end or object of desire. Imagination is assigned to animals simply to explain how they can exhibit quasi-intentional behavior. An illusion-tailored notion of imagination would be without force in such an account. When an animal moves toward water on the basis of an image, talk of perceptual illusion is plainly out of place. As for the first point, it is, I submit, simply false. Certainly, grammar does not legislate that "ἡ βουλευτικὴ φαντασία" (the deliberative imagination) or "ἡ λογιστικὴ φαντασία" (the calculative imagination) denote a kind of thought as against imagination connected with thought. And in light of Aristotle's arguments in De Anima III.3, prospects for identification are rather slim.[37]

To secure the result just reached, however, a closer look at 434a5–10 is in order. The final words of the passage are not straightforward. They may mean that there is something, the deliberative imagination, that is assigned the combinatory function of putting together separate images. On this reading, which is that of Philoponus,[38] ἡ βουλευτικὴ φαντασία (the deliberative imagination) is the subject of the sentence and ἕν is to be completed to ἓν φάντασμα (one image). But neither of these readings is required. Indeed, the first is unlikely, given that the subject of the final sentence is the same as what, in the penultimate sentence, pursues the superior thing. Since this is clearly a rationally endowed animal, that which has the capacity to do this will be an animal with logos (thus "δύναται" is more plausibly completed by something like Hicks's "τὰ λογικὰ ζῷα"). This, of course, squares with our insistence that imagination is not a genuine faculty at all. Construing ἕν as ἓν φάντασμα (one image) is also unnecessary.[39] Strictly, it need only be a necessary condition on deliberation that one be able to bring together, as it were, a number of images in fashioning one plan, thought, or course of action. Indeed, it would be more appropriate to speak simply of images being involved in such single deliberations. To say that many images are involved in a single act of deliberation is not to say that deliberation can be reduced to mentally pasting together images. But even were this the case, deliberation and not imagination would have the active role. We are thus spared Nussbaum's criticism of what she calls Ross's "collage view" of deliberation according to which the person who deliberates "combines elements from different pictures in his head, ending up

37. W. D. Ross is better here, indicating that ἡ λογιστικὴ φαντασία may be involved in thought or deliberation (1961, 317).
38. Philoponus (1897, 592, l. 25, to 593, l. 4).
39. Contra Hartman (1977, 260).

with a single picture" (1978, 263).[40] So again imagination, even deliberative imagination, has no active$_2$ employment and satisfies the canonical theory's condition of functional incompleteness.

3. THE DECAYING SENSE INTERPRETATION OF IMAGINATION

At least since the appearance of Freudenthal's monograph Aristotle has been linked with classical empiricist theories of imagination. Wallace, impressed with verbal parallels, took Hobbes to be paraphrasing Aristotle in claiming that "all fancies are motions within us, reliques of those made in the sense." Hicks (1965, liii) agreed, as did Granger (1963, 17). Recently, Nussbaum has reasserted the traditional line by appropriating Hobbes's idiom in characterizing the canonical theory as a "decaying sense" theory of imagination.

The traditional interpretation has the drawback of imposing severe limitation on the range of the canonical theory. Indeed, the very notion of a deliberative imagination [ἡ βουλευτικὴ φαντασία] suggests that the decaying sense theory cannot hold generally. For not only does deliberation range over objects not immediately perceived but it also concerns future and so unperceived possibilities for objects. It is unclear at best how the decaying sense theory could account for the latter which requires thought but not perception. So if the canonical theory is the theory that imagination is nothing but decaying sense, then it is doubtful that it can cover imagination involved in deliberation. As we shall see, other problems also face this version of the theory.

One response to this situation is to limit the canonical theory to perceptual imagination [ἡ αἰσθητικὴ φαντασία], as Hartman seems inclined to do (1977, 252), and then simply deny generality to the canonical theory, as Nussbaum does. This is, of course, intrinsically undesirable as well as having the disadvantage of suggesting that, when Aristotle argues the dependence of thought on imagination in De Anima III.7 and 8, he is not concerned with the canonical imagination at all. A second response is to deny that the canonical theory itself is a theory of decaying sense perception. An initial ground for doubt is that the functional incompleteness of imagination entails that perceivings, dreamings, rememberings, and the like, cannot be individuated in terms of the images or φαντάσματα that [re]presentationally subserve them. On the decaying sense theory, however, something like this might be thought possible, even if difficult. For the

---

40. Hartman (1977, 253) seems committed to this view as well.

theory might propose to distinguish dreamings from perceivings in terms of the intensity or vividness of the involved image. Although this might be congenial to a classical empiricist, we shall see that it does not appeal to Aristotle.

But more needs to be said, if only because it is unclear, perhaps terminally, what a decaying sense theory amounts to. Nussbaum, for example, employs the idiom extensively but does not fully explain it. So it would be helpful to consider some suggestions for interpretation. My ultimate aim here is to make room for a version of the canonical theory that meets the demands of thought and deliberation. We shall turn to this in the next section.

One thesis we must hold constant, at least until it meets scrutiny in the next section, is

A. Images [φαντάσματα] are forms of perceptual states [αἰσθήματα] or of perceived things [αἰσθητά] or of both.

A second thesis not in dispute here is

B. Images are causal results of perception.

B implies nothing about the status of imagination as decaying sense perception. That thesis will require some sort of relation between images and sense perception; in particular it will require something like

B'. Images are nothing more than the decayings of certain episodes of perception.

Since what decays is the αἴσθημα or perceptual state, we may put B' more precisely:

B". For every image [φάντασμα], x, there is a perceptual state [αἴσθημα], y, such that x is a decayed stage of y.

B" clearly could count as a decaying sense theory of imagination. A first point about B" is that it cannot be argued a priori without embracing the dubious principle that whatever causally results from a given process has the same ontological or theoretical status as the process itself. Even slight familiarity with issues in dualism is sufficient to impugn the principle's plausibility as an a priori truth.

The question, then, is whether independent grounds can be given for attributing B" to Aristotle. Several passages suggest that he has no attachment to B". One, 425b23–25, says that because sensory organs are capable of receiving [the form of] perceived objects without their matter [τοῦ αἰσθητοῦ ἄνευ τῆς ὕλης], perceivings [αἰσθήσεις] and imaginings [φαντασίαι] remain in the sense organs even after the perceived object is removed. Taking B″ at its word, one might have expected that only imaginings would remain or at least that perception and imagination not be rated as *both* occurring.

There are more impressive difficulties. B″ implies that perception and imagination are not different in kind. And this seems a fair characterization of any decaying sense theory, since a decaying sense perception is still a sense perception. But this makes opaque Aristotle's claim that imagination and perception are different in being or kind, even if they are the same in fact or extension. Moreover, it now becomes unclear how to regard the brace of arguments, which occur in *De Anima* III.3 itself, for the distinction between imagination and perception. Clearly, these were not intended to show that the two are extensionally different but rather to separate them intensionally.

Some might object that being-decayed counts as a sufficient difference in being to be consistent with what Aristotle says. Why not just say, for example, that sense perceptions decay into images? After all, a dead man is not a man (*De Interpretatione,* 21a22–23), so why should a decay*ed* perceptual state be a perceptual state? But notice that this is no longer a decay*ing* sense theory. So far it seems to be no more than a general causal claim about the generation of images from perceptual states. The decay*ing* sense theory, B″ anyway, holds, at least, that a given image results from a given perception. Typically, at any rate, this will not be the case for Aristotle. As we saw in chapter 2, many persistings of like-minded perceptual states may be required to generate a given φάντασμα (unlike the dead man). Second, the image thus acquired subserves so diverse an array of cognitive functions that it is surely misleading to describe it as a single decaying perceptual state and it certainly is not several such states. Rather, it is the single structure in the soul that enjoys its own quite distinct ([re]-presentational) role in the cognitive system as a whole.

Although someone might insist that this shows only that the canonical theory alone is a theory of decaying sense perceptions and so that it conflicts with the balance of *De Anima* III.3, a close look at the canonical theory confirms that it does not yield B″ or a similar doctrine. For, we saw above, Aristotle holds that it is the activity of αἰσθήματα that produces the image and, in the idiom of *Analytica Posteriora* II.19, that this can require repeated episodes of appropriate perceptual states or αἰσθήματα persisting to yield the corresponding image.[41] The only role here for decaying sense would be

41. Barnes overlooks this in holding that what persist are properly only φαντάσματα and not αἰσθήματα (1975, 252), and Michaelis takes the persisting perceptual state to be identical with rather than merely required for images (1888, 10). Brentano also makes an identification: "*die Phantasmen und die Sensationen ganz dieselben sind*" (1977, 102).

that of the persisting αἰσθήματα. So the perceptions cannot be the same as the image even though they are required for it. Better, then, to regard them as what I have called [re]presentational devices that one acquires as one develops one's cognitive skills. Such a view is applicable to images as forms but not to images as decaying sense perceptions.

A decaying sense theorist might respond that Aristotle's denial of the identification of imagination and perception is formulated in terms of a strict notion of perception, one that requires presence of the object of perception. Nonetheless, the suggestion goes, a weaker notion is available to characterize imagination. On the weaker notion, we permit ourselves to speak of something like the perceptual state [αἴσθημα] of an episode of perceiving and hold that imagination is just a weakened version of this state. The paradigm case here might be afterimages. Attractive though this suggestion might be to some (only as an account of the canonical theory, of course), there are two difficulties it must meet. First, Aristotle objects at 428a8–9 that perception but not imagination is always present. This causes difficulty for the decaying sense theorist, for the objection is not that in some cases of perception there is no associated image or imagination but rather that some animals simply lack imagination but not perception.[42] Now, given Aristotle's account of the process of perception, there is no reason to suppose that perceptions do not persist even in such animals. What they lack is the capacity to generate images from such repeated persistings. But if the decaying sense theory of images were correct, such animals would have images after all.

Let us suppose that a revised decaying sense theory is able to meet the above objection. A second difficulty remains. For if imagination is construed as decaying sense perception, then any given image or φάντασμα will be different from its correlated proper perception. That is, by our earlier reasoning, it will not co-occur with the perceptual state of a proper sense perception. This would be intuitively plausible, if it means only that one does not have an afterimage while one is properly perceiving something. But what in fact follows, with certain provisos, is that no φάντασμα may occur during an episode of proper sense perception. This Aristotle unambiguously denies. Speaking of the movement that results from sense perception, he says at 428b27–28 (on which see section 1 of this chapter)

42. Contrast this with Nussbaum's unsuccessful attempt to make sense of her rather curious reading that perception is always going on (1978, 256). Here she follows Freudenthal, who is no more successful (1863, 12). Since the line following 428a8–9 develops the point by citing certain animals that have perception but not imagination, 428a8–9 clearly says that perception (by definition) is always present *in animals* but not imagination. Michaelis's view (1882, 18–19) that perception but not imagination is always ready (*immer bereit*) requires interpolation and does not fit with the following lines.

that this movement will be true as long as perception is present.[43] The mentioned movement cannot, of course, be perception because it can occur when perception is absent. The movement, as we have seen, turns out to be imagination. But notice that Aristotle expressly states that images occur while proper perceptions occur. This is at the heart of the canonical theory and flatly contradicts B″. Hence, it cannot be the case that imagination is decaying proper perception because it is co-occurrent with such perception.

Further, if images and perceptual states [αἰσθήματα] differ only in degree, then we ought to expect an introspective criterion for distinguishing them.[44] The decaying sense theory might, we have suggested, propose to distinguish dreamings from perceivings in terms of degree of vivacity of the involved image. But Aristotle shows no inclination to pursue this Humean strategy. He proceeds, rather, in the language of form and content, rating images as forms of sense perceptions. Indeed, given this, it is difficult to see how one could apply a vividness test at all. For, generally, images will be an intrinsic feature of a perception and unavailable for comparison save in special cases such as afterimages. Indeed, not even dream-involved images are properly described under the heading "decaying sense perception." Rather, they are straightforward φαντάσματα which result from residual movements in the sensory organs. Thus, if anything is decayed or, perhaps better, delayed, it is, to reiterate, the movement [κίνησις] that occurs in the perceptual organ [αἰσθητήριον] and that in turn causes the φάντασμα involved in dreaming.

The temptation to regard Aristotelian images as decaying sense perceptions is, I suspect, traceable to contexts where images could not be said to occur in connection with episodes of sense perception. But even in the paradigm cases here, dreams and memory, it will do as well to read images as forms. Indeed, it is unclear how images qua decaying sense perceptions could be fitted into Aristotle's account of memory, for here there is no perceptual process, delayed or otherwise, to work with. That is, suppose I to be a memory-related image, and S, a prior and appropriately related perceptual state. The relation is, roughly, that what was [re]presented through S as the object of perception is what is [re]presented through I as the object of memory. Now although we may dispute the status of I as a behavioral disposition, brain state, [re]presentational structure or whatever, it is simply not possible to regard I as a decayed sense perception. For this would require that I be causally contiguous with S as an actual, albeit

43. See now Watson (1982, 107) who appears to concur on this point.
44. At least one might expect this on Nussbaum's view that the decaying sense theory is committed to the view that images are introspectable. (See following section for more on this.)

weakened, perception. And in the case at hand this cannot occur. Notice that Aristotle provides for this by requiring not just that the image be of the thing perceived but also that temporal distance be indicated.

The result of the last paragraph suggests how to defuse what is generally accepted as certain evidence for a decaying sense theory, namely, *Rhetorica* 1370a27–29's assertion that imagination is something like weak perception [ἡ δὲ φαντασία ἐστὶν αἴσθησίς τις ἀσθενής]. Thus, Beare (1908, 294–95) takes Hobbes's "imagination, therefore, is nothing but decaying sense" to reproduce the line. But notice that Aristotle says only that imagination is *something like* weak perception. This hardly counts, pace Schofield (1978, 120), as a definition. Nor, thus, is it obviously, pace Nussbaum (see note 46 below), straightforward invocation of a decaying sense theory.[45] Notice, further, that the remark occurs in the course of a discussion of pleasure and pleasant things, more precisely in the course of arguing that it is plea-surable to be reminded of certain things and painful to be reminded of others. (Presumably, such knowledge would have utility for the rhetorician.) The argument begins with the premise that being pleased consists in being aware of a certain affection [τὸ ἥδεσθαι ἐν τῷ αἰσθάνεσθαί τινος πάθος]. The point here is not, or at least not obviously, that one is aware of an affection of pleasure. Rather, it is the point echoed at *Ethica Nicomachea* 1105b20–24 that an affection is the sort of thing attended by pleasure or pain. Thus, perception of a lover is pleasurable because the affection involved (the αἴσθημα) is attended by pleasure. To account for the pleasure involved in remembering a lover would require that the affection involved in memory (the φάντασμα of the lover) be attended by pleasure. Aristotle secures this possibility by asserting that imagination is, *in this regard,* like a weak per-ception. Hence, as one can perceive something with pleasure so what one remembers can be pleasurable. Interpreted in this light there is no need to find 1370a27–29 asserting a decaying sense notion of imagination. For imagination is a sort of weak perception on the point of analogy only: as perception can be pleasurable so may remembering, even if in a weaker way.[46] It follows that 1370b27–29 is making an entirely general point about imagination, even about ἡ λογιστικὴ φαντασία or thought-related imagi-

---

45. See Watson (1982, 103n6) for a salutary comment on the line. In particular, I am happy to follow his reading of "αἴσθησις τις." My discussion below (chap. 5, n. 63) of the weakening "τις" is relevant here.

46. We thus spare Aristotle Nussbaum's unflattering judgment: "Although Aristotle in this popular and probably early work invokes decaying sense to explain what *phantasia* is (1370a28), that account does not fit his own usage of the word in these passages [namely, 1379b32 and 1371a19]" (1978, 248n44). Ours is also perhaps a happier way with the passage than Labarrière's simply dismissing it on the grounds that it is the sole such *énoncé* in the corpus (1984, 22).

nation, for one could equally well say that, in point of pleasurability, thinking of a lover is less pleasurable, if only slightly less, than perceiving her.[47]

Finally the closing lines of *De Anima* III.3 are awkward for the decaying sense theorist:

> And because imaginations (*a*) remain [ἐμμένειν] and (*b*) are similar to perceptions [ὁμοίας εἶναι ταῖς αἰσθήσεσι], (*c*) animals do many things in accordance with them [πολλὰ κατ' αὐτάς] (*d*i) some because they do not have reason, for example beasts, and (*d*ii) some because reason is sometimes obscured by passion [πάθει] or disease or sleep.

Notice that *a* cannot mean just that images [φαντάσματα] are decaying impressions of sense because whatever *a* and *b* explain, that is, whatever are the many things in *c*, these are done in circumstances where no such decaying sense theory could apply. An animal in sleep will not even have the requisite sense perception or αἴσθημα that B″ requires. So mention of things perceived in *b* is meant only to explain how, namely, in virtue of similarity,[48] animals act in accordance with images only. Thus, "ἐμμένειν" is to be read "remain (in them)" rather than "remain as decaying sense impression" or something similar. On the other hand, simply as [re]-presentational devices images may remain in the absence of perception because perception is necessary only as a genetic causal condition. So the decaying sense theory is not required to account for Aristotle's canonical theory of imagination.

4. WHAT IMAGES ARE NOT

The decaying sense theory of imagination is frequently tied to a naive view of images as mental pictures. Thus, Nussbaum appears to argue that if the canonical theory offers a decaying sense account of imagination, it must treat φαντάσματα as images and images as mental pictures that are informationally rich.[49] To the extent that the argument of the last section is

47. Compare Cope (1877) who finds 1370b27–29 exclusive of thought.

48. Notice that Aristotle says, carefully, that the imaginations [φαντασίαι] are only like [ὁμοίας] perceivings. Since this is meant to carry the point about what animals do, there is little warrant for finding in the canonical theory a decaying sense version of imagination, at least none that excludes imagination's role in action. And since what animals do is also linked to imagination's being *about* something, there is place for [re]presentational φαντάσματα.

49. Nussbaum's discussion of what I am calling the naive view of images is one of the more successful parts of the essay. It does not, however (which is to the good), touch the notion of [re]presentation as it figures in cognitivism. And it is with this, rather than neo-Humean notions, that I am associating Aristotle's φαντάσματα.

correct we have at least blocked *this* way of wedding the naive view to the canonical theory. Of course, Aristotle may hold the view on other grounds. So it will be well to say something about its alleged occurrence in Aristotle. This is especially important for us because, while urging that φαντάσματα are [re]presentational, our interpretation claims immunity from the undesirable consequences of the naive view. Let us, then, take the naive view as holding (N1) that imagination always involves images that [re]present in virtue of some similarity and (N2) that imagination always involves two logically distinct processes: the having of an image, either produced or somehow impressed, and its inspection or contemplation. N2 has an important corollary, namely, (N2′) that images are informationally dense, that is to say, that they somehow yield information to introspection. In the balance of this section I shall show that the canonical theory can avoid the standard objections retailed by Nussbaum without sacrificing the [re]presentational status of images. We shall then be positioned to address more directly Nussbaum's own "seeing-as" interpretation of imagination.

N2 and its corollary can be dealt with quickly. N2 assumes that there is some mental operation that not merely uses images in performing its function but actually has images as the object of its function. But, as we saw above, the functional incompleteness of imagination simply excludes any such possibility. Even were this sometimes the case, however, N2′ would not follow. One could inspect or contemplate an image, in some minimal sense, without extracting any new information from it. Not even *De Memoria* 449b30ff., perhaps the most likely candidate, supports this. The contemplating geometer may have an image "before his eye," but he does not extract information from it by inspection or any other procedure. Information is forthcoming in virtue of his *doing* something, namely, proving theorems. And although this requires images, the images merely subserve the thinking. They are not what the thinking is about.[50] In this light the functional incompleteness of imagination can be seen as warning against mistaking what is used in thinking about an object for the object thought about.[51] What is involved is simply the occurrence of a triangle image *in the context* of contemplating a triangle.

The need to generate information from mental operations on images is due, presumably, to the mistaken view that this is what counts as thought for Aristotle.[52] This may in turn reflect an impulse to Platonize Aristotle

50. Contrast Proclus, who routinely mentions the φανταστόν (object of imagination) as the object of thought. (See Appendix A)

51. Here I may be close to Watson, who stresses imagination's role in "supplying materials on which the mind builds judgments" (1982, 106n10).

52. See, for instance, Hartman (1977) and Hicks (1965, 457).

by making images serve the function of Platonic forms. This, of course, is mistaken. In any case, Aristotle neither says nor suggests that one can get new information from contemplation, let alone contemplation of images. Contemplation is an activity, complete and self-satisfying in its own right, whereas information acquisition is by its nature a process. Even granting that in discursive thought [διάνοια] new information is gotten by introspection (which we have seen is doubtful), what yields knowledge to inspection are thoughts [νοήματα] and not images [φαντάσματα].[53] In short there is no reason to suppose that Aristotle held either N2 or N2′.[54]

What about N1? Three claims are packed into N1: that imagination always involves images, that images are always [re]presentational and that images are [re]presentational in virtue of similarity. Aristotle agrees, I would argue, with some version of all three claims. On the other hand, the versions are not subject to the standard objections Nussbaum marshals. We have already substantiated the first claim by meeting the standard objection that numerous occurrences of "φαντασία" simply refuse to accommodate images. The remaining claims are best dealt with in discussing the general relation between thought and imagination. We shall turn to this in the next chapter. A few remarks on the second and third claims, however, would be in order at this point.

Nussbaum's objection to N1 is slightly ambiguous. At one point (1978, 224) the mistake is to take similarity as a necessary and sufficient condition for [re]presentation. Because it is clear that Aristotle does not hold it to be a sufficient condition, we need only to deal with the objection to its being a necessary condition. The implication here is that one thing can [re]present another without being similar to it. At another point (1978, 228) the objection is that similarity (resemblance) can be symbolic without being [re]presentational. So being similar to and being [re]presentative of something are logically independent. Again this is surely correct and, again, it does not threaten the particular interpretation we are offering. Besides informational density, which we have already remarked on, [re]presentation involves the semantic notion of reference or standing for something. And it is obvious that a first thing can be similar, even exactly similar, to a

53. For more on the distinction between thoughts and images, see the following chapter.

54. From the cognitive point of view one is free to admit that certain *internal* operations process, as it were, information that is in the form of an image and pass it on for further interpretation within the system. This, however, amounts not to extracting information from an image but only to treating an image as a certain kind of information. In any case, this need not involve any introspecting that *I* do. Rather, it is like what happens when "control" [τὸ κύριον of 460b16–18; see n. 39 of chapter 2] overrules the report of the senses in making certain that no error results. Aristotle is under no illusion that in such cases *I* am aware of what control does. Yet just this is what N2 and N2′ require.

second without being a [re]presentation of it. Aristotle quite agrees. Witness our earlier discussion of images involved in memory. Similarity of image to thing was not sufficient for the image to be a copy *of* or, in present idiom, to be a [re]presentation of that thing. And no operation on the image can make it a [re]presentation because no mental operation on an internal item can give it the semantic property of aboutness. This occurs only, but unsurprisingly, when one remembers or thinks *about* the thing in question. This is a sufficient condition for the image to be [re]presentational with respect to the contemplated or remembered object.

It is still the case, however, that similarity is regarded by Aristotle as a necessary condition on [re]presentation. Before addressing this in the next chapter, something needs to be said about Nussbaum's objection to similarity as even a necessary condition. It is, roughly, that the thesis assumes that there is "one way of seeing the object as it is" (1978, 226). So far as I know Aristotle nowhere says anything of this sort. What he does seem inclined to say, however, is that there is a correct way of depicting an object. But this correct way can accommodate perspective. Just as one has a triangle-image of fairly definite specifications in the course of contemplating or developing some truth about triangles, so one may have a Socrates-image of fairly definite perspective in thinking about Socrates. If logical priorities required making inferences from image to thing imaged, as part of the account of thinking, then quite exact images would seem required. But the functional incompleteness of imagination is sufficient to save Aristotle from this unfortunate view. Still what is required is that when one thinks of Socrates some internal device is necessarily involved and that it is similar to Socrates. Exactly why for Aristotle similarity is a necessary condition on representation will, I hope, become clear in the course of the next chapter.

There is a more intriguing response to the objection that so far from enjoying informational density only perspectival images of objects are available. The response, somewhat surprisingly, is to embrace the alleged objection as a solid piece of Aristotelian doctrine. Indeed, we shall go even further. Recall that on the canonical theory φαντάσματα are generated from the activity of αἰσθήματα and, as A above asserts, that the former are (formally) similar to the latter. But recall also that for Aristotle the proper objects of perception fall within one of five mutually exclusive classes. Colors are seen only, sounds are heard only, and so on. Membership in a given class is a matter of matching the receptivity of a given sensory organ (see 418a24–25). I argued in chapter 2 that φαντάσματα result from perceptual states [αἰσθήματα]. Since the latter are perceptual states resulting from the activity of objects of perception [αἰσθητά], the possibility suggests itself that we have αἰσθήματα principally of objects received through a sensory organ and that perhaps the same holds for φαντάσματα. Something like this is suggested by *De Anima* II.6's discussion of special [ἴδιον], common [κοινόν], and incidental [κατὰ συμβεβηκός] objects of perception. Of these, only the first two rate as proper [καθ' αὑτά] objects of perception. The incidental objects are characterized as follows:

> An object of perception is said to be incidental (if, for example, the white thing were the son of Diares), for (i) you perceive it incidentally because that which you perceive happens to be white [ὅτι τῷ λευκῷ συμβέβηκε τοῦτο, οὗ αἰσθάνεσθαι]. So too (ii) no one is affected by the object of perception as such [οὐδὲν πάσχει ἢ τοιοῦτον ὑπὸ τοῦ αἰσθητοῦ]. (418a20–23)

The first point is echoed in *De Anima* III.1 where we are said to perceive the son of Cleon not because he is the son of Cleon but because he is white and the white object happens to be the son of Cleon. It might, thus, appear that what is incidental about such cases of perception is just that the object so perceived merely happens to be, say, white. But round objects merely happen to be whatever color they are and, nonetheless, they manage to be counted among perception's proper objects. So the crucial condition seems to be ii. Somehow incidental objects do not affect the perceiving agent.

It will not do simply to offer

1. x perceives y & y affects x ≡ y is a proper object of perception

and

2. x perceives y & y is an incidental object ⊃ y does not affect x

as an account of incidental perception. For, unless we take proper objects to be sense data or the like,[55] proper and incidental objects are extensionally the same. So the distinction is an intentional one, focusing on *how* external objects can affect perceivers. Something like the following, rough and partial, characterization might help.

3. x perceives y incidentally ⊃
    a. there is a description, D, of y such that y does not affect x under D[56] &

---

55. As J. A. Smith appears to do in the Oxford translation: " 'being the son of Diares' is incidental to the directly visible white patch."

56. Aristotle's choice of type D descriptions, "the son of Callias" and "the son of Diares," are themselves nonessential signifiers. Thus, pace Cashdollar (1973, 168n24), it is not at all obvious that Aristotle here asserts that a substance is incidental to an accident. For more on such cases, see Wedin (1984).

  b. there is a description, D', of y such that y does affect x
     under D' &
  c. x perceives y because y satisfies D'.[57]

It seems, then, that Aristotle is suggesting that incidental objects do not affect a perceiver because they do not affect the perceiver's sensory organs. Proper objects do, both the special and the common varieties. The first can affect but one organ, the second more than one.

The fact that when Ortcutt perceives Socrates he is not affected by Socrates qua Socrates should not be thought to harbor a skeptical thesis. What is at play is only a technical account of perception and its objects. One perceives Socrates by perceiving, for example, the white thing that is Socrates. But this does mean that perceiving Socrates qua Socrates, perhaps even qua man, involves something more than just proper perception. For one thing it involves the identity of the object, not simply feature identification. So it is likely that belief, thought, and even language may be needed as well. I shall return to these topics in chapter 4.

The immediate point of focus is what consequences to draw for the theory of [re]presentation. If perceptual states [αἰσθήματα] follow the same sort of account and if images [φαντάσματα] track them fairly closely, then it might be argued that when one, say, remembers Socrates, one must do so in virtue of an image but not necessarily an image of Socrates qua ordinary thing.[58] Rather, the [re]presentational image may be of a white thing that is or was Socrates or of an appropriately odored thing that is or was Socrates. In technical terms, an image may turn out to be an image of Socrates only κατὰ συμβεβηκός, or incidentally. Of course, the image occurring must, for Aristotle, bear some similarity to perceptual features of Socrates.[59] Consequently, Nussbaum's objection against N1—that because one may imagine (image?) Valhalla in virtue of an auditory image, say its Wagnerian leitmotif, images need not resemble the remembered objects—misfires. This would simply count as a case of the involved memory image being an image of Valhalla κατὰ συμβεβηκός (incidentally) and, hence, is no objection to a [re]presentationalist interpretation of Aristotle's φαντάσματα.

So far I have commented mainly on Nussbaum's expressed or implied objections to the sort of interpretation I am proposing. Some more general

---

57. As it stands, 3 covers incidental perception of a special object of one sense by another sense (see *De Anima* III.1). So to get just the incidental objects we need a condition to the effect that there is no object, z, such that under D, a subject is affected by z.

58. Contrast Hartman (1977, 260) who misses this.

59. See the account of ὅμοια in *Metaphysica* V.9, 1018a15–19.

remarks on her own positive interpretation are, therefore, in order. It will be enough to mention a few of the leading features of the view. First, she denies that Aristotle has a canonical theory of imagination at all. In particular, the nonmetaphorical φαντασία of 428a1–2 is not given canonical status; indeed, it is not construed as [re]presentational at all. Second, imagination is linked primarily with the notion of how things appear and these contexts are to be read with

> i. x φαίνεται F to z ≡ x is seen as F by z

and

> ii. x φαίνεται F to z ⊃ x is a thing in the world.

We have already indicated divergences over each of these points, so I will add only a few final comments.

The first point is defended by the following sort of claim: "the clear connection of *phantasia* and *phantasma* with a theory of pictorial representative images is limited to a few passages in the *DA* and *PN*, where Aristotle is constructing a physiological hypothesis concerning 'decaying sense'" (1978, 223). This is a curious remark, for it suggests that Aristotle starts out with an interest in something called decaying sense and then has to ring in images in contructing his theory. But the theory offered in CT is too detailed and technical to be regarded as a received set of facts. And what he says certainly seems to aspire to more than an account of dreams or afterimages (assuming these to be genuine image contexts). Or does it have no role in the general program of *De Anima*? Thus, Nussbaum's claim threatens to turn an explanatory theory into the very thing to be explained. Moreover, the account in *De Anima* III.3 is located exactly where one would expect to find a canonical account. So champions of the canonical status of *De Anima* III.3's imagination, even construed [re]presentationally, need only show how the canonical theory accommodates imagination in various contexts. And, of course, we have tried to indicate how this might work. So while Nussbaum is correct to warn against neglecting action contexts as a source of insight (1978, 223), the neglect is due less, I would urge, to the assumption that such contexts have been sufficiently explained once mental images (her expression) have been read into them than to the assumption that once action contexts are sufficiently explained, the role slotted for imagination is covered by the canonical theory. And although this may be an assumption, it is, as this essay urges, a justified one.

These points are important not merely because they reflect on a view contrary to our view that Aristotle is in possession of a canonical theory but also because Nussbaum's own interpretation requires that, *even were* there a canonical theory, it would not be that of *De Anima* III.3. This brings us to i and ii.

It is somewhat unclear how generally Nussbaum wishes to take i. I do not mean to ask whether it accounts for what she sees as the "few passages" in *De Anima* and *Parva Naturalia* that concern decaying sense but whether it covers all cases of perception. If so, then seeing-as will be entirely global. And if this, in turn, gives imagination a global interpretive role,[60] then we ought to expect some sensitivity to the fact that, within certain obvious limits, it follows that no way of seeing the world is any more correct than another.[61] But Aristotle shows little openness to this idea. There are clear constraints on what counts as a correct interpretation of the world—the theory of science depends on this—and what hints he gives us about concept acquisition seem more congenial to a cognitive role for imagination in [re]presenting features of the one world that there is. If, on the other hand, seeing-as is not construed globally, then does imagination take on a skeptical face in the manner of Schofield? This would be less than completely consistent with Nussbaum's view.

It hardly needs mention that ii contrasts with the view urged in the last chapter. For in effect it states that imagination has an object, namely, any object that may appear to someone as something. Such objects would appear to be the φαντάστα countenanced by Chrysippus (see Appendix A) but eschewed by Aristotle. So although there is no special quarrel with ii as it stands, as a reading of the canonical imagination we have rejected it. Nussbaum remarks, "This broad interest in how things appear to sentient beings seems to form the basis for Aristotle's more specialized discussions of envisaging and of the sort of awareness that leads to action" (1978, 231). Perhaps so, but there is no reason it cannot be belief, perception, and the like, that take what appears as an object, leaving imagination to enter the story at a different level of explanation. And in an explanation of why someone believes that x is F or perceives x as F, images, suitably characterized, would have a role. At least this would be so if we were trying to explain how a system must be structured, internally, in order to accomplish believing and perceiving.

Two passages are adduced to show that Aristotle's interest in the truth and falsity of imagination is an interest in the truth and falsity of appearances and has nothing to do with images. *Metaphysica* V.29, 1024b24–26, asserts that things are false either because they themselves are not or because the imagination resulting from them is of what is not [τῷ τὴν ἀπ᾽ αὐτῶν

---

60. See Nussbaum's "the active, interpretive role of the imaginer" (1978, 230).
61. In the style, perhaps, of a Quine, a Goodman, or a Putnam.

φαντασίαν μὴ ὄντος εἶναι]. Nussbaum notes that strictly speaking Aristotle ought to have said not that the imagination is false but that the information it presents (which can be expressed propositionally) is false (1978, 248*n*43). But the passage says that imagination is *of* what is not. Thus, it is arguable that, in the cases at hand, the attendant φαντάσματα are what are not true *of* the relevant things and that, perhaps systematically, they are not overridden by belief or something more authoritative in the soul. And 1025a5, which remarks that a person may be called false if he often gives others a false impression, just as things are called false that create a false imagination [φαντασία], is made to resist introduction of images by a very odd argument. We would, says Nussbaum, have to say that such a man paints in others' minds a picture contrary to what he is. This would, of course, be a feat of considerable report. But it is sufficient that X gets Y to believe something P and that Y's so believing involves images of what is not. They need figure only in the *explanation* of what Y believes or comes to believe. They need not be cognitive darts thrown from without.

If we must make room for seeing-as, better, perhaps, to do so on the side of perception itself, in the nonminimal sense of that term. So it will be a function of this or of belief or of whatever it is that affirms or overrides the reports of individual senses. Although imagination and so φαντάσματα are involved here, they will figure but as lower-level conditions for [re]presenting the object in question. So the general strategy for φαντασία contexts allegedly inaccessible to the canonical theory is clear, at least for those answering to "x φαίνεται F to z." For although it is obvious that expressions for genuine worldly objects are fit substitution instances for the variables, we can insist that the subject has as well a context-related image. What the subject says and does in such contexts is just one of the "many things" that 2d of the canonical theory reports one does in accordance with imagination. What is salient here is, perhaps, less the depictional than the causal role of images: they are part of the internal mechanism that must be countenanced in order to explain adequately what a system does, in particular, its intentional acts.

Let us close this chapter by indicating how two of the most difficult cases might yield to the strategy in question. Thus, consider *Ethica Nicomachea* 1114a31–b1:

> But someone might say that all men strive for the apparent good [φαινομένου ἀγαθοῦ], yet no one is in control of the imagination [τῆς φαντασίας οὐ᾽ κύριοι]; rather how the end appears [φαίνεται] to someone depends on what sort of man he is.

and *Ethica Eudemia* 1235b26–29:

> Pleasure is desired because it is an apparent good [φαινόμενον
> ἀγαθόν]; some believe it is such and to some it appears [φαίνεται]
> such, even if they do not believe it to be so, for imagination [φαν-
> τασία] and belief [δόξα] are not in the same part of the soul.

Let me begin by returning to some old remarks. Those who took *De Anima* III.3, 427b16–21, to talk of imagination's being up to us and this, in turn, to imply a free, active₂ exercise of a faculty will be discomfited by 1114a31–b1's insistence that one does not control the imagination. In the *Ethica Nicomachea* passage what appears good is a function of what sort of man one is, that is to say, of what one believes, desires, and so on. This squares nicely with our general account whereby images, and so imagination, occur only by way of actual₂ exercises of genuine faculties. What images occur depends on what one is believing or thinking. Likewise, the *De Anima* passage counts imagination "up to us"[62] only in the sense that we have committed to memory specific mnemonic places and in the course of recalling something at will an image involved in the original act of memorization is produced. But, again, it is produced by the recalling.

The passage 1235b26–29 resembles the sun example, and so we have already dealt with it to some extent—not entirely, however, for the *Ethica Eudemia* passage (both of the present passages in fact) appears to embrace a propositional sense of imagination. The first suggests, for example, that it might appear good to invest money in the stock market and the second that it might appear pleasurable to eat a third chocolate.

But, now, might not one object that despite such similarities, the propositional context makes all the difference? In particular, it might be argued that here imagination cannot be *De Anima* III.3's canonical imagination. If whatever makes it possible for me to think about, say, the end of human conduct or a complex investment schedule is a φάντασμα, then this will have to be canonically based. But this seems difficult because 1b, 1c, and 1d of CT tie the canonical imagination too closely to perception.

On the other hand, so far from curtailing the canonical theory, this suggests how to extend it. For if Aristotle holds that all thought requires not merely imagination but also images, then appearings whose content is expressible in terms of thought or belief will also require images. And the appearings mentioned in the passages in question are surely of this sort. Of course, the suggested extension depends on the thesis that images are required for thought. It is time to turn to this thesis.

---

62. Recall that the text does not unproblematically recommend φαντασία, as opposed to νόησις (thinking), as what is up to us.

IV

THE RELATION BETWEEN
THOUGHT AND IMAGINATION

As so far interpreted, the canonical theory of *De Anima* III.3 is two sided. On the one hand, it contains a genetic account of the acquisition of those internal devices or [re]presentational structures that are required if we are to be aware of objects in complete intentional acts. On the other hand, it suggests a stronger thesis concerning the logic of such acts, namely, that actual deployment of such structures is a necessary condition for any functionally complete act, that is, for any act that falls within the purview of FFO and the Framework Passage. This receives classic expression in the thesis that imagination is required for thinking.

Aristotle conceives of the relation between imagination and thought primarily in terms of the necessity of images [φαντάσματα] for thinking [νόησις]. That discussion occurs, appropriately, after presentation of the canonical theory in *De Anima* III.3 and the functional analysis of thought in *De Anima* III.4–6. But already, in the B section of *De Anima* III.3, Aristotle has offered a set of remarks that locate imagination, cognitively, with respect to perception and thought, remarks that serve as well to guide the discussion in the following several chapters. So before turning to these later discussions, let us briefly consider these first suggestions.

1. THOUGHT, SUPPOSITION, AND IMAGINATION

Suppose we begin with 427b11–16:

> For (i) perception of the special objects [ἰδίων] is always true and is found in all the animals, but (ii) it is possible to also think [διανοεῖσθαι] falsely and thinking occurs in nothing in which

there is not also reason [οὐδενὶ ὑπάρχει ᾧ μὴ καὶ λόγος], for (iii) imagination is different from perception and thought [διανοίας] and (iv) this [imagination] does not occur without perception [αὕτη τε οὐ γίγνεται ἄνευ αἰσθήσεως] and supposition does not occur without imagination [ἄνευ ταύτης οὐκ ἔστιν ὑπόληψις].

First, a remark on the logic of the passage. Points i and ii are easily seen to support the thesis, mentioned in the preceding line, that thought [νοεῖν] and perception are not the same. It is considerably less clear how iii, in turn, supports them and that is what concerns us.[1] But the following might do. Assume, what we have already seen in the canonical theory, that imagination plays a role in explaining falsehood: because images can be true and false *of* objects, they figure in explaining why we sometimes make false perceptual reports. But if this is so, then imagination had better well differ from perception because the latter, at least for special objects, is always true and so could not figure in any such account. Thus, iii's differentiation between imagination and perception has a place in the argument. The distinction involving thought yields to a similar strategy. If imagination were thought, then, because imagination occurs in virtually all animals,[2] so would thought. Thus iii rules out a hypothetical objection to the claim that only certain animals enjoy thought.[3]

Having distinguished imagination from perception and thought, Aristotle turns in iv to the relationship between them. Imagination does not occur without perception, and supposition [ὑπόληψις] does not occur without imagination. Given 427b24–25—"And there are also different varieties of supposition itself [εἰσι δὲ καὶ αὐτῆς τῆς ὑπολήψεως]: knowledge [ἐπιστήμη], belief [δόξα], intelligence [φρόνησις], and their opposites"—it follows that none of these can occur without imagination. And this squares nicely with the rationale he immediately offers for placing imagination before thought in the order of inquiry: "Concerning thought [νοεῖν], since it is different from perception but imagination and supposition are thought to be contained in it [τούτου δὲ τὸ μὲν φαντασία δοκεῖ εἶναι τὸ δὲ ὑπόληψις], we must determine about imagination before proceeding to the other [περὶ θατέρου] (427b27–29).

Notice that Aristotle does not say that imagination and supposition are

---

1. Hicks (1965), by not translating the "γάρ" that introduces ii, does not even read the text as containing an argument.
2. See the discussion above, chap. 2, sec. 3, on the extent to which imagination and animality are coextensive.
3. Here I concur with Hamlyn (1968, 130).

two kinds of thought. Rather, they seem to be components or structural features of thinking. In effect, the passage can be paraphrased: since imagination and supposition are the two features of thinking and since (427b11–16) the first is presupposed by the second, we must first tackle imagination before turning to supposition.[4]

These initial passages contain several theses governing the relation between thought and imagination. The last considered might be put as

    1. x thinks $p \supset$ x supposes p & imagination is involved in [re]presenting p.

This would, in fact, follow from the claim that to think something is to suppose something together with a second thesis, explicitly mentioned in 427b11–16, namely:

    2. x supposes $p \supset$ imagination is involved in [re]presenting p.

Both 1 and 2 refuse to see the relation between thinking or supposition and imagination in terms of the verb "φαίνεται," thus eschewing formulations such as "p appears to x," "p presents itself to x," or, the seeing-as favorite, "something appears p to x." There are at least two reasons for this. First, if we want to find here a thesis linking thought with the canonical imagination, then the suggested idioms will, we have seen, simply be inappropriate. Second, when Aristotle finally addresses the need for imagination in thought, he does so in the canonical idiom of φαντάσματα or images. The third thesis, drawn from 427b24–26, retails the varieties of supposition:

    3. x supposes $p \equiv$ x knows p v
                     x believes p v
                     x thinks-practically p.

One striking point about 1, 2, and 3 is the prominence of the notion of supposition [ὑπόληψις]. Hamlyn (1968, 130) likens it to the notion of judg-

---

4. The "μὲν... δέ" construction in the bracketed phrase recommends "περὶ ὑπόληψις" (concerning supposition) as the most natural match for "περὶ θατέρου" (concerning the other). Yet what Aristotle goes on to discuss is νοῦς and this appears to argue for reading "περὶ νοεῖν" (concerning mind). In fact, however, it turns out that either reading is probably acceptable from the point of view of doctrine. For De Anima III.4 introduces its topic as that part of the soul in virtue of which the soul knows [γινώσκει] and thinks [φρονεῖ] and a few lines later glosses the part that is called νοῦς, presumably the same, as that in virtue of which the soul thinks and supposes [λέγω δὲ νοῦν ᾧ διανοεῖται καὶ ὑπολαμβάνει ἡ ψυχή]. And although his discussion of thinking focuses on mind's proper objects, the notion of νοεῖν employed in De Anima III.4 may be broad enough to accommodate δόξα and φρόνησις. At least Aristotle addresses, if only to remove from the discussion of thought proper, the sort of thinking that has as its objects things that have matter. More on this later.

ment in absolute idealists such as Bradley. For Barnes (1975, 192) it sometimes goes as a synonym for belief [δόξα] but officially marks out (as in 3) the genus of cognitive attitudes only one of which is δόξα. Hicks (1965, 457) thinks that δόξα, sometimes synonymous with ὑπόληψις, is generally the nearest single notion and so follows Bonitz in holding "ὑπόληψις is a supposition or assumption of belief, whether true or false." And Ross (1949a, 411) reports that ὑπόληψις records a higher degree of conviction than δόξα, "something like taking for granted." This collective commentary contains some but not, I would argue, nearly the whole truth about ὑπόληψις.

Part of the problem is that in *De Anima* III.3 the notion is rung in to explain thinking but remains itself relatively unexplained. What we need to see is how Aristotle himself *uses* the notion, in particular, how he uses the verb "ὑπολαμβάνειν" (suppose) and its variants. We may start with the fact that the verb is used extensively in *De Anima*[5] and elsewhere[6] to report views of predecessors, opponents, and the like. Thus, Democritus and Leucippus are said (404a8) to have held [ὑπολαμβάνοντες] that the soul is what supplies movement in animals and the cohorts of Critias (405b7) to have held that perception is most characteristic of the blood. Sometimes Aristotle selects the verb to indicate what we ought to suppose. At *De Partibus Animalium* 648a14, for instance, it "must be supposed" [ὑπο-ληπτέον] that anatomical variations have to do with an animal's functions and essence or with its advantage or disadvantage, and *Metaphysica* 982a6–8 counsels that we should collect the ὑπολήψεις of the wise man because we hold [ὑπολαμβάνομεν] that he knows all things. In these, indeed in all passages examined,[7] ὑπόληψις means something like taking something to be the case. It is not, pace Hicks, assuming something, which then happens to be true or false; rather it is supposing or assuming *that* something is true. This is clear from the way the notion is pressed into service in Aristotle's discussion of the principle of noncontradiction in *Metaphysica* IV.3. The passage at 1005b24–26 explains that none can hold [ὑπολαμβάνειν] that *p* and not-*p* because what someone says he need not suppose [ὑπολαμβά-νειν], apparently tilting at the antagonist of 1005b35–1006a2 who asserts the possibility of *p* and not-*p* and claims that one can actually suppose as much [καὶ ὑπολαμβάνειν οὕτως].

---

5. In Book I, for example, 402a1, 403b31, 404a8 and 22, 404b8, 405a5, 20, and 30, 405b7, 408a12, 411a1 and 16.

6. See, for instance, *Metaphysica* 1009a10 and 30, 1009b12 and 27, 1010a10 and 26, 1010b10.

7. These include not all but some ninety occurrences of "ὑπολαμβάνειν" or "ὑπόληψις."

Thus, ὑπόληψις can be made to bear the sense "taking or holding something to be the case," appearing to be an essentially propositional notion. This is true even where the supposition is about a single thing. *De Anima* III.11's distinction between a general supposition and reason [ἡ καθόλου ὑπόληψις καὶ λόγος] and one that is particular [ἡ τοῦ καθ᾿ ἕκαστον] does not countenance a nonpropositional kind of supposition. Rather, it mirrors *Metaphysica* I.1, 981a5–12's distinction between the particular supposition[8] that Callias was cured by a certain medicine [τὸ ὑπόληψιν ὅτι Καλλία...] and the supposition that all similar persons, marked off as one class [τὸ ὅτι πᾶσι τοῖς τοιοῖσδε κατ᾿ εἶδος ἓν ἀφορισθεῖσι], were similarly cured. The use of ὅτι-clauses for both singular and general cases clearly indicates propositional force for both.[9]

The general meaning and wide use of "ὑπόληψις" and "ὑπολαμβάνειν" in reporting predecessor views may explain why it has been taken as synonymous with "δόξα." For when Aristotle reports received views, he is reporting what someone took to be the case and often these will be wrong views. Hence, he is easily thought to be equating ὑπόληψις and δόξα. At best this is misleading and suggests an incorrect picture of the relation between ὑπόληψις and its forms. Certainly, *if* one held that supposition competes at the same level as knowledge [ἐπιστήμη], belief [δόξα], and practical intelligence [φρόνησις], then one might hold with Ross that it indicates a sort of conviction selectively firmer or weaker than these. But if 3 means to claim that ἐπιστήμη, δόξα, and φρόνησις are simply species or forms of ὑπόληψις, then such weighting will be inappropriate.

The point is this. Just as there are many figures that count as a plane figure so there are many ways to hold that something is the case. *Analytica Posteriora* I.33 discusses two of them. If, where *p* is necessary, x holds [ὑπολαμβάνει] that *p* and if *p* is held to be the case [ὑπολήψεται] in the way appropriate for definitions in demonstration, then x knows [ἐπιστήσεται] but does not believe that *p*. If, on the other hand, *p* is not held to be the case in the way appropriate for definitions, then x's holding that *p* amounts to x's believing but not knowing that *p*. Left undiscussed here is the case of practical intelligence [φρόνησις], but presumably that will be covered by stipulating that *p* is to be held to be the case on the basis of deliberation. At least one would expect this given *Ethica Nicomachea* VI.5, 1140b13–16's distinction between ὑπόληψις concerning geometrical theo-

8. So καθ᾿ ἕκαστον οὕτω at 981a9.

9. Nonetheless, I have formulated 3 cautiously. Use of the "know *p*" idiom rather than the more natural "know that *p*, and so on, places few constraints on what may serve as *p*. In particular, it allows for the possibility that Aristotle countenances nonpropositional as well as propositional modes of thought. At this point it seems prudent to leave this question open.

rems and that concerning action. So all three forms reported in 3 are discussed by Aristotle. The fact that the doxastic mode is more frequent does not mean that ὑπόληψις is closer to, let alone synonymous with, δόξα any more than a preponderance of squares would render "square" synonymous with "plane figure."

This is confirmed, again, by Aristotle's usage. As a rule "ὑπόληψις" and "ὑπολαμβάνειν" are employed when what matters is not how but simply that something is taken to be the case. In discussing the principle of noncontradiction, for instance, it is sufficient to show that one can't *hold* that p and not-p. To couch the point in terms of knowing might only encourage the silly remark that, nonetheless, perhaps one could believe such. And, in the familiar sun example [428b2–4], we rightly hold something to be the case [ὑπόληψιν ἀληθῆ ἔχει] even though this is "contradicted" by appearances. Although other language could have been used—witness "εἰδόσιν" (know) at 458b28 in *De Insomniis*'s parallel passage—there is no need for it.

Ross is, then, not reflecting Aristotle's practice in claiming that ὑπολαμβάνειν (supposing) implies a higher degree of conviction than δοξάζειν (believing). In the first place, it is unclear that "taking something for granted," Ross's support for the claim, connotes a higher degree of conviction as opposed to a lesser degree of scrutiny. But at least Ross seems sensitive to the wide role accorded ὑπόληψις. So far from taking something for granted, however, the general role is explained in terms of taking something to be the case on one of several grounds. And this requires that degree of conviction be meted out not between ὑπόληψις itself and its varieties but simply between the varieties themselves. *Ethica Nicomachea* VII.2 suggests just this. In the midst of puzzling over the possibility of moral weakness, Aristotle remarks (1145b36–1146a1) that we could forgive the morally weak man "if it is belief [δόξα] and not knowledge [ἐπιστήμη], not the strong but the weak supposition [μηδ' ἰσχυρὰ ὑπόληψις... ἀλλ' ἠρεμαία], that offers resistance."[10]

To return to thesis 1, it is now clear that it asserts that thinking involves, on the one hand, taking something to be the case and, on the other hand, imagination. Because the former extends to singular propositions such as "Socrates is melancholic" and "That is light meat,"[11] thesis 1 can hardly

10. If to anything, ὑπόληψις would seem closer to διάνοια. *Metaphysica* IV.7, 1017a2–4, connects the latter with affirmation and denial, and *Analytica Posteriora* II.19, 100b5–7, gives this notion scope over δόξα (belief), λογισμός (calculation), ἐπιστήμη (knowledge), and νοῦς (mind). Granger (1963) concurs on this point.

11. By inference from the fact that *De Anima* III.11 discusses the supposition about the particular thing [ἡ τοῦ καθ' ἕκαστον ὑπόληψις] as the minor premise of a practical syllogism plus the fact that elsewhere these take the indexical form, "That is F."

award imagination a propositional role and, hence, cannot construe it as a kind of thought. Aristotle confirms the point later, at *De Anima* III.8, 432a10–11, in insisting that imagination is neither affirmation nor denial, for these both amount to taking something to be the case.[12] Thus, 1 would appear to report that when one thinks, one must [re]present whatever it is that one is taking to be the case. If so, one would expect supposition and imagination to be involved in thought in rather different ways. And this appears to be what is caught by the asymmetry in 2 and, thus, what is also reflected in *De Anima* III.4's characterization of the mind [νοῦς] as that in virtue of which the soul reasons [διανοεῖται] and takes something to be the case [ὑπολαμβάνει]. For imagination will enter only as a condition on thinking, never as thinking in its own right.

There is a final point concerning the assertion that supposition and so thought is not without imagination. One could grant that this shows the dependence of thought on imagination but deny that this counts as an extension of the *canonical* theory. Although this already rings untrue given the occurrence of both within a single chapter of *De Anima,* one can fashion an argument for the objection, namely, that 1b, 1c, and 1d of CT tie the canonical imagination too closely to perception to allow for its extension to thought. Although we return to the point throughout the chapter, a response is already at hand.

The place to begin is with the language Aristotle uses in iv of 427b11–16: Thought is *not without* [οὐ γίγνεται ἄνευ] imagination nor imagination without perception. *De Anima* III.8 frames its conclusion in like manner and, thus, appears to opt for the second formulation suggested in the opening chapter of the work: "if this [τοῦτο = τὸ νοεῖν] is a sort of imagination [φαντασία τις] or not without imagination [μὴ ἄνευ φαντασίας], it will not be possible even for thinking to be without body" (403a8–10). Here ". . . οὐκ ἄνευ . . ." is used to express a weak dependence relation between thought and imagination. It is this relation that enables Aristotle to extend the role of the canonical imagination to thinking. To see how this works we need to return to *De Memoria*'s discussion of the relation between memory, thought, and perception.

It will be enough to consider 450a12–14—"So memory, even of objects of thought, is not without an image [οὐκ ἄνευ φαντάσματος] and thus it belongs to mind incidentally [τοῦ νοῦ κατὰ συμβεβηκὸς ἂν εἴη] and properly to the primary thing that perceives [καθ' αὑτὸ τοῦ πρώτου αἰσθητικοῦ]"—with 450a22–25, a text we have already used in a somewhat different context: "To which of the things of the soul memory belongs is,

_____

12. Granger (1963, 14) appears to appreciate this point.

then, clear, namely, that to which imagination pertains [οὗπερ καὶ ἡ φαντασία]. And whatever is a thing of imagination is an object of memory properly [μνημονευτὰ καθ' αὑτὰ ὧν ἐστι φαντασία] while whatever is not without imagination is an object of memory incidentally [κατὰ συμβεβηκὸς ὅσα μὴ ἄνευ φαντασίας]."

The first passage implies that no memory is without an image, and the second suggests that this is so because whatever is an object of memory is either a thing of imagination [ὧν ἐστι φαντασία] or not without imagination [μὴ ἄνευ φαντασίας]. The former echoes, in fact, appears to be coextensive with, the things of perception [ὧν αἴσθησις ἐστίν] in 1d of CT. So we appear to have here a distinction between objects of perception [τὰ αἰσθητά] and objects of thought [τὰ νοητά].

This difference in kinds of objects of memory is paralleled by a difference in how memory functions in each case. Memory belongs properly to perception, specifically to the primary perceptual faculty because, as 450a10–11 states, the image is an affection of the common sense [τὸ φάντασμα τῆς κοινῆς αἰσθήσεως πάθος ἐστίν].[13] It is not an *affection* of the mind, at least not properly, and will be involved with the mind only incidentally [κατὰ συμβεβηκός].[14] This appears to follow from

> 4. If memory of objects [of thought] is not without imagination, then objects [of thought] are only incidentally objects of memory,

given in the second passage, and

> 5. If objects of thought are only incidentally objects of memory, then memory belongs only incidentally to the mind.

What is interesting about these formulations is the connection between the weak dependence relation, "...οὐκ ἄνευ...," (". . . not without . . .") and the notion of one thing holding of another incidentally. Since "οὐκ ἄνευ" signifies a weak relation, it of course applies, as in the first passage, to stronger cases as well.[15] But where, as here, it counts as the strongest relation applicable, Aristotle seems to hold something like

> 6. If φing is not without O & O properly belongs to X, then φing involves X incidentally.

This is a very rough formulation but may, nonetheless, catch the crucial

---

13. See the discussion of this passage at the end of chapter 2.

14. This parallels a point made in the discussion above concerning incidental perception.

15. Also 427b11–16, where it covers the relation between imagination and perception as well as that between supposition and imagination.

point. Thus, as memory of objects of thought is not without images and images belong properly to imagination so memory of objects of thought involves imagination only incidentally. What is important for our purposes is that 6 has a natural extension to the relation between thought and imagination. Because, as 449b31–450a1 reminds us, thinking is not without an image [νοεῖν οὐϰ ἔστιν ἄνευ φαντάσματος] and, as the canonical theory requires, images belong properly to imagination, it follows that thinking involves imagination only incidentally.[16]

Two points deserve emphasis here. First, it *must* be the canonical imagination that is involved in thought, unless one were to claim that it is not the canonical imagination that is involved properly in the perceptual faculties! So the canonical theory is clearly intended to cover the sort of imagination involved in thinking. Second, the ϰατὰ συμβεβηϰός, or incidental, mode of extension in no way impugns either the status of the involved images or the nature of the involvement. This is clear from other contexts. That, for example, I perceive the son of Callias incidentally [ϰατα συμβεβηϰός] does not mean that I perceive an accident or that I need not perceive him, although both points may be true. Perception of special objects counts, after all, as proper or [ϰαθ' αὐτό] perception. Rather, the expression directs our attention to the way in which the son of Callias is perceived, namely, in virtue of perceiving, properly, a white thing that happens to be Callias's son.[17] Likewise for *Analytica Posteriora* I.22's distinction between predications of the form (*a*) "The white thing walks" and (*b*) "The large thing is a log" and those of the form (*c*) "The man walks." If, as Aristotle says, we must legislate, then *a*- and *b*-type predications will not count as predicating at all [μηδαμῶς ϰατηγορεῖν] or they will be cases of predicating incidentally [ϰατὰ συμβεβηϰός] and not strictly [μὴ ἁπλῶς ϰατηγορεῖν].

What is problematic about *a* and *b* predications is neither their meaning nor their truth value. It is, rather, just that they are not in "proper logical" form. They fail to display perspicuously the ontological relations that would make the sentences true[18]—*b* suggests that the genuine subject [ὑποϰείμενον] is the large, whereas it is in fact the log, and *a* fails entirely to mention the genuine subject. It will be true *in virtue of* the truth of two *c*-type predications, say, "Socrates is white" and "Socrates walks," both of which

16. If, in light of 450a10–11, one substitutes "and the image belongs properly to perception," we get the result that thinking involves perception only incidentally. We shall return to this later in assaying the dependence of mind on body.

17. Again, see the discussion referred to in n. 14.

18. For more on this, see my *Aristotle's Argument for the Principle of Non-Contradiction in Light of His Theory of Predication,* deposited in the Regenstein Library of the University of Chicago.

are in proper logical form and so count as strict predication. Here again there is no question of such cases failing to count as predication. (Aristotle plainly rejects the extreme position that they are μηδαμῶς κατηγορεῖν.) By the same token, then, that thinking involves imagination κατὰ συμβεβηκός does not mean to downgrade either imagination or the involvement.[19] It means only that thought involves imagination not on its own terms but in virtue of something else. The point would seem to be that thinking involves imagination in virtue of the fact that it involves images and these, in turn, involve imagination nonincidentally.

It may help to take a yet clearer case: the president is an artist incidentally because he is a pianist and pianists are artists nonincidentally. It would be ludicrous to suppose that, in its first occurrence, "artist" means something different from what it means in its second occurrence. To be an artist incidentally is not to be an incidental artist! Whatever sense attaches to the second must attach to the first. This is important because it shows that Aristotle's strategy for extending imagination to thought preserves a single notion of imagination, namely, the canonical imagination. Thus, it cannot, as Nussbaum assumes, invoke a different sense of the term. There can, then, be no doubt that the canonical imagination is extended to thought on the strength of the thesis that thought requires images.

2. THE NECESSITY OF IMAGES FOR THOUGHT: A RESTRICTED VERSION

The thesis that images are required for thought (call this IM) is part of a more general argument concerning the dependence of mind on body. Roughly, the idea is that images require perception and perception in turn requires physical sense organs. So if thought requires images, then what thinks (presumably mind) will depend on body. Although we may occasionally refer to the general argument, the thesis in question can be scrutinized on its own. Although, as we have already seen, IM appears in *De Anima* I.1, it is mentioned there only as a possible course of argumentation. But in *De Anima* III it appears to be argued twice, at III.7 and III.8. The close proximity of these arguments suggests that they may have slightly different force. Indeed, it turns out that the first argument stands in need of the second.

19. This is reflected in *De Anima* III.10, 433b27ff.'s point that imagination is said to be either rational or perceptual as well as 449b24's remark that memory is a state or affection of perception or supposition [ὑπόληψις]. It enjoys equal status in both roles.

The first or restricted version of IM must be culled from the following portions of *De Anima* III.7.

> Perceiving [τὸ αἰσθάνεσθαι] then is similar to simple assertion and thought [ὅμοιον τῷ φάναι μόνον καὶ νοεῖν]: whenever something is pleasant or painful, [the soul] pursues or avoids it [διώκει ἢ φεύγει] which is like asserting or denying it; and to experience pleasure or pain is to be active with the perceptual mean [ἐνεργεῖν τῇ αἰσθητικῇ μεσότητι] toward the good and the bad. (431a8–11)

> (*a*) Images [τὰ φαντάσματα] serve the thinking soul [τῇ διανοητικῇ ψυχῇ] as perceptions [οἷον αἰσθήματα]. And (*b*) whenever it affirms or denies good or bad, it avoids or pursues it. Hence (*c*) the soul never thinks without an image [διὸ οὐδέποτε νοεῖ ἄνευ φαντάσματος ἡ ψυχή]. (431a14–17)

> That which thinks [τὸ νοητικόν], therefore, thinks the forms in images [τὰ εἴδη ἐν τοῖς φαντάσμασι νοεῖ]. (431b2)

The statement at *c* unambiguously asserts that images are necessary for episodes of thought, and 431b2 returns to the argument and appears to endorse the implication that, if the soul never thinks without an image, then the soul thinks the forms in images. Since forms here are forms of things, the suggested inference would require the further assumption that images are images of things. Although Aristotle does not argue this in *De Anima* III.7, he comes close to doing so in *De Anima* III.8. Indeed, if we approach *De Anima* III.8 in light of the canonical theory, it will turn out to be fairly obvious that images are images of (perceived) things.

Before addressing the argument of *De Anima* III.8 we need to look more closely at *De Anima* III.7. For while we get an argument for IM, it turns out either that the argument fails to establish IM or that IM is not to be given a general interpretation. This can be made clear from a look at the argument's structure. It is governed by the analogy between perceiving, on the one hand, and thought or assertion, on the other. The restriction to simple [μόνον] thought and assertion may serve simply to safeguard the analogy. One might, for instance, have doubts about what sort of perception would be available as an analogue for extremely complex thoughts. Or the restriction may be somewhat more severe, excluding any assertion or thought of one thing of another thing [τὶ κατὰ τινός]. On this reading the analogy would hold between perception and assertions or thoughts expressible only in terms of the schema "This/it is F," where F introduces some perceptible property such as greenness or roundness. The difficulty with the latter view, espoused at least by Hicks, is the lack of evidence that

Aristotle ever departs from his usual practice in order to countenance a simple naming interpretation of "φάναι."[20]

Apparently, Aristotle holds that *a* and *b* *imply* *c*. Unfortunately, it is unclear how this works in detail. Part of the problem is a lack of clarity regarding the meaning of the individual premises. For instance, *a* has at least the following construals:

> *a*1. Images are to the (discursively) thinking soul as sense percep-
>   tions are to the perceiving soul.
> *a*2. Images are to the (discursively) thinking soul as sense percep-
>   tions are to that (the discursively thinking soul).
> *a*3. Images of the (discursively) thinking soul are similar to per-
>   ceptions.

The first two versions trade on the analogy, introduced at 431a8, between perception [αἰσθάνεσθαι] and thinking [νοεῖν], whereas the last appeals merely to similarity between images [φαντάσματα] and perceptions [αἰσθήματα]. But there is no indication that the latter is at issue in the passage. The third construal is also unlikely for the further reason that it simply cannot advance the argument toward *c* via *b*. So better to opt for *a*1 or *a*2. In a sense choice between them is not crucial. For, given Aristotle's eschewal of a faculty psychology, the thinking soul will be extensionally the same as the perceiving soul. Nonetheless, this detracts from the point of analogy which is to draw structural parallels between thinking and perceiving, something that is accomplished by *a*1 only.

The argument seems strong enough for *c*, only if we add to

> *b*. The thinking soul, S, asserts (denies) x → S pursues (avoids) x

both

> *b*1. S pursues (avoids) x → S has an image of x

and

> *b*2. S thinks of x & S thinks x good (bad) → S asserts (denies) x.

The above three premises together yield a weak version of the conclusion, namely,

> *c*1. S thinks of x & S thinks x good (bad) → S has an image of
>   x.

---

20. Contra Hicks (1965, 527), who holds λέγει (say) at 426b21 also to be a case of "the simple naming of a thing." But the latter occurs in an account of an important kind of contrastive judgment, namely, "The sweet is different from the white" and the like, and these surely involve more than mere naming.

This is hardly strong enough to support a full version of IM. So we might try to strengthen the conclusion by manipulating $a1$. One possibility is to combine 431a9–10's remark that the soul pursues what is pleasant and avoids what is painful with the observation in *Ethica Nicomachea* 1105b20–24 that affections, or πάθη, of the soul are those items in the soul that are accompanied by pleasure and/or pain. Thus, if images and perceptions are πάθη, then they will be accompanied by pleasure or pain. This allows us to construe $a1$ in terms of the analogy. Just as in perceiving something one has a perception [αἴσθημα] that is pleasurable or painful so in thinking something one has an image [φάντασμα] that is good or bad. Because being pleasurable or painful is the analogue to being good or bad, just as one pursues the pleasurable and avoids the painful so one affirms the good and denies the bad and, hence, pursues the good and avoids the bad.

Unfortunately the immediately given consideration is too strong. In effect, it suggests strengthening $b1$ to something like

$b1'$. S pursues/avoids x $\longleftrightarrow$ S has an image of x

on the argument that images are affections of the soul and so are either pleasurable or painful. But $b1'$ seems false because of requiring that all images be connected with what can be pursued or avoided. It is totally implausible to suppose that images involved in mathematical operations are pleasurable or painful, certainly not in any sense that is relevant to pursuit and avoidance. Thus, if we make use of b and its ilk in reconstructing the argument, the conclusion will be something like

$c1'$. S thinks of x in action contexts & S thinks x good (bad) $\rightarrow$
    S has image of x.

On the other hand, from $a1$ we could get

c. S thinks of x $\rightarrow$ S has an image of x

by assuming

$a1'$ The perceiving soul never perceives without an αἴσθημα.

Although $a1'$ plus the analogy between perceiving and thinking would be sufficient for c, this last maneuver makes b and its ilk irrelevant to the argument's strategy. The most we can get from the argument of *De Anima* III.7, then, is that Aristotle has shown, for a large number of cases, namely, cases involving action, that thought requires images. There is, however, another way of taking this result. For it tells against the view that the one context in which Aristotle relaxes IM is in action contexts.[21] Thus, we know that, whatever the range given IM by the argument of *De Anima* III.8, IM at least covers action contexts.

3. A GENERAL VERSION OF IM

De Anima III.8 contains an argument for a general version of IM. If all thought requires images, then presumably any operations involving thought will also be operations involving images. Since we have already shown that nonminimal perceptual activity involves images, it would follow that images are required for all nonminimal operations of the soul. Besides generality, the *De Anima* III.8 argument affords some explanation of why images are conceived as forms and not as decaying sense impressions. The chapter ends with an interesting remark on the difference between images and thoughts. We shall want to say something about this but after discussion of the argument.

The argument, located at 432a3–10, has the following, rather literal, form:

> Since (i) there is no thing or fact [πρᾶγμα] apart from sensible extended things [παρὰ τὰ μεγέθη... τὰ αἰσθητά], then (ii) what is thought [τὰ νοητά] will be in the perceptual forms [ἐν τοῖς εἴδεσι τοῖς αἰσθητοῖς], both (iia) those which are spoken of in abstraction [τὰ ἐν ἀφαιρέσει λεγόμενα] and (iib) those which are dispositions [ἕξεις] and affections [πάθη] of things that are perceived [τῶν αἰσθητῶν]. And because of this (that is, ii), (iii) there is no learning [μάθοι] or understanding [ξυνίοι] without perceiving [οὔτε μὴ αἰσθανόμενος] and (iv) whenever one contemplates [ὅταν θεωρῇ], one must at that moment contemplate with an image [φαντάσματι θεωρεῖν]; for (v) images are like perceptual states [τὰ φαντάσματα ὥσπερ αἰσθήματά ἐστι], except without matter [πλὴν ἄνευ ὕλης].

This is a very rich passage and calls for a number of comments. Notice, first, that we have an argument from what exists or what is the case to what one can think about. The apparent effect of the implication from i to ii is to bar thought about what does not exist as a perceptible and extended thing. Two qualifications are in order, however. Since Aristotle elsewhere countenances thought about what does not exist, he cannot be asserting the

---

21. Nussbaum (1978) is unambiguous in holding this view.

strong thesis that thought of particular objects requires that they exist. From *Categoriae* 13b27–33 it is clear that one can think of Socrates, even though he no longer exists. Rather, the point is that one cannot think of things that are of a kind not to have existed or, even more liberally, that one cannot think of things whose salient parts are of a kind not to have existed. This is sufficiently strong for the conclusion that images are required for thought and so seems to be harmless. Indeed, there is some internal support for this qualified reading, for the forms mentioned in iib do not include forms of substances qua substances but rather forms of dispositions and affections of them. The dispositions [ἕξεις] and affections [πάθη] of things that are perceived are arguably nothing other than (certain) accidents of perceptible substances. Thus, the forms here in question may be forms of proper objects of perception since these exclude substances.[22] On the other hand, iia and iib may not be specifying the notion of form introduced in ii but rather indicating that that notion can be extended to include cases that might not prima facie seem covered by ii.

The second, and somewhat more important, qualification concerns the apparent restriction of thought to objects that are extended and perceptible. Although i seems to imply this, especially given "since" [ἐπεί] rather than the less willful "if" [εἴ], the final sentence of the preceding chapter should caution us. For 431b17–19 asks whether mind [νοῦς], if not separate from extension, can think of objects that are separate from extension. Since Aristotle clearly recognizes such objects, this is not an idle question. Even assuming the answer to be affirmative—that consideration Aristotle defers until "later"—the argument in 432a3–10 still makes impressive claims. For if it goes through, the argument would show that thought of anything save perhaps incorporeal substances requires images. This result would have the interesting effect of raising the question of what sort of thought would then be available for such elevated items. Taking our lead from Aristotle, we shall defer discussion of this point until we have a firmer grasp on IM itself.

Something should be said about ii. Ross and Hicks took "ἐν τοῖς ἔδεσι τοῖς αἰσθητοῖς" to refer to perceptible forms and Hamlyn translated the words "among the forms which are the objects of perception." The latter is implausible on two accounts. First, things and not forms are the objects of perception, even if perceiving a thing involves somehow having a form of the thing in the soul (as 431b29–432a1 points out). Second, this makes objects of thought [τὰ νοητά] the same as objects of perception. But 417b22–24 rules this out by rating objects of perception particulars and objects of

22. This recalls our earlier argument that, strictly, there may be no φαντάσματα of substances qua substances. It does not follow from this, however, that forms are so restricted. This would assume, what I shall presently argue is false, that thoughts are reducible to images.

knowledge, which τὰ νοητά surely are, universals in the soul. By the same token "perceptible forms" is at least misleading. Perhaps "perceptual forms" or "forms in or of perceived things" will do, since this indicates only that the forms in question must figure in perceptual contexts, not that they be the objects of perception.

Given the above remarks, especially the qualifying remarks on the i → ii inference, it is fairly clear how iii follows. One can, presumably, learn and understand only what one can think of. So if thought requires perception (because its objects are forms in perceived things), then there is neither learning nor understanding apart from perception. Literally, the participial construction "οὔτε μὴ αἰσθανόμενος" gives iii the force—"there is no learning or understanding unless something is perceived." Although, grammatically, this could support the meaning that one can think about only what one has perceived or is perceiving, the Greek need only yield the weaker and more plausible point that perception is required for acquisition of the materials of thought, namely, τὰ νοητά. And, of course, exactly this process has been accounted for by the canonical theory.

Less clear, however, is how iv fits into the argument. The fact that it is introduced by the connective "τέ" suggests that iv does not follow from i, ii, and iii but has an independent route into the argument. Indeed, this is borne out by the text which gives v as the ground for iv. That iv makes a different point than iii is clear from the fact that, although the latter may be explainable in terms of acquisition of [re]presentational structures, the former surely is not. So it is hardly plausible to limit the canonical theory to a strictly acquisitional role, as some commentators prefer.

Notice that v entails iv only on the assumption

> v'. Whenever one contemplates, one contemplates with something that is like a perceptual state [αἴσθημα] except that it is without matter.

Taking the argument in this way we have still to relate the initial premises with the final defense of IM. That is, IM asserts a connection between thought and imagination that may take one of two forms. Either we could say that thoughts just are images or we could say that thoughts, although not identical with images, require them. I shall argue that it is the latter that must be meant.

Notice, first, that until v there is no mention of αἰσθήματα but only of αἰσθητά—the familiar contrast between the object perceived and the perceptual state. Now were thoughts, the νοητά of ii, identical with images, it would be clear that, because one contemplates a νοητόν, iv would license the conclusion that thought involves images. There are, however, two reasons against this line of argument. First, the dative "φαντάσματι" at 432a8 resists taking images as thoughts.[23] To contemplate with an image is not to contemplate an image [φάντασμα], nor can it be to contemplate a φαντ- ταστόν (object of imagination), which would seem, at least grammatically, to be the candidate for identification with the νοητόν (object of thought). Here we need only invoke the point made earlier that Aristotle simply has no room in his psychology for φανταστά. So there simply is no sense in which one can say that for Aristotle one contemplates images when one is contemplating an object of thought. Second, 431b2, cited above, tells against the identification of thought and images, for it asserts quite un- ambiguously that objects of thought are not images but forms (in the cur- rent context, presumably, of perceived things) *in* images.

So it seems clear that an image is a vehicle for thought without being identical with the thought.[24] It is the means by which the thought is [re]presented to the subject. This, of course, squares rather nicely with the view that imagination is functionally incomplete. One explanation, then, of how iv fits into the argument is by way of the requirement that besides objects of thought, presumably the objects of contemplation par excellence, there must be devices for [re]presenting objects of thought. These are the images. Were this consideration omitted, the argument could be taken as embodying a thesis only about objects of thought, namely, that they must be possible existents in a sensible world. But this, of course, goes no way toward establishing the dependence of thought or mind on body. For this the argument must be made to embody a thesis about the structure of thinking, namely, that whatever is thought about must be [re]presented internally and this is accomplished with an image. Hence, the importance of iv and its sufficient conditions, v and vi.

4. IMAGES, PERCEPTUAL STATES, AND THOUGHTS

Both arguments for IM so far considered are guided by the analogy between perceiving and thinking. One feature of that analogy is particularly im- portant for our purposes. This is the use in v of the form–matter distinction.

23. With Themistius, Hicks, and Smith I follow E against alternative readings of inferior manuscripts, SVWX's "φαντάσματα" and CLU's "φάντασμά τι." Rose (OCT), Hett (Loeb), and Mugnier (Budé), who fails even to list the E reading, like "φάντασμά τι," as do Hamlyn and, now, Lowe and Watson (1982, 109). I can only speculate that the better attested reading was shunned, ironically, for doctrinal reasons. In fact, it turns out to be less difficult.

24. And of course, as we shall shortly see, 432a13 asserts that thoughts [νοήματα] are not the same as images [φαντάσματα].

The distinction is part of the account of how a subject can be aware of objects as opposed to merely registering or responding to them. In particular, it plays a role in the central thesis that when a system is aware of an object it becomes or is somehow the same as the object in question. I refer to this as the Sameness Thesis. The Sameness Thesis applies either to the system as a whole, for example, Socrates, or to one of its parts or subsystems. The first is intuitively unappealing and has no textual support. So it appears that the Sameness Thesis is part of explaining the internal mechanisms of perceiving. It holds for any faculty and its operation. Thus, 430a19–20 asserts that actual knowledge [ἡ κατ' ἐνέργειαν ἐπιστήμη] is the same as its object [τῷ πράγματι]. De Anima III.7 opens with a restrike of the line and ends, in the penultimate sentence, with a slightly different phrasing of the point: "In general the mind in activity is its objects." De Anima III.8 proceeds to explain the force of the sameness. When a faculty is not active or at least not active with respect to a given object, it is only potentially the same as that object. When, however, it is actually₂ (to employ our familiar idiom) directed on an object, the faculty is the same as the object. But the identity cannot hold between faculties and their proper objects. Witness how Aristotle couches the identification at 431b23–24: "In a way [πώς] knowledge is [the same as] the objects of knowledge [τὰ ἐπιστητά] and perception [the same as] the objects of perception [τὰ αἰσθητά]." What the faculty is the same as is not the object proper but rather its form:

> In the soul that which perceives [τὸ αἰσθητικόν] and that which knows [τὸ ἐπιστημονικόν] are potentially [the same as] these [ταῦτα], namely, the known thing [τὸ ἐπιστητόν] and the perceived thing [τὸ αἰσθητόν]. These must be either the things themselves [αὐτα] or their forms [τὰ εἴδη]. They are not the things themselves [αὐτα] because the stone is not in the soul but its form. (431b26–432a1)

There may be some temptation to read into the above passage the view that objects of perception and knowledge are internal to the soul. On this view the true objects of each would be internal objects and external objects are held to be perceived or thought of only inferentially. Three reasons tell against this. First, were this Aristotle's intention it would have been more happily expressed by mentioning αἰσθάματα (perceptual states) rather than αἰσθητά (objects of perception). The former but not the latter are certified internal items. Second, there is no independent evidence that Aristotle treats αἰσθητά in the suggested manner. Indeed, the theory of perception runs squarely against the suggestion. Third, the "these" [αὐτά] in the second sentence is to be read with "τὸ ἐπιστητόν" and "τὸ αἰσθητόν" in the preceding line. And since these are, respectively, proper objects of knowledge and perception, in light of the last sentence neither will be an internal item.

Still it might be insisted that the passage shows only that objects of perception are not in the soul but that objects of thought are. After all, the last sentence proves the point by adducing a case that is clearly an object of perception. I think, however, that Aristotle is counseling that there is a sense in which neither objects of thought nor objects of perception are in the soul. Here are some reasons for thinking so. First, the grammar of the passage is difficult otherwise. Were one to urge that there is one case where the proper objects of a faculty are in the soul, namely, in the case of objects of thought, one would have to read the disjunction in sentence two as not offering an exclusive disjunction for all such objects. But since the "αὐτά" in the final sentence can only pick up its predecessor in the left arm of the disjunction, what is being excluded is that any things themselves are in the soul. This would include those that are objects of thought.

There are two ways to take this last, rather surprising, conclusion. First, one might hold out for a *modified* exclusion of objects of thought as constituents of the soul. This might cover cases of thinking about Socrates or my favorite painting. Besides facing the grammatical difficulty just deployed, another and more serious problem is Aristotle's insistence that the objects of knowledge are universals. Thus, we find at 417b22–24 "actual perception is of particulars [τῶν καθ᾽ ἕκαστον] while knowledge is of the universal [τῶν καθόλου]; and the latter are somehow [πώς] in the soul itself [ἐν αὐτῇ τῇ ψυχῇ]."

This passage seems to conflict with the interpretation of 431b26–432a1. The conflict is, however, only apparent. For the immediate passage does not find Aristotle saying that universals are in the soul in any straightforward way. Rather they are in the soul *in some way*. We have already seen that the rider cuts deeply; for perception and the objects of perception to be the same *in some way* was not for them to be the same in any standard sense of sameness. By the same token Aristotle here is saying, in effect, that universals are not in the soul itself in any standard sense of being in. On reflection this is prudent policy since anything that is in a particular soul (the impact of "the soul *itself*) will be a particular and not a universal after all. Thus, just as knowledge is *somehow* the same as its objects so also universals are *somehow* in the soul, and so there is a quite straightforward reconciliation between 431b23–432a1 and 417b22–24.[25] We can, I think,

25. I do not pretend to have explained either thesis. See chapter 5 for an attempt at this.

now begin to see the crucial role of images as the vehicles of thought because they, of course, are particulars in the soul.[26]

The form-matter distinction is put to a variety of uses by Aristotle, but none are more interesting than the role he gives it in *De Anima*'s account of awareness of an object. A main principle governing this account is that whatever one is aware of, especially perceptually, must be some thing or feature that is independent of the perceiver. Thus, while granting that there are no actual flavors or sights without actual tastings or seeings, he insists (426a20–21) that it is misleading to say that there are no flavored or colored things without such tastings and seeings. The identification of object of perception and faculty of perception holds only for actual episodes of perception. So the identity is only contingent or, as Aristotle prefers to put it, "The activity or actuality of the object of perception [ἡ ἐνέργεια τοῦ αἰσθητοῦ] and of that which can perceive [τοῦ αἰσθητικοῦ] is one but the being of each is different" (426a15–17; also 425b26–27). And this identity is possible only because the sense organ [τὸ αἰσθητήριον] is able in each case to receive the thing perceived without its matter [τοῦ αἰσθητοῦ ἄνευ τῆς ὕλης] (425b23–24). By 431b26–432a1, above, we know that what is received is the form of the thing perceived. Elsewhere, at 418a5–6 for example, he speaks of the faculty becoming like and being such as the perceived thing [ὡμοίωται καὶ ἔστιν οἷον ἐκεῖνο]. In terms of our earlier account of perception what we can say is that when the movement in the organ of perception reaches the starting point [ἀρχή] of perception, the faculty of perception is like the perceived thing by having the same form as the perceived thing. In terms of the relationship between faculty and object of perception we can say that actualization$_2$ of one is neccesary and sufficient for actualization$_2$ of the other. But the relation between the faculty and any given object is still contingent. And although it may be extensionally symmetrical, intensionally the relation is asymmetrical, for the faculty is actualized$_2$ *because* the object is actualized$_2$, not conversely.

Aristotle's examples cover sounds, tastes, smells, and the like. So it would be overly simple to think of the notion of form or likeness involved here as visually pictorial. That seems at best only one possible case of likeness and, indeed, one involving common sensibles because it requires the notion of shape or magnitude. The impulse to make forms into pictures may stem from a need to explain perception of outer objects in terms of inferences made on the basis of inner [re]presentations. But this is no part of Aristotle's account. Rather, he operates from the assumption that per-

---

26. In chapters 5, especially sec. 7, and 6, sec. 6, I return to this point in considerably more detail.

ception is in general perfectly reliable (and when it isn't we tend to know that as well) and, moreover, that it is perception of the actual features or qualities of things. Aristotle is no skeptic. His account is an *explanation* of the conditions that a system must satisfy in order to accomplish such perception. These include that in actual perceivings we actually have the forms of perceived things but not that *we* use them to make inferences, reliable or otherwise, about the world.

Having a form in one's soul when one perceives something involves having an appropriately related αἴσθημα. So we may say that the αἴσθημα, or perceptual state, is or embodies the form of the perceived thing. What else would it mean to say that the soul receives, and so becomes like, the perceived thing without its matter? This, however, gives an overly simple view of the role of forms in object awareness, for it allows that images are just weakened versions of such received forms. The situation is rather more complicated.

To the principle

> *d*. A perpetual state [αἴσθημα] is (similar to) the perceived thing without its matter

or, perhaps,

> *d'*. A perceptual state [αἴσθημα] is (embodies) the form of the perceived thing

Aristotle adds, from v of 432a3–10,

> *e*. An image [φάντασμα] is (similar to) the perceptual state [αἴσθημα] without its matter

or

> *e'*. An image [φάντασμα] is (embodies) the form of the perceptual state [αἴσθημα].

That the primed versions are in order is clear from the fact that *d'* is the most plausible way of construing 432a2–3's interesting remark that perception is the form of perceived things [ἡ αἴσθησις εἶδος αἰσθητῶν]. This, plus the parallel between *d* and *e*, warrant asserting that imagination is the form of perceptual states [αἰσθήματα], which is just what *e'*, says.

On the decaying sense theory of imagination one would have expected Aristotle to have characterized images and perceptions strictly in terms of their relationship to forms of perceived things, perceptions as relatively vivid forms and images as relatively weak forms.[27] This, of course, embraces the awkwardness of applying vividness talk to forms at all. What, for instance, would it mean to claim that the *form* embodied in a blueprint is less vivid than that embodied in the actual building? Indeed, vividness seems to apply only to the matter of perceptions, if to anything. So in their roles as *forms* of perceptions images cannot be weakened sense perceptions because qua form they are no weaker than the perception. In short, the form-matter distinction seems ill suited to the decaying sense theory of imagination. So to the extent that *e'* is Aristotle's settled view, the decaying sense theory is not.

On the basis of the above paragraph we can decide between two rather different corollaries to *e'*, namely,

> *e1'*. If x is an image, then it is possible that there is a perceptual
> state z such that x has the form of z but not the matter of z.

and

> *e2'*. If x is an image, then there is a perceptual state z such that
> x has the form of z but not the matter of z.

Unless we are talking about acquisition of [re]presentational devices, which is not our concern here, *e2'* is implausible. It requires for occurrence of an image that there be a concurrent or, perhaps, immediately prior perception. This is obviously too strong a condition for those who wish to widen the range of the canonical theory. On the other hand, *e1'* requires only that it be possible that an image embody the form of a perceptual state and so, because the notion of form here employed is transitive, that it can embody the form of perceivable things.

Certain commentators—Hartman (1977, 254) is a recent example—think 432a9–10 asserts that perceptions [αἰσθήματα] are somehow material but that images are not. Thus, they deny the appropriateness of *e'*. This is obviously an undesirable view, for it contradicts a guiding assumption of the whole of *De Anima*, namely, that if thoughts are dependent on images, then thought itself is dependent on body. This makes no sense if images are immaterial. Fortunately, there is no need to foist this embarrassment on Aristotle. The words "ἄνευ τῆς ὕλης" (without the matter) must have the same force at 425b23–24 and 432a9–10, the textual correlates for *d* and *e*, respectively. Since the words must mean "without the matter of the perceived thing" in the first occurrence, they must mean "without the

---

27. Granger may be committed to something like this insofar as he thinks that images and perceptual states can be distinguished phenomenologically (1963, 15).

matter of the perception [αἴσθημα]" in the second occurrence. Hartman cannot rejoin that at 425b23–24 "ἄνευ τῆς ὕλης" means that perceptions are immaterial because it is the *material* sense organ that receives the perceived thing without its matter. This would also contradict his own claim that perceptions or perceptual states are physical. What 425b23–24 does show is that something can be without matter [ἄνευ τῆς ὕλης] without being immaterial. Images, as well as perceptions, are just such items: φάντασμα is related to αἰσθήμα and αἴσθημα to αἰσθητόν as form to matter. At each remove the form is increasingly abstract. This explains why images are capable of occurring in a much wider range of intentional acts than perceptual states. It also explains why one might be tempted to think of images as immaterial. For just as we saw in chapter 1 that, in general, form cannot be reduced to matter so also it appears here that, in particular, the forms of cognitive states cannot be reduced to what they are forms of, in the case of αἰσθήματα, or to their internal realizations, in the case of φαντάσματα. Yet here, as there, it would be a mistake to conclude that, by dint of enjoying a measure of abstractness, images are immaterial in any serious sense. Consequently, Aristotle is not suddenly ranking images as immaterial items and we are spared the task of unraveling an inexplicable puzzle.

5. DISTINGUISHING THOUGHTS AND IMAGES

One advantage of adopting the form–matter rather than the decayed sense impression model is enhanced utility for the notion of imagination. For we can employ it in a variety of contexts where it is simply implausible to apply a decaying sense model.[28] An obvious case is extension of the model to the case of thought. This is, however, not completely straightforward business. Thus, immediately following the *De Anima* III.8 argument for IM Aristotle puzzles over the relation between thoughts and images:[29]

> But (vi) imagination [φαντασία] is different from assertion [φάσεως] and denial [ἀποφάσεως]. For (vii) truth and falsity involve the combination of thoughts [συμπλοκὴ νοημάτων]. But (viii) what distinguishes the first thoughts [τὰ πρῶτα νοήματα] from images [φαντάσματα]? Clearly (ix) neither these nor any other thoughts [τἆλλα] will be images; but (x) they cannot exist without images [ἀλλα᾽ οὐκ ἄνευ φαντασμάτων]. (432a10–14)

28. Recall the remark at 2d of the canonical text that in virtue of imagination one can do many things.
29. I do not understand Mugnier's comment that at 432a10 Aristotle distinguishes between memory and imagination (1953, 54).

There is much of interest in this passage. Notice that it continues the discussion of 432a3–10 introduced in section 3 above—a discussion that construes the image-perceptual state relation as a certain kind of form-matter relation. It is thus arguable that the form-matter distinction might apply to the relation between thoughts and images, much as it applied earlier to the relation between images and perceptions. Thus, we would have something like

> f. A thought [νόημα] is (like) an image [φάντασμα] without its matter

or

> f'. A thought [νόημα] is the form of an image [φάντασμα].

Statement f, modeled on e, cannot be replaced in favor of something, nearer to d, to the effect that a thought is (like) an object of thought [νοητόν] except without matter. For objects of thought, at least paradigm cases such as objects of knowledge [τὰ ἐπιστητά], are already without matter (see De Anima III.4, especially 429b29ff.). In light of ix, f cannot be interpreted as an identification of thoughts and images. It should, thus, be read in the weaker, parenthesized, sense. Equally so, I suggest, for d and e as well as for the primed versions of these. This means, of course, that there is more than a mere difference in degree between images and perceptions, and thoughts and images. In the case of images we saw that it had to do with the enhanced role they could play as [re]presentational devices in the full range of cognitive acts that a subject is capable of. The ability to [re]present a given object is required by and in part enables us to, for example, remember, think about, desire, and dream about the object.

How, then, do images and thoughts differ? First a polemical remark: ix and x make it clear that it is misleading at best to assert, with Hartman, that "the simplest case of having a thought is having an image of the object of thought" (1977, 243) or that "thought is an unexplained attitude of a person toward an image." The first cannot be true simply because objects of thought are universals whereas images are not (De Anima II.5, 417b22–24). Indeed, it is not even clear that one could have an image of this sort of thing.[30] One might have an image of an object of perception and images might be required vehicles for thought, but they cannot be objects of thought. The second point is misleading, for it suggests that by operating on an image, the subject is somehow able to produce a thought. This, as

---

30. The account of the next section allows images to be exemplars of thought without requiring that they be images of objects of thought.

we would expect from our discussion of the incompleteness of imagination, is indeed difficult to explain. Of course, if one insists on conceiving of images as suitable objects of a faculty's operations, then it is tempting to follow some such line. But the temptation vanishes on realization of the incomplete and strictly [re]presentational role of images.[31]

Getting clear on the distinction between thoughts and images requires a closer look at the discussion in 432a10–14. Aristotle begins, in vi and vii, by distinguishing imagination from assertion and denial by an argument that has the following two explicit premises.

> 1. If S is an assertion or denial, then S is either true or false

and

> 2. If S is true or false, then S involves combination of thoughts.

But 1 and 2 are not enough for the conclusion

> 4. If S is [an instance of] imagination, then S is neither an assertion nor a denial,

unless we supply the argument with something like

> 3. If S is [an instance of] imagination, then S does not involve combination of thoughts.

The operative premise is 3 rather than something like

> 3′. If S is [an instance of] imagination, then S is neither true nor false

because 3′ would make 2 irrelevant to the argument. So it is 3 that marks out the crucial difference. To appreciate this is also to appreciate that Aristotle is only denying imagination the kind of truth or falsity that involves combination. He is, in other words, denying propositional truth and falsity to instances of imagination but not, or at least not here, true-of and false-of. This, of course, tallies with our earlier discussion of the sense in which truth and falsity apply to images.

Obviously, 4 does not claim that imagination is different from thought. Rather, Aristotle uses 4 to introduce what is a crucial distinction between thoughts and images, namely, that the first are combinable in ways that yield truths and falsehoods and the second are not combinable or at least not in ways that yield truths and falsehoods. I think this notion of combinability is crucial and that Aristotle took it to be. For he anticipates the

---

31. For exactly how images are employed, see the next section.

objection that all 3 shows is that if thoughts are to be combined so as to yield truths, it cannot be the imagination that does this. Hence, it is still open to argue that the thoughts combined are, nevertheless, images. Thus, he raises in viii and resolves, negatively, in ix the question whether the [primary] thoughts or the thoughts that are to be combined can be counted images.

The view just advanced is plainly interpretation and needs further support. In particular, we need to say something more about the identity of primary thoughts. After all Aristotle makes special mention of them. Nussbaum appeals to the *Metaphysica* IX.10 discussion of what she takes to be the simplest and most basic things [ἀσύνθετα]. Thoughts about such items are, presumably, the primary thoughts. It is, however, not completely clear what counts as an instance of such a thought. What Aristotle says (1051b30–32) is that concerning what is strict being or actuality [ὅπερ εἶναι τι καὶ ἐνέργεια], we simply think them or we do not think them [νοεῖν ἢ μή]. In the first case the thought is true of an object and in the second case it is not. But in neither case are thoughts combined, and so propositional truth or falsity does not apply to these thoughts. Nonetheless, we can inquire into the nature [τί ἐστι] of such items.

Metaphysica IX.10 is best read in light of *De Anima* 430b26–31:

> An assertion [ἡ φάσις] that says something about something [τι κατά τινος], as does an affirmation [κατάφασις],[32] is true or false. But this is not the case for all thought [ὁ νοῦς οὐ πᾶς]; thought of the nature [ὁ τοῦ τί ἐστι] of the essence [of a thing] [κατὰ τὸ τί ἦν εἶναι] is true but does not say something about something [οὐ τὶ κατά τινος]. But just as perceiving a special object is true, while perceiving that the white thing is a man or not is not always true, so also with what is without matter.

The *Metaphysica* passage allows that one can think of ἀσύνθετα without thinking of their natures: how else could one investigate these natures? The *De Anima* passage suggests that even when we think of the nature of such an item, it is misleading to say that we are thinking something about something. Thus, propositional truth and falsity are inapplicable not only to thought of an object *simpliciter* but also to thought of the nature of its essence. The first seems to be what Aristotle means at *Metaphysica* 1051b24 under the notion of truth as contact [θιγεῖν]. Here something like grasping the object by or in itself is guarantee of truth. This seems to match the

---

32. Hamlyn (1968) translates "denial," adopting Ross's substitution of "ἀπόφασις." But he is curiously unconcerned to preserve the parallel with *Metaphysica* IX.10.

analogy with perception of a proper object of sense, for there also direct acquaintance with the object guarantees truth. The second case where propositional truth and falsity is inapplicable seems to correspond to the *Metaphysica* 1051b24–25 notion of truth as assertibility [φάναι]. Aristotle is careful to distinguish assertion [φάσις] from affirmation [κατάφασις], the latter but not the former being a case where something is said about something. The most plausible interpretation to make of this is that successful assertion of the nature of the essence (of a thing) is guarantee of truth.

It might appear, then, that certain thoughts about any necessary object or essence, for example, a triangle, will count as thought about an uncombined object [ἀσύνθετα]. If we can take the further step of equating truth and falsity involving combination of thoughts (vii of 432a10–14 above) with truth and falsity involving saying something about something, then the primary thoughts of viii will include those expressing a thing's essence.

There are two difficulties with this view of primary thoughts. First, it is simply not clear what would be the point of asking in viii how first thoughts qua essential propositions differ from images. We can, however, meet this objection by ruling out those thoughts that enjoy truth as assertibility and restricting viii to those that enjoy truth as "contact." Attention to the details of Aristotle's language in 432a10–14 allows us to do this. Notice, first, that the *Metaphysica* IX.10 passage contrasts affirmation and denial with assertion of what is uncombined [ἀσύνθετα] and *De Anima* 420b26–31 contrasts the same pair with what does not assert something. So assertion [φάσις] and affirmation [κατάφασις] are clearly opposed. Second, vi does *not* oppose imagination to affirmation and denial, what we would expect from the above-mentioned texts; rather it contrasts imagination with assertion [φάσις] and denial [ἀπόφασις]. This has led commentators to gloss "φάσεως" at 432a10 as "καταφάσεως" (Hicks, 1965, 546, for example). But this is undesirable in light of the explicit rejection of the gloss in the closely parallel passage at *Metaphysica* 1051b30–32. We can avoid this uneasiness and give the *De Anima* passage a better interpretation by retaining in vi the sense given "φάσις" (assertion) at *Metaphysica* 1051b24–25. For vi can now be seen to contrast imagination not only with thoughts corresponding to affirmation and denial but also with those corresponding to assertion of a thing's essence. Hence, what remains are just those thoughts whose purchase on truth is through the notion of contact or acquaintance. Thus, the primary thoughts of viii do not include propositions expressing a thing's essence.

What we have so far established is that primary thoughts will not be propositional in character. This would also make sense in light of *De Anima* III as a whole. Chapter 3, section 3, began the discussion of imagination by locating it as one of the elements of episodes of thinking. Thus, if supposition, the second element, is propositional and if grasping the uncombined objects [ἀσύνθετα] does not count as supposition [ὑπόληψις], then it is clearly in order to puzzle over the difference between primary thoughts and images. For he is asking how one thing that is nonpropositional, namely, the second, [re]presentational, element of thinking, differs from another thing that is nonpropositional. We have not, however, explained whether all or only some of the survivors are to be counted as primary thoughts. Any answer to this must make some sense of what is *primary* about the primary thoughts [πρῶτα νοήματα].

Trendelenburg (1877, 439) took primary thoughts to correspond to the most general universals such as being and unity. But these thoughts, as Freudenthal pointed out, are the least likely to be confused with images, yet viii indicates that they should be especially difficult to distinguish from images. If, on the other hand, viii demands not a safeguard against a likely confusion but only completion of an unresolved feature of the preceding account of the difference between thoughts and images, a variant of this interpretation suggests itself. For suppose that primary thoughts correspond to formal or strictly combinatory universals. Having dealt in vi and vii with thoughts that can be combined in assertions, Aristotle turns in viii to those thoughts that do the combining.

There are, however, a number of problems with this suggestion. First, Aristotle does not typically regard being and unity in the formal or combinatory mode. A glance at his discussion of these notions in *Metaphysica* V.6 and 7 is testimony to this. Second, if images are [re]presentational structures, then it is neither required nor relevant to ponder how thoughts that in effect play a syntactic role differ from images. Third, even more puzzling is explaining the sense in which such thoughts have images in the first place. We have to rule out the suggestion that these thoughts have images in the sense that discussion of the combinatory feature of sentences proceeds itself in terms of sentences or assertions and that these can serve as images for the thought discussed. This may be true, but it is beside the point. The context of discussion is governed by the combination of thoughts *in* assertions and denials. Hence, the identity of primary thoughts is to be located within these boundaries and cannot be secured by an ad hoc switch to an alternative candidate.

Torstrik (1970) took the thoughts to correspond to those first universals gotten from the data of experience. Thus, they are linked with the πρῶτον καθόλου of *Analytica Posteriora* II.19. Hicks (1965, 548) prefers Freudenthal's suggestion that the primary thoughts are not those corresponding to the earliest won universals but rather any simple, uncompounded thoughts—

Freudenthal's *unverknüpfte Begriffe*. Although this suggestion is attractive, it still calls for an explanation concerning what is primary about these primary thoughts. If to be an *unverknüpfter* thought is to be no more than a thought that is not the product of other thoughts, then such thoughts will amount to the first universals Torstrik favors. For *Analytica Posteriora* II.19 at least appears to explain occurrence of higher universals as resulting from induction on lower universals. It is, of course, unclear that this is sufficient to make higher universals such as being-a-color logically complex. So if "primary" has the force "logically primary" rather than "epistemologically primary," this objection loses force. If, then, to be an *unverknüpfter* thought is simply to be a thought that is not combined with others *in an assertion or denial,* then the references of "τᾶλλα" and "τὰ πρῶτα νοήματα" may be explained as combined and uncombined thoughts, respectively.

   With this maneuver we still need to say what is logically primary about these primary thoughts, for thoughts of almost any complexity can be a constituent of an assertion. This is a less serious difficulty than it appears. For if we restrict assertions and denials to single assertions and denials, then we may deal only with cases where one thing is asserted or denied of another thing. This is the familiar *De Interpretatione* condition (18a13ff.) that a single assertion is one in which one thing is said of one thing [ἓν καθ' ἑνός]. Any thought satisfies the combinatory conditions so long as it is not a *truth-functional* compound of more basic thoughts. So being a man, despite implying being a two-footed animal, is one thing, whereas being a tall man is not one but two things. Hence, "*a* is a tall man" contains two assertions, "*a* is tall" and "*a* is a man."[33] Assuming, then, that the account addresses thoughts combined in single assertions, the primary thoughts are the constituents of such assertions and the other thoughts [τᾶλλα] will presumably be the combined thought or assertion itself.[34] It is unsurprising that the latter is not confused with an image because it is a combined thought and images do not correlate with assertions as wholes. This is ·a natural consequence of the incompleteness thesis of imagination.

   Some will feel uneasy about this interpretation of primary thoughts because it will appear to them to saddle Aristotle with what Lloyd (1981) has called "an enigma of Greek philosophy," namely, nondiscursive thought. Sorabji (1982, 296–99) is typical in worrying about any thought that involves contemplating something without thinking anything *about* it. It is partly for this reason that he argues for the view that the thought of un-

---

33. See *De Interpretatione* XI and the discussion in Wedin (1978 and 1984).
34. Thus, Aristotle here appears to echo *De Interpretatione* 1's thoughts in the soul that are neither true nor false because they are uncombined thoughts corresponding to names by themselves (for example, "man" and "white").

combined objects [ἀσυνθετά] and the undivided objects [ἀδιαιρετά] of *De Anima* III.6 is propositional after all. Notice that this would square with our interpretation so long as the incomposites are not counted among the primary thoughts because the latter, we have argued, are *not* propositional. Nonetheless, Sorabji's account deserves attention not because it is without difficulties but because the nature of its difficulties suggests a view of so-called nondiscursive thought that is not subject to the usual complaints.

What Sorabji worries about, rightly I think, is the fairly common view that, in *De Anima* III.6 and *Metaphysica* IX.10, Aristotle endorses "the contemplation of isolated concepts." The view is made to rest on 430b28's remark that thought of the essence is not a matter of one thing being about another [οὐ τὶ κατά τινος]. Sorabji thinks that this fails to establish the "isolated" nature of nondiscursive thought and offers his own two-part account. First, thought involving incomposites is thought involving their definitions, and so nondiscursive thought will amount to contemplation of these definitions. But these are surely propositional. Second, the propositional nature of such thoughts can be squared with the claim that they are not τὶ κατά τινος because Aristotle views statements of definitions as statements of identity. Rather than predicating one thing of another, they "involve simply referring to the same thing twice."

Despite its initial appeal, there are some problems with this account. Let me start by looking at two of the texts where Sorabji finds support. The first is *Analytica Posteriora* I.4, 73b5–10, in particular, 73b9–10, which says that what is not predicated of a subject is to be called essential [τὰ μὴ καθ' ὑποκειμένου καθ' αὑτὰ λέγω] and that what is so predicated is to be called incidental. By itself this line does appear to support Sorabji's claim. But since the line clearly refers back to 73b5's "what is not predicated of some *other* subject [ὃ μὴ καθ' ὑποκειμένου λέγεται ἄλλου τινός]," it is not obvious that it concerns identity statements. The passage yields

a. F is essential ⊃ F is not predicated of a subject other than itself

and this leaves open, if it does not imply,

a'. F is essential ⊃ F is predicated & F is predicated of itself.

Both a and a' are glosses on one of the two senses of καθ' αὐτό that are developed earlier in the chapter. In particular, they concern what we earlier (in chapter 1, n. 15) called the per se₁ relation: A belongs καθ' αὐτό· to B ≡ A is an element in the essence of B. Not all pairs of terms that satisfy this relation can be said to yield identity statements, even in the loose sense that Sorabji appears to have in mind. Thus, where A stands for plane figure and B for triangle, we have the corresponding essential statement "A triangle is a plane figure" and this is hardly to be taken as referring to the same thing twice.

A second passage used by Sorabji occurs in *Analytica Posteriora* I.22. It is easy to see how the passage has been taken to support the identity of statements of definition, especially if one translates the crucial lines 83a24–25 as Mure (1932) does: "Predicates which signify substance signify that the subject is identical with the predicate or a species of the predicate." But the Greek, Ἔτι τὰ μὲν οὐσίαν σημαίνοντα ὅπερ ἐκεῖνο ἢ ὅπερ ἐκεῖνό τι σημαίνει καθ' οὗ κατηγορεῖται, is more cautious and suggests only

b. F signifies substance ⊃
   (b1) F signifies precisely what a thing is v
   (b2) F signifies precisely a sort of what a thing is.

Line 83a30 exemplifies b1 with "Man is precisely animal" [ὅπερ ζῷόν ἐστιν ὁ ἄνθρωπος] and, given that this is contrasted at 83a31–32 with analogues, for the case of incidental predication, to *both* b1 and b2 ("Man is not precisely color" and "Man is not precisely a certain color," respectively), "Man is precisely animal" is not meant to be the same as "Man is precisely a sort of animal." The point of these remarks is that the b1 cases do not specify identity statements but, at most, statements such as "Man is animal" or "Triangle is a plane figure." Notice, further, that at 83a21–23 Aristotle leads us into the discussion by pointing out that both accidental and essential predications are cases where one thing is said of another [ἓν καθ' ἑνὸς κατηγορεῖν] and this is to apply equally to the b1 and b2 versions of each. This is very difficult to square with *De Anima* III.6's insistence that thought of incomposites is not τὶ κατά τινος. So, even were Sorabji correct in holding that statements of definition are identities, they cannot be cases of thinking an incomposite.

Now there are passages where Aristotle, explicitly or implicitly, denies that definitions involve predication. But, pace Sorabji, these do not involve *statements* to the effect that a such and such is, by definition, a so and so. Rather, in such contexts Aristotle is referring simply to the *definiens*. Witness *Analytica Posteriora* II.3, 90b34–38: "in definition [ἐν τῷ ὁρισμῷ] one thing is not predicated of another, for example, not animal of biped nor it of animal; nor even figure of plane (because plane is not figure nor figure plane)." Aristotle says much the same at *De Interpretatione* 5, 17a11–15. So it seems clear that where Aristotle explicitly separates definition and predication, he has in mind a clearly nonpropositional sense of definition. It would seem, then, that he might also have this in mind in *De Anima* III.6's discussion of undifferentiated objects of thought.

Does this mean that we are committed to finding "isolated" discursive thought in Aristotle after all? Not necessarily. Notice, first, that *De Anima* III.6 begins a discussion of a certain kind of object of thought and that by the end of III.8 we are told that thoughts must be combinable in judgments that are true or false. So one constraint on interpretation is combinability. A second constraint is forthcoming from *Metaphysica* IX.10's point that one hits or misses the incomposite objects but cannot be in error with respect to them [περὶ ταῦτα οὐκ ἔστιν ἀπατηθῆναι at 1051b31]. I would like to suggest, somewhat in the spirit of conjecture, a way to honor both constraints without falling into the isolated nondiscursive thought Sorabji, sensibly, dislikes.

Let me begin by enlisting the support of

c1. The flower in the vase is a daffodil,

or, perhaps,

c2. Daffodils are bulbous herbs.

The major point of conjecture is this: because thoughts are essentially combinable (*De Anima* III.8), incomposite objects can be thought of only in combination with other objects. That is, I think of daffodils only insofar as the νόημα daffodil occurs in a propositionlike complex. But if this is so, and it is not at all certain, then why does Aristotle deny ordinary truth or falsity to such thoughts? Unlike Sorabji, who finds the answer to lie in a special sort of combining, namely, combining in identity statements, I favor the following line. In order to combine the thoughts in c1 one must already be acquainted with the thoughts themselves. And acquaintance is an all-or-nothing affair. But, and this is the crucial point, we are conjecturing that the acquaintance occurs only in contexts like c1 and c2 and, thus, we must find room in such contexts for the immunity to error enjoyed by thought of the incomposites.

We can see how this works by considering two ways we might override someone who falsely asserts c1. We might improve his local epistemic situation, perhaps, by turning on the light and allowing him to see that what he had taken to be a daffodil was, in fact, a tulip. This would amount to correcting an error in judgment—in Aristotle's terms, our near-sighted subject had combined thoughts but not so as to get truth. But suppose, after we have taken all reasonable measures, that our subject continues to assert c1. In such a case we would not say that he has made an error in judgment because errors in judgment presuppose that one grasps the concepts or thoughts involved in the judgment. Rather, we would discard his report simply because he does not know what daffodils are. So the question of his mistaking the flower for a daffodil doesn't arise because he is not even capable of such an error. In Aristotle's terms, he has failed to hit the object at all. Thus, the incomposites' immunity from error, at least Aristotle's version of it, can be accommodated within a "propositional" context without rendering the thought itself of an incomposite propositional thought. Thus, so-called nondiscursive thought is, after all, not isolated contemplation. On this account, a nonessential term such as "white" could count as an incomposite and, indeed, just this is implied at 1051b18–21. And this would appear to hold, generally, for what we have called primary thoughts.

For those who feel uneasy about the sense of primacy we have accorded primary thoughts, Torstrik's interpretation may be more appealing. The thoughts other than the primary thoughts will, then, either include combined thoughts or be limited to nonprimary constituents of thoughts. In either case it is clear why the primary thoughts would be less easily distinguished from images. In the first case, as noted, there simply is no image that matches the entire assertion. In the second case, precisely because primary thoughts correspond to universals gotten directly from experience, the difference between thought and image is more likely to be blurred in such cases. Whether we follow Freudenthal or Torstrik on the identity of primary thoughts, the thesis IM, that thought depends on images, can be stated in its full generality. So let us turn to this.

IM contains two subtheses. One of them governs the difference between thoughts and images,

> 5. If x is a thought and y is an image, then x≠y,

and the other their dependence,

> 6. If x is a thought and x occurs at t, then there is a y such that
> y is an image and y [re]presents x at t.

Subthesis 5 is unambiguous in claiming that thoughts are not images. The explicit mention of πρῶτα νοήματα (primary thoughts) in effect excludes interpreting a thought as an image in combination. By the same token it excludes the Hartman-type interpretation that thought is some sort of attitude toward an image, for by the current argument not even regarding an image in combination with others could count as the attitude in question. And if this fails, anything stronger surely will.

Subthesis 6 requires images for thought but leaves unspecified the exact nature of this requirement. It has at least the following variants:

> 6a. If z thinks x at t, then at t there is a y such that y≠x & y≠z
> & y is an image & y [re]presents x

and

> 6b. If z thinks x at t, then at t ◇ (there is a y such that y≠x &
> y≠z & y is an image & y [re]presents x).

Variant 6b might be proposed by those who would impress upon us that, while the capacity to *produce* the appropriate images might be necessary, a good many of our thinkings seem to proceed without requirement or benefit of actual images. As formulated, however, 6b is too weak to catch even this, for it implies nothing about what the subject must be able to do. Suppose, then, we exchange 6b for

> 6c. If z thinks x at t, then at t ◇ (z reports that there is a y such
> that y≠x & y≠z & y is an image & y [re]presents x).

Introduction of z's reportage capabilities in 6c is meant to catch the intuition that one can think, say, the Pythagorean Theorem without visualizing anything but must, nonetheless, be able to produce a visualization, as when explaining it to another or rehearsing it to one's self. Strictly speaking, of course, what 6c has the subject report is something slightly different. It is more in the order of what the theory would say about such reports. Bearing this in mind, 6c will serve well enough as an expository device.

What attractiveness 6c has is due to the impulse to give a dispositional account of knowledge and the like. My knowing the Pythagorean Theorem, for example, does not require constant visualization of the proof but it does require the ability to visualize or produce the proof. Thus, such an item of knowledge counts as the disposition, given appropriate conditions, to produce the theorem's proof. Other, nonnegligible, problems aside, this consideration fails to enhance the claims of 6c because IM concerns actual exercise of knowledge rather than the potential for such exercise. Although the latter may submit to a dispositional analysis, the former certainly will not.

Notice that on 6c we are committed to images only if someone reports on the thought. Nothing prohibits thinking an object without an image or images so long as one does not articulate this. Taking the notion of reporting in a suitably wide sense, we may say that 6c commits Aristotle to the view that one could be said to think an object even where no articulation, internal or otherwise, could be forthcoming. On this view IM would not assert that images are required for all thought but only for thought that can be articulated. On the face of it this is incompatible with what Aristotle argued in *De Anima* III.8. So we are advised to look at 6a as the most likely candidate for IM.

There are other reasons that favor 6a along with its corollary

6a'. If z thinks x at t, then at t there is a y such that y≠x & y≠z
& y is an image & y [re]presents x & ◇(z reports . . .).

Both 6a and 6a' share the requirement that every object of thought have an
associated image, but 6a' adds that the subject must be able to report on
what is being thought. Thus, it catches what is salutary in the disposition-
alist's impulse without sacrifice to a fully general IM. Or, in terms of 4* of
section 7 below, 6a' reflects the fact that νοεῖν involves something like formation of a linguistic intention. It adds images to the equation, at least
partly because they are required for difference and so determinateness of
objects of thought.

Although 6a' makes thought dependent on images, occurrence of an
image even in souls capable of thought is not sufficient for occurrence of a
thought. Certain kinds of human perception are accommodated by this as
well as all perceptual activity of most animals not endowed with thought.
But even were the conditional, 3, strengthened to a biconditional, it would
still distinguish thoughts and images insofar as primary thoughts, but not
images, are combinable in assertions and denials. If we link this with Aristotle's insistence that thoughts are universal, we can see the significance
of distinguishing them from images. The point is that thoughts must be
shareable, public items that support communication and objective judgments. Otherwise there is no point to the claim that they are true or false.
Images, by their very nature, lack these qualities. They are particulars
proper to a given mind or soul and may differ in various ways from mind
to mind without threat to their [re]presentational utility. Thus, two persons
need not have absolutely similar triangle-images in order for their talk of
triangles to be talk of one and the same thing, namely, the universal triangle.[35] The image may be subjective so long as it bears sufficient similarity
to the form or universal to enable successful discourse. If we seek a modern
analogy, better to find here an anticipation of Frege's distinction between
thoughts and ideas than allusions to decayed sense data and the like.

Thoughts and images are particularly difficult to distinguish because
universals are neither perceivable in their own right nor correlates of things
that are perceivable in their own right in the way that perceptual states
[αἰσθήματα] are. Hence, the match or lack of match between image and
thought cannot be determined in any perceptual or quasi-perceptual way.
So in a given episode of thinking the image seems virtually indistinguish-
able from the thought it embodies.[36] As in the case of αἰσθήματα the dis-

35. For more detail on how this works, see the next section.
36. That the difficulty in distinguishing thoughts and images concerns actual, thinking
emerges with particular clarity in Aristotle's *Metaphysica* XIII.10 discussion of the object of
episodes of thinking. See chap. 5, sec. 7, for discussion of the problem.

tinction requires conceiving of the image in its wide role: although the image [re]presents an object of thought in the case considered, it might have [re]presented an object of desire, perception, memory, and so on, or possibly even a different object or thought.

The difficulty of distinguishing image from thought, as well as image from perception [αἴσθημα], should not be surprising. For if images are nothing more than [re]presentational structures, there will be no feature of the internal state in an episode of perception or thought that can be introspected as the image as opposed to the αἴσθημα or the νόημα. This would be more difficult than trying to distinguish *in strictly perceptual terms,* in single episodes of perceiving, the form of a painting from the painting or even the form of a house from the house. So this will parallel, for the case of thoughts, the close unity of form and matter that Aristotle elsewhere upholds.

A potential difficulty with the current account of the difference between thoughts and images is that it depends on the thoughts being universal. Some such assumption may be involved in their being combinable in assertions, for the latter are by nature intersubjective. But might not intersubjectivity be gained at the price of limiting objects of thought to universals *only* and might not this be undesirable? We need to address this point because, even if Socrates qua particular is not technically an object of thought [νοητόν], still the theory must accommodate the possibility that sensible particulars be objects of thought or of something analogous to thought. Otherwise, we shall be without any account of such common locutions as ". . . is thinking of . . . ," and so on. In such cases, then, might it not be the case that images and thoughts converge? After all the object of this sort of thought is a particular and so, presumably, for the thought as well. Hence, in this case the identification of thoughts and images cannot be denied by appeal to the particularity of the latter and so IM is not completely general after all.

A number of things can be said about this line of objection. For one thing, although *De Anima* III.4 makes place for them, Aristotle does not pay much attention to the sense in which particulars are objects of thought. Of course, he is unambiguous on the point that they are objects of perception. This follows directly from the causal role played by the object of perception [αἰσθητόν] in actual perceivings. On the other hand, there are certain particulars that may be objects of thought only. Thus, the unmoved mover, if an object of awareness at all, must be such a particular. What this suggests is that it is not part of the logic or structure of thought that its objects be universals, even though they must be shareable, public items. Rather, the crucial point seems to be whether an object is properly to be received by the senses or by the mind [νοῦς]. Since the determining factor here is the physical nature of the sense organs, nonsensible particulars as well as universals may be received by the mind.

So the least to be said is that *thought* about a sensible particular would not be thought about something that is a proper object for the mind's receptivity. But a deeper and more interesting point lurks here. Recall our earlier discussion of the sorts of things that are proper "objects" of images. There it was clear that Aristotle recognizes no *proper* images of sensible substances but only of those features that count as proper or common objects of sense. On the other hand, *if* we grant that one thinks of Socrates, then one is thinking of a sensible particular. It follows that the image or images involved in such thought cannot be identical with the thought. Thus, 5 holds after all.

6. THE MECHANICS OF [RE]PRESENTATION
IN *DE MEMORIA*

A set of passages in *De Memoria* contains some of Aristotle's most detailed remarks on the internal mechanisms of [re]presentation. At 449b31–450a7 he explains how the image can function [re]presentationally in thought and he closes the book by distinguishing this from its [re]presentational role in memory. The passages deserve attention, if only for the light they shed on Aristotle's view of internal cognitive structure. But they demand our attention for another reason as well. According to several commentators the passages do not merely require images for thought but actually identify them. This does not sit comfortably with the message of *De Anima* III.8.[37] What I suggest, on the contrary, is that both 449b31–450a7 and the passages on the dual use of images construe imagination not as a kind of thought but as what supplies certain items essential to thought, namely, devices for [re]presentation.

Let us look first at 449b31–450a7:

> (g) thinking is not possible without an image [νοεῖν οὐκ ἔστιν ἄνευ φαντάσματος], for (h) the affection that occurs in thinking [συμβαίνει γὰρ ἐν τῷ νοεῖν] is just the same [τὸ αὐτὸ πάθος] as that involved in constructing a diagram [ἐν τῷ διαγράφειν]; for (i.1) while we draw it as a determinate size, we make no use there of the fact that the triangle is of a definite size and (i.2) similarly

37. Hicks (1965, 457) makes the identification. He resolves the contradiction by simply invoking, unsatisfactorily to my mind, a wide and narrow sense of thinking [νόησις].

when one is thinking, though he may not be thinking of a quantity [κἂν μὴ ποσὸν νοῇ], a quantity is put [τίθεται] before the eyes but he does not think of it as a quantity; and (i.2′) should the nature of what he thinks about be quantitative, but indefinite, a determinate quantity is put before the eyes but he thinks of it as a quantity only [νοεῖ ᾗ ποσὸν μόνον].

What strikes one immediately about this passage is its preoccupation with what goes on when one thinks.[38] The relevant mechanisms appear to be just those that functionally, not physiologically, subserve thinking. They are, moreover, mechanisms that imply IM (that is, h). So the underlying thesis seems to be that thinking about something involves being in an internal state that bears a relation both to, say, actual constructed triangles and to the triangle as an object of thought. This reflects, on the one hand, De Anima III.8's demand that thought be about what is extended and perceptible and, on the other hand, Analytica Posteriora II.19's story of concept acquisition. In effect, IM has at least three different lines of support—ontological, cognitive-psychological, and concept-acquisitional.

Notice that Aristotle does not say that I place an image before the eye, at least not as a result of Hicks's "free play of the imagination." For i.1 to support h at all we must assume that the πάθος (affection) involved in geometrical construction results from my constructing a chalk triangle. As its actual size is irrelevant to its utility in proof so also for the attendant image, should we care to say it has a size.[39] Equally, then, when one thinks without aid of physical devices, the required image occurs simply by dint of my doing a proof, and the size of the internal image, apparent or otherwise, is irrelevant to the function it performs. Thus, when Aristotle says the geometer does not think of the image quantitatively, he does not mean to record an operation that the geometer performs. The point, rather, is that the operation the geometer does perform simply does not include any such feature of the image. This will be so for both i.1 and i.2 and 2′.

The most 449b31–450a7 warrants, then, is that images are employed in thinking because, although deriving from actual particulars and so, perhaps, enjoying certain determinate features, such features are irrelevant to their [re]presentational function. In this way they may [re]present the object of thought without being identical with it, exactly what one would expect in light of viii–x of the above section and chapter 1 generally.

38. Kahn (1981) seems inclined to take the passage primarily as a description of concept *acquisition*. But he offers no argument and *g* alone hardly will bear that reading.

39. By this account, *h* mirrors the earlier suggestion that for an image to have a size is simply for it to be an image that would be true of a certain-sized triangle perceived under fairly standard conditions.

There is, however, a final line of objection open to friends of identification. Aristotle closes *De Memoria* by raising, and resolving, a puzzle concerning his theory of memory. Since, for many, the resolution appears to identify images with thoughts, we need to take a look at the remarks in question.

The puzzle concerns the fact that memory is a certain kind of disposition [ἕξις] or affection [πάθος] of perception or supposition. When one actually remembers something, what he directly has in mind or is aware of is just a certain πάθος, something like an internal impression or picture [ὅμοιον ὥστερ τύπος ἢ γραφὴ ἐν ἡμῖν]. How, then, does awareness of this [ἡ τούτου αἴσθησις] count as memory of something different [μνήμη ἑτέρου] and not merely as memory of itself [ἀλλ᾽ οὐκ αὐτοῦ τούτου]? How, in short, is it possible to remember, not the affection [πάθος], but that which caused it [ἐκεῖνο ἀφ᾽ οὗ ἐγένετο]? A theory that fails to accommodate such cases is hardly a theory of memory.

Aristotle responds by distinguishing two different ways images function in cognitive acts. These, he says, parallel two different attitudes one can hold toward pictures. A figure in a drawing [γεγραμμένον ζῷον] may be contemplated as a likeness [ὡς εἰκόνα θεωρεῖ] of, say, Coriscus and, thus, as about Coriscus [ὡς Κορίσκου]. But it may also be contemplated simply as a picture. We must, to explain memory, suppose that the same sort of thing applies to images. Thus, the internal image [τὸ ἐν ἡμῖν φάντασμα] is something in its own right and an image of something else [αὐτό τι καθ᾽ αὑτὸ εἶναι καὶ ἄλλου φάντασμα].[40] Taken as in its own right [ἢ καθ᾽ αὑτό] it is a θεώρημα or φάντασμα; taken as about something else [ἢ ἄλλου], namely a likeness [οἷον εἰκών], it is also a memory state [μνημόνευμα]. Then at 451a1–2 the distinction is drawn in terms that encourage identification of thought and image: what is in the soul occurs, on the one hand, as a thought only [ὥσπερ νόημα μόνον], and on the other hand, because it is a likeness, as a memory state [μνημόνευμα].

Obviously, these remarks deserve scrutiny. Notice, first, however, that Aristotle says of the one case that the image occurs *as* a mere thought [ὥσπερ νόημα μόνον at 461a1] and at 450b27–29 we have the even more cautious "so, whenever its movement is actualized₂[41] [ὅταν ἐνεργῇ ἡ κίνησις αὐτοῦ], its soul [ἡ ψυχὴ αὐτοῦ][42] perceives it [the image][43] in this way,

40. Not bracketing φάντασμα with Freudenthal (1863) and Ross (1955).

41. Presumably, this occurs when the movement reaches the ἀρχή, or starting point, to employ an already familiar idiom.

42. This should be understood to suggest only that it is the soul in which the movement occurs, not that the image itself has a soul.

43. Although I understand image here, the subject is strictly one and the same thing (450b22) that is both θεώρημα and εἰκών or μνημόνευμα. This, of course, turns out to be just the image regarded in different ways.

namely as in its own right—it seems to occur like a kind of thought or image [ὅιον νόημά τι ἢ φάντασμα φαίνεται ἐπελθεῖν]."

These passages show enough reserve to preserve consistency, particularly given the context of the point. After all, Aristotle mainly wants to isolate an other-directed use for images, so one might not expect him to devote complete detail to the contrasting case. Still that discussion does associate φαντάσματα (images) very closely with θεωρήματα (theoretical concepts). To the extent, then, that the latter count as νοήματα (thoughts) we need to say more.

Let us begin by reminding ourselves that Aristotle is spelling out the internal cognitive mechanisms required, functionally, for something to accomplish memory. His "δεῖ ὑπολαβεῖν" (it is necessay to suppose) at 450b24 reflects not the fruit of observation but the need for explanation. We appear, then, to have Aristotle arguing for the presence of a certain kind of internal item because it is required by theory. The passage, in effect, offers an explanation of what goes on internally, at a lower level of the system, when thinking occurs. Not only are internal [re]presentations required but so also are internal interpreters of these [re]presentations. Thus, some part of the soul is said to interpret[44] an image in a certain way, when we have a case of thinking, and in another way, when we have a case of memory. Since the image is the same in each case, the interpretation is essential.

It is crucial to specify the item, that is, the image, so as to allow for its occurrence in different cognitive acts. When it occurs qua in its own right [ἢ καθ' αὑτό] it seems to occur as a theoretical concept [θεώρημα] or thought [νόημα]; when it occurs qua about something else, it appears as a likeness or memory state.

Beare (1908) translated "θεώρημα" as "object of contemplation." But the θεώρημα is no more this than the μνημόνευμα is the object of memory or the νόημα the object of thought. All are internal states necessary for a cognitive act to be directed on such an object. Beare also implied that in its ἢ καθ' αὑτό (qua in its own right) use the image is not about something, by arguing that to regard the γεγραμμένον ζῷον, or drawn animal, as ζῷον, or animal, the parallel case, must be to regard it as a picture generally, not as a picture of an animal: "To restrict the meaning here to painted *animals* would spoil the illustration, since then ζῷον (animal) would be relative at once and from the first." Apparently, the idea is that to regard the picture as a picture of an animal, or perhaps an animal picture, already involves

44. Lest there be any doubt that Aristotle ascribes some sort of internal cognitive capability to the soul, note that he uses "αἴσθηται."

regarding certain marks, colors, and so on, as standing for an animal. And, thus, there would be two things regarded ἢ ἄλλου (qua about something else) and none ἢ καθ' αὑτό (qua in its own right).

I think Aristotle is holding precisely what Beare disliked. First, to regard a picture ἢ καθ' αὑτό (qua in its own right) does not exclude regarding it as a picture of something or other. Pictures are intrinsically dog, cat, or triangle pictures. We need, in short, to assume only that Aristotle eschewed the modern notion of uninterpreted marks and color volumes. But the modern point of view also suggests something more interesting. For Aristotle may be indicating that certain input comes already determined; hence, not everything must be interpreted by internal structures, at least not from the ground up.[45] What *is* being excluded is that, so regarded, the picture is about some *particular* dog, cat, or triangle. The Coriscus example suggests just this. Taken one way we have a picture of Coriscus; taken another, a picture of a man.

There are several advantages to this line of interpretation. First, we can explain why images in their ἢ καθ' αὑτό (qua in their own right) use function so well for thought. If an image can serve simply as an image of a triangle, then it can function in general thought about triangles. Second, we see why images and thoughts are so hard to distinguish. For just as the other-directed use of images treats them as about something and, thus, as [re]presentations so also is the image [re]presentational in its η καθ' αὑτό use. What it [re]presents in that use are just the features or properties, or at least certain of these, that any triangle has qua triangle. One could say it [re]presents triangularity without requiring the object triangularity. How? Because it itself exemplifies the set of properties that it [re]presents. This, I conjecture, is just what Aristotle means by the notion of regarding the image qua in its own right [ἢ καθ' αὑτό]. Thus, it is unsurprising to find the image ἢ καθ' αὑτό linked closely with the theoretical concept [θεω-'ρημα] and thought [νόημα] but in language that warns against outright identification.[46]

An additional advantage of this interpretation is that it makes some sense of *f* and *f'*. A thought is like an image in the sense that the properties in virtue of which the image exemplifies the thought are those that tell us what it is to be, say, a triangle. So we may say that the image exemplifies its form. Or, with 431b2, we may say that the mind thinks the forms in the

---

45. On this see the discussion of "Hume's problem" in Dennett (1978).
46. The ἤ in 450b26's "θεώρημα ἤ φάντασμα" (theoretical concept or image) is probably to be taken explicatively and so as weakening the association with θεώρημα.

images [τὰ εἴδη τὸ νοητικὸν ἐν τοῖς φαντάσμασι νοεῖ].[47] Moreover, because the image is particular, which is the point of granting it apparent size, it enjoys something analogous to the subject [ὑποκειμένον] of the object of perception that is in the perceptual system qua perceptual system when one perceives something (425b24 and 426b8–11). Thus, while it cannot exemplify independently of something like a material aspect, what it exemplifies can be something immaterial. As universals, precisely this is required for exemplification of objects of thought. It would be a mistake to suppose that images merely prompt the mind to entertain an independently existing object of thought. Aristotle's point is much deeper and much more anti-Platonist. There simply is no such thought to be intuited, grasped, or touched apart from the image. Thus, images really are essential for thought.

7. LANGUAGE AND THOUGHT

The account just given of thought's dependence on imagination itself gives rise to a problem. Because they are shareable and intersubjective, thoughts are, as *Metaphysica* 990b24 says, one [τὸ νόημα ἕν]. Little and Small are same thinkers, in thinking any given thing, because they think the same object. Yet how can this be, if one thinks forms or thoughts only in or through images, for these may vary with occasion and agent of thought. So far as I can determine two possible answers are available to Aristotle here, one linguistic and one mechanistic. The latter, already partially unpacked, turns on the fact that mechanisms for generating and using thoughts are reliable and do not vary between normal members of the species.[48] Reliability will mean something like producing internal devices for [re]presenting the structure of the world. It is, in effect, a systems design answer; because we are by nature well-designed systems and because fitness of design is a specieswide feature, different members of the species can be expected to operate in the same way.[49] Thus, of the process described in

47. Notice, again, the cognitivistic nature of the idiom. Aristotle is explaining how *we* think on the basis of what an internal part of the system does.

48. There is a nice statement of faculty reliabilism in *Rhetorica* I.1. Speaking of the faculty [δύναμις] whose peculiar domain is the true or that which is true, Aristotle remarks, at 1355a14–17, that men have a natural capacity sufficient for truth [πρὸς τὸ ἀληθὲς πεφύκασιν ἱκανῶς] and in most cases attain it.

49. If this is the meaning of Aristotle's dictum that nature does nothing in vain (see *De Anima* III.9, 432b21–26), then he is closer to the evolutionary picture than is usually thought. For the latter explains the development of reliable faculties in terms of the evolution over time of physical structures that subserve their operations. Those better suited to subserve a faculty's operations are more favored from the point of view of selection. What is common to both pictures is the system design feature; what is peculiar is the etiology of the feature. It is the common point that favors, in both cases, a cognitivist view of the soul.

Analytica Posteriora II.19, whereby a single universal is gotten from the multiplicity of experience, Aristotle says simply that the soul is capable of undergoing this and *Ethica Nicomachea* VI.11 holds the development of intellectual capacities, such as νοῦς and φρόνησις, to be the actualizations₁ of certain of our innate, natural endowments.

These passages suggest, at most, that Aristotle held we must be capable of developing the internal structures that subserve thought. They do not require that we make inferences from internal structures to the nature of the world. Aristotle does not have the soul, as it were, saying "Ah, yes, this image derives from a reliable process beginning with things of a certain sort in the world and qua things of that sort the process regards one as no different from another (that is, one triangle does not differ, qua triangle, from another), so a triangle, or whatever, will just be a such and such." This is to have Aristotle confuse explanation of *how* a system thinks of triangles with explanation of what "triangle" means or justification of knowledge claims about triangles. It is clear that for Aristotle justification is a function of scientific demonstration and so is a shared or public affair. And, of course, it is widely agreed that meaning is a matter of public practice. This suggests, because thoughts [νοήματα] are combinable in public judgments, that Aristotle may be open to the possibility that part of what the soul undergoes in acquiring a universal is acquisition of linguistic competence. So, while the mechanical account clearly dominates the psychological works, it is an account of a system that, as a whole, is unique in enjoying linguistic capability.[50] This brings us to the second response.

There can be no doubt that for Aristotle thought and language enjoy a close connection. It is, for example, a common theme that of the animals man alone possesses both. But what this amounts to is less than clear. It does not, for instance, amount to the claim that animals possess no "semantic" capabilities. Witness 420b29–34: "not every sound [ψόφος] made by an animal is articulate sound [φωνή] . . . but the striking [of the windpipe] must be done by something with a soul [ἔμψυχον] and with a certain imagination [μετὰ φαντασίας]. For articulate sound is a certain significant noise [σημαντικός τις ψόφος ἐστὶν ἡ φωνή]." Nonetheless, one should be wary of making too much here of attributions of significant noise[51] despite

50. See, for instance, *Rhetorica* I.1, 1355b1–2, which makes much of the fact that use of speech is more characteristic of the person [μᾶλλον ἴδιον ἀνθρώπου] than nonlinguistic physical action.

51. Hamlyn (1968, 109) finds the passage urging the excessively strong point that all articulate sound must have meaning rather than the more reasonable point that such sounds must be in some sense intentional. One motivation for taking the passage in his way would be the belief that Aristotle regards images, in effect mentioned by "μετὰ φαντασίας," as thoughts and, perhaps, meanings. But, as we have seen, this is an implausible move at best.

Historia Animalium IX.1, 608a17–21, and *De Partibus Animalium* 660a5–b1 which permit certain animals (birds are the example) to learn from, teach, and communicate with one another via their sound [φωνή].[52] In isolating man as the owner of logos, *Politica* 1253a9–15 gives a rather modest role to animal communication. Nature has fitted man with logos because he alone needs a means, the logos, of revealing the advantageous and the disadvantageous, the just and the unjust. But sound [φωνή], as an indicator of pleasure and pain, is found in the other animals as well: "for their nature concerns perception of pleasure and pain and indicating these to one another [ταῦτα σημαίνειν ἀλλήλοις]" (1253a12–14). So despite talk of teaching, learning, and the like, the official doctrine appears to be that nonhuman animals are capable of indicating in speechlike sound (536b11–16 licenses, in very cautious language,[53] the description) nothing beyond a positive or negative reaction to a particular situation. They have, to follow *Ethica Nicomachea* VII.4, 1147b4–5, only imagination and memory of particulars [τῶν καθ' ἕκαστα]. This at least exceeds the response of minimal perceivers, who also react bivalently to immediate stimuli, because it is conditioned by imagination and memory. Thus, it at least has the look of intentional behavior.

Not restricted to episodes of memory and imagination that concern particulars only, man has both logos and νοῦς. Thus, it is unsurprising to find Aristotle at the end of *De Anima* III.10 countenancing, on man's behalf, a calculative imagination [λογιστικὴ φαντασία]. The following chapter expands on the notion:

> Imagination concerned with perception [ἡ αἰσθητικὴ φαντασία] is found in the other animals too but that concerned with deliberation is found in those capable of reasoning [ἡ βουλευτικὴ ἐν τοῖς λογιστικοῖς] (for whether to do this or that is already a job for reasoning [λογισμοῦ] and one must measure by a single thing [ἑνὶ μετρεῖν]; hence, one is able to make one thing out of many images [ὥστε δύναται ἓν ἐκ πλειόνων φαντασμάτων ποιεῖν]). (434a5–10)

Rather, Aristotle's point is simply that certain sounds, if they are to count as more than mere noise, must be associated with internal structures or states of the animal such that the animal can be said to be doing more than merely registering or reacting to parts of its external environment. For this images are required but not in a way that renders the account unacceptably strong. An ordinary animal's noise must only embody certain very minimal recognitional qualities such as a dog's anticipatory yelps at mealtime or a lion's fear-inducing growls at an enemy's approach.

52. Indeed, if one is to believe Ax (1978, 258), the first passage may not be genuine.

53. ἡ ἐν τοῖς ἄρθροις, ἣν ἄν τις ὥσπερ διάλεκτον εἴπειεν.

Several scholars[54] take the last line to assert that human animals must be able to fashion one *image* out of many and that this defines the calculative imagination [λογιστικὴ φαντασία]. From our point of view this is undesirable to the extent that it encourages the view that imagination has an active₂ use. In fact, however, this is not the line's most likely reading. For one thing it is because deliberation requires measuring by a single standard that deliberators must be able to make one thing out of many images. If, on the one hand, the single standard is just the same thing as the one thing made from many images, then the latter can hardly be an image because what one measures by in deliberation is not an image but a logos. If, on the other hand, the single standard merely implies that deliberators be able to make one thing from many images, it still need not be an image. More likely it is a universal required for the logos that serves as the deliberative standard.[55]

What Aristotle has in mind under λογιστικὴ φαντασία is simply a quite distinctive use of imagination. The key to seeing this is that the context of discussion is action. Sometimes for persons, and always for other animals, the goal or end of an action results simply from perceiving or perhaps remembering something. Since, we have seen, images are standardly involved in such cases, the perceptive imagination [αἰσθητικὴ φαντασία] bears simply on the production of images in cognitive acts of an exclusively perceptual persuasion. Persons, on the other hand, are able to arrive at ends and goals on the basis of deliberation. So it must be possible to have as an end something that is not in one's immediate perceptual or mnemonic field. When I decide that some light meat would be good for me, there need be no morsel at hand. Yet I do desire some light meat and so must be able to [re]present this as the object of desire. Since the object cannot reasonably be construed as a particular (I do not after all desire any specific bit of meat) and since the image may well be like that involved in cases where one does desire a specific piece of meat, Aristotle can have in mind here only a distinction in *how* the image is produced.

Although not the single standard itself, the image is routinely involved when one forms a desire on the basis of the single standard, that is, on the basis of a judgment about what one needs. Such judgments do involve a logos and so are characteristic of human animals only. Accordingly, because images are involved in my [re]presenting the objects of these cognitive acts, the calculative [λογιστική] or deliberative [βουλευτική] imagination is distinctively human as well. But this means simply that *operation* of imagi-

54. Hamlyn, Hicks, Hett, and Barbotin (Budé), but not Smith in the Oxford translation.
55. In the manner sketched in *Metaphysica* I.1 and *Analytica Posteriora* II.19.

nation in calculative or deliberative contexts is distinctively human. What is salient is not the imagination but the logos it subserves. So the difference between man and the other animals lies less in the distinction between two types of imagination than in the former's capacity for logos.[56]

To get a clearer idea on what this amounts to we need to turn again to *Metaphysica* I.1. At 980b25–27 animals are accorded little of experience [ἐμπειρίας μετέχει μικρόν], suggesting rather that they live by imagination and memory alone. In man, however, experience develops out of memories. Counted as a kind of knowledge or understanding of particulars [ἡ ἐμπειρία τῶν καθ' ἕκαστόν ἐστι γνῶσις at 981a15–16], experience differs from art and science whose knowledge or understanding is of the universal variety. To generalize from Aristotle's example, knowing that a particular F is G is a matter of experience, whereas knowing that all Fs are G is a matter of art or science. Nonetheless, because experience entails knowing *what* a particular thing is, it presupposes acquisition of universals. These would appear to be 981a5–6's many notions of experience [πολλὰ τῆς ἐμπειρίας ἐννοήματα] from which the universal *judgments* of art and science are gotten.

Several comments are in order at this point. First, if experience is about particulars, then a fortiori so is the imagination of 980b25–26's animals other than man. Indeed, they appear to be denied any notion of *what* something is to the extent that this involves judging that something is a this or a that. This tallies with our earlier estimate of their meager cognitive capacities. Granted, Aristotle says just that animals have *little* of experience. But, in a backhanded way, this supports our point, for it is hard to take this as more than a prudent caveat reflecting Aristotle's sensitivity: certain animals behave *as if* they know what something is.[57]

Second, the crucial point of differentiation is man's capacity to acquire universals and this is explicitly tied to his ability to make, first, singular and, then, universal suppositions [ὑπολήψεις]. If, by 427b24–26 (see 3 of the chapter's first section), these singular suppositions count as belief [δόξα], then, by 428a22–24, they will depend on logos. Elsewhere, in *Analytica Posteriora* II.19, for example, the distinction is couched in terms of certain perceivers[58] acquiring a logos from experience or the universal that

56. Contrast Labarrière (1984) who gives pride of place to the distinction between types of imagination.

57. *Ethica Nicomachea* VII.3, 1147b4–5, is even more emphatic, insisting that beasts have only imagination and memory of particulars [τῶν καθ' ἕκαστα φαντασία καὶ μνήμη].

58. Presumably, these will be mind-endowed perceivers. Barnes (1975) translated "ἐν τῇ ψυχῇ" at 100a1 as "in their minds," which curiously suggests that it is a sufficient condition for having a mind that a perceiver have ἐν τῇ ψυχῇ (in the soul) something or, retaining "ἐν τι" at 100a1, some one thing in the soul. But since what is held in the soul must be that from whose retention [ἐκ τῆς τῶν τοιούτων μονῆς at 100a2–3] the λόγος comes and since in some

has been acquired in the soul [ἐκ ἐμπειρίας ἢ ἐκ παντὸς ἠρεμήσαντος τοῦ καθόλου ἐν τῇ ψυχῇ] (100a6–7). By itself, the *Analytica Posteriora* passage might suggest that one can have a universal without a logos because, after all, the logos is said to come about *from* the universal. But the logos of interest to the writer of the *Analytica Posteriora* is obviously one fit for duty in scientific explanation, one that is "a principle of art and science" (100a8). These will be just the universal suppositions of *Metaphysica* I.1. Thus, it will still hold generally that, as universals "somehow" in the soul, thoughts depend on logos.

Does this mean, then, that thought depends on language, in particular, that concept acquisition requires acquisition of appropriate linguistic abilities? The answer to this depends partly on how one construes "logos," so far left untranslated. The two most likely candidates, at least for this discussion, are "reason" and "language." There will be no argument that the first is frequently in order, but the appropriateness of the second is anything but settled. So it will demand some close attention.

Many passages in the corpus link logos with language. *De Partibus Animalium* II.17, 660a2–3, remarks that logos through sound consists of combinations of letters [ὁ λόγος ὁ διὰ τῆς φωνῆς ἐκ τῶν γραμμάτων σύγκειται], and *De Generatione Animalium* V.6, 786b19–22, reports that nature has endowed man most of all with the capacity for sound because he alone of the animals uses logos [διὰ τὸ λόγῳ χρῆσθαι μόνους τῶν ζῴων] and sound is the matter of logos [τοῦ λόγου ὕλην εἶναι τὴν φωνήν]. *Politica* I.2, 1253a9–15, reaffirms the link, implying that nature has gifted man with sound that indicates more than pleasure and pain because man alone has logos and logos is for revealing advantage and disadvantage, and so on [ὁ λόγος ἐπὶ τῷ δηλοῦν ἐστὶ τὸ συμφέρον...].

Although such passages undeniably relate logos and language, it is anything but clear that they show language to be a requirement for rather than a reflection of logos. The last two passages suggest that man has language because he has logos, not conversely, and the first two may only imply that, if logos is given material expression, it will be in the form of sound, indeed, human sound.

Some interpreters have tried for a stronger connection. Labarrière (1984), for instance, uses *De Anima* III.3 428a22–24—"every belief entails conviction [πίστις], conviction being persuaded, and persuasion entails logos; and some beasts have imagination but none logos"—to argue for language as a

---

perceivers such retention does not yield a λόγος [τοῖς δὲ μή at 100a3], only the first can be said to have minds, yet both hold perceptions in the soul. The latter is clear also from the fact that 100a1 resumes discussion of the case introduced earlier of perceivers capable of retaining the perception [99b36–37's μονὴ τοῦ αἰσθήματος].

necessary condition of thought, or at least of that variety that counts as belief. Roughly, the idea is that for belief to presuppose persuasion is for it to presuppose an intersubjective space in which discourse goes on. Thus, Labarrière urges that here *logos* is to be read as *une certaine oratio* rather than *ratio* partly on the strength of his claim that animals may share to some extent in the latter. But the passages that can be adduced in support of this claim all indicate that Aristotle has little interest in attributing ratio to beasts in anything but an "as-if" manner.[59] In any case, the thesis argued is, unfortunately, more attractive than the argument for it. Why might not one convince oneself, by deliberation, demonstration, or other means, of the truth of a certain belief? While this would surely involve reason, why need it involve public discourse?[60]

A passage in *De Sensu,* also used by Labarrière, may provide the best evidence for the thesis that language plays a necessary role in explaining how the mind acquires knowledge of the world. At 437a1 it is claimed that for creatures with practical intelligence [φρόνησις] the three so-called external senses, hearing, sight, and smell, are (functionally) designed to serve the (or a) good end. They do this by reporting [εἰσαγγέλλουσι] numerous distinctions from which develops a grasp [φρόνησις] of objects of thought [νοητά] as well as of practical things. Then Aristotle says (437a5) that concerning mind [νοῦς] hearing is the most important of the three. This is explained as follows:

> Hearing gives differences in noise (ψόφου) only; in some cases this is also articulate sound [φωνή]. Although only its incidental function, hearing contributes the most to development of intelligence [πρὸς φρόνησιν]; for language that is audible [ὁ λόγος ἀκουστὸς ὤν] is the cause of learning [αἴτιος τῆς μαθήσεως] not in its own right but incidentally [οὐ καθ᾽ αὐτὸν ἀλλὰ κατὰ συμβεβηκός]. For language consists of words each of which is a symbol [ἐξ ὀνομάτων γὰρ σύγκειται, τῶν δ᾽ ὀνομάτων ἕκαστον σύμβολόν ἐστιν]. (437a9–15)

59. See, for example, the discussion on this later in this chapter.

60. Labarrière (1984) also appeals to 434a10–12, "καὶ αἴτιον τοῦτο τοῦ δόξαν μὴ δοκεῖν ἔχειν ὅτι τὴν ἐκ συλλογισμοῦ οὐκ ἔχει," which he translates "La raison pour laquelle les animaux semblent ne pas posséder l'opinion, c'est qu'ils n'ont pas cette sort d'imagination qui procède du syllogisme, tandis que celle'ci suppose la première." But so far from mentioning imagination, the passage simply says that animals do not have beliefs about the end of their actions that have been formed on the basis of deliberation. Depending on the weight one gives to "μὴ δοκεῖν" (not to believe), the passage squares with the view that animals have some attenuated sort of belief or with the view that capacity for any belief at all entails capacity for holding beliefs on the basis of deliberation.

The passage is clear on the point that the hearing of articulate sounds plays an important role in developing intelligence. It is also clear that this amounts to acquiring a grasp of objects of thought [τῶν νοητῶν]. This in turn implies that one acquires the corresponding thoughts [τῶν νοηματῶν]. Although language figures explicitly here, the question is whether it figures as a *necessary* condition for thought. The passage appears to recommend nothing more than the dependence on language of those thoughts or pieces of knowledge that are acquired *by instruction*.

Or can the passage be made to yield something stronger? We might try exploiting two slightly different ways to take the participial construction in 427a12–13. Taken attributively, with "λόγος," "ἀκουστὸς ὤν" gives us something like

    1. logos that is audible is the cause of learning.

Taken circumstantially, with the verb, we get

    1'. logos is the cause of learning because it is audible.

This appears to imply that logos is something that is audible, hence, something linguistic. But context makes it unlikely that, in either case, the line expresses a general thesis about logos. This appears to be so whether one reads the final three lines as

    2. (*a*) logos that is audible is the cause of learning, (*b*) not the cause in its own right but incidentally, for (*c*) it consists of words each of which is a symbol.

or as

    2'. (*a*) logos is the cause of learning because it is audible, (*b*) not audible in its own right but incidentally, for (*c*) it consists of words each of which is a symbol.

The English translators, Smith in the Oxford and Hett in the Loeb, like 2'. Mugnier and Labarrière, on the other hand, appear to favor 2. It seems to me that 2' is more plausible because what it explains is the fact that hearing contributes most to development of intelligence and that it does so incidentally. This would be explained by saying that although one hears the logos, the thing that must be grasped in order to understand, one does not hear it directly but only *in virtue of* its audible expression, only κατὰ συμβεβηκός. It is less clear how 2 bears on the salience of hearing in this process. Appropriately, *c* then explains how one can grasp a logos in the manner required.

Do we have indicated here a stronger connection between thought and language? On its own, c might suggest this, since "σύγκειται" (consists) takes logos as its subject. But the entire passage addresses the occurrence of logos in the context of instruction, so we should probably read nothing stronger than logos qua audible. The passage, thus, says, in effect, that we do not directly hear the logos, but nonetheless we can grasp it because what we do hear are words that symbolize it. So taken, the passage does establish that communication of a logos depends on language and, although it does not require language for logos, neither does it imply that logos may proceed independently of language. It is simply neutral on the point and so that possibility remains alive.

Another factor has been introduced into the discussion by c. Because linguistic tokens are, or may serve as, *symbols*, certain strings of words convey a logos. Perhaps this notion can further illuminate the connection between thought and language. For the moment it will be sufficient to mention two points, one an observation and the other an argument. The observation is that Aristotle nowhere uses "σύμβολον" (symbol) to characterize the behavior or output of nonhuman animals. Since the same holds for "λόγον," Aristotle appears committed to the thesis that something has the capacity for logos if, and only if, it has the capacity to employ symbols.[61] More plainly, something can reason if, and only if, it can communicate.

The above observation invites argument, for it is obvious that equivalence between capacities does not entail equivalence between their employments. From

    3. x has logos-capability$_2$ $\equiv$
       x has symbol-capability$_2$

it does not follow that

    4. x reasons that p $\equiv$
       x employs an appropriate string of symbols that express p.

What does follow, with certain provisos, is something like

    4'. x reasons that p $\supset$
       x is able$_2$ to employ an appropriate string of symbols that express p

and

    4". x employs an appropriate string of symbols that express p $\supset$
       x reasons that p.

61. See Labarrière (1984) for a useful discussion of this point.

Both 4′ and 4″ reflect, I submit, the truth according to Aristotle; 4″ is implicit in *De Interpretatione* 23a32–35:

> if what is in the sound follows what is in the mind [τὰ ἐν τῇ φωνῇ ἀκολουθεῖ τοῖς ἐν τῇ διανοίᾳ] and there the contrary is the belief of the contrary (for example, that every man is just is contrary to every man is unjust), then the same must hold in the case of affirmations in sound [ἐπὶ τῶν ἐν τῇ φωνῇ καταφάσεων]

and 24b1–2:

> So if this is how it is with belief, and affirmations and negations in sound are symbols of things in the soul [σύμβολα τῶν ἐν τῇ ψυχῇ], it is clear that . . .

It also figures prominently in the semantical model that opens *De Interpretatione:*

> Sounds [τὰ ἐν τῇ φωνῇ] are symbols [σύμβολα] of affections [παθήματα] in the soul and written marks are symbols of sounds. And as written marks are not the same for all, neither are sounds the same. But what these are signs [σημεῖα] of in the first place, the affections in the soul, these are the same for all; and what these are likenesses [ὁμοιώματα] of, actual things [πράγματα], these are also the same.

The first two passages introduce and conclude, respectively, a long discussion of contrariety, so it appears that Aristotle will explain that what is in the sound follows what is in the mind because affirmation and negation in sound are symbols of things in the soul. This is precisely what one would expect from the semantical model. There written marks and spoken words are symbols of something in the soul. The latter are arguably thoughts [νοήματα]. For one thing, this is what the text recommends: 16a9–10's immediate mention of νοήματα in the soul that are neither true nor false refers not to 17a3–7's prayers and poems but to what 16a14 calls thoughts without combination or separation, thoughts that correlate with individual symbols such as "man" and "white." In the second place, the affection in the soul must support communication and intersubjective meaning. What is a symbol of what is a matter of agreement. In Aristotle's idiom, the symbol is a sound significant by convention [φωνὴ σημαντικὴ κατὰ συνθήκην (16a19). This is enough to ensure some sort of intersubjectivity because it amounts to establishing a public criterion for usage. But more is needed because, for Aristotle, meaning is globally invariant and usage does not guarantee this. So whereas convention varies, or might have varied, signification does not. Thus, the likeness relation holding between affections and things is not a symbolic relation and affections in the soul are signs, but not symbols, of actual things. It is thus only that grasp of alien conventions is sufficient for grasp of meaning.

What is interesting about the model is that the relation between affection and thing lends itself to a mechanical and not a linguistic explanation. So the model as a whole combines the two approaches we mentioned at the section's outset. Of the available candidates, only thoughts [νοήματα] are suited for this dual role. The perceptual state [αἴσθημα] and image [φάντασμα] enjoy too much particularity and neither is combinable in assertion and denial. This does not license elimination of φαντάσματα from the story because they are crucial to the mechanical account. They explain how a particular, perhaps thoroughly idiosyncratic, system can [re]present objects of thought in an intersubjective and publicly available way. They do so by exemplifying the thought in the manner shown in the previous section, thus enabling thoughts to occur as affections of the soul and as the proper significations of symbols. Use of symbols appears, then, to imply grasp of universals and this is just what 4″ reports.

What about 4′? First, a negative remark. The fact that logos is expressed in speech only incidentally [κατὰ συμβεβηκός] implies neither that logos is otherwise expressible nor that 4′ is false[62]—no more than the fact that the son of Diares is seen incidentally implies that he can be seen in some other way or without seeing a special object of sense. And thought may involve imagination only incidentally, yet be dependent upon it.[63] What can be said by way of support for 4′? This is a live question, if only because of Aristotle's idiom. At 23a33–35 language is said to follow what is in the soul because, 24b1–2, language consists of symbols of thoughts in the soul, and *Metaphysica* IV.3, 1005b24–26, implies that what one says need not be what one believes or reasons. Passages such as these, and they are not the only ones, suggest that language reflects but may not be required for logos.

Nonetheless, there are signs that Aristotle is open to something like 4′. In fact, I want to suggest that he sees having a logos as something like formulating a linguistic intention. Thus, 4′ turns out to be true because of the truth of

---

62. And, pace Ross's comment (1961), it is misleading to say that language (human speech) is not inherently meaningful but has meaning attached to it by convention. This suggests that we first are given words and then we assign meaning to them. An odd story at best. Rather, to be given a word, better, sentence, just is to be given something that is meaningful, albeit by convention. For this, see *De Interpretatione* 16a26–28. Steinthal (1890, 1:187) held a similar view and is now followed by Ax (1978, 264).

63. Indeed, precisely this formula was adduced in chap. 4, sec. 1, to explain the dependence in question.

4*. x reasons that $p \supset x$ formulates the linguistic intention that
p.

The notion of a linguistic intention is admittedly vague, but perhaps it is
enough to say the following. By formulating a linguistic intention I have in
mind, roughly, formulation of an intention to utter or otherwise produce a
sentence expressing that p or to perform a speech act to the same effect.
While this spares Aristotle 4, it does commit him to 4' and so assumes
that formulation of such intentions makes no sense apart from the ability$_2$
to express it symbolically. Is this a defensible assumption?

One place to start is with the style of his attribution of cognitive abilities
to nonhuman animals. Given certain assumptions about goal directedness
and economy of functional design, attribution is based mainly on what
cognitive capacities seem required to explain what animals *do* or appear to
do. Two points about Aristotle's discussion are especially salient here. First,
nowhere does he unambiguously attribute to beasts practical intelligence
[φϱόνησις], discursive thought [διάνοια], mind [νοῦς], and the like. His
language is cautious and deliberately qualified to avoid outright ascription
of such capacities. Second, what we have to go on in the case of animals
is bodily behavior plus a minimal sort of φωνή, or voice. These two points
set the boundary conditions on ascription. Since we know that Aristotle
denies possession of universals to nonhuman animals, we must assume that
there simply is no basis in their behavioral repertoire for such attribution.

So on what grounds *would* one be justified in attributing universals to
an animal? Well, surely, on the grounds that the animal has logos. But that
is the very point under discussion! In virtue of what do we attribute *that*
to a system? So far as I can tell, this requires including in the animal's
behavioral repertoire linguistic behavior that displays grasp of universals.
This in turn calls for judgments, singular or otherwise, that make use of
universals.[64] This is implicit in *Rhetorica* I.1, 1355b1–2's reminder that logos
is more characteristic of man than the use of his body. Because that discussion concerns the use of logos in debate, logos clearly has linguistic force
there. It is explicit in *Historia Animalium* IV.9, 536a32–b5, which asserts not
only that no other animals enjoy discourse, a clearly public notion, but also
that it is *characteristic* of man [διάλεκτον οὐδὲν ἔχει, ἀλλ' ἴδιον ἀνθϱώπου
ἐστίν]. If one makes the reasonable assumption that human discourse is a
form of linguistic behavior involving symbols, then the assumption underlying 4' seems warranted.

Use of symbolic or conventional linguistic behavior as a mark of reason

---

64. Recall here our earlier discussion of *Metaphysica* I.1's distinction between singular and
universal ὑπόληψις, both of which involve universals.

[λογισμός] has recently been challenged by Ax (1978) who makes much of the fact that passages such as 536a33–b5 appear to be contradicted by 536b14–19:

> And among small birds some do not sing in the same voice [φωνή] as their parents, if they have been raised apart and have heard other birds sing; and a mother nightingale has already been observed [ἤδη ὦπται] giving singing lessons to a young bird. Thus, speech is not natural in the same way that voice is [ὡς οὐχ ὁμοίας φύσει τῆς διαλέκτον οὔσης καὶ τῆς φωνῆς] but is able to be molded.

One point of conflict can be dealt with quickly. A contradiction is forthcoming only on the assumption that the above passage countenances outright possession of speech by other animals. But the assumption is unjustified. Although b9–10 enlists the passage in the task of distinguishing sounds [φωναί] from speech [διάλεκτοι], b11–12 appears to sanction incorporation of nonhuman sound in a weak way at best: it is simply articulated sound that one "might call speech" [ἡ ἐν τοῖς ἄρθροις ἦν ἄν τις ὥσπερ διάλεκτον εἴπειεν].

But there is, apparently, a second and more crucial problem. Avian speech, attenuated though it be, is held to be, in Ax's words, "not the result of innate nature [Physis] but rather a product of a changeable environment and educational shaping—and thus, in the last analysis, a product of convention" (1978, 266; my translation). If correct, certain sounds of certain beasts are significant by convention, and thus we have a clear and grave contradiction between 536b14–19 and passages that award to man alone the conventional use of symbols. Ax's diagnosis of Aristotle's inconsistency, that the various parts of Aristotle's *Sprachtheorie* must be culled from texts devoted to different topics and written at different periods, pales in light of the fact that the contradictory claims under immediate consideration are separated by some ten lines of Bekker text. An alternative response would be welcome.

I wish to suggest that we have here only the appearance of contradiction. Notice, first, that for Aristotle the case shows only that speech is not natural *in the same way as* [ὁμοίας][65] voice. Unlike the latter, which is invariant

---

65. Reading "ὁμοίως" with P and Dᵃ, Ax gets "als wäre διάλεκτος nicht ebenso φύσει wie die Stimme" (as if discourse were not just as much "by nature" as voice) on the grounds that the distinction is plainly between the natural and the non-natural. This assumes, what we have given reason to doubt, that no qualification attaches here to attribution of speech. In any case, I fail to see how "ὁμοίως" gets the reading Ax wants (Smith reads "ὁμοίως" without getting it). In particular, I see no basis in the Greek for the counterfactual cast.

specieswide, "speech" can be molded in different ways. But why cannot certain natural things be so molded and yet remain natural or, more directly to the point, why must voice [φωνή] that is subject to molding be for that reason conventional?

So far as I can determine there are two considerations Ax might appeal to. One is the arbitrariness of words on the conventionalist account and the second is the characterization of words as nonnatural. If, then, a young bird is taught "speech" that is different from its native tongue, then its (unlearned) native speech would hardly have counted as anything but arbitrary in the first place. Two observations counter this. First, "ἤδη ὦπται" (has already been observed) may, for all we know, indicate a certain ironical attitude toward reports of mother bird's pedagogic feats. It certainly keeps Aristotle at a safe distance from the claim. But the more serious point is that arbitrariness of word follows from but does not entail linguistic conventionalism. More is needed.

Perhaps, then, the second consideration can establish the conventional nature of avian "speech." We have already argued that at most such speech is said to be natural in a way different from voice, but more can be said. *De Interpretatione* contains several remarks pertinent to the topic. Consider, for example,

  a. The name (or logos) is a sound significant by convention [φωνὴ σημαντικὴ κατὰ συνθήκην] (16a19),
  b. No sound is a name by nature but only when it has become a symbol [φύσει τῶν ὀνομάτων οὐδέν ἐστιν, ἀλλ᾽ ὅταν γένηται σύμβολον] (16a27–28).

and

  c. Every sentence is significant [σημαντικός] not as a tool but by convention (17a1–2).

Statement *b* is explicitly given as the reason for *a,* so we may infer that Aristotle opposes sounds significant by nature equally to symbols and to sounds significant by convention. In *c* we get a second opposition. What is significant by convention is not significant in the way a tool is. Since something is hardly a tool by nature, this constitutes a new point of difference. A tool is significant because of what *it* does, what *its* function is. Its significance is, nonetheless, tied to an end it serves. Thus, like words, they do not enjoy intrinsic significance. It is for this reason that Aristotle is careful to distinguish the two cases. In order to accomplish a given task a tool must satisfy certain constraints. One can cut wood only with what is hard, sharp, serrated, and so on. Thus, certain properties of the tool itself are relevant to its discharging its function, hence, to its significance as a tool.

Significance by convention, on the other hand, is thoroughly nonnatural. A word's success is independent of any of its material properties and is a function of agreement alone. This feature of a word is nowhere put more clearly than in *De Sophisticis Elenchis* I.1, 165a6–8: "It is impossible to bring in the things themselves [αὐτὰ τὰ πράγματα]; rather we use names of things as their symbols [συμβόλοις]." Words can deputize or stand for things. Significance by convention amounts, then, to agreement about what word is to deputize for what thing. Significance as a tool is anything but this. And because words manage to do this in virtue of their being symbols of thoughts, what they stand for need not be anything in a speaker's immediate perceptual or mnemonic field. It is this *Stellvertreterfunktion* that is denied nonhuman speech, for these animals live by imagination and memory of particulars only. This holds for the avian "speech" of 536b14–19. The fact that voice [φωνή] is subject to molding in no way entails that it can reveal or express more than immediate states of a subject. The fact that, as symbols, nouns, verbs, and sentences are not so restricted also enables them to [re]present items that are combinable in full thoughts, for among the latter we surely include general thoughts as well as thoughts about nonpresent particulars. Ax has not, then, dislodged the thesis that humans alone are capable of linguistic behavior involving symbols.

If they do not prove the point, the passages we have considered strongly suggest that attribution of logos to a system depends on that system's displaying certain linguistic behavior. This is not simply a matter of producing sounds, saucy or otherwise, as does the parrot. Rather, the ability to discourse with a fellow speaker appears to be the critical factor. This makes complete sense, if one bears in mind Aristotle's general account of how one acquires faculties in the first place. Just as *De Anima* II.5 suggests that Smith's knowing the Pythagorean Theorem amounts to his being able to produce it so now his inability to give public expression to the theorem removes all temptation to credit him with it.

If what has been said so far is correct, or close to correct, then it would be plausible to conjecture that Aristotle views acquiring a logos, universal, or whatever, as depending not only on the operation and development of cognitive mechanisms (the story supplied in *Analytica Posteriora* II.19) but also on the acquisition of certain kinds of publicly scrutable linguistic behavior. To dispel any suspicion of incompatibility here it is enough to remark that the mechanisms develop in the context of and ultimately subserve public discourse. This is, moreover, fully consistent with the semantic model of *De Interpretatione*. For if public language consists of symbols of thoughts in the soul, then acquiring a language would explain how one acquires concepts. So long as, of course, the mechanical development does not go awry.

A further indication that Aristotle looks at matters in this way is found in 536b3–8 which continues the *Historia Animalium* passage already introduced. Two points command our attention. First, the deaf are also dumb because, even if they have sound, they are devoid of discourse [φωνὴν μὲν οὖν ἀφιᾶσι, διάλεκτον δ᾽ οὐδεμίαν]. The point is not the trivial one that because they can't hear they are unable to receive as well as volunteer their thoughts. That does not require that they be deaf from birth [ἐκ γενετῆς]. Rather, as context makes clear (after all, birds constitute their comparison class), they lack what is characteristically human, namely, logos and thought. So too, then, for children. They lack not merely the physical skill to express thoughts they have in hand but rather what is characteristically and fully human.

The suggestion that development of logos and thought tracks development of linguistic competence may also be at work in *Ethica Nicomachea* VI.11. There the capacities and conditions that are characteristic of humans, judgment [γνώμη], understanding [σύνεσις], practical intelligence [φρόνησις], and mind [νοῦς], are said to emerge in a person at the same time (1143a25–28), namely, when the child or person reaches the "age of reason." These are natural abilities, indicated by the fact that we think our various powers correspond to particular times of life (1143b6–8). To this I would attach only that development of linguistic competence follows the same route and, indeed, is arguably the basis for the shared opinion of the last passage.[66]

One advantage of the current suggestion is that it goes some distance toward removing a difficulty that Barnes (1975, 255) rightly finds in *Analytica Posteriora* II.19, namely, 100a17–b5's use of the chain, man → animal → . . . → substance, to illustrate how induction generates higher from lower universals. The difficulty is lack of an account explaining how the initial universal in this kind of series could be gotten by strict induction on the sensory given. Restricted, as Barnes suggests, to special and common objects, the sensory given would appear to support generation of nonsubstantial universals only—colors, shapes, and the like. But, as a substance

66. In this regard one might note the parallel drawn in *Physica* I.1's final lines between linguistic competence and conceptual development. After commenting on the need to advance from what is more knowable to us to what is more knowable in nature Aristotle says, "Words stand in something of the same relationship to definitions. A name, for example, "circle," indiscriminately signifies a certain whole, whereas the definition analyzes it into particular (elements). And children at first call all men 'father' and all women 'mother,' only later discriminating each of them."

sortal, man provides a principle of individuation for objects. If it is to be gotten by induction, the inductive base will have to include incidental as well as proper objects of perception. Yet incidental objects appear to call for more than purely perceptual mechanisms.

Aristotle himself hints at a solution in 100a16–b1: "While what is perceived is the particular, perception is of the universal." This remark, delivered in the midst of the mechanical account, implies that the perceptual system can inductively generate universals only because perception is of types, not tokens. But notice that the remark also suggests—what is particularly crucial for the case of substance universals—a way to wed the mechanical and linguistic accounts. Precisely because it embodies universals, language can make explicit what is implicit in perception. Thus, we have here at least a suggestion as to how language acquisition could play a role in concept acquisition. It is in some such way that we are able to be aware of Socrates qua man and not merely Socrates qua colored or shaped thing.

I am not suggesting, on Aristotle's behalf, the rather recent view that our conceptual scheme or, perhaps, our ontology is wholly dependent on our language and that because our language could vary, or could have varied, in important ways, so might our settled conception of the world be other than it is. In a sense Aristotle would not dispute the last point except when extended to deny the possibility of a correct version of the world. Aristotle's νοῦς is charged with grasping the world in its essential structure and language reflects this.[67] But νοῦς does not operate independently of a linguistic context. Thus, in the theory of science, where νοῦς is assigned the job of grasping the principles from which demonstration ultimately proceeds, it is implausible in the extreme to suppose that νοῦς manages this independently of demonstration. Rather, it is only by reflecting, as it were, on actual patterns of demonstration that νοῦς even knows what is called for in the way of first principles. So the public, justificatory context is central.

I have ventured to inject language acquisition into the discussion of concept acquisition partly because the alternative account of how νοῦς gains awareness of features of the world that exceed the strictly sensible is wholly mysterious. Clark (1975), for example, weds the individual with the divine mind that reveals the nature of reality. For those of us accustomed to leaner fare, however, other explanations would be welcome. This is, of course, not to deny νοῦς a role in the process. But it will be mind with language

---

67. Of course, not all usage does so. But where it fails, Aristotle favors adoption of perspicuous alternatives. For more on this see Wedin (1978 and 1984).

as its vehicle of intuition and interpretation, not mind operating in splendid isolation or divine company.

The canonical theory provided for acquisition or development of [re]-presentational structures or devices, namely images, as a part of Aristotle's account of how a subject can be aware of objects in functionally complete acts. But acquisition of a [re]presentational system is not equivalent to acquisition of concepts, at least not under the interpretation of the above section. Acquiring images [φαντάσματα] is a necessary but not sufficient condition for acquiring concepts. For if Aristotle provides at all for concept acquisition, it is in terms of acquisition of νοήματα. The latter, however, differ from φαντάσματα, and given the nature of the difference, acquiring images does not entail acquiring concepts. Since the crucial point of distinction was the combinability of νοήματα in judgments, I have suggested that completion of the theory of concept acquisition may involve νοῦς and its role in language acquisition.

I am, then, attributing to Aristotle what might be a partial parallel with Kant, namely, the dictum that νοήματα without language are blind. It would, on the other hand, be mistaken to assume that linguistic practice alone is sufficient for understanding or possession of a concept or νόημα—if, that is, by linguistic practice alone is meant *nothing more* than the grammatically correct use of sentences. On Aristotle's view use alone is not enough. Internal cognitive states are also necessary and these are the thoughts or νοήματα. So, to complete the Kantian parallel, Aristotle also appears to adopt the dictum that language without νοήματα is empty. Implicit in the semantical model of *De Interpretatione,* the point is fully explicit at *Physica* II.1, 193a4–9:

> To show [δεικνύναι] what is clear by what is unclear is the sign of one who is unable to discriminate [κρίνειν] between what is known by itself and what is not [τὸ δι' αὐτὸ καὶ μὴ δι' αὐτὸ γνώρι-μον]. It is certainly possible for this state to be effected, for one who is blind from birth might reason inferentially [συλλογί-σαιτο] about colors. It is, therefore, necessary that for such people the discourse be about words [ὥστε ἀνάγκη τοῖς τοιούτοις περὶ τῶν ὀνομάτων εἶναι τὸν λόγον]; nothing is thought [νοεῖν δὲ μηδέν].

Suppose, as is reasonable, that there is some internal state in virtue of which the congenitally blind are able to reason about colors. In light of Aristotle's explicit use of "συλλογίσαιτο" this will, presumably, amount to their knowing the logic of color terms. But in such a case there will be no genuine understanding because without perception there can be no images or φαντάσματα and without these no νοήματα. In short, whatever internal state is involved, it will not be part of a [re]presentational system. Since the state in question could surely be a functional state, Aristotle is, in effect, arguing that genuine understanding requires internal states that are more than functional states and that these require a system of [re]presentation. Thus, something like linguistic intentions do seem to be essential if language is to be about something nonlinguistic. The congenitally blind are portrayed as simply moving linguistic tokens about.

From the modern point of view it looks as if Aristotle would be happy to distinguish between genuine and merely simulated understanding. I think this is correct, but it need not mean that he would be unwilling to allow that differently realized systems might enjoy genuine understanding. He would, rather, urge caution because such attribution commits one to fairly high-powered internal cognitive states, namely, νοήματα. At least this would be consistent with his attribution of φαντάσματα to nonhuman animals on the basis of their behavior (we do not, after all, *observe* these internal states). In short, nothing prevents differently realized systems from having systems of [re]presentation that support genuine νοεῖν or understanding.

So if νοῦς has a place in concept acquisition, it is very likely through its role in acquiring genuine, as opposed to "merely inferential," linguistic understanding. A number of commentators have, however, pursued a somewhat different course, tying concept acquisition to *De Anima* III.5's distinction between productive and receptive mind, some awarding concept acquisition to the first, some to the second. The next chapter argues, however, that the distinction has little, if anything, to do with concept acquisition. It is, rather, part of a theory of the functional organization of the mind.

V

THE MIND

The single most vexing problem in Aristotle's psychology is the status of νοῦς. This is especially so for those who wish to find in Aristotle a coherent and systematic theory of intentional attitudes and behavior generally. For scholarly opinion is virtually unanimous in holding that De Anima's treatment of νοῦς is driven in opposite and irreconcilable directions by Aristotle's naturalistic and his transcendentalistic tendencies. His naturalistic side wants an account of νοῦς to be an account of strictly individual noetic activity without mention of factors or entities extrinsic to embodied persons. Here the mind is to be studied as any other psychological capacity$_2$. Despite stirring about the possibility that νοῦς is independent of body, the naturalistic side dominates the work. Indeed, with appropriate weighting, the independence of νοῦς can, for the most part, be assimilated to the dominant strain. This is unsurprising if, as we have urged, Aristotle is proposing an essentially cognitivist account of mental activity, for, as we have seen, such an account will remain within the bounds of Aristotelian physics.

In De Anima III.5, however, Aristotle's transcendentalistic side allegedly surfaces in the figure of productive mind [νοῦς ποιητικός]. Here commentators have taken up, roughly, four lines of interpretation. For some, III.5 remains exclusively interested in the individual mind and simply—in fact, of course, not so simply—countenances the immortality of one of its parts.[1] For others, curiously undaunted by Aristotle's silence on the point, productive mind, although not properly a part of the *individual* mind, is required to complete the account of individual noetic activity.[2] Still others

1. Aquinas, sections 742–43; W. D. Ross (1961, 47–48), Rodier (1900, 2:465); Guthrie (1981, 19); Renehan (1980, 136); Hyman (1982); Berti (1973, 105–06); possibly also Sorabji (1982). Also Robinson (1983, 143–44).

2. Clark (1975, 184–86); Brentano (1977); Joachim (1951, 290–91); Guthrie (1981, 322–24); Hamlyn (1968, 140). Also Kahn (1981; 1985, esp. 327*n*24).

find that in III.5 Aristotle gestures toward the transcendent intelligences of *Metaphysica* XII without intending any connection whatever with individual noetic activity.[3] And some, finally, retreat to the position that Aristotle has simply saddled himself with a contradiction.[4]

None of these routes is successful in restoring theoretical coherence to the *De Anima* account. Nor does any one of them appear, beyond a doubt, to capture what Aristotle wants to say. Arguing this to full effect will obviously require detailed discussion. Thus, the next chapter devotes considerable attention to one of the prominent contending interpretations. In this chapter, however, I shall proceed, for the most part, directly with interpretation. The target is mainly *De Anima* III.4 and 5 and the interpretation's thrust is that *together* these chapters provide the essentials of what is recognizably a cognitivistic account of individual noetic activity. More particularly, I shall suggest that because productive mind figures in a general cognitivistic account of the mind and its operations, it must itself yield to a nontranscendentalistic analysis. In short, the mind is to be systematically incorporated into the psychological theory of *De Anima*.[5] I begin with some remarks on III.4 and continue in the balance of the chapter with III.5.[6]

3. Wilkes (1978, 115–16); Anscombe (1963, 58); and, possibly, Barnes (1971–72, 113).

4. For example, Düring (1964). Jaeger (1923, 331–34) diagnoses the alleged inconsistency by urging that *De Anima* III's discussion of νοῦς is an unscientific holdover from Aristotle's early Platonistic period. But such developmental theses should be the court of last resort.

5. My approach to productive and receptive mind differs markedly from those commentators who find the distinction irrelevant to Aristotle's psychological theory. For Watson Aristotle introduces, under the heading of productive mind, something that is "suspiciously like nothing" (1966, 10). And Wilkes would exorcise the distinction as "the one outstandingly difficult dualism of the work," urging that it is "imposed upon his psychology by his ethical, theological, and metaphysical preoccupations" (1978, 116). Apart from its dubious merit as a general strategy for achieving consistency in interpretation, such an outright dismissal here counsels dismissal elsewhere of the relation between divine and human thought. Are none of these to be taken seriously, not even those passages not party to ethical and theological discussion? Even worse, if we are right in taking *De Anima* III.4 and 5 as a continuous analysis of thinking [νόησις], it would follow on Wilkes's reasoning that the entire analysis of νοῦς is "not essential to Aristotle's argument." Surely, this is too expensive a way to avoid dualism. As antidote to Wilkes's strategy, it will, I think, be sufficient to note Cooper's equally curious claim that *Ethica Nicomachea* X isolates, unhappily, theoretical activity alone as the final good because Aristotle was in the grip of the technical psychological theory of *De Anima*. We can't have it both ways. Better, then, to insist on interpretation rather than elimination of the troublesome distinction. (On how to handle Cooper's thesis, see Timothy Roche's *Aristotle on the Human Good*, deposited in Shields Library at the University of California, Davis, 1984.)

6. I do not deny the relevance to my topic of *De Generatione Animalium*'s III.3's discussion of νοῦς entering from without, of the suggestion at 408b18 that νοῦς comes about in us as a sort of substance, and in general of those passages allegedly attributing divinity to human νοῦς. Such passages can, I believe, be brought into line with the present account: the last two are discussed in the following chapter and the first is itself an attempt to naturalize the genetic account of the origin of human νοῦς.

I. MIND AS A FACULTY:
DE ANIMA III.4

Aristotle is the first philosopher whose views are sufficiently sophisticated and systematic to constitute a genuine theory. As such, he is, we have urged, the first serious cognitivist in the philosophy of mind. Primarily, an account of the soul is to concern itself with what various sorts of creatures can do. Those capable of more intricate, linguistically informed behavior are said to be endowed with νοῦς. A cognitivist account of νοῦς will not, of course, consist solely in a list of kinds of noetic behavior but rather will attempt to explain how an entity must be structured to be capable of producing such behavior. Whether we must introduce into the explanation a separate entity as the doer of noetic acts is an interesting but, at the outset, independent question.

In general Aristotle downgrades the ontological question in favor of the cognitivist program less because that question is especially difficult than because answers, if any, to the ontological question will follow from the demands of the cognitivist theory.[7] Thus, at the start of *De Anima* III.4 (429a10–12) he proposes to examine the distinguishing features of νοῦς and to say something about how thinking comes about, *whether or not* mind is separate extensionally. So it is clear that Aristotle thinks the cognitivist program can be pursued without settling the ontological question. Especially suggestive for my purposes is the division of labor indicated in the line. For the question of what features are distinctive of νοῦς is kept separate from the question of how thinking occurs, and thus the possibility arises that *De Anima* III.4 is meant to address the first and *De Anima* III.5 the second question. It is this suggestion that I want to exploit.

De Anima III.4 divides roughly into three sections: 429a10–b9 discusses the mind's operational features and retails some of its properties; 429b10–22 distinguishes between the objects of theology, physics, the special senses, and mathematics; and 429b22–430a9 raises and resolves some "paradoxes" of thought. I say something about the paradoxes in sec. 6 of this chapter and 429a10–b9 will receive attention throughout. The passage at 429b10–22 not only differentiates kinds of objects but also concludes that what is most characteristic of mind is that it is concerned with things insofar as they are distinct from matter: ὅλως ἄρα ὡς χωριστὰ τὰ πράγματα τῆς ὕλης, οὕτω καὶ τὰ περὶ τὸν νοῦν. Thus, the process of differentiation is plainly intended to lead up to an answer to our first question concerning what is

---

7. One might, for instance, try to argue for mind's dependence on body from the functional role of images in thought. This was, in fact, the form of argumentation that was discussed in chap. 4, sec. 1.

distinctive of νοῦς. Note, in accordance with FFO, that the answer comes by way of isolating a set of objects proper to νοῦς. The more precise nature of these objects is discussed further in *De Anima* III.6. This will parallel Aristotle's treatment of the second question. For, as I argue in chap. 5, sec. 6, although the puzzles are technically "solved" in 429b22–430a9, how the mind can do what the solution requires is not explained until *De Anima* III.5.

Among the features *De Anima* III.4 marks out as distinctive of mind are the following:

    1. Thinking is something like being affected (429a14–15)

and

    2. One can think of what one wishes (429b7).

The first follows from the analogy, adduced early in III.4, between perceiving [αἰσθάνεσθαι] and thinking [νοεῖν].[8] The analogy, often granted strict governance over the III.4 account, is in fact crucially imperfect. For, as 417b19–21 makes plain, what produces the activity [τὰ ποιητικὰ τῆς ἐνεργείας] of perceiving is invariably something external, whereas in the case of thinking it is somehow something in the soul. Since this in turn is held at 417b21–24 to imply 2, which has no counterpart at all for perception, the analogy itself should not be taken too literally. On one point, however, Aristotle takes the analogy quite seriously, namely, on the causal role of the object of thought. This is clear from 429a14's requirement that thinking be (something like) being affected *by the object of thought* [ὑπὸ τοῦ νοητοῦ] together with 429a17–18's remark that the relation between mind [νοῦς] and objects of thought [τὰ νοητά] is similar to that between that which can perceive [τὸ αἰσθητικόν] and objects of perception [τὰ αἰσθητά]. (See also *Metaphysica* 1072a30 where mind is said to be moved by the object of thought [νοῦς δὲ ὑπὸ τοῦ νοητοῦ κινεῖται].) Thus, just as, causally, it is the object of desire or perception that produces actual desiring or perceiving so also it is the object of thought that produces actual thinking. Let us, then, enter as a third feature of mind:

8. Notice that the analogy generates two alternatives: either thinking will be a certain being affected [πάσχειν τι] or it will be something different like this [τι τοιοῦτον ἕτερον]. It is clear, as 1 requires, that Aristotle wants the second alternative. *De Anima* II.2, 417b6–7, announces that perception itself is not an instance of πάσχειν in the strict sense because it does not involve the destruction of something by its contrary. Rather, perception involves something (the faculty of perception) developing into itself and into actuality. The latter is called "being affected" by convenience only because "there is no name for the difference" (418a1). See also *De Sensu* 4, 441b23, which compares perception to thinking (it is κατὰ τὸ θεωρεῖν), but not to learning (it is not κατὰ τὸ μανθάνειν).

3. Actual thinking is produced by the object of thought (429a13–14).

Three further features central to the *De Anima* III.4 account are

4. Mind is nothing actual until it thinks (429a24),
5. Mind is the same as its object (430a3–5),

and

6. Mind thinks itself (429b9).

Feature 4 is said to follow from (at least) three other theses. Ordered in terms of consequence, they are that mind's range is unrestricted, that it is unmixed [ἀμιγής] with anything, and that its sole nature is that it is potentiality. This last thesis most likely means simply that mind's sole nature is the potentiality to be the same as any possible object of thought.[9] After all, its nature could hardly consist in being identical with any given set of objects. Nor can its nature consist in some noetic activity that is invariant over variation in content or object of thought, for, as Aristotle insists at 430a5–6, we do not always think. So the account of mind's nature is functionally in line with his account of other faculties. Both are to be defined as potentialities$_2$ (developed potentialities) or, in his alternative idiom, as actualizations$_1$ of certain potentialities$_1$ (undeveloped potentialities). The difference is just that faculties other than mind are actualizations$_1$ of distinct physical structures, namely, sensory organs.[10] It is this that explains the limitation on the range of objects accessible to the non-noetic faculties.

Note that it need not, indeed cannot, be implied that the mind is devoid of all modifications, particularly those connected with learning, memory, and the like. How else could the theoretical man come to contemplate this rather than that truth? The point, rather, is that although receptive mind is modified, such modifications are no part of its nature. Unlike the physical structures that partially determine other faculties' operations, these modifications in no way set boundary conditions on what the mind can do. How this works is explained by the particular way in which the notion of form applies to systems capable of thought. Early on in *De Anima* III.4 Aristotle approves of those who call the soul the place of forms so long as they refer to the part of the soul that thinks [ἡ νοητική] and assert of it that it is the

9. One could think of this as, in effect, granting completely general scope to 5 (what we are calling the Sameness Thesis).

10. Thus, Aristotle is here not claiming, contra Norman (1969, 64), that mind is *completely* independent of body. See 429a22–25, which implies that where a faculty is mixed with body, it will be something actual prior to thinking, namely, the structure or structures over which it is defined (of which it is an actualization$_1$).

place of forms potentially rather than actually [οὔτε ἐντελεχείᾳ ἀλλὰ δυνάμει τὰ εἴδη]. At *De Anima* III.8, returning to the point on his own terms,
Aristotle describes the mind as the form of forms [ὁ νοῦς εἶδος εἰδῶν] just
as perception is described as the form of objects of perception [τὰ αἰσθητά].
So the mind is to be understood as the form of potential rather than actual
forms.

Now one could, I suppose, hold that the mind characterized as the form
of potential forms is the mind of the knower$_1$ of the Framework Passage
(chapter 1, section 2), that is, the initial potentiality a thing has, by dint
of being born into a certain species, to *develop into* a system that can right-
fully be said to know and exercise particular pieces of knowledge. But this
is unlikely. Rather, Aristotle means to be talking about the mind of the
knower$_2$, for this alone counts as a faculty and no more than the perceptual
faculties can the mind actually$_2$ think more than one object of thought
(though it may be propositionally complex). So both the mind and the
faculty(s) of perception are forms and both are forms of their respective
objects, potentially. Notice that, by failing to mention the form's realization,
this formulation differs from the standard definition of the soul and its
faculties as the actualization$_1$ of a body, or bodily parts, with the capacity
for life. There is a reason for this, namely, the fact that the mind has no
such simple realization.[11] Nonetheless, both mind and perceptual faculty
can be characterized as the form, potentially, of their respective objects
because this just means that they are the forms of systems that are capable
of cognitively grasping these objects. Indeed, the "form of forms" formulation mirrors, for the mind, the FFO condition (chapter 1, section 2)—
a condition that is tailored for fully operational faculties. As the form of
systems capable of grasping αἰσθητά, perceptual faculties will be forms or
actualizations$_1$ of physical structures and as such will be subject to constraints on the range of objects thus grasped. Not so for the mind. What I
mark, for the sake of reference, in the formula "form$_2$ of forms$_1$," as forms$_1$
are the proper objects of thinking [νόησις]. Characterizing νοῦς as the form$_2$
of such forms calls for a theory of the mind as a certain sort of functional
structure. That the mind is subject to modification is clearly not a comment
on its functional structure. For the potential forms$_1$ are those that a subject
can entertain at will, namely, already acquired forms, and thus the modification on the mind is simply a function of what forms$_1$ have already been
acquired and, so, can be contemplated at will. Hence, to consider the mind
as the form$_2$ of forms$_1$ is to consider it as the form$_2$ of already acquired

11. And this is one reason why early on in *De Anima* II, at 413b24–27 and 415a11–12,
the reader is reminded that the standard account of a faculty will not do for νοῦς. Another is
the singular way in which νοῦς is brought to activity.

forms₁. But since there is no limit, in principle, on what we can think, there is no limit on the forms₁ that can be acquired. It is thus that the mind's modifications set no boundary conditions on its objects.

Finally, the fact that the mind is not defined as the actualization₁ of any set of physical structures explains why it is indeed nothing actual until it thinks. For all other faculties there is at least something that is actual even when the faculty is not operative, namely, the particular physical structures whose actualizations₁ they are. Notice that the mind may well depend on a complex of physical structures, say, in virtue of its dependence on images, without being the actualization₁ of any such structures. So 4 need not be made into the paradoxical claim that mental content is somehow created out of nothing.

Let me now turn to 5 and 6. Thesis 6, that the mind thinks itself, does not enjoy a settled interpretation among Aristotle's commentators. For the moment I shall avoid the thick of the debate by restricting comment on 6 to the discussion at hand.[12] Notice, first, that in finding 6 at 429b9 I reject the translators' popular substitution of "thinks by itself" for "thinks itself." Although the difference does not affect my main thesis, the former enables one to take Aristotle as claiming only that when one is a fully capable noetic agent one can think by oneself. It cannot, of course, be denied that this makes sense in context:

> When mind has become each thing [ἕκαστα] as one who actually₂
> knows [ὁ ἐπιστήμων ὁ κατ᾽ ἐνέργειαν] is said to be—and this
> happens when he can actually₂ exercise his potentiality₂ by him-
> self—it is still in some sense a potentiality₂ but not in the same
> way as before it learned or discovered [that is, not as a po-
> tentiality₁]. Then it is capable₂ of [actually₂] thinking itself [αὐτὸς
> δὲ αὑτὸν τότε δύναται νοεῖν]. (429b5–9).[13]

12. Chapter 6 discusses the divine version of 6, and both 5 and 6 are major players in Aristotle's cognitivist theory of thinking.

13. This parallels De Anima II.5's Framework Passage and so, pace Kahn (1981), concerns less the issue of concept acquisition than the operations of a fully functional mind already possessed of a rich stock of concepts. This is quite clear from Physica VIII.4, 255a30–b5, which bridges the two De Anima passages. Hardie and Gaye (1930) translate: "the term 'potentiality' is used in more that one sense . . . One who is learning a science [ὁ μανθάνων ἐπιστήμων] knows it in a different sense from one who while already possessing the knowledge is not actually exercising it [ὁ ἔχων ἤδη καὶ μὴ ἐνεργῶν] . . . e.g., the learner becomes from one potential something another potential something: for one who possesses knowledge of a science but is not actually exercising it knows the science potentially in a sense, though not in the same sense as he knew it potentially before he learnt it [ὁ γὰρ ἔχων ἐπιστήμην μὴ θεωρῶν δὲ δυνάμει ἐστὶν ἐπιστήμων πως, ἀλλ᾽ οὐχ ὡς καὶ πρὶν μαθεῖν]. And when he is in this condition, if something does not prevent him, he actively exercises his knowledge [ἐνεργεῖ καὶ θεωρεῖ]." The passage also makes clear that the account in the psychology not just of faculties generally (the thrust of the Framework Passage) but of the mind in particular (the thrust of our quoted passage, 429b5–9) is conceived of as part of physics.

There are, however, cogent reasons to resist the substitution. Not the least of these is thorough manuscript agreement for reading "δὲ αὑτόν" ("itself") rather than the needed "δι' αὑτοῦ" ("by itself") in the final line of the passage. The emendation also makes the line curiously otiose, for Aristotle has just said that a subject can exercise his mind by himself. Finally, the fact that 5 is introduced in the first line indicates that the topic of discussion is the relation between mind and its objects. So 6 is hardly out of place here.[14] In particular, it will bear on the special way in which the mind is brought to active thinking. Aristotle appears to regard the scope of 429b5–9 as entirely general, and certainly so for 5. It follows, then, that 6 also is asserted as a general thesis. So implicitly the passage is committed to something like the following:

> 7. Whenever one actually thinks (that is, when one's mind is the same as the object of thought), then the mind thinks itself.

Although I shall later have more to say that bears on 7, let me now comment further on 6. Notice that in 429b5–9 Aristotle asserts but does not explain 6. Indeed, at the chapter's end 6 is regarded as something of a puzzle. Thesis 1 plus mind's simplicity makes it problematic how the mind can think at all. To this is immediately attached the question of how mind can think itself. In light of our preceding paragraph this is an appropriate query: if for the mind to think an object is for it to somehow think itself, then perplexity regarding the first will spill over to the second. The two problems require joint illumination.

Aristotle in fact offers a solution of sorts in De Anima III.4. The problem was that, ordinarily, in cases of being affected two actual things are involved, a first thing that is affected and a second thing that causes the first to be affected.[15] In the case of mind, however, there is only a single actual thing, for in any episode of thinking the mind is actually the same as the object that produces the thinking. Since whatever else it *may* be affected by, namely, any other potential object of thought, is no actual thing, the problem of how mind can think and yet be simple is supposedly met. The problem of mind thinking itself submits to similar resolution: since, in the case of things without matter, mind is the same as its object, it follows that in such cases mind thinks itself.

Notice, however, that this solution solves the pair of puzzles strictly in terms of the language in which they are set. What it does not do is provide any picture of how the mind can do what the solution requires of it. In

14. For a persuasive case against emendation, see Owens (1976, 107–18).

15. See, for instance, 417a17–18: "Everything [that is affected or moved] is affected or moved by something that is able to produce this and is in actuality."

effect we still lack a theory about the functional organization of the mind. The next several sections of this chapter argue that *De Anima* III.5 contains just such a theory. In the chapter's penultimate section I return to the dilemmas that close *De Anima* III.4 and show how they are resolved by treating *De Anima* III.5's productive and receptive mind as part of the internal, functional organization of the mind. The chapter closes by addressing the special character of Aristotle's thesis that the object of thought is a universal.

2. THE FUNCTIONAL ORGANIZATION
OF MIND: *DE ANIMA* III.5

What sort of picture of mind underlies an account containing the features we have just discussed? In particular can we sketch a picture that gives productive mind a natural and nontranscendentalistic role in a cognitivist theory? So far as I can tell this is possible only by taking seriously Aristotle's distinction in *De Anima* III.5 as a distinction between receptive and *productive* mind. The standard translation of "νοῦς ποιητικός" by "active mind" is, I suggest, off the mark doctrinally as well as linguistically (here "creative mind" fares much better). So I shall assume that there is a definite sense in which one aspect or part of the mind is productive or creative and that, as the explicanda, 1–7 figure as constraints on what is reasonable to say about this aspect.

Very roughly, the underlying view I have in mind (call it *M*) is this:

> At *t a* thinks (noetically)[16] of something P if, and only if, at *t a*'s mind not only produces P but also produces itself by producing P.

The central idea is that in producing an actual object of thought the mind also produces itself as an actual thing. Qua actual, the mind is nothing other than the activity whose content is the particular object of the given episode of thinking. Even this characterization threatens to mislead insofar as it allows for what I call the searchlight model of mind. Here the mind is thought of as sweeping through noetic space until encountering an object, at which point content materializes. Not only is this less apt as a characterization of a *productive* noetic function but also it counters Aristotle's com-

16. The caveat is simply to hold at bay passages, such as *De Anima* III.2, 426b22 and 426b31–427a1, and *Physica* VI.1, 224b18–19, that appear to countenance αἰσθητά as objects of thought.

mitment to the thesis of intentionality which requires objects for all genuine mental acts.[17] So noetic activity is necessarily activity under a certain objectual mode and a mind producing itself is always a mind producing itself *as producing an object*.

Of course M does not entail any strong thesis about the identity, in general, of a's mind, for such talk is talk about the essential nature of a's mind and this we know to be pure potentiality. Perhaps criteria of identity for such an entity will be forthcoming from facts about the person a but in no case will they appeal to facts about an alleged episode-independent entity. And in any case Aristotle displays little interest in the identity conditions for any such entity and so, presumably, no more in its actual existence. This is just what one would expect from a fundamentally functionalist account.

It appears, then, that M explains 4, 5, and 6. It also honors 3's causal requirement because actual thinking is produced by the mind's production of the object of thought. The object of thought that produces thinking is, of course, actual, and so M squares with the requirement, familiar from the *Physica* and elsewhere, that the productive factor in cases of being affected be something actual. The gloss on 1 required that mind's object be internal to it. M satisfies this by legislating that the mind itself produces its object,[18] and 2 squares with M in like manner. The causal role of the object of thought in episodes of actual thinking is no threat to mind's thinking what it wishes precisely because it is the mind itself that produces the object. In fact, on this point, M seems tailor-made for the dilemma, raised at *Physica* VII.3, 247b5–8, concerning how that which knows potentially comes to know actually not by moving itself but by the presence of something else. Since mind's objects are internal, the only way to avoid the outlawed case of the mind moving itself is to have it somehow produce, internally, the object that affects it. (More on this in the next chapter.)

Stressing that the analogy between perceiving [αἰσθάνεσθαι] and thinking [νοεῖν] is directed at the causal aspect of each provides a rather nice

17. Indeed, the prime mover's self-thinking may simply be an advanced expression of the commitment.

18. That M does not here commit Aristotle to the absurd thesis that mental content is created from nothing is clear from the fact that M is a thesis about fully capable noetic agents, the sort for whom the model of thinking sketched in 429b5–9 holds. For such agents do not simply create objects of thought on their own; rather, objects of thought are already part of the public domain to be entertained at a thinker's discretion. Indeed, this is at least part of the effect of the otherwise difficult lines 430a19–21: "Actual knowledge is identical with its object but potential knowledge is prior in time in the individual but not prior even in time in general." Although Hamlyn brackets the sentence, presumably because the point of their inclusion is unclear, it is quite appropriate as a warning against mistaking the sense in which mind produces objects of thought.

account of how the αἰσθατόν–αἴσθημα (object of perception–perceptual state) relation is in its turn analogous to the νοητόν–νόημα (object of thought–thought) relation. The point of the latter analogy lies, I suggest, in the causal role of the object of perception [αἰσθητόν] and object of thought [νοητόν] in the account of perceptual activity [αἴσθησις] and noetic activity [νόησις], respectively. Just as the αἰσθητόν is the immediate cause of perceiving [αἴσθησις] so also the νοητόν is the immediate cause of thinking [νόησις]. And just as the resultant state of the perceiving subject is occurrence of a certain αἴσθημα or perceptual content so also the resultant state of the thinking subject is occurrence of a certain νόημα or mental content. As παθήματα in the soul both αἰσθήματα and νοήματα are, we know from *De Interpretatione* 1, objective and, thus, the analogy cannot mean to underscore an objective–subjective distinction. And since objects of perception are external but objects of thought not, neither does the analogy mean to distinguish νοητά and νοήματα as external versus internal items. Thus, the analogy between perceiving and thinking supports *M*'s emphasis on the causal role of certain internal and objective items, and, more to the immediate point, it gives a straightforward account of at least part of what the νοητόν–νόημα distinction consists in.

It is also worth noting that although the νοητόν–νόημα distinction is not that between objective and subjective items of awareness, it does play a role in allowing Aristotle's theory to maintain both the objectivity of objects of thought and their sameness with the thinking subject (properly, with the subject's mind). First, stress that the Sameness Thesis, the thesis that mind and its object are the same, is part of Aristotle's theory of νόησις or the activity of thinking. In particular, it is part of the account of mental content. Thus, the sense of identity called for will be a function of the role of the thesis in the wider theory. So far as I can see nothing more than formal identity is required. Then, in order to *distinguish* x's thinking P from y's thinking P without threat to the objectivity of P (the νοητόν that is the same for x and y), an additional feature is called for. This is just the νόημα that is formally the same for x and y but that, as a causal result of the νοητόν P in distinctive noetic structures, is numerically different.[19]

19. *De Sensu* VI confirms this interpretation. In answering the objection that it is impossible for different persons to see, hear, or smell the same thing [τὸ αὐτό], Aristotle says at 446b21–29: "The answer is that in perceiving that which is the primary cause of movement [τοῦ κινήσαντος πρώτου], all do perceive something that is numerically one and the same [τοῦ αὐτοῦ καὶ ἑνὸς ἀριθμῷ αἰσθάνονται πάντες]; the stimulus peculiar to each is numerically distinct but the same in kind [τοῦ δὲ δὴ ἰδίου ἑτέρου ἀριθμῷ, εἴδει δὲ τοῦ αὐτοῦ] and this explains how many persons see, smell, and hear the same thing at the same time. And these are not bodies but an affection [πάθος] or kind of movement [κίνησίς τις] . . . although they do not occur without body." Although the πάθος in question here is the αἴσθημα, the point is completely general and extends to the νόημα as well.

Some might find it preposterous to propose, as *M* does, that the mind creates itself in producing its objects. Discontent may stem, partly, from neglecting the fact that the mind thus creates itself only as something actual and, partly, from failing to appreciate sufficiently Aristotle's commitment to functionalism. Given a predominant concern with what noetic agents can do, *M* does provide a partial account of the facts. Conjoined with Aristotle's taste for ontological parsimony, these reminders do something to enhance *M*'s plausibility. What, for instance, would be gained by postulating an episode-independent mind? Certainly not clarity.

There is another line of support for *M* besides its usefulness in explaining 1–7. Numerous passages tout the mind's immunity to error. With respect to its proper objects at least, νοῦς divines truths only. This is a difficult point for the Platonist who countenances the independent existence of objects of thought. For here there is logical space to drive a wedge between thinker and object of thought. The usual device for coping with this possibility, namely, endowing νοῦς with an intrepid ability to fathom distinct objects, is notoriously unsatisfactory. Aristotle's solution is more attractive. If the mind not only creates but also is the same as its objects, then there simply is no logical space for the error-enabling wedge.[20]

In any case the infallibility of mind with regard to its objects is problematic at best.[21] Reflexive self-reference, however, fares rather better. One simply does not have any idea how to concoct the required discreditation story, however farfetched. Sincere uses of the reflexive pronoun "I" are ipso facto referentially successful uses. So there is a certain sense in which mistakes are not possible here. I raise this point because it suggests a surprising line of support for *M*, a line recently drawn with some elegance by Robert Nozick (1981) in a somewhat different context.[22] Nozick suggests that infallibility of genuine reflexive self-reference is among the most salient features of full selfhood and that the notion of the self best explaining the feature is the notion of something that constitutes itself in the very act of reflexively referring to itself. This is surely a close cousin of *M*.

What is more to the point, however, is that there is some evidence that Aristotle himself would welcome such an account. In at least one place, *Ethica Nicomachea* III.1, 1111a7–8, Aristotle suggests that although I can be

---

20. Of course, the gain is not without cost. For may not the gap be relocated at the point of contact between objects of thought and the world? Subjectivity is not so much the issue—Aristotle seems open to a model of concept acquisition that is globally intersubjective—but rather the details of how the model works are what are in question. As we saw in the last chapter, nowhere does Aristotle give us a sustained and adequate account of his views on concept acquisition.

21. In fact, it is possible to simply "miss" them. On this, see chap. 4, sec. 5.

22. Especially "Self-Synthesis," 87ff.

mistaken about almost any other feature of an action I perform, I cannot be mistaken about the fact that *I* am performing the action. Since here, and elsewhere, he displays techniques suitable for handling mistakes in reference via descriptions (and, by straightforward extension, proper names), he may have something like reflexive self-reference in mind at 1111a7–8. Aristotle's concerns do not take him deeply enough into problems of reflexive self-reference, nor personal identity for that matter, to find him anticipating Nozick's theory of the self. But they do go far enough to add support for attribution of *M* to Aristotle.

So far I have leaned heavily on Aristotle's usage. This at least has allowed us to explain why productive mind is *productive*. But *De Anima* III.5 contains substantive discussion of productive mind and the question that now looms is whether our interpretation can be squared with these remarks. The discussion of productive and receptive mind divides roughly into three stages: 430a10–14 introduces the distinction in terms of a connection between nature and the mind; 430a14–17 explicates the latter term of the connection; 430a17–25 retails the crucial features of productive mind.

3. MIND AND NATURE

Suppose, then, we begin with the connection between nature and mind.

> Since [as = ὥσπερ] in the whole of nature [ἐν ἁπάσῃ τῇ φύσει] there is, on the one hand, something that is the matter for each thing of a given kind [τι τὸ ὕλη ἑκάστῳ γένει] (and this it is that is potentially all the things of the kind), on the other hand, something different that is the cause and that which produces [τὸ αἴτιον καὶ ποιητικόν] by making all of them [τῷ ποιεῖν πάντα] in the way that an art is disposed with respect to its matter, so must these differences hold in the soul. (430a10–14)

It is unsurprising that the above passage has been aligned with the view that productive mind is the prime mover, particularly if one retains the bracketed "ὥσπερ" in 430a10. For one might then take the passage to assert no more than an analogy between mind and nature. Just as there is a single thing that makes all things in nature so also in the soul something, presumably the divine mind, makes all things. On this view there is no reason to expect that the mind will submit to any principles that are genuine principles of Aristotelian physics and so no reason to locate the study of the mind within physics—at least *as far as this passage is concerned*. But two considerations counsel otherwise. First, the conditional structure of the passage urges elimination of "ὥσπεϱ"[23] and requires that what is said about the mind follows from the general rule on whatever is in nature. Second, the fact that Aristotle writes "each *kind* of thing" rather than "each thing" makes it clear that he is not at this point introducing anything as grand as the unmoved mover but merely issuing a rule on any production whatever, namely, that it occur within a genus.[24] This is a standard and familiar requirement.[25]

So there is, initially, no warrant for linking productive mind and the divine mind. In fact, the opposite would seem to be the case. For the distinction between productive and receptive mind is explained as an instance, in fact, of course, a very special instance, of a distinction that holds generally in the domain of nature. And this at least leads one to expect that the distinction will play a role in a psychological, as opposed to a theological, account of thinking. What Aristotle does want to focus on is the *way* productive mind produces its objects. *De Anima* III.4 approves of those who describe the mind as the place of forms so long as the forms are understood as potentially and not actually present. Thus, the general point seems to be that productive mind retrieves, as it were, from receptive mind a given object of thought and so renders it actual. That this is a rather special sort of production is clear from the fact that is is likened to the way an art produces its result. On the standard account of *De Generatione et Corruptione* I.7 there are two kinds of productive agent [τὸ ποιοῦν]: where what produces does not have the same matter as what is affected, it is possible that it move without being moved itself (324a24–34). Thus, whereas wine produces health by itself being affected, the doctor manages this without suffering change. So too for the *art* of medicine (324b5–7), which, thus, rates as an unaffected producer [τὰ ἀπάθη τῶν ποιητιμῶν].

23. Some might retain "ὥσπεϱ" on the grounds that sometimes it is used to soften or apologize for introduction of a locution that is out of context (see *LSJ*, 2040). For in the present case a principle from the theory of nature is suddenly enlisted to explicate a point about the mind. I note that Furley (1963, 49) reads the relation between mind and nature as one of analogy.

24. Even had Aristotle written "each thing" rather than "each *kind* of thing," there would be no warrant for identifying the productive factor in nature with the prime mover. Exploiting the scope ambiguity of the quantifier expressions "ἐν ἁπάσῃ τῇ φύσει" (in the whole of nature), "ἑκάστῳ" (in each case), and "τῷ ποιεῖν πάντα" (by making everything), we could adopt [1A] (y) (∃x) (y is in nature ⊃ x produces y) rather than [1B] (∃x) (y) (y is in nature ⊃ x produces y) as the correct (partial) reading of the text. Besides this, 1B would, for the case of mind, require that some account be forthcoming of the relation between individual thinking and the master activity of a single global productive mind. But Aristotle nowhere even hints at the need for such an account (in contrast, incidentally, to Averroës and Avicenna), and it is difficult to see what it would consist in. In particular, adoption of 1B, or something like it, would seem to preclude an account of *individual* noetic activity. But see the next chapter for a current attempt to resuscitate 1B.

25. See, for instance, *De Generatione et Corruptione* I.7 and *Metaphysica* IX.8.

Aristotle appears, then, to be urging that productive mind will, like an art, produce thinking or an object of thought without itself being affected. Since this was one of the features of the mind advertised in *De Anima* III.4 as well as in III.5, it is unsurprising, given our hypothesis, that III.5 should explain this in terms of one of the mind's structural features.[26]

There is a related point here. In *De Anima* III.2 and elsewhere Aristotle points out that it is not necessary for what produces movement to be moved itself. Just as the object of perception is not affected when it causes perception so also the object of thought is unaffected when it brings a system to active thought. The difference is that the first is a system-external item, whereas the object of thought is, in some sense, internal to the system. But in both cases the appropriate faculty is actualized, by the presence of the object—other things being equal, of course. For productive mind to "operate" is just for an object of thought to be present. Consequently, were it affected in so doing, there might be some temptation to suppose that the object produced was also affected in bringing the mind to thought. But this would run against the rule. It would also have the consequence that one could never think of quite the same object that one had "in mind," as it were. For in the very thinking the object would be affected.

It might be objected that although the first part of the passage allows for the above interpretation its sequel does not. So we must square our account first with Aristotle's characterization of the two parts of mind and then with the traits assigned to productive mind. The passage at 430a14–17 explains the first as follows:

> And there is, on the one hand, a mind that is of this sort by becoming all things [ὁ τοιοῦτος νοῦς τῷ πάντα γίνεσθαι] and, on the other hand, one that is of this sort by making all things [ὁ τῷ πάντα ποιεῖν], as a sort of disposition such as light [ὡς ἕξις τις, ὃιον τὸ φῶς]. For in some way, too, light makes colors that are potential [τὰ δυνάμει ὄντα χρώματα] into colors that are actual [ἐνεργείᾳ χρώματα].

Since I am suggesting that the above passage, and *De Anima* III.5 in general, attempt an explanation of individual noetic activity, the mind or minds here introduced must be the same as that discussed in *De Anima*

26. It is clear from *Metaphysica* IX.8 that producer unaffectability is the intended point of analogy. The passage at 1050a30–b1 distinguishes production that results in something apart from the producer from that which does not. In the former, exemplified by building, the activity [ἐνέργεια] is in the result; in the latter, exemplified by theoretical thinking, the activity is in the producer [ἐν τῷ θεωροῦντι]. See also 417b8–9's remark that the man of practical intelligence no more changes when he thinks than does the builder when he builds. Compare Düring (1966, 581).

III.4. For the latter is clearly the individual mind. In particular the distinction between productive and receptive mind is to be connected with the mind described in 429b5–9 (see section 1 of this chapter) and with 429b22–25's puzzle about how the mind can think at all if thinking is something like being affected.

An additional remark on this passage is in order. The point I wish to stress is that even when the mind is actually$_2$ thinking of, say, a triangle, it is potentially thinking all other objects of thought. This is essential to any account of the activity of thought because the mind cannot actually$_2$ think two objects of thought at one and the same time, yet it must be possible for it to actually$_2$ think another object at a later time. If, to reinvoke our puzzle, thinking were *only* being affected, the latter condition could not be met. Since, we have seen, it is clearly the case that thinking is at least something like being affected, there must be some other feature of thought that allows for the actually$_2$ thinking mind to think other thoughts. This additional feature is, I submit, nothing other than the productive mind of *De Anima* III.5.

Obviously, nothing like productive mind would be required were thought like perception in point of the causal efficacy of its object. For perceivings change at change of object perceived and without agency on the part of the subject. But nothing of this sort is available in the case of thought, where the mind itself creates the object that produces thinking. So, if *De Anima* III.5 attempts an answer or partial answer to the puzzle raised at 429b22–25, then it is unsurprising that the distinction between productive and receptive mind completes the account of individual mind sketched in *De Anima* III.4.

On the interpretation here offered, that productive mind makes all things simply states a condition on the mind actively thinking an object. The mind is productive just in the sense that the object it happens at t to actually think was prior to t potentially an object of such thought and, in accordance with M, in producing the object at t it produces itself as well.

Other commentators have attempted stronger readings. Ross, for example, suggests that productive mind "*divines* the existence of abstractions that are never presented in experience" (1961, 47). He claims support for this reading by urging its power to explain why receptive mind cannot survive death, namely, because it depends on sense perception. Mathematical thinking does not, however, and so is made the exclusive business of productive mind. Philip objects that Ross's view is prima facie implausible because it has no antecedents in the history of commentary on *De Anima* (1962, 199). But there are more conclusive objections to Ross's view. First, restriction of productive mind to mathematical thinking requires reading "τῷ ποεῖν πάντα" (by making all things) as short for "by making all *mathematical* things."[27] This is implausible at best. Second, the alleged support actually tells against the reading. For Aristotle makes clear that images are required for mathematical thinking. Thus, it would follow that such thought and, hence, by Ross's own argument, productive mind cannot survive death.

Hartman takes a slightly different line. Following Aquinas, he charges productive mind with the task of concept acquisition. Productive mind constantly contemplates all the species and genera in nature (1977, 268) and somehow implants them in receptive mind in conjunction, presumably, with formation of images from experience. For a number of reasons this will not do. First, although mind does seem required for acquisition of concepts, it need not operate in this particular, and admittedly mysterious, way. We have already indicated that mind's role in concept acquisition may lie, at least partially, in its role in language acquisition. Second, there is not even the hint of such a role for productive mind in the "mechanical" account of acquisition of universals in *Analytica Posteriora* II.19. Third, *De Anima* is concerned not with concept acquisition but with activities and functions of individual operating souls. So an interpretation fitting productive mind into such a program will be plainly preferable. Fourth, *De Anima* III.5 itself excludes the suggestion because acquisition of concepts involves acquiring a capability$_2$ but productive mind is concerned with exercising already acquired capabilities of this sort.[28] This was the point of connecting *De Anima* III.5 with the description at *De Anima* III.4, 429b5–9, of individual noetic activity. There simply is no contextual ground for finding in productive mind a concern with concept acquisition.[29]

Nor am I following Barnes's converse suggestion that receptive mind is charged with the task of concept acquisition (1971–72, 112). Of course, mind must somehow acquire concepts and, of course, actively thinking something presupposes a stock of thought-ready concepts. Barnes's suggestion has the merit of locating acquisition in structures that are linked with induction; but I prefer a receptive mind that contains the results of induction

27. I have noted that Furley (1963, 49) lodges a similar complaint.

28. Bullinger makes a similar point (1882, 34). Brentano, on the other hand, makes productive mind the directive cause of our thought insofar as it is the "light which, by illuminating images, makes the spiritual element of the sensible graspable for the eye of our spirit" (1977, 180).

29. Hartman attempts to motivate his view contextually by claiming that the account of productive mind is "in the middle of the treatment of thought and abstractness" (1977, 265). But this is curious, for these pages contain no discussion of abstraction in the sense needed for Hartman's version of productive mind. The same point applies to Aquinas's account (1951, 428).

rather than one that guides the process. I am not, thereby, denying that νοῦς may play an active role in concept acquisition. My point is simply that *De Anima* III.5 is not concerned with concept acquisition at all. Barnes argues for the view on the strength of 429b5–9, but that passage shows no interest in the topic of concept acquisition but only in that of actual concept use.[30] *De Anima* III.5 plays out the two aspects of such use.

4. THE ANALOGY BETWEEN PRODUCTIVE MIND AND LIGHT

Aristotle pursues the account by analogizing productive mind to light. The force of the analogy is easily missed if we neglect certain features of Aristotle's views on light. For our purposes it will be sufficient to consider 418b9–13:

> Light is the activity [ἐνέργεια] of this, the transparent qua transparent [τοῦ διαφανοῦς ᾗ διαφανές]. Potentially, whenever this is, there is also darkness. Light is a sort of color [οἷον χρῶμα] of the transparent, whenever it is made actually transparent [ὅταν ᾖ ἐντελεχείᾳ διαφανές] by fire or something like the body above [that is, the sun]

with 418a31–b2:

> All color is capable of changing that which is actually transparent [τοῦ κατ' ἐνέργειαν διαφανοῦς] and this is its nature.

and 418b18–19:

> Since darkness is the privation of this sort of disposition [τοιαύτης ἕξεως] from the transparent, light is the presence of this [ἡ τούτου παρουσία].

On a number of points it is clear that Aristotle means the analogy to be taken seriously and in some detail. The passage at 418a31–b2, for instance, supports our linking of the "puzzles" of *De Anima* III.4 to the doctrine of productive mind by urging that it is in the *nature* of the actually transparent that it change from one color to another. Analogously, it is in the *nature* of an actually₂ contemplating mind that its object change. Indeed, this is a requirement productive mind is tailored to fit. Further, because what is

---

30. This is clear from parallel passages in *De Anima* II.5 and *Physica* VIII.4. (See n. 13 above.) We return to 429b5–9 in the next chapter.

actually transparent will always be a certain color, the actually transparent does change qua red, say, but not qua transparent. Similarly, the actually₂ contemplating mind does change qua, say, triangle because it may contemplate a different object. But qua productive mind itself it cannot change.

Note, also, that although light is the actuality of the transparent qua transparent, it does not follow that light is potentially something else but only that the actual *transparent* that is light is potentially dark. This is important for it counters the long-received view that productive mind is always active. Light, necessarily active whenever occurrent in any sense, need not be and, in fact, is not always occurrent. On our interpretation it is unsurprising to find *De Anima* III.4 already extending this feature of the analogy to the individual mind. Line 430a5 states plainly that subjects, and here is meant individual contemplating minds, are not always thinking. So unless we assume that the analogy is suddenly not to be taken seriously, additional support is forthcoming for our interpretation.

Even more important, however, is the following. Attention to the account of light in *De Anima* II.7 reveals that light is not a causal factor, in any standard sense, in the account of vision. Rather, it is a certain sort of activity that results from the operation of such a standard causal factor on the transparent.[31] Nowadays, this causal factor, characterized by Aristotle as fire and the like, would be described as the source of light itself. Nothing of this sort applies to Aristotle whose theory of light excludes any notion of the propagation of light. The fact that *De Anima* III.5 omits this factor from the mind–light analogy suggests Aristotle's desire to keep us from taking productive mind to have a *standard* causal role. Certainly, *M* gives it no such role.

What Aristotle *does* want to incorporate from the *De Anima* II.7 account is the characterization of light as both an activity and a disposition [ἕξεως, at 418b19]. What can be made of this, at least prima facie, curious dual nature of light? Light, I suggest, is strictly an activity but one that might be called a dispositional activity. Although it does not occur without some color, it need not occur as any given color. For Aristotle light does not come in kinds such as blue light, red light, and so on. The official view that light is a sort of color of the transparent qua transparent does not imply[32] that light is a color that is different from ordinary colors. Rather, it is an activity that, though active, is disposed to take different manifestations and must manifest some color. Referring us back to the *De Anima* discussion, *De*

31. So *De Sensu* VI, 446b27–28: Light exists because of the presence of something but it [light] is not a process [τῷ ἐνεῖναι τι τὸ φῶς ἐστίν, ἀλλ' οὐ κίνησις].
32. Pace, for example, Rist (1966, 12).

Sensu 439a18–19 puts the point more strongly: light is the color of the transparent κατὰ συμβεβηκός, or incidentally.

Indeed, just this view seems to be entailed by a pair of II.7's opening theses. The first (418a29–31) asserts that color, the proper domain of the per se visible, overlies something else (presumably the transparent) that also is per se visible, not in the definitional sense of per se but because of having in it the cause of its visibility. The second thesis (418b4–6) asserts that the transparent is visible not in the strict (presumably definitional) sense of per se visible but because of the color of something else. This is why, as the *De Sensu* passage says, light is the color of the transparent only κατὰ συμβεβηκός. Together these theses imply that light never occurs without some color or other and that it itself is visible only insofar as a given color is visible. Analogous points hold for productive mind and its objects.[33]

The picture I want to extract from the analogy is that of productive mind as nothing more than the activity alone of episodes of individual thinking. In terms of *M* it is the inclusion of productive mind as a structural feature that explains how the mind creates its objects simply by its activity. For this just is its activity.[34] It is also productive mind that explains how thinking is possible, thus, cashing the second promissory note issued at the outset of *De Anima* III.4.

Let me enhance the picture by showing how it accommodates the difficult last sentence of the chapter. Then we shall be in a position to address the more notorious attributes of productive mind. Here is how I read the sentence: "But we are not mindful [οὐ μνημονεύομεν] because this [τοῦτο = νοῦς ποιητικός] is not capable of being affected [ἀπαθές] while receptive mind [ὁ παθητικὸς νοῦς] is perishable; and without this there is no thinking [ἄνευ τούτου οὐθὲν νοεῖ]."

The interpretation I shall suggest fits the lines 430a23–25 into an account of the function and activity of an individual mind. It does so with an ease that is surprising, given the bewildering variety of interpretations so far

---

33. Contrast W. D. Ross, who finds the characterization of productive mind as both ἕξις and ἐνέργεια to be "the most conspicuous instance" (1961, 296) of the carelessness he finds pervasive in III.5.

34. Two passages outside of *De Anima* support our interpretation of what it means to characterize productive mind as a hexis. The first, *Metaphysica* V.20, lists as the first sort of hexis "a sort of activity of the haver and of what he has [ἐνέργειά τις τοῦ ἔχοντας καὶ ἐχομένου]" and says, in agreement with *M*, that this sort of having cannot be had on pain of infinite regress. The second passage, *Metaphysica* XII.7, 1072b19–23, explains the thesis that νοῦς thinks itself (in language, incidentally, that closely reflects feature 7 above) on the grounds that for the mind to be actual is just for it to possess the object of thought [ἐνεργεῖ δὲ ἔχων]. Since this is just the hexis mentioned above, being a hexis of a certain sort is nothing other than having an object. So on this point *M* and *De Anima* III.5 go hand in hand.

advanced. First, I assign as the object of "οὐ μνημονεύομεν" (we are not mindful) productive mind or, more precisely, episodes of productive mind. Whereas we do remember receptive mind or, better, episodes involving receptive mind by virtue of its capacity for images, there is nothing analogous for productive mind. The reason for this is that productive mind is nothing more than the activity, as opposed to the content, of a given episode of thinking. If, for example, I think about something at a given time and later recall the prior thought, what I remember is the object or content of the thought and not the thinking itself. We may be reflexively aware of the activity itself while engaging in it but it drops out as a candidate for memory.[35] It is also clear why Aristotle would raise the issue. Probably only philosophers give attention to the pure activity involved in thinking.[36] Nonreflective thinking, fixed on the object of thought, excludes such thought about thinking and, hence, most thinking subjects are unaware of it. So when Aristotle says that we are not mindful of such thought, he is paying tribute to the fact that we do not notice that aspect of episodes of thinking which is without content.[37]

Second, I take the perishability of receptive mind to amount to the perishability of what occurs in receptive mind rather than to the perishability of receptive mind as a whole (although one *could* talk about *receptive* mind as perishing whenever thinking stops). The passage contrasts what is unaffected [ἀπαθές] with what is perishable [φθαρτός]. So what is perishable is what is capable of being affected, and this, I submit, means just that one state of receptive mind gives way as another comes to be. Appropriately, *De Anima* III.4 requires precisely this of an account of the operation of the individual mind.

Third, the final clause of the sentence, "καὶ ἄνευ τούτου οὐθὲν νοεῖ," fits the entire chapter into an account of individual minds. Exactly how this works, however, is not completely clear. Hicks took the contrast to be between being perishable [φθαρτός] and being eternal [ἀΐδιον] and, hence, reasoned that the final clause asserts the dependence of the conditional part of the contrast (receptive mind) on its unconditioned correlate (productive

35. In this sense 430a23–25 plays out the message of *De Memoria* 450a12–13 that even memory of objects of thought requires images.

36. The analogy with light further supports this line of interpretation. *De Anima* II.7, 418b4–6, says that the transparent is not, strictly speaking, visible in itself [οὐ καθ' αὑτὸ δὲ ὁρατὸν ὡς ἁπλῶς εἰπεῖν] but only because of perceiving the color of something else. Analogously, mind is not, strictly speaking, thinkable in its own right. Thus, not only is it the case that the suggestion that we remember the activity of productive mind turns out to be a nonstarter, but also we have here a view that is obviously of a piece with Aristotle's own account of what is involved in mind thinking itself.

37. Contrast this with Hamlyn (1968, 141), who is unable to find a plausible way to make productive mind the object of "οὐ μνημονεύομεν."

mind). Thus, 430a25 would get the reading "and without the productive mind the mind does not think."[38] Interpretation aside, grammar urges reading ἀπαθές (unaffected) in contrast to φθαρτός (perishable). This plus the fact that receptive mind is that feature of mind which doesn't answer to the activity itself of thinking requires that the last clause be read "and without the productive mind there is no thinking." Thus, the account of De Anima III.4 is finally completed by explaining how one can think autonomously even though thinking is something like being affected: in addition to receptive mind, which is essential for mind's being affected, the individual mind must also be capable of the sort of activity that goes under the heading of productive mind. I do not, of course, mean to imply by this that the two can proceed independently of one another.

Finally, this interpretation gives productive mind a natural and important place in Aristotle's theory of individual noetic activity. It also explains why productive mind appears almost exclusively in De Anima III.5. Since productive mind is required for a conceptually complete analysis of individual νοῦς, the obvious place to introduce the condition is after the discussion of De Anima III.4, which retailed but did not explain the salient features of individual noetic activity. Where explicit analysis of individual mind is not undertaken, no point would be served by mention of productive mind. On the other hand, were νοῦς ποιητικός god or divine reason, one would expect the notion to occur in other contexts. But it is notoriously absent.[39]

5. THE ATTRIBUTES OF PRODUCTIVE MIND

The theory of productive mind just offered faces a final interpretive task. The remaining lines of De Anima III.5, namely, 430a17–23, attribute a number of characteristics to productive mind, characteristics that most commentators assume hold only of an entity such as god or the prime mover. Even Hamlyn accommodates this intuition by making productive mind an abstract entity required as the metaphysical ground of thought. So it will be necessary to show how these prima facie transcendental characteristics can apply to productive mind construed as the activity only of episodes of individual thought. It also turns out that the lines lend support

38. Although Hicks does not say exactly this, it is what he is committed to (1965, 509–10). Hamlyn (1968), on the other hand, explicitly adopts the reading.

39. And if productive mind is elsewhere mentioned, it would appear to be in explicit discussions of thinking, such as Ethica Eudemia 1248a18–29 and, perhaps, Metaphysica XII.7, 1072b19–22. In any case, these passages agree nicely with our interpretation (see chap. 6, sec. 3, on the first passage, and n. 34 above, on the second).

to the hypothesis that III.5's distinction between receptive and productive mind is part of a lower-level explanation of the sort of mind that III.4 discusses, namely, the mind of an ordinary thinking person.

The characteristics I have in mind are, then, typically located in the following passages:

> And this mind [οὗτος ὁ νοῦς] is (a) separable [χωριστός] and (b) not capable of being affected [ἀπαθής] and (c) unmixed [ἀμιγής] since (d) in its being it is activity [τῇ οὐσίᾳ ὢν ἐνέργεια], for (e) what acts [τὸ ποιοῦν] is always superior to what is acted upon and the principle to the matter. (430a17–19)

> And (f) actual knowledge [ἡ κατ᾽ ἐνέργειαν ἐπιστήμη] is the same as the thing but (g) potential knowledge is prior in time in the individual case [ἐν τῷ ἑνί], although in general it is not prior in time [ὅλως δὲ οὐδὲ χρόνῳ]; but (h) it is not the case that it sometimes thinks and sometimes does not [ἀλλ᾽ οὐχ ὁτὲ μὲν νοεῖ ὁτὲ δ᾽ οὐ νοεῖ]. (430a19–22)

> (i) When separated [χωρισθείς] it is just that very thing that it is [μόνον τοῦθ᾽ ὅπερ ἐστί] and this alone [τοῦτο μόνον] is (j) not capable of death [ἀθάνατον] and is (k) eternal [ἀΐδιον]. (430a22–23)

I shall begin with remarks on the possibility that productive mind is here accorded some sort of ontological independence. Easily read in this way is a. Even if this is correct, it is relatively harmless. Given that a is grouped with b and c, the notion of separation here awarded productive mind is too weak to support a Cartesian notion of mind, let alone any doctrine of pre- or postexistence. For suppose b and c referred back to De Anima III.4's arguments for the independence of mind. Can we now take these arguments to pertain to productive mind? Recall that the mentioned arguments show only that mind is independent of body in the sense that mind is not the actualization₁ of any set of physical structures.[40] This is precisely what it means for a faculty to be mixed with body. It also explains the fact that intense objects induce fatigue in faculties that are actualizations₁

---

40. Indeed, as the sense given to "χωριστός" (separate) at the outset of Aristotle's analysis (II.1, 413a3–7), it would appear to govern discussion of separation in the balance of the work. Unless, of course, other indications are forthcoming, as in the "χωρισθείς" (having been separated) at 430a22, discussed below. This is in complete agreement with Aristotle's suggestion (II.2, 413b24–27, and II.3, 415a11–13) that the theoretical part of the soul calls for a different account because this means that, unlike other parts of the soul, νοῦς cannot be treated simply as an actualization₁ of a given set of physical structures.

of physical structures but have no affect on the mind. Such objects produce in the physical structures in question durational states that exclude reception of certain inputs. (See, for instance, *De Anima* II.12, 424a28–32.) In Aristotle's idiom the faculty ceases to be in a mean with respect to these inputs (objects). That the mind in general is not subject to such fatigue requires that receptive mind as well as productive mind be independent of any physical structures in the sense that neither is an actualization$_1$ of such structures. Otherwise, contemplation of a particularly fine object of thought would, after all, inhibit the mind's capacity for thought of lesser objects. It follows that the (receptive) mind is dependent on body in the weak sense that it is not the actualization$_1$ of any specific set of physical structures but only requires such structures as a causal condition for its [re]presentational devices (images). Thus, in no serious sense does *a* countenance separate existence for productive mind. Hence, we remove one temptation to identify productive mind with a transcendent entity.[41]

The sense just given to separation in *a* is especially plausible in light of *d,* which gives as the reason for the separateness of productive mind that its being is activity. No mention of separate existence need be found here. And *b* squares obviously with our interpretation, as does *c,* whether the latter has the sense "unmixed with body" or the sense "unmixed with receptive mind (alternatively, images)."

There is, however, an additional point that demands comment, namely, the fact that *De Anima* III.4 has already listed *a, b,* and *c* among the mind's characteristics. This has inclined a number of commentators toward the view that both receptive and productive minds are separate, unaffected, and unmixed and that they differ on the point, mentioned in *d,* that productive mind is, additionally, activity.[42] Unfortunately, problems arise here. First, the view overlooks the fact that *d* is given not just as another, even if distinguishing, feature of productive mind but rather as the *reason* for productive mind being separate, unaffected, and mixed.[43] Second, III.5 certainly appears to deny just these features of receptive mind, so how can

41. It might be urged that *b* and *c* manage to contrast productive and receptive mind, even if *a* is understood not as separate from body but as separate from receptive mind. Here productive mind would not be dependent even in this weak sense. But there is no reason to find in this a claim stronger than that the noetic feature determined by productive mind does not properly involve images. It is sufficient to hold that the purely active feature of an episode of thinking can, for purposes of analysis, be separated from its given content at any given moment. This, incidentally, is quite like the manner in which light is distinct from the transparent and from any given color of the transparent.

42. For example, Hicks (1965, 502), and Rodier, who goes so far as to urge that *a, b,* and *c* apply in *different* senses to receptive and to productive mind (1900, 460–63).

43. This, at least, appears to be the most natural reading of the participial clause, "τῇ οὐσίᾳ ὢν ἐνέϱγεια," at 430a18.

III.4 be supposed to attribute them to it? The mind of which *a, b,* and *c* are properties, namely, productive mind, is referred to by means of the indicator expression "οὗτος ὁ νοῦς" ("this mind"), and this would seem to imply that they are *not* properties of that "other" mind, namely, receptive mind or the mind that becomes all things. Finally, there is III.5's assertion that receptive mind is perishable. If, as Brentano (1967) thought, *a-, b-,* and *c-* characterized items are eternal (a somewhat dubious proposition), then III.4's mind could hardly be the same as III.5's receptive mind. Brentano's rather drastic solution was to deny that the mind that becomes all things, what he called the *aufnehmende Vernunft* and took to be the subject of III.4, is the same as that which is said to be perishable (ὁ παθητικὸς νοῦς at 430a24). This he took to be the imagination.[44] Unfortunately, Brentano's solution would have us believe that Aristotle introduces in the final sentence of the chapter, without warning or explanation, a completely new sort of νοῦς. This is difficult at best. Moreover, the context of *De Anima* runs counter to Brentano's solution. For *De Anima* III.3 argues against the identification of νοῦς with φαντασία and III.8 is emphatic in denying that thoughts are images. Since the latter are just what the canonical imagination generates, III.8 would appear to be equally emphatic in denying extension of νοῦς to φαντασία—unless we are to suppose that the notion of νοῦς employed in *De Anima* III.4–5 is different from that found in flanking chapters. Surely, this is undesirable.[45]

My solution would be to deny that III.4 means to address receptive mind in the first place. Here it is important to emphasize that we do not take the mind in potentiality [νοῦς δυνάμει] of 429b30–31 in III.4 to be the same as III.5's νοῦς that becomes all things. And since we do not take receptive mind to differ from ὁ παθητικὸς νοῦς, neither is the latter meant to be

---

44. Thus, he appears to follow Proclus, although unaware of the fact.

45. Driscoll has now reminded me that Brentano (1967, 141) tries to meet the objection that νοῦς cannot be stretched so far as to include φαντασία: "That the imagination, though it belongs to the sensitive part, should be called νοῦς is in no way remarkable. In the *Ethica Nicomachea* Aristotle once called sensation . . . itself νοῦς [Z 12, 1143b4]. But imagination he often counts with thinking . . . as, for example, in chapter 3 of *De Anima* [427b27], and calls it νοῦς and a kind of knowledge [νόησις], as, for example, in chapter 10 of the same book. 'But it appears,' as he says there, 'that one of these two is the source of movement, either the desire or thinking (νοῦς), if indeed one regards imagination as a kind of thought (ὡς νόησίν τινα) and comprehends it under that name [433a9–10]" But, as chap. 3, sec. 2, shows, the *De Anima* passages do not establish the point and the passage from the *Ethica Nicomachea* is notoriously difficult. In context, it probably means to underscore the point that agents must be capable of recognizing, on sight, the means determined by a practical syllogism and that this, in turn, requires the ability to recognize specific *kinds* of things. Thus, the passage need say no more than what we have already witnessed, namely, that νοῦς is involved in judgments of the form "This is F." This hardly amounts to treating αἴσθησις as a kind of νοῦς.

addressed in III.4. Rather, the "potential" mind of III.4 is simply the ordinary, intentional-level mind that happens not to be actually$_2$ thinking. As
such, the expression "νοῦς δυνάμει" gives us a way of talking about what
a subject is capable of, noetically speaking. Receptive and productive minds
are mechanisms rung in to explain how that capability is exercised. So the
subject of III.4 is simply the individual mind of the ordinary person and
III.5 provides a (partial) account of how it must be organized to function
in the way it does. To reintroduce the language of levels of explanation, we
might put the point as follows. Where S is a person, we may characterize
S as an 0-level system. Suppose we then say that S thinks in virtue of one
of its subsystems, say S$_1$. My proposal is that the mind of III.4 is just S$_1$.
But when we reflect on what S does or, better, on what S$_1$ enables S to do,
we realize that a more complex account is required. In particular, we must
be able to account for the fact that S is able to think of its (in principle)
unlimited objects *autonomously and spontaneously*. To explain this S$_1$, the mind
must be broken down yet further into lower-level subsystems, S$_2^R$ and S$_2^P$,
and these are just the receptive and productive minds of *De Anima* III.5.
Properties of the higher-level system, in this case the ordinary mind, are
explained by appeal to lower-level features. So the reason that individual
mind is separate, unaffected, and unmixed will be that productive mind
has these characteristics.

The structure of the passage can be made to support this in the following
way. Notice not only that *d* is the reason for productive mind enjoying *a*,
b, and *c* but also that *e* explains *why d* is the reason. This suggests that
Aristotle's reasoning involves the following principles:

8. If (i) what produces is superior to what is affected & (ii) productive mind is the purely active feature in thinking & (iii)
   what produces in the case of thinking is the purely active feature, then (iv) productive mind is superior to receptive mind[46]

and

9. If iv & (v) individual mind has superior qualities *a, b,* and *c*,
   then (vi) productive mind has *a, b* and *c*.

Asserted in the passage are i and ii, and iii follows from the general principle
that what produces must always be something actual. So, if we may assume
that separateness, unaffectedness, and unmixedness are superior qualities,
at least in the context of III.4, then we may assert vi. Thus, the passage

46. As we shall see in the next chapter, *Metaphysica* XII.9. 1074b17–21, makes use of 8,
or at least something very like it.

can be construed without requiring that receptive mind also is separate, unaffected, and unmixed.

More needs to be said, however, for 9 allows us to say that productive mind has the features in question but not that this explains why *individual* mind has them. And just this is demanded by our interpretation. The following principle, stated at *Metaphysica* 993b24–27 and *Analytica Posteriora* 72a29–33,[47] may help:

PT. If x has F because of y, then a fortiori y has F.

Just as the *Analytica Posteriora* ranks as better known those propositions in virtue of which another is known so also might not Aristotle here hold that, if individual mind is separate, unaffected, and unmixed because of productive mind, then a fortiori productive mind has these features? And just as the *explanation* of P's knowability involves appeal to the superior knowability of some Q so also the . . . *explanation* of individual mind's separability involves appeal to the superior separability of productive mind.

The above interpretation would benefit from a more direct account of how PT applies to the case at hand.[48] Taking the lead from *d,* the suggestion I want to advance is this: it is because of the nature of its *activity* that individual mind must be separate, unaffected, and unmixed; and it is because individual mind enjoys such activity *in virtue of* productive mind that productive mind itself must be separate, unaffected, and unmixed.

Roughly, the idea is that, unlike other kinds of cognitive activity, noetic activity is not the activity *of* any set of physical structures.[49] Recall that faculties are distinguished in terms of their objects. Since, for all cognitive faculties, the activity, or faculty in activity, is somehow the same as its object, restriction on range of objects will entail restriction on range of activity and this in turn, I am suggesting, enforces a corresponding restriction on the physical structures that are the *loci* of the activities in question.[50] It would, thus, follow that any faculty whose range of objects is limited must itself be unseparate, affected, and mixed *because* its activity is, in part

47. "A thing has an attribute more than other things, if it is in virtue of it that the same quality [τὸ συνώνυμον] belongs also to the other things" and "for that by which an attribute belongs to something always has it more," respectively. I note that Proclus cites PT (11 of Morrow).

48. It is, for instance, clear from examples alone how PT applies to the case of scientific knowledge. For Q to be more knowable than P is, at least, for Q to be logically independent of P, but not conversely. Thus, the proposition that planets are proximate heavenly bodies can be known apart from propositions it explains, propositions such as that planets twinkle.

49. Thus *De Generatione Animalium* II.3, 736b22–29, especially b28–29: "for the activity of mind has nothing in common with bodily activity."

50. This move needs more argument. Perhaps the discussion in *De Anima* III.1 concerning the exhaustiveness of the five senses contains the seeds of such an argument.

at least, the activity of certain physical structures. In short, object individuation goes hand in hand with organ individuation.

The fact that mind's objects are unrestricted means, then, that its activity is not the activity *of* any set of physical structures. Now, of course, one might respond that this supports the view that receptive mind also is *a-*, *b-*, and *c-* characterizable. In view of the above paragraph, however, it is unclear why anyone would say this. For, if I am right, ascribing *a*, *b*, and *c* to receptive mind will not, in any case, *explain* why individual mind has these qualities, for such an explanation must proceed in terms of noetic activity and here it is productive mind that plays the crucial role. So it is indeed understandable that III.5 would attach *a*, *b*, and *c* to productive mind alone.

We come now to *f*, *g*, and *h*. Although Ross brackets the entire passage, it is in fact quite at home in the chapter.[51] First, Aristotle has just finished a discussion whose interpretation makes use of the thesis of sameness of object and active faculty (the Sameness Thesis); second, the sameness is one of the features (namely, 7 above) III.4 attributes to individual mind; and

51. Ross's arguments for bracketing 430a19–21 are curious at best. First, 430a19–20 reappears at 431a1–3. Although Alexander obelizes the latter lines (Brentano and Rodier are comfortable with them at both places), Ross thinks they fit better in III.7 because that chapter he regards anyway as a "collection of scraps." This is surely a bizarre sense of fit. Second, the text is alleged to read more smoothly without the lines: "this sort of mind is separable . . . and when it has been separated . . ." But notice that the first argument does not justify bracketing 430a22 (our *h*) and the second argument requires bracketing from "ἀεὶ γὰρ..." in 430a18 (our *e*). Thus, Ross's arguments recommend bracketing a full third of the chapter! (I have noticed that Furley (1963) complained about the first bit of bracketing.)

Surely a more acceptable alternative should be sought. I prefer to keep the lines at both places, admittedly for self-serving reasons. In III.7 they are followed by "ἔστι γὰρ ἐξ ἐντελεχείᾳ ὄντος πάντα τὰ γιγνόμενα" (for everything that comes to be is from something that is complete). This line is plainly intended to explain the fact, registered in *g*, that in the individual case potential knowledge is temporally prior but in general not. The idea, I suggest, is that prior to actually thinking O, a subject S is only potentially thinking O because S's actually thinking O requires that there be something complete that causes it to so think. Since in the case at hand it is not actually thinking O, the requirement can be satisfied only if something complete causes S, or perhaps, S's νοῦς to actually think O. This, I submit, is just the νοητόν produced by productive mind. In short, then, the distinction between productive and receptive mind is part of Aristotle's account of how νόησις squares with the general principle enunciated in the "ἀεὶ γὰρ" clause. Notice that *g* does not imply that actual knowledge *is* temporally prior in general, although of course it may be, but only that potential knowledge is not. This is all he needs to assert in order to make the point we are attributing to him. Finally, this interpretation is supported by what Aristotle does in the lines following the clause. Addressing the case of αἴσθησις, Aristotle asserts that it is the αἰσθητόν that raises the perceptual faculty from potentiality to actuality [τὸ αἰσθητὸν ἐκ δυνάμει ὄντος τοῦ αἰσθητικοῦ ἐνεργείᾳ]. So not only are arguments for excision of the lines weak, but retaining them strengthens our general interpretation of the theory of νοῦς in III.4 and 5. Indeed, if Aristotle wrote III.7 with III.4 and 5 in mind (in the manner we have suggested), then he might have registered this by replicating earlier idioms.

third, the solution to how mind can think itself is given in terms of the Sameness Thesis. So, if nothing else, *f, g,* and *h* serve to make exact the sense we are to give to the sameness of mind and object.

Earlier promises notwithstanding, it is appropriate to say something here about the thesis (call it A) that mind thinks itself because of its connection with the thesis (B) that mind and object of thought are the same. That there is a connection is clear enough: the entailment from A to B is asserted at 429b5–9 and explained at 430a2–5. What is in question is the meaning of B. There are, initially, four ways one might take B: (B1) mind introspects or intuitively grasps itself; (B2) mind studies itself as just another object of scientific investigation; (B3) mind can retail its contents and this amounts to mind knowing itself; (B4) mind thinks itself in thinking any proper object of thought (an object without matter). Since I favor B4, something should be said about the alternatives. B1 is a difficult doctrine in its own right and there is virtually no evidence to support its attribution to Aristotle. Indeed, our discussion so far (see n. 36 above) indicates that we are aware of the mind only insofar as we are aware of particular thoughts it has. B2 is true, witness *De Anima* itself, but irrelevant. III.4 and 5 do not even pretend to be addressing the *program* of *De Anima* but clearly are treating a specific topic that arises in the course of carrying out the program. Further, Aristotle's explanation of the possibility of B, namely, a certain version of A, suggests not B2 but B3 or B4. But B3 is difficult because, if to know mind's contents is for mind to know itself, then it seems that mind will have to know some complete set of objects. But this is an implausible reading of A, for 429b5–6 says whenever the mind has become *each* thing [= ἕκαστα and not ἅπαντα which would be better for "all"]. Besides this, B3 denies B any interesting theoretical role in the account of noetic activity. B4, on the other hand, squares with the explanation at 430a2–5 and makes B part of a theory of thought.

Taken together, *f, g,* and *h* appear to be addressing the following interesting issue. At the end of III.4 (430a6) Aristotle says that we must consider why we are not always thinking. Since this query comes on the heels of the assertion that theoretical knowledge is one with its object and since this is just what *f* says, the passage as a whole might be cashing the III.4 promissory note. This, at any rate, is the suggestion I want to try out.

Given the sameness of actual knowledge and its object (*f*) and the fact that what is known is an eternal feature of the world, there may be some temptation (registered, we may suppose, in the promissory note) to think that individuals are also eternally in possession of actual knowledge. After all, the mind in activity is said to be the same as its object. But *g* neatly rules this out by emphasizing that in the individual case, which is the case that concerns Aristotle, potential rather than actual knowledge is temporally prior. There are, however, at least two ways to take this. Read with, for example, *Metaphysica* IX.8, 1049b17–1050a3, *g* might mean to assert that actual knowledge is prior in general because for any individual to acquire the knowledge that P is for him to acquire the ability to exercise that knowledge and this presupposes that tokens of such actual knowledge already exist. How else would one learn? Since, however, III.4 and 5 show little interest in knowledge acquisition as opposed to its exercise, an alternative account would be preferable.

Metaphysica VII.1 suggests a nongenetic notion of priority in time. Adapted to the case at hand, we get something like the following:

> PR. x's potential knowledge that P is prior in time to x's actual knowledge that P ≡ x's potentially knowing at t that P does not depend on x's actually knowing at t that P & x's actually knowing at t that P does depend on x's potentially knowing at t that P.[52]

In our earlier idiom, being an actual₂ knower entails being an actual₁ knower but not conversely. On this reading, *g* is about episodes of thinking and heads off a potential difficulty for the account of individual thought.

But if this is correct, what role is *h* supposed to play? What else but a transcendent entity could do justice to such an impressive characteristic? Since *we* plainly are not always thinking, the subject of "νοεῖ" (thinks) would appear to be god or an appropriate transcendent analogue. This, at least, is the received view. But so far from implying, as this requires, that the subject of "νοεῖ" is always thinking, *h* need yield nothing more than what it literally says, namely, that *it is not the case that there is something that at one time thinks and at another time does not think.*[53] In effect, *h* simply denies the existential proposition that there exists a special entity for thinking such that it sometimes thinks and sometimes does not. Again, the parallel with light is instructive. For there it is obviously mistaken to suppose that light

52. The passage at 1028a33–34 glosses the primacy in time of substance: "of items in the other categories, none can exist separately, but only substance." This comes out, roughly, in the formulation "x is an accident (particular) & x exists at $t \supset$ there exists at t a substance y & x is in y." I am pleased to note that Patzig (1977, 43) now suggests a similar reading.

53. Most recently, Sorabji takes the unduly strong reading (1982, 305). It is also the view of Merlan (1967). In fact, *h* is almost universally held to say that productive mind is always thinking. But, as we have shown, *h* says no such thing at all and, were it to, it would flatly contradict *De Anima* III.4, 430a5's assertion that we are not always thinking. Hicks (1965, 505) registers but does not resolve the "glaring contradiction." W. D. Ross (1961) leaves *h* without comment but probably bracketed it for the same reason (see n. 51 above). Others, for example, Brentano (1977), avoid contradiction by making divine mind the subject of *h*. But this proliferation of subjects is not needed.

is the sort of thing that is sometimes active and sometimes not. It just is a sort of activity and, hence, is either active or simply nonoccurrent. This is exactly what Aristotle needs to say at this point. For having shown in *g* that his theory does not have the undesirable consequence that individual mind is always thinking, it might then be supposed that individual productive mind must sometimes exist but not think. So Aristotle is quick to point out that productive mind simply isn't an entity of this sort. Socrates may well be such an entity but productive mind surely is not. Indeed, it is not an entity in the usual sense at all. After all, it is odd to talk of light as an entity. So *h* can be reconciled with construing productive mind as the activity solely of individual episodes of thinking.[54] It hardly needs pointing out that anyone who held *M* would also be committed to *h*. Aristotle's explicit mention of *h*, thus, counts in favor of attributing to him *M* or something like it.

What about the admittedly more difficult *i*, *j*, and *k*? Surely, it would seem, immortality and eternality attach to none but transcendent entities. That appearances may well deceive in this case is, however, suggested by the fact that in *i* Aristotle introduces *j* and *k* by a quite deliberate use of the aorist participle "χωρισθείς" rather than the "χωριστός" (separate) already available from 430a17. Indeed, the latter would have Aristotle simply repeating himself.[55] Clearly something new is afoot, but what? Recall that the sense given to "χωριστός" in *a* was not strong enough to yield immortality and eternality. So Aristotle's choice of the aorist participle arguably signals not only that some different sense of separation is meant but also, and in particular, that the separation is sufficient for some sort of ascription of immortality and eternality to productive mind. What is needed is an account of *i* that accommodates *j* and *k* within our general naturalistic reading for *De Anima*.

The first of two strategies I shall suggest for accommodation assumes with Zabarella and Hicks that occurrence of the aorist participle in *i* imposes at least one constraint on interpretation, namely, that the separation is to have occurred in past time. (But see note 56 below.) But, of course, productive mind may rate either as an individual or as a divine affair. This

---

54. Lacking an interpretation of the line, Torstrik (1970) urged excision of "οὐχ" (not), thus, making *h* a repeat of *De Anima* III.4. Brentano (1977, 183) retains "οὐχ" but takes the subject of "νοεῖ" to be divine νοῦς but not productive mind. This view, which commits *De Anima* III.5 to three where only two kinds of mind are indicated, is offered strictly *faute de mieux*.

55. Although some would translate "χωριστός" in *a* as "separate," "separable" is happier in light of the "χωρισθείς" in *i*. But either is acceptable given a sufficiently weak reading for "χωριστός."

plus the option of reading "χωρισθείς" either extensionally or notionally yields the following possibilities for *i:*

*i*1. when divine productive mind is extensionally separated
*i*2. when divine productive mind is notionally separated
*i*3. when individual productive mind is extensionally separated
*i*4. when individual productive mind is notionally separated.

On *i*1 it would follow, given the aorist participle, that at some time in the past divine mind, singly or severally, was separated and so that it was previously unseparated. Since to be unseparated from receptive mind is to be unseparated from matter, *i*1 requires that at one time the divine mind was not separate from matter. But by definition, as well as by proof (of the unmoved mover), it is impossible that divine mind be connected with matter. So *i*1 will not do.

If we construe notional separation as separation by abstraction, then *i*2 is not better off. For Aristotle abstraction is always abstraction from something, typically something material. So, again, it can't be divine mind that is separated by abstraction. And this certainly squares with *j* and *k,* for what would be meant, in any case, by attributing, *in abstraction,* immortality and eternality to the divine mind?

The third possibility, *i*3, commits Aristotle to some sort of individual immortality, not for all individual mind but at least for individual productive mind. Since here there will be no memory, perception, and the like, proponents of *i*3 must urge that what thus postexists the individual is entirely without content. This, of course, raises serious problems about the individuation of such allegedly individual entities. If we finally cannot say what would count as having two as opposed to one such entity on our hands, then either *i*3 is internally objectionable or it collapses into *i*1. In either case it fares ill. It would also be rather odd for Aristotle to interject discussion of individual immortality into a context where it serves no apparent purpose. Such objections notwithstanding, for our purposes it is sufficient to provide a credible nontranscendentalistic interpretation.

The remaining candidate is *i*4. As Hicks (1965) indicates, there is nothing objectionable about taking the aorist of the active verb to cover separation by abstraction. Less clear, however, and what Hicks doesn't address, is how *j* and *k* can be fit into the abstractionist account. One place to start is with the *Metaphysica* VI.1 contrast, discussed in chapter 1, between the objects of mathematics and the objects of theology. The objects of theology are extensionally separate [χωριστά] and changeless [ἀκίνητα]; those of mathematics are not. They may, however, be considered as if they were separable and changeless. Since 1026a10 glosses the latter with "eternal" [ἀΐδιον],

we may suppose Aristotle to be saying that mathematics considers its objects as *if* they were separate, changeless, and eternal. *Physica* II.2 takes us
a step further, for there such objects are said to be rendered changeless by
dint of their being separated in thought [χωριστὰ τῇ νοήσει at 193b34]
from change. So the separating is what yields the changelessness and eternality of the objects of mathematics and, on the assumption that "ἀκί
νητον" and "ἀθάνατον" are here interchangeable, we get an exact parallel
with *i, j,* and *k.* Thus, just as separation in thought is what gives the objects
of mathematics apparent transcendental characteristics so also is this the
ground for attribution of immortality and eternality to productive mind in
j and *k.* And just as the objects of mathematics are not extensionally separate
so also for productive mind.

In effect, I am suggesting that we relativize ascription of divine properties, counting them as indicators of the most divine thing in us, not of
anything absolutely divine. In particular, I am urging this even for what
seems to me to be the most difficult case, namely, ascription of immortality.
There is, in fact, independent evidence for relativization. *Ethica Nicomachea*
X.7 grants human beings a restricted share in divinity on the basis of an
ability to engage in *theoria* and urges, therefore, that we do whatever we
can to immortalize [ἀθανατίζειν] ourselves. This can hardly count as making us immortal in the sense of the gods. Hence, it falls short of ascription
of any transcendental property to νοῦς. This is even clearer from *Protrepticus*
B108 (Düring, 1961), which counts νοῦς and φρόνησις alone, of the things
in us, as candidates for divine status. For Aristotle says only that this alone
seems [ἔοικεν] to be immortal and divine. The most this warrants is ascription of a sort of "as-if" immortality to human νοῦς, especially in light
of the following sentences, B109 and 110, which characterize man as a god
relative to other animals because of his νοῦς. (More on these passages in the
next chapter.)

So far, then, from demanding a transcendentalistic interpretation *i, j,*
and *k* can be made to support the opposite. The only sense in which apparent transcendental attributes hold of the mind is that in which a certain
feature, namely, productive mind, has them and, even then, only in the
weak sense of having them in abstraction. It is also clear why, pace Aquinas,
productive but not receptive mind may be so considered. Not everything
is a candidate for abstraction. In particular, nothing whose definition includes or entails matter can be properly considered in abstraction. (See our
discussion in chapter 1.) And, of course, the feature of mind that so requires matter is receptive mind, for an adequate account of receptive mind
will require mention of at least general physical structures. In the idiom of
Metaphysica VI.1 it falls to the study of nature to investigate a certain kind

of soul, namely, that which is not independent of matter. Only productive mind can be *adequately* considered without mention of matter (note here the "τοῦτο μόνον" [this alone] at 430a22) and even then, only if held separate in its own right from receptive mind. Of course, the general account of mind cannot proceed free from such mention because both receptive and productive mind are required for the general account.

A final word is in order regarding how this first strategy makes Aristotle ascribe immortality and eternality to individual productive mind. The parallel with mathematical abstraction is by itself not enough, for we must have some idea of what such an ascription amounts to in its own right. In other words, $i4$ must be held to the condition that an object is suitable for consideration in abstraction, only if there is no such actual object but nevertheless we have some idea of what such an object would be like. For objects of mathematics the condition is unproblematically satisfied; indeed, it is worth conjecturing that they would be suspiciously like Platonic forms. (In this light Plato's "mistake" was to construe notional separateness as ontological separateness.) Individual productive mind seems rather more recalcitrant. Nonetheless, it satisfies the condition in much the same manner. Although not actually immortal and eternal, productive mind may, in abstraction, be safely so regarded because not only do we know what such an object would have to be like but also we have actual examples in the divine intelligences and the unmoved mover.

The second promised strategy for accommodation drops Zabarella's assumption that the separation is to have occurred in past time.[56] Thus, it is able to read i as notionally separating divine productive mind (that is, $i2$). How exactly does this work? Assume that productive mind is a generic or determinable notion whose determinations are, or include, individual as well as divine mind. This requires only that in certain general features individual and divine productive mind are alike. Of course, they differ in certain respects as well. In particular, only the divine version will satisfy j and k. In i, then, separation is an analytical operation specifying for consideration the divine kind of productive mind. Thus, we may paraphrase

---

56. The first strategy can be pursued even if, as I suspect, Zabarella is wrong to insist that the aorist carries a past time constraint. It is enough, to rule out $i1$ and $i2$, that the separation occur at some time. This would, however, not exclude a view on which productive mind, while neither individual nor divine, is nonetheless singular. Here there would be but one productive mind for all individual thinkers (presumably in the way that there is, some argue, just one substantial form per species) and differences in individuals will track differences in receptive minds. Although I applaud the nontranscendentalistic possibilities of this view, it fails to provide any account of how individual thinking comes about. Moreover, if this single productive mind is always thinking (and, as activity, it would have to be), then we have no account of why we are not always thinking. But we have been promised both accounts.

the entire passage as follows: "When one has specified that type of productive mind that can, when all alone, be just what it is, then (unlike
individual productive mind, which is the type that can be separated only
in the weak sense of *a*) we have something that is not capable of death and
is eternal (namely, divine mind)." In short the separating in *i* is something
we do when we consider one rather than another variant of productive mind.
This means, of course, that divine mind makes an appearance in *De Anima*.
But it does so by way of removing itself from the sort of productive mind
that ʾs germane to the *De Anima* account. So that account remains stub-
bornly naturalistic.[57]

I have been arguing that Aristotle's program in *De Anima* does not call
for transcendent entities or properties and that this holds for III.5's productive mind as well.[58] By way of conclusion let me add a final bit of
confirmation for this thesis. In *De Anima* I.1, 403a2–15, Aristotle introduces the topic of mind's separability from body in terms of its dependence,
or lack of dependence, on imagination. If thought depends on imagination,
then even νοῦς will not be separable extensionally. *De Anima* III.8 then
appears to establish the point by arguing, as we have seen, that all thought
requires images. But this may well not be conclusive because the argument
for thought's dependence on images employs a premise that Aristotle himself considers false, namely, that there are no actual things apart from extended things. Recognition of the unmoved mover alone falsifies this.

So it may be that III.8 is not intended to argue a thesis for all thought
but, perhaps, for human thought only. That, in any case, this does no harm
to my argument is clear from the fact that the final sentence of the preceding
chapter raises, but immediately *defers,* the question whether the mind can
think separate objects should it itself lack separateness.[59] What is most
striking here is Aristotle's staunch neutrality on the extensional separability
of νοῦς. Moreover, this is precisely his attitude toward the question at *De*

57. Some readers will notice that I do not consider the possibility that productive mind
is eternal in the way that the species is regarded as eternal, namely, as eternally instantiated
by some member or other of the species. This is because the point will hold not only of
productive mind but also of receptive mind. Indeed, it would appear to hold of all psychological capacities that are characteristic of persons.

58. If I am correct in taking *M* as a general thesis on productive mind, then we may want
it to cover divine mind as well. It turns out that *M* does indeed apply to the unmoved mover
as a self-thinker and in a rather surprising way. We know from *Metaphysica* XII.6 that the
unmoved mover must always exist and by *M* we know that, as a purely thinking thing, it can
manage this only if it always thinks itself. It will, in short, guarantee its eternal existence by
continuously producing itself through eternally thinking itself. So the unmoved mover is just
the limit case of *M*.

59. Thus, pace Düring (1964, 95–96), Aristotle is not championing "Platonic" separation
either for his productive mind or for his forms.

Anima II.2, 413b13–16, and in III.4. In light of this, the contention that III.5 countenances extensional separateness for productive mind loses plausibility, for it asks us to find there an outright assertion of such separateness even though flanking chapters unabashedly promote neutrality. Surely this is asking too much. Besides, if we have succeeded in locating *De Anima* III.5 within a fundamentally functionalist account of individual noetic activity, the question need not arise at all.

6. *DE ANIMA* III.5 AND THE "PARADOXES" OF THOUGHT

Let us end the chapter by returning to a promissory note issued earlier. Section 1 of this chapter closed with the observation that Aristotle's solution to a pair of puzzles left untouched the question of how the mind is able to do what the solution requires. The puzzles concern two questions: (Q1) how will the mind think? and (Q2) can the mind itself be thought? In *De Anima* III.4 Aristotle solves Q1 by exploiting an important difference between thinking and ordinary cases of being affected. Thus, in the case of perception two actual things are involved, one that is affected and another that causes the first to be affected. In the case of thinking, however, there is only a single actual thing because in actual$_2$ thinking the mind is the same as the object that produces the thinking. Q2 appears to enjoy a similar resolution. Where what is thought is an object without matter, the mind is the same as its object and so in such cases it thinks itself. In short, both puzzles are treated by applications of what we have called the Sameness Thesis.

In two respects, however, the solution is unsatisfying. First, in *De Anima* III.4 the Sameness Thesis is used but not explained. The materials for an account of the Sameness Thesis are available elsewhere, but it is enough now to remind ourselves that the thesis is part of an explanation of the internal mechanisms by which we manage to [re]present objects in cognitive acts. The second point of dissatisfaction is that we are given virtually no indication of *how* the mind can operate in a way that avoids the puzzles. Without this, Q1 and Q2 do not have a theoretically satisfying resolution and, thus, Aristotle's theory will fall short of *explaining* mental operations. Of course, these questions count as puzzles only on certain assumptions. In this final section, then, I shall offer a version of the puzzles that makes clear the role of the major assumptions and suggest how the cognitive theory of *De Anima* III.5 is formulated to avoid the puzzles.

Let us begin with the text that generates the first puzzle, 429b22–26:

If the mind [ὁ νοῦς] is simple [ἁπλοῦν] and unaffected [ἀπαθές] and, as Anaxagoras says, has nothing in common with anything [μηθενὶ μηθὲν ἔχει κοινόν], someone might raise the question: how will it think [πῶς νοήσει], if thinking is a kind of being affected [εἰ τὸ νοεῖν πάσχειν τί ἐστιν] (for it is insofar as two things have something in common that the one is thought to act and the other to be affected [τι κοινὸν ἀμφοῖν ὑράπχει, τὸ μὲν ποιεῖν... τὸ δὲ πάσχειν])?

Q1 generates a puzzle given three properties of the mind:

    i. the mind is simple,
    ii. the mind is unaffected,

and

    iii. the mind has nothing in common with anything,

plus two governing assumptions about the structure of thought, namely,

    iv. thinking is a kind of being affected,

and

    v. x acts on y ⊃ x and y have something in common.

We might call ii and iii Anaxagorean assumptions. Line 429a18 appears to attribute a variant of iii to Anaxagoras, namely, that the mind is unmixed [ἀμιγής], and 405b21 appears to credit him with both ii and iii. This raises the immediate question of whether the puzzle about thinking follows from the conjunction of i, ii, and iii or from each separately. In what follows I take the conservative route and develop a version of the puzzle for each of the properties. The properties themselves I take to be properties asserted of the ordinary mind of the ordinary person,[60] and the solution in each case will call for the distinction between productive and receptive mind.

    Let us take the two simplest cases first. The dilemma concerning the property of being ἀπαθές (unaffected) can be formulated simply. From

    1a. iv & (vi) mind thinks ⊃ (vii) mind is affected,

and

    2a. ii ⊃ ~vii

---

60. This is supported to the extent that ii and iii are Anaxagoras's properties, for it is surely implausible to credit him with the lower-level distinction between productive and receptive mind.

we get

    3a. ii & iv &vi ⊃ vii & ~vii.

Because vi is implicit in question Q1, it can hardly be a candidate for rejection. So it must be ii or iv that comes in for scrutiny.

Let us worry about this after looking at the puzzle concerning iii—mind's having nothing in common with anything. Relabeling, we begin with the same initial premise

    1b. iv & vi ⊃ vii,

adding

    2b. vii & (v′) in any case of being affected something, x, acts and something, y, is affected & v ⊃ (viii) mind has something in common with something.

Then, because of

    3b. iii ⊃ ~viii,

it follows that

    4b. iii & iv & vi ⊃ viii & ~viii.

So both Anaxagorean assumptions appear to lead, by virtually parallel arguments, to contradictions.

Finally, what of the mind's alleged simplicity? Is it also intended to set a puzzle for thinking? Some, for example, Hicks, appear to think not. In fact, however, it contains the seeds of a puzzle and one that is especially suggestive for our purposes. For it appears to call for just the sort of cognitive organization that we have taken *De Anima* III.5 to recommend. To see this we need to recall that, insofar as possible, Aristotle wants discourse about the soul to reflect principles of physics. Suppose, then, we begin with two principles from *Physica* VIII.4, 255b30–35 and 255a5–15, respectively:

    1c. (ix) x is affected by y ⊃ x ≠ y v x = y,

and

    2c. (x) x affects y & x = y ⊃ (xi) x has parts, z . . . w, such that z affects w (or, perhaps, y).[61]

61. *Physica* 255a14–15: "it is only insofar as a thing is divided that one part of it is by nature active and another passive [ἢ κεχώρισται, ταύτῃ τὸ μὲν πέφυκε ποιεῖν τὸ δὲ πάσχειν]" with 254b31–33: "It seems that, just as in ships and things that are not organically continuous [e.g., flesh, worms], so also in animals that which causes motion is separate from that which undergoes motion [διῃρημένον τὸ κινοῦν καὶ τὸ κινούμενον] and that in this sense the animal as a whole moves itself [καὶ οὕτω τὸ ἅπαν αὐτὸ αὑτὸ κινεῖν]."

Roughly, the idea is that something can affect itself only insofar as some part of it affects it or another part. But because of

3c. i ⊃ (xii) mind has no parts,

it appears to follow that

4c. i ⊃ mind does not affect itself.

Now, for argument's sake, we take the other disjunct from 1c's consequent,

4c'. (xiii) x is affected by y & x≠y ⊃ (xiv) mind has something
      in common with something else,

whose consequent appears to entail that x is not simple,

4c''. xiv ⊃ is not simple.

So we have

5c. xiii ⊃ is not simple,

which appears to entail

6c. i ⊃ mind is not affected by something different.

In general, then, the mind's simplicity has the apparent consequence that it is not affected. At least

7c. i ⊃ mind is not affected (that is, ~vii)

follows from 1c, 4c, and 6c. But because we still have our familiar, though again relabeled, premise

8c. iv & vi ⊃ vii,

we end up with the contradiction

9c. i & iv & vi ⊃ vii & ~vii.

All the puzzles use iv and vi. Since vi is obviously true, we might expect Aristotle to reject or, at least, modify iv. I think this is, in fact, the case, but before seeing how iv is to be modified in all three puzzles, I would like to look at our last puzzle in more detail. For its diagnosis yields a good deal of information about the structure of a mind that is, in fact, able to think. Let us begin with the observation that Aristotle can't exit from the dilemma by rejecting 4c', that is, the implication that mind needn't have something in common with something else, thus, blocking the move to ~vii in the second half of the dilemma. What Aristotle can do, however, is simply deny xiii, the antecedent of 4c', for mind. This forces us to look at x and its entailment, xi.

My suggestion is that Aristotle wants to adopt a version of xi for mind and so he will countenance a sense in which the mind is not simple after all. Here, roughly, is the proposal. Prior to thinking, the mind has no parts, at least no actual parts, for it is a pure potentiality; when actually₂ thinking, the mind has no parts because it is then nothing but activity. These are both points about the ordinary or, we might say, level-1 mind. Nevertheless, the mind has parts in the following sense. The change from potentiality₂ to actuality₂, what the Framework Passage labeled the change from knowing₂ to knowing₃, requires that productive mind renders a potential₂ object of thought actual₂ and this, in turn, requires mention of both productive and receptive minds. But this distinction operates at a lower level of the system, say, level 2. If "ἁπλοῦν" (simple) in our puzzle-setting passage tracks the use of "ἁπλῶς" in De Anima II.5, then it means something like "without distinction." Thus, Aristotle's dilemma trades on a levels conflation. The notion of simplicity that operates at one level is inappropriate at another. The crucial complication, from our point of view, is that the explanation of *how* thinking comes about requires distinct mechanisms at a lower level of the system of precisely the kind De Anima III.5 recommends.

It is important to reemphasize that we do not take the νοῦς δυνάμει, or mind in potentiality, of 429b30–31 in III.4 to be the same as III.5's νοῦς that becomes all things. Rather, it is the level-1 mind that is not actually₂ thinking. As such it is simply a way of talking about what a subject is capable of, noetically speaking. Receptive and productive mind are mechanisms rung in to explain how the capability is exercised. This, of course, is just our view that III.5 provides a functional organization for just such a mind. Above all, it explains what mechanisms are required for it to make the switch to thinking.

Now, as we already indicated in section 1, 429b29–430a2 purports to extricate mind from our three paradoxes without, however, explaining *how* the mind is able to do what the solution requires. This, we have argued, is the business of De Anima III.5. But because the extrication contains further support for our view of III.5's role, we should take a slightly more extended look at the passage. Following Hamlyn, it reads

> Now being affected in respect of something common [τὸ πάσχειν κατὰ κοινόν τι] has already been discussed—to the effect that the mind somehow is potentially the objects of thought [ὅτι δυνάμει πώς ἐστι τὰ νοητὰ ὁ νοῦς], although it is actually nothing [ἀλλ'

ἐντελεχείᾳ οὐδέν], before it thinks [πρὶν ἂν νοῇ]; potentially in the way that there is writing on a tablet on which nothing actually written exists; that is what happens in the case of the mind [ὅπερ συμβαίνει ἐπὶ τοῦ νοῦ].

Because it focuses on the notion of being affected by something common, this passage appears to suggest that resolution of the puzzles lies in tinkering with iii. I think, however, that it is the *being affected by* rather than the having of something in common that is salient. So we can take the solution as involving a variation on iv or, perhaps, vi. What is crucial is the particular style of mind's being affected. We know that the solution involves two claims: (α) somehow the mind is potentially the objects of thought and (β) in actuality it is none of them before it thinks or perhaps (β⋆) in actuality it is nothing before it thinks. In this context β and β⋆ may well amount to the same thing. Prior to thinking, the mind is a special kind of pure potentiality$_2$ and, hence, is no actual thing simply because it is not yet thinking, that is, simply because it is not yet the same as an object of thought. In any case, 429a22–24 suggests as much by remarking that that in the soul which is called νοῦς is none of the actually existing things before it thinks [οὐθέν ἐστιν ἐνεργείᾳ τῶν ὄντων πρὶν νοεῖν].

How do α and β/β⋆ solve the puzzles? Take the first of the three, that concerning ii, the property of being unaffected [ἀπαθές]. Ross suggested blocking the move to ~vii by simply dropping ii. But ii ⊃ ~vii, only if ii means that the mind is unaffect*able*. If "ἀπαθές" means simply "unaffected," then the inference to "the mind is unaffected" (that is, ~vii) fails.[62] So long as we understand 2a as something like

2a′. The mind is unaffected by O at $t_{(t<t1)}$ ⊃ ◇the mind is affected by O at $t1$,

where O is an object of thought. We may then read 3a as

3a′. The mind is unaffected by O at $t_{(t<t1)}$ & iv & the mind thinks O at $t1$ ⊃ the mind is affected by O at $t1$.

Not only is there no inconsistency here but also 2a′ and 3a′ faithfully reflect the distinction between α and β/β⋆. What is most important, for our purposes at least, is that the solution to the first puzzle requires, but does not say *how* the mind is able to switch from an unaffected to an affected state, how, that is, it is able to actually think.

Might not one object that 2a′ and 3a′ will have analogues for all other

---

62. See Driscoll (1987) for an excellent commentary on this.

faculties as well? Certainly, but this counts in favor of my reading because Aristotle indicates that they are unaffected in rather different ways. Both the sensory faculties and νοῦς satisfy 429a15–16's condition that they be ἀπαθὲς καὶ δεκτικόν τοῦ——, where the blank is filled by a term standing for the faculty's object. If this is an intense object of perception, the faculty is immediately παθὲς καὶ μὴ δεκτικόν (affected and not further capable); not, however, if it is an intense object of thought.

We shall make more of this difference in a moment. But, first, what about the puzzle concerning iii, the supposition that the mind has nothing in common with anything? Ross (1961, 294) again recommends strong medicine and opts for dropping iii, thus blocking the move in 3b to viii & ~viii. Prima facie there are good reasons against a wholesale scrapping of iii. One is that Aristotle seems to like iii at 429a18ff., where the mind is said to know all things and, hence, to be unmixed with anything. If this in turn implies that the mind has nothing in common with anything, then Aristotle can hardly be completely hostile toward iii. Then, at 405b21, left without comment by Ross, Aristotle appears to endorse the Anaxagorean properties ii and iii, complaining that more needs to be said; in particular, he asks, how will the mind know and by what cause [πῶς γνωριεῖ καὶ διὰ τίν' αἰτίαν]?

Armed with 429b29–430a2's distinction between α and β/β*, we can read iii as

iii'. The mind has nothing in common with anything *else*.

When iii is read this way, 3b should be modified accordingly. But, then, the consequent of 3b will be the denial, not of viii, but of

viii'. The mind has something in common with something else.

Because this is not the negation of viii, the contradiction in 4b is avoided. Unless, that is, one were to insist that principle v entails viii'. This would require replacing v' in 2b with

v". x acts on y ⊃ x≠y & x has something in common with y.

But Aristotle's solution rejects v" for the case of mind: where x is an object of thought and y the mind, x is the same as y. This means that what brings νοῦς to activity cannot be something different from it, for then it would have something in common with something else.

Again, the puzzle is blocked and, again, the explanation of how mind can accomplish this is deferred to *De Anima* III.5. Early on in III.4, however, Aristotle hints that it will involve a rather different sort of being affected. To the extent that thinking [νοεῖν] is like perceiving [αἰσθάνεσθαι] it will, says Aristotle, be something like being affected by the object of thought [πάσχειν τι ἂν εἴη ὑπὸ τοῦ νοητοῦ] or something different like this [ἤ τι τοιοῦτον ἕτερον]. Even were Aristotle to opt for the first alternative, thinking will hardly be a standard sort of being affected. First, the indefinite "τι" has a weakening effect here and indicates that thinking is not a kind of being affected in the standard sense at all.[63] Second, De Anima II.5 has, in any case, already counseled that perceiving and thinking are not standard cases of being affected but that they gain the name by courtesy only. (See the discussion in chapter 2, section 2.) If, however, it is the second alternative that fits νοεῖν, then the parallel with αἰσθάνεσθαι is even further weakened, for thinking will involve something different from the already weakened or courtesy notion of being affected that De Anima II.5 applies to perceiving. My suggestion is that this second alternative means precisely to capture the idea that the mind itself produces the νοητόν or object of thought that brings it to activity. This is undeniably a nonstandard sense of being affected [πάσχειν] but it is exactly the sort of thing that is required in order to explain how actual thinking is autonomous and yet caused by the object of thought. It also squares with 429b29–430a2's requirement that the mind can have something in common with what causes it to act without having anything in common with something *else* and, of course, when the mind has done this, it is the same as the object that brought it to activity.

7. THINKING AND THE OBJECT OF THOUGHT

We have observed that Aristotle solves the puzzle concerning how the mind can think itself by insisting that in the case of things without matter the mind in activity is the same as its object and, hence, thinks itself. The solution, in effect, amounts to an application of the thesis that a faculty in operation is the same as its object (the Sameness Thesis). But we also know that what brings the mind to activity, namely, the object of thought, is a universal that is somehow in the soul. Let these theses be more or less contained in the following

    1. a thinks P $\rightarrow$ a's mind is the same as P,
    2. y is a universal $\rightarrow$ y is somehow in the soul itself,

and

---

63. Thus, the indefinite pronoun has the same effect as at 417a14–17, where Aristotle talks of change as sort of an activity [ἡ κίνησις ἐνέργειά τις], and at *Rhetorica* I.1, 1355a4–5, where persuasion is said to be sort of a demonstration [ἡ πίστις ἀπόδειξίς τις]. In neither place can "τις" be supposed to pick out a standard case.

3. *a* thinks → (∃y) (y is a universal & y is the cause of *a*'s mind thinking y.

The theses raise an important question concerning the status of the Sameness Thesis where P is an object without matter. For if P is a universal and is-the-same-as is identity, then there will be, we have pointed out, no individual minds. It is for this reason that we have interpreted sameness as something like formal rather than numerical sameness. But we still have the problem of explaining what it means for a universal to be "somehow in the soul" and how P, the object of an actual₂ operation of a particular system, can be a universal, especially given 3's requirement that this bring the system to activity. Let me sharpen the issue by, first, citing an additional passage that unequivocally separates thinking from perception in terms of the universal and particular nature of their respective objects and, second, turning to two passages that appear to contradict it. The target passage is from *Analytica Posteriora* I.31:

> Knowing is not through perception [οὐδὲ δι' αἰσθήσεως ἔστιν ἐπίστασθαι]; for even if perception is of the such [τοῦ τοιοῦδε] and not of the particular [μὴ τοῦδέ τινος], still what is perceived is necessarily a particular, at a place and at a moment [ἀναγκαῖον τόδε τι καὶ ποῦ καὶ νῦν]. And it is impossible to perceive what is universal [τὸ καθόλου] and holds of everything [ἐπὶ πᾶσαν], for that is not an individual nor at a moment; for then it would not be universal, for it is what is always and everywhere that we call universal. . . . what is perceived is necessarily particular [αἰσθάνεσθαι... ἀνάγκη καθ' ἕκαστον], while knowledge is cognition of the universal [ἡ ἐπιστήμη τὸ τῷ καθόλου γνωρίζειν ἐστίν]. (87b28–39)

This passage, plus others like it, clearly conveys the message that the mind's proper objects are universals. The point obviously needs clarification. We shall turn to this in a moment, but a matter of more immediate and serious concern is that Aristotle himself appears, at least twice, to contradict the message of the target passage. Hamlyn, for instance, locates one contradiction in *De Anima* II.5, 417a28–29, where Aristotle announces that the knower₃ actually₂ and in the strongest sense knows "this particular A" [τόδε τὸ A]. This appears to contradict 3's claim that the object of thinking is the universal. But is 3 really gainsaid by Aristotle's use of "τόδε τὸ A" at 417a28–29 to signify the object of contemplation? Hamlyn takes the phrase to imply that actual knowledge is of a particular, thus, fueling his charge that "Aristotle's confusions in this passage are evident enough, but they are endemic in his thought" (1968, 103). Certainly, the use of upper-case A is not itself sufficient for the point. After all, *Analytica Posteriora* uses them as stand-ins for *general* terms. And the context "τόδε τὸ A" by itself falls short as well. *Metaphysica* VII.3 requires that substance be τόδε τι (individual) and separate, yet substance turns out to be form [εἶδος] as opposed to both the universal compound and the concrete individual, the latter being τὸ καθ' ἕκαστον: Aristotle says at 1035b33–1036a1 that "only parts of the form [εἶδος] are parts of the logos and the logos is of the universal [τοῦ καθόλου]," and in the following lines he remarks that there is no definition of the concrete circle that is one of the particular things [τῶν καθ' ἕκαστά τινος]. Thus, pace Hamlyn, the A in τόδε τὸ A need not be a particular because to be individual [τόδε τι] is not ipso facto to be particular [τὸ καθ' ἕκαστον].

Hamlyn's argument notwithstanding, there is cause for concern because the second point of conflict, a passage from *Metaphysica* XIII.10, seems less amenable to the immediate resolution:

> For knowledge [ἐπιστήμη], just like knowing [ἐπίστασθαι], is twofold—being, on the one hand, in potentiality$_2$ [τὸ δυνάμει] and, on the other hand, in actuality$_2$ [τὸ ἐνεργείᾳ]. The potentiality$_2$ [ἡ δύναμις], being like matter, is universal and indefinite [καθόλου καὶ ἀόριστος] and is about the universal and indefinite [τοῦ καθόλου καὶ ἀορίστου]. But the actuality$_2$ [ἡ ἐνέργεια], being definite, is about the definite and, being individual, is about the individual [τόδε τι οὖσα τοῦδέ τινος]. But sight sees the universal color [τὸ καθόλου χρῶμα] incidentally [κατὰ συμβεβηκός] because the individual color that it sees is color [ὅτι τόδε τὸ χρῶμα ὃ ὁρᾷ χρῶμά ἐστιν]; and the individual alpha that the grammarian investigates is alpha [ὃ θεωρεῖ ὁ γραμματικός, τόδε τὸ ἄλφα ἄλφα]. (1087a15–21)

The first thing to note about this passage is that the final line's "τόδε τὸ ἄλφα" ["this alpha"] appears to match the "τόδε τὸ A" ["this A"] from *De Anima* II.5, for both expressions are linked to the practice of grammar. This appears to neutralize the solution suggested two paragraphs back. So that passage must be read in terms of the fuller account provided by the *Metaphysica* XIII.10 text. In his *De Anima* commentary Ross (1961) does not mention 1087a15–21, but his commentary on the *Metaphysica* makes much of the fact that the passage conflicts with Aristotle's usual doctrine and finds *De Anima* 417a28–29 to be guilty of the same offense. Thus, he joins Hamlyn in accusing Aristotle of an internal inconsistency.

There is, however, something especially alarming about the charge. For one instance of the inconsistency links 417a28–29 with "The reason for this is that active perceiving is of particulars [τῶν καθ᾽ ἕκαστον ἡ κατ᾽ ἐνέργειαν αἴσθησις], whereas knowledge is of universals [ἡ ἐπιστήμη τῶν καθόλου] and these are somehow in the soul itself [ἐν αὐτῇ πῶς ἐστι τῇ ψυχῇ]" (417b22–23), a scant twenty-four lines away. Are we to suppose Aristotle so shortsighted as to have missed this? Hicks (1965) thought not and proposed, in his comment on 417b23, that the way in which [πῶς] universals are in the soul is that explained by De Anima III.8, namely, "in the soul potentially." But this removes the contradiction only if 417b22–23 does not claim that universals are the objects of active₂ knowing. And Ross seems correct to take the lines as implying this. Besides, Hicks's suggestion fails to distinguish appropriately between thought and perception. De Anima III.8 discusses a single sense in which both knowledge and perception are all things, namely, potentially. But because the very point of 417b22–23 is to distinguish knowledge and perception, the way in which the universal is there said to be in the soul must differ from the way in which an object of perception is there said to be in the soul. Hence, appeal to De Anima III.8 will be of little help.

What we need is a consistent account of how knowledge₃ or the mind in active₂ operation can be taken to have universals as its objects. Part of the story is that universals, as opposed to particulars, are in the soul in a way that makes thinking up to us. This is one of the features of thought, registered in 2 of this chapter's first section, that Aristotle's theory was to account for. Since thinking is just a certain style of cognitively grasping universals, grasping or contemplating a universal must be up to us because of its peculiar way of being in the soul. We have already suggested an explanation of this: the mind is able to think autonomously because productive mind at a sublevel of the noetic system produces the νοητόν, or object of thought, that brings the mind or noetic system as a whole to activity. Can we reconcile the apparently conflicting passages in a way that squares with our general theory?

We may begin with the observation that the two senses of knowledge isolated in the Metaphysica XIII.10 passage correspond to those had by the knower₂ and knower₃ of the De Anima II.5's Framework Passage. This is clear from the fact that potential knowledge [δυνάμει] is contrasted with active knowledge [ἐνεργείᾳ] rather than the broader actual knowledge [ἐντελεχίᾳ]. What exactly is involved in the claim that knowledge₃ concerns individuals must be gleaned from the examples given in the passage. For the fuller account of sight we appear to have Aristotle licensing

4A. S sees this/that C & this/that C is C ⊃ S sees C incidentally,

where C is a general term and S, presumably, sees this/that C per se or
καθ' αὐτό. Use of the indexical expressions "τόδε τὸ χρῶμα" (this color)
and "τόδε τὸ ἄλφα" (this alpha) is critical to Aristotle's point and is designed to ensure that the designation of the whole expression is related to
its constituent general term as token to type. As designating expressions,
they are privileged in the sense that they pick out their subjects in terms
of their essence kinds. Even so, 4A will have different readings depending
on whether C = this particular (bit of) color, a certain patch of red, for
example, or whether C = this particular color itself, for example, red. In
the first case, what S sees incidentally will be the universal red; in the
second case, it will be the universal color. Because the object of seeing is
an external particular, the first reading is very likely correct.

We appear then to get an embarrassing parallel for knowledge:

4B. S knows$_3$ this/that α & this/that α is A ⊃ S knows$_3$ A incidentally.

Because it appears to strike an exact parallel between thinking and perceiving, 4B seems to solidify rather than solve the contradiction. But the
embarrassment is, in fact, merely apparent. One point to notice is that the
text does not actually assert that one thinks the universal A only incidentally.
This was forthcoming only on the assumption that an exact parallel was
intended. But suppose, for the moment, that we have, rather, the contrasting case

4B'. S knows$_3$ this/that α & this/that α is A ⊃ S knows$_3$ A per
se.

If we further strengthen 4B' to a biconditional, then we have the beginnings
of an account of what it is to know a universal: namely, it is to know, for
any arbitrary instance of the universal, that it is an instance. One advantage
of this line of argument is that it squares rather nicely with remarks in the
Analytica Posteriora I.1 to the effect that knowledge of universals is a kind
of potential knowledge, namely, knowledge of potential instances of the
universal or universal proposition in question.[64]

If we take 4B' as above, then the following picture emerges. Both actual$_2$
perceiving and knowing (or thinking) are operations of discrete, particular
systems. Nonetheless, both involve universal features but in quite different
ways. The proper object of a perceptual function is a particular, but the
explanation of how the system accomplishes perceiving invokes the claim

---

64. For more on this, see Barnes (1975), especially his commentary on chapter 1, and
Ferejohn (forthcoming).

that what is perceived are instances, as it were, of *kinds* of perceptual input. So 4A fits nicely enough into the theory. What about knowledge? On 4B′ its proper object will be a universal yet the object of actual$_2$ knowing is, in some sense, individual. The need to explain this remains even on 4B, for, in any case, we must preserve the thesis that universals are the objects of knowledge.

What we need is an account of how the actual$_2$ operation of a particular system can amount to knowing something nonparticular. This is not an invented problem but one that genuinely puzzles Aristotle. And it is a problem that arises naturally on the condition that the solution take the form of a certain account of the operations of the particular system in question. So the question is how an operation on exclusively particular structures can amount to knowing something universal. The answer is that the particular structure is regarded as a [re]presentation or, in the style of *De Memoria* (see chapter 4, section 6), as an exemplar of the universal in question. The difference between the two cases is brought out by the different ways each depends on the particular object or item involved in bringing the faculty to activity. It fails to count as perceiving c, if c is replaced by c⋆, even where c and c⋆ are qualitatively identical. It does not, however, fail to count as knowing A, if the particular structures that [re]present A are replaced by other such structures. Nor would it have failed to count as knowing A, had they been different all along. This holds true whether the particular structures are external items, such as marks on a slate board, or internal items, such as images [φαντάσματα]. The fact that any set of appropriate physical structures will do *plus* the fact that φαντάσματα, which are always involved anyway, are [re]presentationally adequate on their own means that operations on physical structures can, in the case of knowledge$_3$, be taken as universally valid because the particular structure or [re]presentation involved in an episode of knowing can be taken as proxy for the object *in any episode*. On this account, for a universal to be in, say, S's soul amounts to saying that S has a certain ability to do something on his own. Not to call up, as it were, the universal itself, this is the Platonist's mistake, but to do something that does the same job but at considerably less cost. This requires endowing S or, better, S's soul with the internal machinery to accomplish the job. This will involve memory, φαντάσματα, and, of course, productive and receptive minds. In short, it will amount to providing a cognitive model for thought. Thus, so far from issuing in contradiction, our account shows how *Metaphysica* XIII.10, and so the mention of τόδε τὸ A in *De Anima* II.5, are part of an explanation of what it means to say that the object of knowledge or thought is the universal.

Not only, then, do the solutions to the "paradoxes" of thought indicate the need for certain internal mechanisms that explain *how* the mind can think; but so also does the alleged inconsistency in Aristotle's notion of the object of thought itself. Locating *De Anima* III. 5's productive and receptive mind at a lower explanatory level in the system is at least part of the story. The fact that these puzzles call out for such an account is surely evidence in our favor. On the other hand, the theory of receptive and productive minds here proposed is anything but standard, especially the theory of productive mind. The attempt to give a naturalistic account of Aristotle's remarks on the mind will be particularly unpopular with those who want to forge a close link between human and divine thought. So in the next chapter we turn to this issue and to two of the chief contenders to our view.[65]

65. Some of the material in this chapter appears in Wedin, 1986 (© 1986 by D. Reidel Publishing Company, Dordrecht, Holland). I am grateful to D. Reidel for permission to use the material.

VI

HUMAN AND
DIVINE MIND

One of the unkept secrets of the corpus is Aristotle's penchant for treating thought as somehow divine. His discussion of mind [νοῦς] and thinking, at least in its theoretical variety [θεωρεῖν], frequently enlists the language of divinity. How, then, can the functionalist account of *De Anima* III.5 expect to succeed? In particular, how can productive mind be given a *non-transcendental* role in such an account? This is answered in part by recalling that *De Anima* III.5 provides a lower-level functionalist account of thinking, one that is tailored to explain the various attributes of acts of thinking at the intentional level. One such attribute of the theoretical variety is its alleged divinity. But what this calls for on the side of productive mind depends on what the attribution of divinity amounts to at the intentional level in these cases. In short, I am suggesting that we interpret the divinity of productive mind in terms of the divinity of the thought it subserves.

The obvious place to begin is with the language of Aristotle's attribution of divinity to human thought. It turns out that this does not call for full-blown divine status for νοῦς. We shall then be in a position to address a deeper argument for upgrading the status of productive mind. This is, roughly, that the divine thought analyzed in *Metaphysica* XII.7 and 9 is essentially the same as human (theoretical) thought and that productive mind must, therefore, be fully divine, perhaps even identical with god. This is sometimes coupled with the claim that only so would productive mind explain how *we* think necessary truths. In the course of this chapter I shall take issue with each of these claims.

1. THOUGHT AND THE LANGUAGE OF DIVINITY

The divinity of human thought is asserted in several places but the locus classicus is *Ethica Nicomachea* X.7 and 8. The formula that controls the entire discussion is given at 1177a13–16. Pinpointing the sort of activity that is to count as happiness, Aristotle says it will be the (best) activity of νοῦς or something else in us that is thought to naturally rule and guide [ὃ κατὰ φύσιν δοκεῖ ἄρχειν καὶ ἡγεῖσθαι] and to have thoughts of the fine and the divine [ἔννοιαν ἔχειν περὶ καλῶν καὶ θείων] *whether* this is also something divine itself or the most divine thing in us [εἴτε θεῖον ὂν καὶ αὐτὸ εἴτε τῶν ἐν ἡμῖν τὸ θειότατον]. The activity is, of course, theoretical activity. But while theoretical activity may have the divine as its object,[1] it does not, as a matter of course, follow that this is activity *of* something that is fully divine. The disjunctive formulation at 1177a13–14 is deliberately cautious and demands nothing more than the best of human equipment. So at the very least the passage establishes that mention of the most divine element in us is not ipso facto mention of god or something divine without qualification.

Nonetheless, one might argue, subsequent discussions establish the full divinity of νοῦς or its better. But this is not borne out by the texts. The passage at 1177a20–b26, which supports the positive claims of *theoria,* does not even mention its divinity. And 1177b26–1178a2 cautions that such a life, the life of theoretic activity, is beyond the human level, for one is capable of this activity not qua man (that is not qua a composite thing) but only qua having something divine in him [ἢ θεῖόν τι ἐν αὐτῷ ὑπάρχει]. Here again Aristotle employs the weak arm of the governing disjunction and proceeds to gloss νοῦς, the best in us at 1177a20–21, as only relatively divine [θεῖον ὁ νοῦς πρὸς τὸν ἄνθρωπον]. Notice, also, that, even thus downgraded, we are urged to achieve immortality only as far as possible [ἐφ᾽ ὅσον ἐνδέχεται ἀθανατίζειν]. If, as we are suggesting, productive mind is to be rung in to explain the relative divinity of theoretical thought, then it must also account for the sense of immortality accorded this activity. And just as that is manifestly weak, something like an "as-if" immortality, so, too, I suggest, the productive mind of *De Anima* III.5 need be given no stronger sense of immortality. The facts to be explained require nothing stronger.

Aristotle closes the case for θεωρία by identifying it explicitly as the activity of god. But his remarks, 1178b7–23, fall short of claiming that the human activity is the same in kind as the activity of the gods. Without need for action or production, the gods are left with θεωρία only. Therefore,

---

1. This is actually too strong. The passage implies that the highest activity, the activity that ranges over the divine, is to count as θεωρία but not that all θεωρία is to count as the highest activity. There are numerous uses of the verb that require a less lofty status, and presumably this is what is left open by 1178b32's εἴη ἂν ἡ εὐδαιμονία θεωρία τις (happiness would be a kind of contemplation).

says Aristotle, "The activity of the god, which surpasses everything in blessedness, will be theoretic activity [ὥστε ἡ τοῦ θεοῦ ἐνέργεια, μακαριότητι διαφέρουσα, θεωρητικὴ ἂν εἴη]" (1178b21–22). Given the placement of the relative clause, the claim is that the activity of the god surpasses everything and turns out to be theoretic activity. It does not say that theoretic activity surpasses everything and turns out to be the activity of the god. The difference is not slight, for it keeps open the possibility that the godly brand of theoretic activity differs in kind from its human counterpart. That we should keep this possibility alive may have already been intimated in 1177b34–1178a2's characterization of the humanly divine as small in amount but it is unambiguously confirmed at 1178b23–24 where the human activity that rates as most eudaimonic is only *most akin* to the activity of the god [καὶ τῶν ἀνθρωπίνων δὴ ἡ ταύτῃ συγγενεστάτη εὐδαιμονικωτάτη].

So far, then, from showing that we ever do anything that the gods do, the most *Ethica Nicomachea* X shows is that we sometimes do something like what the gods always do. This falls far short of establishing that human νοῦς, in any sense, enjoys transcendental ontological status. With the addition of *De Generatione Animalium* 761a4–5's attribution of divinity to bees and 408b28–29's implication that νοῦς is something *more divine* than the perishable composite,[2] it begins to look like attributing divinity to a creature's activity has little, if any, bearing on the ontological status of the creature or its parts.

2. SEPARATIST PASSAGES IN *DE ANIMA*

In several passages Aristotle has been found to argue more directly for the ontological separateness of mind. A passage early in *De Anima* has proven particularly tempting:

> Mind seems to come about as a sort of substance [οὐσία τις] and not to be destroyed. For it would be destroyed by the feebleness of age, if by anything; but, as things are, it is similar to the case of the sense organs. For if an old man acquired a certain sort of eye, he would see as well as a young man. Thus, old age is due to something having happened not to the soul [οὐ τῷ τὴν ψυχήν τι πεπονθέναι] but to what it is in. . . . Thus, thinking [νοεῖν] and contemplating [θεωρεῖν] decay because something else within [ἄλλου τινὸς ἔσω] is destroyed, but in their own right they are

2. More on this passage below.

unaffected [αὐτὸ ἀπαθές]. But discursive thinking [διανοεῖσθαι] and loving and hating are not affections of this [οὐκ ἔστιν ἐκείνου πάθη] but of that individual which has it [τουδὶ τοῦ ἔχοντος ἐκεῖνο] in so far as it has it [ᾗ ἐκεῖνο ἔχει]. Hence when this [τούτου] is destroyed there is neither memory nor love, for these did not belong to it [οὐ γὰρ ἐκείνου ἦν] but to the composite thing [τοῦ κοινοῦ] which has perished. But mind [ὁ νοῦς] is probably [ἴσως] something more divine [θειότερον] and is unaffected [ἀπαθές]. (408b18–29)

Hamlyn took the first sentence to argue that productive mind is an imperishable substance, largely on the strength of *De Anima* III. 5. We have, of course, provided an alternative interpretation of that chapter. Even putting that aside, we should caution against making too much of Aristotle's mention of substance here. First, note that Aristotle downgrades his claim, saying only that mind comes about as a *sort* of substance.[3] Thus, Barnes is probably right to stress that here Aristotle has in mind activity or form and that neither demands a full-blown substantialist interpretation of mind (1971–72, 113).[4] There is, however, a second and, perhaps, more intriguing point. For mind to be produced in us as a sort of substance suggests, minimally, that mind is produced in us as something complete and whole. We do not get it in stages. Implicitly, then, we have a contrast with production of cognitive capacities$_2$ that occurs over time and involves alteration of initially given structures of innate capacities$_1$. These appear to be just what are mentioned in the penultimate sentence and its predecessor. Taken with *Ethica Nicomachea* VI. 11, one might suppose the point to be that, dispositionally, we reach the age of reason all at once, as it were, not by gradually becoming more and more reasonable. Taken with the last chapter, we might (with Hamlyn) see 408b18–19 as anticipating *M*'s insistence that, episodically, the mind is produced whole and complete *whenever one thinks*. Neither view demands special ontological status for νοῦς but at most reflects an emergent or nonreductionist account. This at any rate is what Aristotle seems to be driving at in the balance of the passage.

Notice, first, that even were we to follow Hamlyn in taking ὁ νοῦς as productive mind, it follows only that productive mind is *more* divine. Presumably, it counts as more divine than something perishable and, thus, the perishable is granted some measure of divinity. Thus, being divine cannot

3. This is another use of what I have called the "weakening" τὶς. See n. 63 of chap. 5.
4. This goes some distance toward allaying Hick's worry about "the anomalous position of νοῦς as οὐσία τις ἐγγινομένη when the composite substance of the animal already has a form" (1965, 276).

entail being durationally eternal but only having certain qualities to a certain degree. Although these may be had paradigmatically and in the highest degree by unending items, Aristotle appears to grant that lesser items have something similar. So, here again, attribution of divinity does not secure transcendental status for productive mind.

In fact, however, Aristotle does not appear to have productive mind in mind because the opposition implied in the last sentence is governed by thinking [νοεῖν] and contemplating [θεωρεῖν], on the one hand, and discursive thinking [διανοεῖσθαι], loving [φιλεῖν] and hating [μισεῖν], on the other hand. And *De Anima* III.4 characterized νοῦς as that in virtue of which the soul discursively thinks [διανοεῖσθαι]. The idea, I suggest, is that Aristotle wants to focus on activities and operations of the soul and how they are affected by breakdowns in the systems that subserve them. Thus, the point is better put: insofar as the soul thinks and theorizes it is imperishable; insofar as it discursively thinks, loves, hates, and so on, it is perishable.[5] In any case, however, thinking [νοεῖν] and theorizing [θεωρεῖν] are held subject to decay and perishing. So neither the first line's denial of perishability nor the last line's attribution of divinity entail the eternality of mind.

What is at issue is the manner of mind's demise. Properly, διανοεῖσθαι, or discursive thinking, is an affection not of what thinks and theorizes but of the whole individual that does this. Thus, when certain structures decay or perish, structures crucial to perception and action, so does discursive capability. The fate of διανοεῖσθαι appears closely linked to perceptual rather than strictly intellectual capabilities. Presumably, this is because a good deal of discursive reasoning proceeds in contexts requiring use of perceptual faculties. Thus, there is some sense in which breakdowns in the physical system effect διανοεῖσθαι. If this is correct, then Aristotle appears to be arguing, in modern idiom, that it makes no sense to talk of directly destroying the form or functional description of a given physical system. One can manage this only in virtue of destroying the structures that subserve the form or function. In short, a form or function cannot be destroyed in its own right but only κατὰ συμβεβηκός (incidentally). This holds equally for perceptual and noetic systems. Νοεῖν and θεωρεῖν are better off simply because they are further removed from the scene of action. Neither requires standard perceptual equipment, but both require [re]presentational structures. As φαντάσματα or images these are physiologically based. Hence,

5. The fact that here νοῦς is attached to the first role only is either a concession to its more proper employment or, more likely, a reflection of the wide role of διανοεῖσθαι, including here practical reasoning and action. Compare Joachim (1951, 290), who finds the passage to reflect a consistently sharp distinction between νοῦς and διανοεῖσθαι.

although unaffected in its own right (the weight of ἀπαθές in the last line), breakdown in the [re]presentational system results in breakdown in θεωρεῖν.[6] Thus, there is no suggestion in the passage that νοῦς is an intellectual substance that may exist without body.[7]

Let me turn now to 413a8–9, a notorious crux that has vexed all but the most staunch of Aristotle's dualist interpreters. The single sentence reads "Furthermore, it is unclear whether the soul is the actuality of the body [ἐντελέχεια τοῦ σώματος] as the sailor is of the ship [ὥσπερ πλωτὴρ πλοίου]." Hamlyn, referring us to Descartes's *Meditation* VI, conjectures that the puzzling remark is nothing more than a lecturer's aside (1968, 87), and Bolton is content merely to register puzzlement (1978, 262).[8] In the same vein, Hicks thinks Aristotle may simply be stimulating without satisfying our curiosity (1965, 320). For Ross, the line introduces a flat contradiction and, indeed, raises a point that Aristotle never returns to (1961, 214f.). The ancient commentators were equally puzzled. How, they wondered, could Aristotle hold at 413a6–7 that nothing prevents certain parts of the soul from existing separately should they not be actualizations, of any body and, in the immediately following sentence, imply that, even as an actuality of the body, the soul, or certain of its parts, might be separate?

The puzzle arises on the assumption that the point of analogy is ontological separateness. But the assumption is false. This is perhaps best seen by taking a look at a recent argument for the thoroughgoing dualism of the sailor–soul analogy. Robinson (1983) takes the analogy to urge that the sailor is the final cause of the boat. But he wishes to avoid a simpleminded two-substance view, whereby one substance, the sailor, is neatly separable from the other, the boat. Rather, the soul is "essentially connected to the body," and thus we should think of the sailor as always and thoroughly boat-ridden. Failing the sailor, a boat is an "essentially incomplete" object. Its nature requires mention of the sailor who, thus, gives the ship its end [τέλος] and actuality [ἐνέργεια]. Thus, the analogy establishes the "genuinely dualistic point" that the soul cannot be identified with the body. I have no quarrel with the last clause of this claim. Immediately above and in chapter 1, I urged that form or functional organization cannot be given a strictly physicalist interpretation. But although this may counter *explanatory* reduction, it by no means entails ontological dualism as Robinson asserts.[9] In any case, this is not the point of the analogy in the first place.

---

6. Compare Joachim's overly Platonistic view that unfavorable bodily conditions "interpose . . . a kind of veil" (1951) preventing man from experiencing the functioning of his *nous*.

7. Contrary to Robinson (1978, 120–21, and 1983, 143).

8. Later, on p. 267, he appears to take a stronger stand in favor of dualism.

Notice, to begin, that it may be ill advised to promote the essential incompleteness of moored boats. A house is for shelter, but is it any less a house for the absence of its dwellers? Does an axe cease to be an axe without choppers? Hardly. It simply ceases to be used. When Aristotle specifies an instrument's end by reference to its function, whether cutting or conveyance over water, he doesn't mention persons who employ the artifact in that function—and for a perfectly good reason, namely, that this bears simply on the exercise as opposed to the explanation of its function. Thus, pace Robinson, the sailor does not give the ship its τέλος and ἐνέργεια so much as he exercises them. Second, and more important, it has *already* been established that the soul is the actualization [ἐντελέχεια] of the body and in very intimate terms, indeed, in the very terms Robinson finds introduced by the soul–boatman example. This gives the remark an extremely odd cast. For one of the few clear things about the passage is that it proposes a new consideration.

What, then, is the force of the analogy? We may begin with a point of usage, namely, the fact that the terms of analogy are boat and sailor [πλωτήρ], not boat and captain [πλωτάρχης]. This prompts two observations. First, Aristotle is not perplexed about whether the soul directs or guides the body in action.[10] Rather, the second point, he wonders whether, when the soul moves the body, it does so as the sailor moves the boat. So far from formal causality he is concerned with the soul's efficient causal role.

A number of considerations favor this interpretation. First, pace Ross, the topic of efficient causation is one that Aristotle returns to and when he does, in *De Anima* III.10, it is indeed an unclear and sticky problem.[11] Second, the soul–sailor analogy is used elsewhere to address the topic of efficient causation but never that of final or formal causation. *Physica* VI.10, 240b8–20, argues that what is without parts can be in motion incidentally [κατὰ συμβεβηκός] in the way that a man sitting in a boat moves even though he cannot move in his own right [καθ' αὑτὸ οὐκ ἐνδέχεται]. In some such way, presumably, can the soul be *moved*. At least twice in *De Anima* the analogy is adduced to illustrate how the soul can move *itself*. Discussing the possibility that the soul moves or can move itself, 405b31–406a8 distinguishes between the motion of a ship and the motion of the

9. See Robinson (1983, 144), where Aristotle is represented as countenancing an immaterial intelligence that is able to survive the body.

10. See Hicks (1965, 321), who objects that Aristotle would not say, in any case, that the directive role of the soul is unclear.

11. See Furley (1978) for a nice discussion of the problem. He does, however, take a slightly different line on the analogy.

sailors [πλωτῆρες] in the ship, calling the latter movement καθ' ἕτερον. As the oarsman moves the boat without moving himself so the soul moves the body. At 408a29–34, in a slightly more assertive tone, the soul may move itself but only incidentally [κατὰ συμβεβηκός], namely, by moving what it is in. Since the last clause affirms the soul's role as ἐντελέχεια or actualization, of the body, the causal role under discussion in the first clause must be efficient causation.[12] So likening the soul to a sailor has little bearing, dualistic or otherwise, on its ontological status.

3. MIND AS A SELF-MOVER

The considerations just advanced may be thought pertinent to the soul's role in action only. In fact, however, they bear on Aristotle's theory of thinking. Notice that the 408a29–34 passage says that the soul is restricted to incidental movement for movement in place [κινεῖσθαι κατὰ τόπον]. There it is intended to preserve the thesis that certain creatures are self-movers. *Physica* VIII.2, 253a11–12, and VIII.6, 259b1–16, make much of the thesis, and it seems to be a presupposition of Aristotle's theory of voluntary action. But the account we get in *De Anima* III.10 is much more complicated. Besides that-which-is-moved [τὸ κινούμενον], the animal, we also find mentioned that-whereby-it-is-moved [ᾧ κινεῖ], the body, and that-which-moves [τὸ κινοῦν]. From what we have seen so far, one would expect to find under the latter the soul as an unmoved mover. What we find, however, are two cases—the object of desire, which counts as an unmoved mover, and the faculty of desire, which counts as a moved mover. One reason Aristotle needs to distinguish these elements is to meet an otherwise insuperable difficulty to animal self-movement. Something can move itself only insofar as it is divided, such that one part produces and the other receives [ἀλλ' ᾗ κεχώρισται, ταύτῃ τὸ μὲν πέφυκε ποιεῖν τὸ δὲ πάσχειν] (255a14–15). Thus, an animal is able to move itself because one of its parts moves another.

But this does not explain the need for two kinds of movers. Indeed, since the faculty is the moved variety, what becomes of the thesis that animals are self-movers? In a word, nothing. As Furley (1978) has pointed out, the movement in question will not be one of the standard sorts of movement involving objects in the external world but will involve the actualization, of

12. See now Tracy who argues, conclusively, it seems to me, for the efficient causation view of the analogy and provides a persuasive case for taking the critical sentence to say: "It is as yet unclear whether the soul, being in the way described above (οὕτως) entelechy of the body, is as it were (ὥσπερ) the 'boatman of the boat'" (1982, 111).

an already developed faculty. Hence, it will not even be the sort of movement that the thesis was designed to cover, namely, locomotion, qualitative change, increase and diminution (see 406a12–13). So even though the object of desire, the ὀρεκτόν, is required as an unmoved mover, the animal remains in some sense a self-mover.[13] One reason, suggested by Furley, that Aristotle wants the ὀρεκτόν as the primary cause of motion is to ensure that animal self-movings do not count as absolutely autonomous beginnings of actions and, thus, threaten the singularity of the cosmic unmoved mover. Another and, I think, a more important reason is that conformity with naturalistic causal principles provides a general and plausible explanatory framework. Here the fact that objects of desire and perception are external is an obvious desideratum. In particular, we save the principle that what produces change is something actual, the object of desire. Nonetheless, because the object is something like a final cause the soul itself, more precisely the faculty of desire, remains the efficient cause of the animal's movement. It is precisely in this sense that animals are self-movers.

When Aristotle turns to thought, he wants to preserve the general view that the mind is a self-mover in the sense of thinking by itself. He also wishes to preserve the causal principles featured in the general account of animal self-movement, but he must do so without the luxury of external objects. A more complicated account is called for. Because noetic self-movement is required for the autonomy of thinking, it is an essential feature of the mind. The mind, in short, is essentially a self-mover. It does not follow that the mind cannot be moved incidentally. This is clear from *De Anima* 406b7–8's cautionary remark: "But that which in virtue of its essential nature is able to be moved by itself cannot be moved except incidentally." These demands are met by the distinction between productive and receptive mind. First, the mind has parts, one productive and one receptive, and so can be a (noetic) self-mover. Second, the causal principle is secured by the fact that what produces the thinking, namely, the νοητόν, or object of thought, is produced by something located, functionally, at a lower level in the system, namely, productive mind. Thus, at the intentional or system-wide level, the productive factor in thinking is something actual[14] and unmoved, namely, the νοητόν. I am, then, distinguishing between self-mover and unmoved mover. Mind at the intentional level is a self-mover, not an unmoved mover. It is only productive mind, located at a lower level in the system, or, better, what it produces that is the *analogue* to the unmoved mover.[15]

13. For more on this see Furley (1978).
14. That Aristotle extends the principle to thought is clear from 431a1–4.

So far we have argued that what Aristotle says about human thought entails neither fully divine status nor ontological separateness on the part of νοῦς. We are also urging that νοῦς is the recipient of divine description precisely because one of its parts, productive mind, turns out to be something like the soul's unmoved mover. In short, attribution of divinity is a consequence of the mind's ability to think spontaneously or, in terms of the previous chapter, it follows from M.

A group of interesting but surprisingly underdiscussed passages in *Ethica Eudemia* confirm this. In the course of puzzling out whether luck can be said to cause everything, Aristotle argues that there must be some intrinsic starting point of movement in the soul. The passage divides into three parts. The first sets a puzzle, the second issues constraints on its solution, and the third identifies something that satisfies the constraints:

A. He who is deliberating has not already deliberated and in turn deliberated prior to that but there is a certain starting point [ἀρχή τις]; nor has he who thinks already thought prior to thinking [οὐδ' ἐνόησε νοήσας πρότερον νοῆσαι] and so on to infinity [καὶ τοῦτο εἰς ἄπειρον]. Thought, then, is not the starting point of thinking [οὐκ ἄρα τοῦ νοῆσαι ὁ νοῦς ἀρχή]. (1248a18–21)

B. Or is there a certain starting point [τις ἀρχή] with no other outside it [οὐκ ἔστιν ἄλλη ἔξω], being essentially the sort of thing that is capable of doing this [αὕτη τοιαύτη τῷ εἶναι τὸ τοιοῦτο δύναται ποιεῖν]? What we seek is thus a certain starting point of movement in the soul [τίς ἡ τῆς κινήσεως ἀρχὴ ἐν τῇ ψυχῇ]. (1248a22–25)

C. It is then clear that as god ⟨is the starting point of movement⟩ in the universe so it is in the soul, for somehow the divine element in us moves everything [κινεῖ γάρ πως πάντα τὸ ἐν ἡμῖν θεῖον]. The starting point of logos is not logos but something superior and what could be superior to knowledge and thought [νοῦς] but god [θεός], for virtue is an instrument of mind. (1248a25–29)

Although these passages deserve thorough scrutiny,[16] I shall limit myself

15. The cosmic unmoved mover's (UMM) thinking is not self-movement for it is no sort of movement at all. Contrast Waterlow (1982, 243), who finds that Aristotle wishes to stretch the notion of self-mover to include the UMM. As we shall see, this is certainly not the case in *Metaphysica* XII.7 and 9.

16. See Woods (1982) and Dirlmeier (1962) for general commentary on the passages.

here to what is pertinent to our discussion. A clearly sets a problem concerning efficient causation, in effect arguing against the causal claim that every episode of thinking is caused by some previous episode. Since the argument turns on avoiding the entailed infinite regress, Aristotle would presumably be no happier with the weaker claim that every episode of thought is preceded by a previous episode.[17] The final sentence of A implies that, were νοῦς the starting point of thinking, the vicious regress would ensue, presumably because νοῦς is counted as a thinking. This makes sense if one takes νοῦς here as the νοῦς of De Anima III.4 and bears in mind that what causes something to occur must itself be actual. Hence, because νοῦς is nothing until it thinks, only when actualized$_2$, that is, only when thinking, could it play any sort of causal role. In short, if νοῦς is the starting point, it must have been brought to action, allowably, in this context, by something outside it.

The last point anticipates the set of constraints laid down in B. The second sentence makes explicit the interest in efficient causation that was implicit in A, and the first sentence requires that something be *capable* of causing movement *on its own*. Both points of emphasis are crucial. The second suggests that the ἀρχή must be a self-mover and the first that this can be thought of as a capability of the system. In terms, again, of De Anima III.5 this looks like a description not of νοῦς but of productive mind. And because the ἀρχή must be *capable* of initiating thought by itself, it cannot always be doing so. Hence, it cannot be the same thing as the eternal unmoved mover.

C might appear to contradict, in its first sentence, what has just been said. But the "ὥσπερ" (as god . . .) construction indicates nothing more than analogy, especially in light of the fact that the analogy is introduced on the strength of the claim that the divine element *in us* makes everything.[18] The "τὸ ἐν ἡμῖν θεῖον" (the divine element in us) hardly justifies finding mention here of the eternal unmoved mover and because the phrase governs the interpretation of θεός (god) in the following sentence, neither is it the cosmic unmoved mover that is said to be superior to knowledge and νοῦς. It is, however, something that moves everything in the soul's domain. The idiom suggests, again, the presence of productive mind, for not only does this make each thing in the soul but also it is the superior part of the faculty of νοῦς.

17. To this extent the passage squares with the claim in De Anima III.4 that we are not always thinking. It also supports our reading of 430a22 (see *h* of chapter 5).

18. Here I agree with Verdenius's gloss: "Just as in the universe God ⟨is the starting point of motion⟩ and everything ⟨is moved⟩ by him ⟨so there is a similar starting point in the soul⟩" (1971, 288n6).

There are, in fact, two ways to take θεός in C. We may take it with τὸ ἐν ἡμῖν θεῖον (the divine element in us) and so relativize the notion of god to human beings. There is some warrant for this. On account of the apparent divinity of νοῦς *Protrepticus* B108–110 (Düring) reports that man *seems* to be a god relative to other creatures [δοκεῖν πρὸς τὰ ἄλλα θεὸν εἶναι τὸν ἄνθρωπον], citing Anaxagoras's "Reason is the god in us" [ὁ νοῦς ἡμῖν ὁ θεός].[19] On the other hand, θεός may be mentioned by way of making a rather different point, namely, that we should try insofar as possible to employ knowledge [ἐπιστήμη] and mind [νοῦς] in the service of the god.[20] The last line may suggest something like this. In neither case does the ἀρχή of movement in the soul emerge as the eternal unmoved mover.[21] And because the ἀρχή does look like productive mind, the *Ethica Eudemia* passages confirm the view that productive mind manages to be the soul's analogue to unmoved mover without ranking as an eternal unmoved mover.[22] Notice, finally, what Woods (1982, 197–98) has emphasized, that 1249b17's insistence that external goods aid θεωρεῖν rules out the possibility that that which theorizes [τὸ θεωρητικόν] can be in any way identified with god qua the unmoved mover of *Metaphysica* XII. For the latter, we shall soon see, is entirely self-sufficient and, thus, could not be the beneficiary of goods of any sort.

4. THE ALLEGED ISOMORPHISM OF PRODUCTIVE AND DIVINE MIND

The view of mind, particularly of productive mind, that I am proposing is not the traditional one. Common to a number of traditional interpretations is the thesis that productive mind is rung in to explain how we *acquire* concepts and knowledge. This view runs from Alexander's identifying *De Anima*'s productive mind with *Metaphysica* XII's god at least through Aquinas's assigning it the task of extracting species and genera from experience.

19. Verdenius (1971, 289) approves of Düring's suggestion (1966, 92) that Iamblichus is responsible for adding the citation.

20. This alternative would anticipate the discussion at 1248b6–23, the book's end, of the value of living by reference to or contemplation of the god and that this is done best by maximizing the activity of the theoretical part of the soul. That νοῦς is here not counted as fully divine is clear from Verdenius's analysis.

21. Compare Hamelin (1953, 30f.).

22. *Physica* VIII.6 recognizes noneternal unmoved movements [τι τῶν ἀκινήτων κινούντων at 259b20–21], so there is no objection in principle to productive mind in this way causing the mind as a whole to move itself.

It has surfaced anew in an engaging discussion by Kahn,[23] who cautions against framing Aristotle's theory in anachronistic post-Cartesian, post-Humean terms.[24] If only by way of contrast, it is important to take a look at this so-called traditional reading. I shall do so by following the most recent version.

Kahn (1981, 399) begins with our familiar actualization$_1$–actualization$_2$ distinction, in his idiom (a) the initial stocking of the mind with concepts or *noeta* and (b) the putting of these to use in actual$_2$ thinking, respectively. While he allows that productive mind is intended to account for a,[25] he thinks that b is the problematic case and regards it as equivalent to the problem of acquiring νοῦς as a *hexis*. Moreover, he finds that Aristotle is asserting just this at *De Anima* III.4, 429b5–9:[26]

> When mind has become each thing [ἕκαστα] as one who actually$_2$ knows [ὁ ἐπιστήμων ὁ κατ᾽ ἐνέργειαν] is said to be and this happens when he can actually$_2$ exercise his potentiality$_2$ by himself— it is still in some sense a potentiality$_2$ but not in the same way as before it learned or discovered (that is, not as a potentiality$_1$). Then it is capable$_2$ of (actually$_2$) thinking itself [αὐτὸς δὲ αὐτὸν τότε δύναται νοεῖν]. (429b5–9)

The mind of the first line is what 430a1 likens to a blank tablet and this Kahn takes to be a mere potentiality$_1$, the mind before it has learned or discovered *anything at all*. This contrasts with the potentiality$_2$ "of an intellect that has become all things, like someone actually in possession of a science" (1981, 400). The transition between these is what is to be explained.

A number of puzzles beset this reading of the passage. First, it is dis-

23. Principally in his 1981 essay. Düring also assigns concept creation to productive mind and, thus, sees an outright contradiction between this and the empirically based inductive process of *Analytica Posteriora* II.19 and *Metaphysica* I.1 (1964, 95).

24. Although well-taken, the caution is not without a certain irony, for the earliest tradition is not the Hellenic, post-Christian tradition that shapes the medieval discussion but that of Theophrastus. And here what is salient is the problem of causation in thought. This is plain from a glance at the Theophrastus texts collected in Hicks's Appendix (1965). They portray a thinker troubled by the kind of causation involved in thinking. He sees, for example, that the question πῶς νοητὸν ὑπὸ νοητοῦ πάσχει (Priscianus 28, 29, 31) follows naturally from Aristotle's doctrine that ὁ νοῦς ἐστὶ τὰ νοητά (Priscianus 28, 3) and worries (Priscianus 29, 12–15) about how νοῦς can be a potentiality unless what moves it is something other than νοῦς. These are the sorts of issues we have found Aristotle addressing in the theory of productive mind.

25. Apparently, Kahn takes this as following from the supposed fact that we are always thinking (see 1981, 400).

26. I leave in subscripts, familiar from the last chapter, to keep clear the difference between our views.

cussing the capabilities of the mind that has become *each* thing [ἕκαστα], not all things. We can, in effect, treat ἕκαστα as a quantifier. This suggests that Aristotle is not so much concerned with concept acquisition globally, but rather with what is involved in *a*'s knowing P, for arbitrary P. Thus, rather than Kahn's "like someone actually in possession of a science," ὁ ἐπιστήμων ὁ κατ᾽ ἐνέργειαν has the sense, especially in light of *De Anima* II.5, "the man of knowledge as he is actually exercising his knowledge." Second, the passage focuses on the capabilities of the mind when [ὅταν] it has already become a potential₂ (actual₁) knower. It betrays little interest in the transition to this stage but much in what the mind can do once the transition is made. What makes mind so distinctive is that, unlike other faculties, even at this developed stage (potentiality₂), it is still like a blank tablet. There is nothing there until it actually₂ thinks, until productive mind produces an already acquired object of thought. This, of course, reflects *M* and the interpretation of the above chapter. But it remains the case that one is hard pressed to find any discussion of concept acquisition in the balance of the chapter. What one does find, on the other hand, is considerable discussion of the various ways objects are grasped in actual₂ episodes of knowing. So, pace Kahn, one could say that the chapter is almost exclusively interested in the topic of actual₂ thinking.

Of course, Kahn wants to read productive mind back into the story of III.4:

> For this explanation he requires the agent intellect (i.e., for *a*). If the transition from *hexis* to exercise does not receive separate attention, that is perhaps because Aristotle does not think of it as constituting a distinctive problem. It is, after all, only by repeated acts of *noesis* that we acquire the *hexis* of *nous*. (1981, 400)

One apparent virtue of this suggestion is its use of the notion of a hexis as disposition—a notion that is familiar from the ethical works and elsewhere. Just as we acquire virtue by performing virtuous acts so also, runs the suggestion, we acquire νοῦς by performing noetic acts. While this proposal may be attractive for νοῦς as the grasp of scientific principles, it will not do for ordinary concept acquisition. At least not as Kahn explains it: "The relevant acts of conceptual thinking will be roughly the same in kind before and after the *hexis* is stabilized . . . , except that a phantasm or memory image will replace initial sensory input" (1981, 400*n*16).

There are several difficulties with this. It appears, for example, to clash with *Metaphysica* IX.8, 1050a12–14's assertion that acts performed by a subject whose theoretical dispositions are not fully developed (in Kahn's idiom, not yet stabilized) are not really cases of theorizing at all. Learners who, as it were, practice acts of theorizing in order to develop theoretical capabilities "do not theorize" [οὗτοι δὲ οὐχὶ θεωροῦσιν]. Besides this, we are asked here to suppose that νοῦς is developed in us as a disposition by dint of our performing noetic acts that do not involve images! There is simply no evidence to support this possibility and a good deal that tells against it. For one thing, the suggestion counters what Aristotle says in *Analytica Posteriora* II.19 and *Metaphysica* I.1 about the development of cognitive structures.[27] For another, Aristotle consistently asserts that images are required for all episodes of thinking. So it is not open to Kahn (he is not explicit on the point) to resort to the claim that images are necessary for the acquisition but not for the use of concepts.[28] Indeed, he would appear to be committed to something even stronger, namely, that images are involved in acquisition not of noetic structures but of stable noetic structures only (whatever these are).

A final point about νοῦς as a disposition. One way to explain the *development* of actual₁ noetic capability would be to stress the linguistic side of mental acts and tie this to language acquisition. In this way one could avoid the anomaly facing Kahn's view and say that Smith actually₁ knows something not when the appropriate images have finally settled into place but when he is able to say what he knows. On the other hand, it is hard to see how productive mind fits into the acquisitional account at all. Kahn appeals first to metaphor. Productive mind makes actual what is potentially intelligible as light makes colors visible. The metaphor is explained by way of a two-part process. Stage one involves sense perception and the image as a "mere go-between" required to establish contact between external object and mind. In stage two productive mind somehow extracts—for Aquinas, abstracts—the forms and, thus, we have acquired a concept.

I fail to see how this picture works. For one thing it assumes that the light metaphor supports an abstractionist or acquisitional account. But this can hardly be true. Light illuminates objects already present. It does not put them there. Equally, then, for productive mind. Rather than acquiring concepts or objects of thought, productive mind illuminates what is already there potentially₂. Certainly, *De Anima* III.5's characterization of productive mind as a disposition like light is of no help for the acquisitional theory.[29] Indeed, it presses a dilemma on Kahn's view. For the hexis in question must either be a disposition, the sort of thing that is gotten over time, or a having. If the first, productive mind itself will be a potentiality₂. If the second, it is merely a having, not an extracting, not a process of any kind. Indeed,

27. See above, for example, chap. 4, sec. 7.
28. His n. 22 (1981, 405) betrays an inclination in this direction.
29. See my account in chap. 5, sec. 4.

how, on the view under discussion, are we to distinguish between productive mind's actually₂ thinking P and its acquiring the concept P?

Even if the evidence so far retailed is persuasive, proponents of the traditional view will undoubtedly summon a final argument in its defense. Kahn runs it out as follows. From the causal principle

> i. Where an actual thing is produced from a potential thing it is always by something that is[30]

it follows that

> ii. Productive mind, as the causal agent actualizing₂ noetic forms, must itself be actual₂ noetic form

and, hence, that

> iii. The causal agent is always actually₂ thinking the object of thought.

Since iii holds for any object of thought, it follows that

> iii'. Productive mind is always actually₂ thinking every object of thought.

Let us begin by pointing out, again, that Aristotle does *not* say that productive mind is always thinking.[31] So iii and iii' will have to ride on the merits of the premises alone. Apropos of i let me reiterate what has been said above. Clearly, Aristotle wants to preserve some version of i for the account of thinking. But he does so by making the νοητόν, or object of thought, the causally effective factor (a point, incidentally, left entirely undiscussed by Kahn) and by assigning to a lower-level feature of the system, namely, productive mind, the job of producing the νοητόν on occasions of thought. Aristotle nowhere says anything that implies that productive mind already *is* all objects of thought but only that it is something that can produce them. So we may accept ii because it need mean nothing more than this. In particular, as we have seen, it need not entail iii or iii'.

How good, in any case, is the so-called traditional alternative to our reading of *De Anima* III.4–5 as an early cognitivist analysis of thinking? One way to gauge this is by examining two related consequences that are

---

30. *Metaphysica* IX.8, 1049b24–25: "ἀεὶ γὰρ ἐκ τοῦ δυνάμει ὄντος γίγνεται τὸ ἐνεργείᾳ ὂν ὑπὸ ἐνεργείᾳ ὄντος." Kahn's translation, "What exists in act always arises from what exists potentially by (the causal action of) something which is itself in act," implies that every actually existing thing is produced from something that is potential!

31. See above, chap. 5, sec. 5. Note also that *Metaphysica* IX.3's objection to the Megarian view of potentiality goes directly against this.

claimed to follow from the view, for if they prove untenable, so also may the view. The first, what Kahn calls the "psychological consequence," at once distinguishes between productive mind and human acts of thinking and asserts that the former is "in no sense part of us" (1981, 412). How then, one wonders, could it play any causal role in explaining concept acquisition, concept use, or, for that matter, anything we do? The least to be said is that the Alexandrian variant is excluded. Were productive mind and the god of *Metaphysica* XII *numerically* identical, god would *act on* us otherwise than as an end. Since god would initiate a causal process and since this in turn is governed by Aristotle's general theory of motion and change (412), not only does the god lower itself by delving in the lesser reaches of human affairs but also he does so in an efficient causal way. The first point gives cause for doubt, the second for denial. Aristotle is consistent in indicating that god can affect human affairs as final cause only, as something we strive after.[32] But this is unhelpful to latter-day Alexandrians precisely because the very point of introducing productive mind was to compensate for our inability to inductively generate concepts by our own devices. Surely it borders on fantasy to suppose that some inchoate cognitive desire to know, or even to acquire concepts, would be sufficient human equipment for getting the godly truth.

But there is more to be said. Even *were* iii' true *and* the Alexandrian identity dropped, what remains is more inspiration than explication. How does a productive mind that in no sense is part of us manage to causally effect human thinking?[33] This is a live question for productive mind's role both in actual$_2$ episodes of thinking and in concept acquisition. Here the causal principle, i, is of no more than nominal assistance. It is of little help to explain that concepts are acquired or actually$_2$ used in virtue of something that is actually$_2$ thinking all things. Appeal to a mind actually$_2$ thinking all things can explain human concept acquisition or use only if there is a causal route between them. But there is none and, thus, there is no answer to *De Anima* III.4's promise to explain how thinking comes about. Thus, it seems clear, pace Kahn, that Aristotle is primarily concerned with a mechanical problem, the problem of thought's efficient cause.[34] This and

32. For more on this, see Owens (1979).
33. Clark's idea of divine mind entering us from the outside (1975, 182) and of our receptive minds receiving the light that "eternally *is* conscious reality" (184) is suggestive but succeeds too well in preserving the mystery of mind. Sellars (1949, 561–62) does somewhat better in his account of a transcendent productive mind illuminating receptive mind. But Mure's suggestion (1932, 175) that productive mind is a pure substance common to all men and located midway between man and the astral intelligences enjoys neither doctrinal pedigree nor intrinsic plausibility.
34. One source of the difficulties with Kahn's account is his insistence that actualization$_2$

not the problem of acquisition is the "response . . . to his metaphysics of potency and act."[35]

The second of the two promised consequences of the Kahn view is cosmological. There must, if iii is true, be a strict isomorphism between productive mind and the structure of the natural world. Apart from its intrinsic and historical interest, the view deserves attention because it is a variant of an increasingly popular, but nonetheless mistaken, view of the relation between human and divine thought. More about this later but first the isomorphism.

The argument for isomorphism proceeds, in Kahnian terms, roughly as follows. From

> iv. (a) we grasp a scientifically relevant form or structure $S \supset$ (b) S is actualized$_{1/2}$ in us,
> v. $b \supset$ (c) the immutable cognitive act of productive mind causes S to be so actualized,
> vi. $c \supset$ (d) productive mind is structurally identical with S,

and

> vii. $d \supset$ (e) productive mind is isomorphic with the actualized scientific knowledge of the world,

we infer

> viii. $a \supset e$.

Despite our preference for saying that mind, rather than productive mind, is the same as its object, viii is acceptable enough, but only *if* we read *e* as a thesis about given pieces of actualized$_2$ scientific knowledge. This, however, falls short of establishing what Kahn wants, namely, that productive mind actually is isomorphic with the *totality* of scientific truths, with the totality of truths that can be and are actualized$_2$.[36] What this makes clear is that the isomorphism argument turns on v's very tight constraints on concept acquisition. Not only is productive mind essential to acquiring S but also it is essential in virtue of an immutable act of thinking S. However, the single text cited in support of the immutability claim, 430a22, simply

---

of thought is an unproblematic affair for Aristotle. I am rather more inclined to follow Burnyeat's estimate (1981, 130–33) that in general Aristotle regards concept acquisition as a more or less straightforward matter.

35. I prefer to see the response in terms of his general physical principles. In this light *De Anima* III.4–5 can be seen as an early try at the naturalization of νοῦς. On this, see Wieland (1967, 333n17).

36. Because this will hold, even where no one actually$_2$ knows any scientific truths—the opposite pole of the ideal we aspire to (411).

does not assert that productive mind is always thinking. Thus, we are, in effect, left with the admonition that there is no alternative to v; hence, it must be true.

The availability of alternative accounts notwithstanding, serious questions arise concerning iii′ and c. What sort of thinking are we dealing with here? Is the thought in question, call it the "maximal" thought, the thought, *simultaneously,* of all the various principles of all the different sciences or is it the thought of some only? How could it be the first and by what criterion could a precise selection be made for the second? And why, at all, would experience be such a crucial factor in Aristotle's announced theory of concept acquisition? Despite Kahn's statement to the contrary,[37] no reason is given why productive mind can't do the job alone. And, pace Kahn, the superrationalism of Aristotle's account ought to make it less dependent on experience than Plato's theory of recollection.[38] But, in fact, it is more dependent. On the other hand, construed with the last chapter as the activity, strictly, of episodes of thinking, productive mind need not accommodate any such maximal thought. On our view Aristotle's theory requires only that the human mind can come to reflect the essential structure of the world. And it does this insofar as it can come to grasp, via induction, demonstration, or whatever other process, truths that are expressible in propositions whose structure mirrors the structure of the world. There may be many ways to gain knowledge of these propositions but none obviously requires the superrationalism of productive mind. Nor can one say without risk that productive mind grasps only the concepts that *constitute* the propositions of science—perhaps the primary universals or uncombined concepts discussed two chapters back. For now there will be no isomorphism because, simply, productive mind will cease to reveal the *structure* of the world.

There is, finally, a corollary to the thesis of isomorphism, one that, in Kahn's words, is of "capital consequence for the content of the divine act of νόησις νοήσεως" (thinking of thinking). It is that productive mind and the divine mind are the same in kind, indeed, that they are strictly isomorphic. So let us close the section with a look at this rather bold claim.

---

37. "And this process of learning and exercising science, although it has a metaphysical cause and even a metaphysical guarantee in the alleged super-rationalism of the active intellect, must be achieved in our own experience by the ordinary processes of induction and hard work: there is no epistemic button we can push in order to tune in on the infallible contemplation of noetic forms by the active intellect" (1981, 411). But if Kahn is correct about productive mind, the looming question is "Why not?"

38. Whereby I do not mean to assert that Plato saw the theory as a theory of concept acquisition.

This will prepare the way for consideration in the next section of a weaker version of the sameness-in-kind thesis.

The core of Kahn's argument is

ix. (*f*) productive mind and divine mind are the same in kind & (*g*) the content of productive mind is identical with the essential and formal structure of the natural world ⊃ (*h*) the content of the divine thought is identical with that same structure.

One thing that is clear by now is that *f* is not entailed by the language of Aristotle's attribution of divinity to human νοῦς. Nor is it the case that *f* and *g* entail *h* because sameness in kind need not mean sameness of content. So what is the support? First, because both are in their very essence actuality, productive and divine mind must be same in kind and, second, it would otherwise "be difficult to see how our divine noetic activity could be a likeness (*homoioma*) of the divine *energeia* (*Ethica Nicomachea* X.8, 1178b27), so that as we are at our best moments, 'so is god always, and even more so' (*Metaphysica* 1072b25)" (Kahn 1981, 414).

The first consideration fails for the simple reason that things different in kind may both well be, essentially, activity. *Eudaimonia* comes to mind and it hardly counts as god. Light is another. The second consideration is both curious and somewhat misleading. It is curious insofar as one might equally argue that precisely because human thinking is only a likeness of divine thinking it cannot be the same in kind. After all certain animal behavior mimics human behavior.[39] Are we to say that, therefore, it is the same in kind? Certainly, none of the passages we have canvassed demands this relation for human and divine thought. The consideration is misleading to the extent that the full *Metaphysica* passage says that our wonder is compelled if god is always in the best state we sometimes are in, all the more if it is in a better state [εἰ δὲ μᾶλλον.] Then, Aristotle adds, "and it is" [ἔχει δὲ ὧδε]. Kahn omits this phrase—both here and in Kahn (1985, 327n24). So god is apparently always in a state better than the best state we are ever in. Surely, room is left open here for difference in kind. I conclude, then, that neither *f* nor *g* has been established. Hence, other grounds must be found for asserting the isomorphism of *h*.[40] And, in any

---

39. See chap. 3, n. 13, above for more on this.

40. In fact, if Armstrong is correct in finding Albinus the source of Alexander's point, then the Alexandrian tradition is a *reaction to* the very sort of minimalism that Kahn would deny Aristotle's god. Armstrong writes, "He [Albinus] accepts from Aristotle that God's thought must be self-thought but it seems to him (I conjecture) as it has seemed to many critics of Aristotle since, that a bare νόησις νοήσεως is a limited, sterile and unsatisfactory conception. So by boldly combining the Aristotelian doctrine of the identity of thought and its object in the case of immaterial beings . . . with the doctrine of the Ideas as the thoughts

case, were *h* true, it would follow that the unmoved mover (UMM) is not only final but also formal cause, indeed, formal cause of everything. Given the absence of evidence, a good deal of argument will be required to keep this from retiring, on its own, the claim of strict isomorphism.

Kahn's thesis of isomorphism was advanced primarily on the strength of his analysis of *De Anima* III.5. In effect, the interpretation of productive mind is taken as the key to unraveling the mysteries of divine thought. Given Kahn's view of productive mind, the isomorphism cannot be taken as holding between *human* and divine thought. So sameness in kind would not, in any case, have turned out to be sameness of human and divine minds.[41] In fact, it is not clear that much would follow anyway from the suggested isomorphism. Suppose, for example, that the UMM were to think purely abstract sets only and that these happened to enjoy a one-to-one, structure-preserving correlation with human theoretical thought. Would this make the two same in kind? Not recognizably, at least not for anyone experiencing the thinking. The sameness-in-kind claim must be tied to sameness in content thought, and because, as I urge in the next section, this requires images for the human but not the divine case, human and divine thought are importantly different.

5. THE SUPPOSED SAMENESS-IN-KIND OF HUMAN AND DIVINE THOUGHT

Differences in outcome notwithstanding, few will doubt the wisdom of interpreting *Metaphysica* XII.7 and 9 in light of *De Anima,* especially III.5[42] This strategy, briefly exploited by Kahn, is employed extensively by Norman in developing a weaker version of the sameness-in-kind thesis. But with a twist: *De Anima* III.5 is neglected entirely in favor of III.4 with its exclusive focus on human thought. One effect of this is to keep open what Kahn's account foreclosed, namely, the sameness of *human* and divine thought. Because Norman purports to reach this result by an independent argument, we need to consider his account in its own right.

---

of God . . . he arrives at the doctrine that for God to think himself is to think the ideas, that is the whole of intelligible reality" (1957, 404). Pace Kahn, the suggestion, which is certainly plausible, places the Alexandrian tradition in support of a minimalist reading of Aristotle's UMM.

41. This is to the good because any system that is isomorphic with respect to human thought will have to accommodate the troublesome fact that human thought is sequential and moves from thought to thought. This is something the divine mind does not do.

42. Hicks (1965) is representative in reporting that a close study of the *Metaphysica* chapters are "almost indispensable to the elucidation of" *De Anima* III.5.

Norman (1969) argues that the divine thought of *Metaphysica* XII.7 and 9 is essentially no different from human thought of the theoretical variety. In particular, he is interested in what it means for god or the UMM to think itself. It means, he claims, that the UMM does nothing different from what we do when we think an object in the theoretical mode, that is, when we think an object that is without matter. Roughly, his argument divides into three stages: (A) *De Anima* III.4 distinguishes two kinds of thinking, one of which fixes the sense of self-thinking appropriate to the *Metaphysica* account; (B) *Metaphysica* XII.7 establishes that the UMM's thinking differs in degree only from human thinking; (C) *Metaphysica* XII.9 then argues that god thinks itself simply because its thought is strictly of the theoretical sort.

Let us take stage *A* first. It begins by asserting that 429b5–9, a passage that loomed large in Kahn's analysis (see previous section), distinguishes two kinds of thinking. In the first, mind "takes in the forms and, being itself mere potentiality, it is actualized by becoming those forms" (1969, 65). In the second, mind, "having become τὰ νοητά . . . is now able to think itself." No argument is advanced for reading the passage in this way. Indeed, the so-called first sort of thinking looks rather more like concept acquisition and, hence, can hardly be called thinking at all. Thus, some of our objections to Kahn's reading of 429b5–9 apply here as well. If we bear in mind *De Anima* II.5, then, although 429b5–9 invokes the actualization₁–actualization₂ distinction, it does so mainly to set up discussion of the second. There is nothing, to reiterate, in *De Anima* III.4's sequel that looks like a discussion of concept acquisition. The remark at 429a22–24 that until it thinks mind is nothing concerns the actually₁ developed mind that has already acquired a stock of concepts. Surely had Aristotle meant otherwise he would have reinvoked the language of *De Anima* II.5 or something equivalent to Norman's "takes the thoughts up."

Moreover, Norman is forced to saddle Aristotle with a view he does not appear to hold, namely, the proto-Lockean view on which objects of thought [νοητά] turn out to be suspect mental entities, the "stuff of which the mind is composed" (66). Right to scorn the view, Norman is wrong to attribute it to Aristotle. The grounds for attribution are, roughly, that the first stage of thinking is dependent on something external, what is taken as equivalent to holding that it is a kind of being affected by the object of thought [πάσχειν τι ὑπὸ τοῦ νοητοῦ], and that although mind *becomes* identical with τὰ νοητά in this stage, in the second stage it is *already* identical with them. The first ground assumes, what is anything but obvious, that πάσχειν τι ὑπὸ τοῦ νοητοῦ takes an external object as νοητόν. Of course, one must assume this, if one insists that the actualized₁ mind *already* is identical with its objects. But *Metaphysica* XII.7, 1072a30's use of the formula contains no hint of restriction to external objects. Indeed, it would seem to counsel against this, and our parallel passage in *De Anima* II.5, 417a22–29, suggests that the Sameness Thesis is meant to hold for *episodes* of thinking only, namely, for the man who is already contemplating [ἤδη θεωρῶν], that is, who is actually [ἐντελεχείᾳ] and in the strongest sense knowing *this particular A* [τόδε τὸ A]. Moreover, in perceptual contexts, identity of faculty and object is asserted for actual episodes only, and it is an obvious desideratum to preserve this parallel. So even for theoretical thought, Norman's second stage, the νοητόν seems to play a causal role in episodes of thinking.[43]

It is unsurprising that the grounds are weak for attributing proto-Lockeanism to Aristotle, for he says only that objects of thought are *somehow* [πώς at 417b23] in the soul. The emphasized phrase cautions against precisely the sort of view Norman hangs on Aristotle. Aristotle consistently ties ontological commitment to particularity and explicitly counts objects of thought as universals. *Analytica Posteriora* I.11, 77a5–10, makes it clear that there is no inclination on Aristotle's part to count the latter among the entities that exist independently.

There seems, then, little reason to follow Norman on *De Anima* III.4, particularly 429b5–9. Nonetheless, we need to look at stage *B* of the argument because *De Anima* III.4 does urge that one thinks oneself insofar as the object of an *episode* of thinking is without matter, that is, insofar as one is engaged in theoretical thinking.

Norman finds two claims in *Metaphysica* XII.7, one implicit, the other argued. The implicit claim is that when the UMM thinks itself "what is meant is not self-contemplation but simply that sameness of νοῦς [mind] and νοητόν [object of thought] that characterizes all abstract thought" (69). But this is hardly conclusive, since it is still an open possibility that the UMM enjoys a unique sort of theoretical thought, one deserving of the name "self-contemplation." Norman attempts to block this twice over by arguing, first, that XII.9 in fact contains a contrary message and, second, that XII.7 implies—this is its argued claim—that human and divine thinking are the same in kind. Let us take the latter first.

What is proposed is that the UMM thinks itself because it is engaged, eternally, in the activity of theoretical thinking, and all theoretical thinking, human or otherwise, is characterized by sameness of thinker and object of thought. Although I would not quarrel with this result, I fail to see that it

---

43. This is clearly the message of *Metaphysica* XII.7, 1072b20–23 (see below).

establishes the essential sameness (sameness in kind) of human and divine thought. The crucial passage divides into two parts, the first of which is:

> And thinking in itself [ἡ νόησις ἡ καθ' αὐτήν] deals with that which is best in itself, and that which is thinking in the fullest sense with what is best in the fullest sense [ἡ μάλιστα τοῦ μάλιστα]. And mind thinks itself [αὐτὸν νοεῖ ὁ νοῦς] in virtue of sharing in the object of thought [κατὰ μετάληψιν τοῦ νοητοῦ], for it becomes an object of thought by contacting and thinking the object [νοητὸς γίγνεται θιγγάνων καὶ νοῶν], so that mind and the object of thought are the same [ταὐτὸν νοῶς καὶ νοητόν]. For that which is *capable* of receiving the object of thought and the essence is mind [τὸ δεκτικὸν τοῦ νοητοῦ καὶ τῆς οὐσίας νοῦς]. But it is *active* when it possesses this object [ἐνεργεῖ δὲ ἔχων]. Therefore, the possession rather than the receptivity is the divine element which mind seems to have [ὃ δοκεῖ ὁ νοῦς θεῖον ἔχειν], and the act of theorizing is what is most pleasant and best. (1072b18–24)

This passage specifies in what sense thought in general is divine, namely, as activity rather than potentiality.[44] The point of these remarks, which recognizably reflect the theory of *De Anima,* is to prepare the way for identifying the UMM as the activity of thought in 1072b26–27: if activity is the aspect of thought that seems divine in the human case, then surely the UMM will be exclusively activity.

I wish to argue, contra Norman, that the path is left open for counting divine thought as different in kind. First, a remark on the strategy of argumentation. Norman rightly finds in 1072b22–23's distinction between the essence of mind as the capacity to receive the object of thought and the activity of mind as its possession an echo of *De Anima* III.4, presumably, of the remark that even when actualized mind is still in some sense potential. But because the *Metaphysica* passage understands by possession of the νοητόν the episodic activity of thinking and equates this in turn with the sameness of mind and object of thought, *De Anima* III.4, 429b5–9, must also be restricting the thesis of sameness to actual₂ episodes of thinking.[45] Thus, the thesis cannot be extended to mind and *all* of its acquired objects. But this is exactly what Norman requires. It also forces him to allow, on the one hand, that *De Anima* III.4's theoretical thinking is "in a sense

---

44. Note, again, Aristotle's cautious language at 1072b23: mind *seems* to have a divine element.

45. For a detailed account of how the sameness thesis is related to the thesis that the mind is caused to be active by contact with the object of thought, see Wedin 1988.

potential" (65) and to claim, on the other hand, that it is the same as god's theoretical thought. This alone may be sufficient to retire the view.

Second, the sameness of mind and object of thought holds, presumably, for anything that counts as the first line's ἡ νόησις ἡ καθ' αὑτήν (thinking in itself). Yet the sentence goes on to distinguish thinking what is best from thinking what is best *in the fullest sense,* so it is tentatively left open that divine mind may differ in kind from human thought. The second part of the passage is even more definite:

> If, then, god is always in a good state such as we sometimes are [εἰ οὖν οὕτως εὖ ἔχει ὡς ἡμεῖς ποτέ, ὁ θεὸς ἀεί] that is amazing; and if in a better state [εἰ δὲ μᾶλλον] that is more amazing.[46] And god is in that state [ἔχει δὲ ὧδε]. (1072b24–26)

Norman comments that god's state is not generically different from man's. It is greater in degree only "because in man 'theoretic' thought is mixed with the activity of ὁ δυνάμει νοῦς [the mind in potentiality], in god it is completely pure" (68). This simply won't work. First, *if* Norman is correct about sameness in degree, then man's theoretic *activity* will be the measure of the god's. For *as activity* the fact that our mind is also a potentiality does not enter the picture and that is what is relevant here. The point, rather, is that the two sorts of *activity* differ—unless, what Norman cannot allow, admixture of potentiality affects, downward, the *quality* of human theorizing. So human thinking will have to differ, after all, simply by its failure of continuity. But the passage indicates a difference in the state itself and, thus, certainly appears to countenance difference in kind.[47]

It is possible, of course, that holdouts for sameness-in-kind will insist that "εἰ δὲ μᾶλλον" (and if in a better state) at 1072b25 has merely quantitative force and, thus, that divine and human thought differ, finally, simply in point of the former's eternality. This maneuver, however, is effectively blocked by a passage in *Ethica Eudemia* I.8. At 1218a10–15 Aristotle supposes, on behalf of the Platonist, that what the good-itself has, beyond simply being the common definition, is eternality and separateness. But this, he protests, can in no way enhance the status of the good-itself because "that which is white for many days is no more [οὐθὲν μᾶλλον] white than what is white for one, thus neither ⟨will the good be any more good by

46. Norman's translation, "It is remarkable enough if God's happiness should be eternally what ours is sometimes, but still more remarkable *that it* is even greater," by an unwarranted reading of "εἰ δέ" at the italicized phrase and by a failure to include the last sentence of the passage, gives a misleading representation of the text.

47. Kraut strikes the right note: "This last passage (i.e., 1072b24–26) makes it clear that the difference between divine and human contemplation does not consist solely in the former's greater duration; a difference in kind also exists" (1979, 472).

being eternal)."[48] It is clear that here μᾶλλον cannot have merely quantitative force and, thus, that for the good-itself to be a greater good [μᾶλλον ἀγαθόν] is for it to be something more than an eternal version of ordinary goods. Thus, Aristotle's admonition at 1218a22 that the fine or good will be present more in unmoving things [ἐν τοῖς ἀκινήτοις μᾶλλον τὸ καλόν] registers more than their endless possession of the attribute. They must have it in a qualitatively superior way. By parity of reasoning, for god's thinking to be better [μᾶλλον] than ours is not for it to be just an unceasing version of what we episodically do.

So far, then, from showing difference in degree only, the argument of *Metaphysica* XII.7 is aimed in the other direction. What XII.7 does not do, however, is spell out the nature of the difference in kind. That, I will argue, is part of what XII.9 is all about. But to fully appreciate this we need first to see why the argument for the essential sameness of human and divine contemplation comes up short. And here we return to stage *C* of Norman's argument.

Aristotle opens *Metaphysica* XII.9 by stating that the UMM is the *most divine* of phenomena and asking what this entails about its nature. The balance of the chapter, at least the section down to 1074b35, plays out the entailment. Notice, what Norman overlooks, that the UMM is characterized as the *most divine* thing [θειότατον]. Thus, at the chapter's outset the possibility is still alive that god is more divine than anything human. In particular, what seems alive is the possibility that XII.9 develops XII.7, 1072b24–26's remark that god is in a better state than our best state. But let us see where the argument takes us.

The unfolding of the UMM's nature begins with the apparently innocuous point that the UMM must think of something rather than nothing [μηδέν]. Both the dichotomy

1. (a) mind thinks (something) v
   (b) mind thinks nothing (1074b17–19)

and the reason for excluding the latter, that νοῦς would have no greater dignity than a sleeping man, are more interesting than meets the eye. The fact that Aristotle even mentions *b* may suggest that what the UMM does is so formal and abstract that it may well appear to be thought of nothing. It would, to anticipate, be especially prudent to raise and rule out *b*, were the UMM nothing but purely reflexive thinking for *b* is tantamount to mind not thinking at all, since the contrast is expressed by "εἴτε μηδὲν νοεῖ...

48. With Woods (1982) and others, I keep the emendation in angle brackets: τὸ ἀγαθὸν μᾶλλον ἀγαθὸν τῷ ἀΐδιον εἶναι οὐδέ. And, in any case, the point is implied by the course of argumentation.

εἴτε νοεῖ" (either thinks of nothing or thinks)—thus, the parentheses in *a*. Consequently, rejection of *b* not only preserves the dignity due the UMM but also reflects the principle, familiar from *De Anima* and elsewhere, that activities as well as faculties are determined by their objects.

This principle, our old friend FFO, is implicit in the next move which generates two alternatives for *a*:

2. *a* ⊃ (*c*) something else determines mind to think v
   (*d*) ~something else determines mind to think,[49]

and argues against the first by pointing out that mind would then be a mere potentiality. Thus, at 1074b18–20 we get

3. *c* ⊃ (*e1*) the substance [οὐσία] of mind is not thinking but capacity [οὐ νόησις ἀλλὰ δύναμις[.

This is combined immediately (1074b20–21) with

4. *e1* & (*e2*) the value mind has lies in its thinking [νοεῖν] ⊃ (*e3*) what determines mind to think will be of greater value than mind

to reject *c*.

Both 3 and 4 are instances of quite general principles. In particular, the inference appears to be underwritten by something like

PT★. If x is valuable because of F &
   x does not have F in its own right &
   x has F in virtue of z,
   then z is more valuable than x.

We have already seen a variant of PT★ at work in *De Anima* III.5 (see 8 in chapter 5, section 5), where it was used to establish the superior nature of productive mind. To that extent we get further confirmation for our interpretation of productive mind as that which determines thought by producing the object of thought. Of course, occurrence of the principle here does not establish sameness of productive mind and divine mind. For it is rung in to exclude the candidacy of mind qua determined by something else. Regardless of what, if anything, fits the latter description (thought initiated by objects encountered in experience comes to mind), *both* human and divine thought survive the rejection of *c*. Hence, both may count as autonomous thought, not determined by anything else.

This is confirmed by the fact that Aristotle is now poised to discuss

49. At 1074b18–19, *c* translates "τούτου δ' ἄλλο κύριον."

what mind thinks [τί νοεῖν], *whether or not* its substance is νοῦς or νόησις. Norman follows the commentators in taking this to distinguish potentiality from actuality. Thus, we get two alternatives for *d*:

> 5. *d* ⊃ (*d1*) the substance of mind is an activity$_2$ v
> (*d2*) the substance of mind is a potentiality$_2$.

Aristotle does *not* say that there is anything intrinsically wrong with *d2*. In fact, if οὐσία is construed definitionally, then *d2* captures precisely the *faculty* of human νοῦς. By the latter I mean to include the potentiality$_2$ to think theoretically as well as otherwise.

Here we differ widely from Norman. First, he takes the *d1–d2* distinction to parallel the *c–d* distinction and reads the former as opposing (i) thought whose object is something external to (ii) thought whose object is its own mental contents. But, as we have just seen, the parallel is not asserted by Aristotle and, though Norman's i may match *c,* there is no ground for his pairing i with *d2*. Without appeal to his interpretation of *De Anima* III.4, 429b5–9, and *Metaphysica* XII.7, both of which we have challenged, there is nothing in the text of *Metaphysica* XII.9 to support his reading of *d1* and *d2* as distinguishing two kinds of actual thinking as opposed to the capacity$_2$ for thought, on the one hand, and its exercise, on the other.

At this point it will be helpful to make explicit two constraints Aristotle issues on divine thought:

> *Di.* The UMM thinks only of *the* most divine and honored thing
> [τὸ θειότατον καὶ τιμιώτατον]

and

> *Dii.* The UMM's thought does not change [οὐ μεταβάλλει].

What Aristotle's argument will show is that only the UMM's self-thinking, characterized by the formula "thinking of thinking," satisfies both constraints. Before contending with the formula let us look at the argument.

At 1074b22–23 Aristotle suspends for the moment his interest in deciding between *d1* and *d2* and asks simply what will count as the object of divine thought. He begins the answer by issuing

> 6. (*e*) mind thinks itself [αὐτὸς αὑτόν] v
> (*f*) mind thinks something different [ἕτερόν τι]

and

> 7. *f* ⊃ (*f1*) mind thinks the same thing always v
> (*f2*) mind's object changes.

From 1074b23 to 33 he argues against f, sometimes directly, sometimes against its entailments $f1$ and $f2$. Thus, after introducing 6 and 7 he immediately cautions against a wide-open reading of f. Lines 1074b23–26, invoking Di, require at a minimum that the divine mind not think of anything that falls short in worth or honor. So far nothing prevents these objects from being "ἕτερόν τι."

And $f2$ runs into trouble because *were* the object of divine thought to change it could be only for the worse, thus infringing against Di. Besides, he adds, this would already count as a movement. I wish to emphasize two points here. The first is that it is opaque how the prohibition against change could even apply to human theoretical thinking. When Smith shifts the object of theoretical thought, he does not, so it would seem, shift to something of lesser value. Equally, *were* the UMM to do so, why should that count as a descent on a scale of value? And since it is a fact that we do shift, even in theoretic thought, from one to another object, it appears that the prohibition does not sit well with the sameness in kind of human and divine mind. The only way around this would be to insist that *we* are always thinking all things that the UMM thinks. But this response drives us back to the isomorphism rejected in the last section. And even then isomorphism was asserted only for productive mind, which is not even addressed by Norman's theory. A second point is that any interpretation must accommodate the notion of human thinking as at least something like a movement.[50] We have suggested it involves something like a moved self-mover. Thus, the additional qualm that $f2$ already introduces movement appears to separate it from divine but not human thinking.

We come at last to two final objections to f. The first comes by way of objecting to $f1$: "if it ⟨divine thought⟩ is not the act$_2$ of thinking [νόησις] but the potentiality$_2$, then it is reasonable to suppose that the continuity of its thinking [τὸ συνεχὲς αὐτῷ τῆς νοήσεως] would be tiring" (1074b28–29). Roughly, the idea is that any mind that thinks something different from it, the mind of f, has a measure of potentiality. Here Aristotle returns to $d2$, in effect, asserting its equivalence with f.[51] Thus, his point is that even were the $d2$ characterized mind to think the same thing continuously, as $f1$ supposes, it would find this tiring.[52] Since the UMM obviously finds

50. See *De Anima* III.4 and our discussion in the last chapter.

51. Sandbach (1954) notices the slight discontinuity in the argument that I deal with by having Aristotle return to an earlier point. His remedy, transposing lines 28–30 [πρῶτον... τὸ νοούμενον] to follow ἡ ἀρίστη οὐσία εἴη in line 20, does not affect the logic of Aristotle's argument; so I stay with the standard order.

52. Perhaps because it would have to move from a potential$_2$ state to its actual$_2$ exercise and then keep from switching to another object or back to its original potential$_2$ state. It would, in short, be obliged to keep its attention fixed. Note also that this does not conflict

nothing tiring, it cannot be construed as f (that is, $d2$) even read just with $f1$.

The second, more direct, objection consists simply in pointing out that f's introduction of potentiality into mind has the consequence that something will be more valuable than the act of thinking, namely, what is thought: "it is clear that there would be something else more honored than mind [ὅτι ἄλλο τι ἂν εἴη τὸ τιμιώτερον ἢ ὁ νοῦς], namely, the thing thought [τὸ νοούμενον]" (1074b29–30). This is supported and explained immediately by a very difficult passage: "for thinking [νοεῖν] and the act of thinking [νόησις] will belong to one who thinks the worst of things; so if this is to be avoided the act of thinking will not be the best thing" (1074b31–33). So far as I can determine these lines simply drive home the point that f entails that the act of thinking cannot be the best of things.[53] That is *all* the argument intends to show and, incidentally, all it needs to show. Since this result followed from the distinction between mind and object of thought[54] and since, whatever else it is, the UMM is thought and the finest of things, we may reject f and so adopt e.

This takes the argument down to its famous conclusion at 1074b33–35: "Therefore, it thinks itself [αὐτὸν ἄρα νοεῖ], since it is the highest [εἴπερ ἐστὶ τὸ κράτιστον], and the thinking is a thinking of thinking [καὶ ἔστιν ἡ νόησις νοήσεως νόησις]." Norman reports "the conclusion 'αὐτὸν ἄρα νοεῖ' has nothing to do with any 'self-contemplation' but is simply a reference to that abstract thinking in which mind 'thinks itself.'" Perhaps, but there is cause for doubt. For one thing, the mentioned "simple reference" assumes that *De Anima* III.4 and *Metaphysica* XII.7 together exclude difference in kind between divine and human thought. But this, we have seen, is unlikely at best. Thus, even if the phrase "αὐτὸν νοεῖ" refers to abstract thinking in which mind "thinks itself," it may be a unique brand of this that Aristotle has in mind for divine thought.

There are some prima facie reasons in favor of this in 1074b33–35 itself. Notice, first, that we do not simply get a conclusion. Rather, we get a conclusion plus a justification for it as well as an explication of what counts as the divine mind thinking itself. Two points about the justification merit

---

with *De Anima* III.4's claim that, unlike other faculties, mind is not incapacitated by an intense object [σφόδρα νοητόν] because the incapacitation in question is not the same as weariness due to *continuity* of thinking. The latter says nothing about intensity of object.

53. Roughly, the argument goes: If thinking and object of thought differ and if the object of thought can be good or bad, then thinking will be good just insofar as its object is good. Hence, it will be good *because* its object is good and so the object will be of greater value than the thinking.

54. It is, incidentally, precisely what is missed in Norman's summary of the argument (1969, 71).

mention. The first is that Aristotle appeals not to any general feature of abstract or theoretic thought but to the fact that the divine mind is the highest thing.[55] In *De Anima* III.4 the mind thinking itself is connected with matter-free objects, but there is no mention of these being the highest or most divine and honored things. So something new may be in the offing. But, the second point, even were the objects of *theoria* so described, *Metaphysica* XII.9 never speaks of the objects of divine thought. It is *the* most divine thing [τὸ θειότατον at 1074b16] and its object is *the* most divine and honored thing [τὸ θειότατον καὶ τιμιώτατον at 1074b26]. By itself, of course, this is hardly conclusive, for it is well known that Aristotle occasionally uses the singular form as a variable formula with open extension. Nonetheless, the point counsels caution. After all, *Ethica Nicomachea* VI.7, 1141a18–20, defines wisdom as mind plus knowledge concerning the highest objects [τῶν τιμιωτάτων] and *Metaphysica* I.1, 982a1–2, reports that they are the principles and causes [ἀρχαί καὶ αἰτίαι]. Even *Metaphysica* VI.1, 1026a30–32, incorporates the attributes of being qua being [τὰ ὑπάρχοντα ἢ ὄν] into the study of primary philosophy.

But it is the explanation of divine mind's thinking itself that tells most against Norman's view. Notice, first, that he has little to say about the unusual nature of the formula "ἡ νόησις νοήσεως νόησις" (the thinking is thinking of thinking), in particular why Aristotle would employ it, if he is merely counting the UMM's self-thinking as a reference to theoretic thinking in general. Surely this calls for an explanation. Why did Aristotle not simply say that the UMM thinks all of the highest truths and, because it is identical with these, thinks itself? No need here for the puzzling phrase. What Norman does say suggests that he thinks divine mind's thinking of thinking [ἡ νόησις νοήσεως νόησις] is meant to be *explained by* its thinking itself [αὐτὸν νοεῖ]. But this *reverses* the order of explanation demanded by the text. So it appears that the formula is introduced to mark the special status of the UMM's αὐτὸν νοεῖν. Its activity does not merely range eternally over higher objects but is of a rather different form.

We should say something about the two remaining sections of the chapter, 1075a5–10, which closes the discussion by returning, explicitly, to the nature of the difference between human and divine thought, and 1074b35–1075a5, which contends with an objection to the characterization of the UMM as thinking thinking of thinking. Since Norman seizes on the latter as conclusive evidence for his view, a few remarks are in order.

The passage raises and removes the objection that knowledge, perception,

55. So he clearly means to be answering his opening question, namely, how (divine) mind is to be characterized if it is to be the most divine of phenomena.

opinion, and understanding all have something else as their object. For objects without matter, paradigmatically those of the theoretical sciences, knowledge and the object of knowledge are the same. Thus, in this context at least, thinking and thing thought are the same. Norman takes this as establishing the sameness in kind of human and divine thought. But that is because, so far as I can tell, he thinks that 1074b35–1075a5 explicates the divine thought that is ἡ νόησις νοήσεως νόησις. This is not obvious.[56] The passage meets an objection but it is an objection to the *general* possibility mentioned in *e,* namely, to the possibility of any mind whatever thinking itself. The strategy for defusing the objection is to show that in the clear case of human theoretical thought *e* is satisfied. Thus, the objector cannot complain: "How can you characterize god as ἡ νόησις νοήσεως νόησις when, by any notion of thought that makes sense to me [read 'to anyone'], what is thought about is always something different." So rather than explicating the UMM's thought, the passage meets an objection to one of its conditions.

A symptom that something has gone wrong is Norman's account of the distinction between self-contemplation and the ordinary theoretical thinking shared by human thinkers and the UMM. Given that an act of thinking contains (a) the subject that thinks, (b) the thought it thinks, and (c) that about which it thinks, Norman argues, "To describe the Prime Mover's activity as 'self-contemplation' suggests that (a) and (c) are the same. But the sense in which mind 'thinks itself' is rather that which amounts to an identity of (a) with (b)" (1969, 72). This is a curious argument. For while (b) would appear to match up with Aristotle's νόημα and (c) with his νοητόν, the identity of thought and object of thought is standardly formulated as a thesis about νοῦς and its νοητόν and never as a thesis about it and its νόημα. Norman's account at least has the virtue of reading the formula ἡ νόησις νοήσεως νόησις as a characterization of the UMM. Anscombe, on the other hand, dismisses it as an absurdity derived in "one of his dialectical passages" (1961, 59). Apart from lack of indicators as to the alleged dialectical nature of the passage, her suggestion that the sequel, 1074b35–1075a5, contains Aristotle's final word on the subject is curious for several reasons. First, Aristotle nowhere indicates that he is withdrawing the claim that the UMM is ἡ νόησις νοήσεως νόησις. Second, he in fact begins, as we have just seen, with an objection to that thesis. Thus, when he moves to meet the objection, he is also moving to save the thesis. So although there may be disagreement as to its interpretation, the formula is

56. The Oxford translation may, thus, be hasty in reading "ἡ νόησις" at 1075a4–5 as the divine thought.

clearly meant to apply to the UMM. There is some irony in Anscombe's appeal to Meinong's dislike of the formula, presumably on the grounds that all thinking needs an object, because Aristotle generates the formula partly out of his insistence that all thought be of something (see 1 above).

In the final lines of the chapter Aristotle moves to sharpen the contrast between human and divine thought. Can divine thought, he wonders, have as its object anything that is composite [σύνθετον]? This would require that it change from part to part of the whole [μεταβάλλοι ἂν ἐν τοῖς μέρεσι τοῦ ὅλου] and any sort of change has already been excluded by Dii. This can hardly be a question about whether the UMM has extensional parts, so Aristotle appears to be asking whether the object of divine thought can be notionally composite. Can it be a composite thought? If Ross is correct (1924, 398–99), these will be or include objects of scientific knowledge and so, properly speaking, will be apprehended by διάνοια (discursive thought) rather than νοῦς.[57] It follows that, whatever else counts as abstract thinking, it cannot cover objects of science. Indeed, if what results from any combination of thoughts counts as a σύνθετον, then precious little of human thinking remains even as a candidate for identification with divine thought. So it is far from obvious that when the UMM thinks itself, it is "doing nothing different from what we do when we think in the abstract" (Norman, 1969, 71). Moreover, to insist otherwise is to undermine the appeal to De Anima III.4, for there abstract thought was held to enjoy a rather wider role. In fact, just such a wider role may be suggested in 1075a6's denial of change to divine but not, we can arguably infer, to human thought. After all, De Anima III.4 defines thinking as something like being affected.

Aristotle answers his admittedly rhetorical question, first, by remarking that everything without matter is indivisible and, then, by contrasting human and divine styles of thinking the indivisible. Human thought occurs in a certain period of time [ἔν τινι χρόνῳ]. It is also thought of, or perhaps by, something composite [ὅ τῶν συνθέτων].[58]

I want to address two points concerning the human style of thinking the indivisible, both of which suggest why it falls short of divine thought. The first concerns De Anima III.6, 430b6–16's distinction between actual and potential indivisibles. Although one may grasp in a single period of time an actual undivided object, the object is potentially a divided object. For it

57. Ross's reason, that it is doubtful that νοῦς would be described as apprehending composite objects [τὰ συνθέτα], is not particularly impressive, if we read human νοῦς. It is, after all, that in virtue of which the soul supposes something to be the case [ὑπολαμβάνει] and discursively thinks [διανοεῖται] (De Anima III.4, 429a23).

58. Ross followed Alexander in taking τῶν συνθέτων at 1075a8 as the subject of human thinking but found it "awkward" that at 1075a5 σύνθετον clearly refers to the object of thought. I confess that I fail to see why this is a difficulty.

could be, or could have been, grasped in terms of its parts in two different periods of time. Equally, then, what is divided, and surely a σύνθετον will be such, can be grasped in an undivided thought. Neither of these can apply to divine thought because both admit potentiality.

The second point, which seems to me more crucial, urges that because we are composite things we must grasp everything in a certain period of time and, thus, that our thought of even indivisibles inevitably harbors potentiality. That we must think everything in time is clear from *De Memoria* 450a7–9: "we cannot think of anything apart from continuity [ἄνευ τοῦ συνεχοῦς] nor of what is not in time [τὰ μὴ ἐν χρόνῳ ὄντα] apart from time [ἄνευ χρόνου]." Because of this condition, any indivisible object of human thought is also a potentially divisible object. Thus, as Berti (1978, 151–54) suggests, even *De Anima* III.6, 430b14–15's objects that are undivided in form alone cannot be thought of apart from continuity and time. *Physica* IV.12, 221b3–4, counts what always exists [τὰ ἀεὶ ὄντα] as things that are not in time [οὐκ ἔστιν ἐν χρόνῳ], and 222a4 cites the incommensurability of the diagonal with the side of the square as an always existing thing. Consequently, human thought of such objects necessarily involves potentiality, and this will include most of the objects of the theoretical sciences. *De Anima* III.6, 430a30–31, distinguishes between, on the one hand, the incommensurable [τὸ ἀσύμμετρον] and diagonal [ἡ διάμετρος] that were previously separate [κεχωρισμένα] and, on the other hand, what results from their being combined [συντίθεται]. So it is obvious that the latter, as a σύνθετον, will not qualify as an object of divine thought. And, if we take seriously *Metaphysica* VII.10's talk of parts of the form [εἶδος] or essence [τί ἦν εἶναι], then, pace Kahn and Norman, neither will divine thought have these as its object.

Whether or not this establishes a difference in kind, it drives a wedge between human and divine thought that is sufficiently deep to cast grave doubt on the competing view. For it is simply false that we sometimes engage in exactly the same sort of thinking that the UMM always engages in. Thus, *Metaphysica* XII.9's final lines signal only that the divine thought is eternally actual where ours is only episodically so. The nature of their respective activities remains, nonetheless, quite distinct. And since the point is made by reinvoking the formula "ἡ νόησις νοήσεως νόησις" [αὐτη αὐτῆς ἡ νόησις at 1075a10] to sharply distinguish divine from human thought [ὁ ἀνθρώπινος νοῦς at 1075a7], that formula can hardly be meant to cover human thinking. Accordingly, the UMM must think itself and in a purely reflexive way. Were it to think one of the formally undivided, atemporal things that we think, why would it not still be subject to the potentiality that infects the human case? Aristotle's response is, in effect, that the question does not arise because only purely reflexive formal thinking answers to the demand that the UMM be activity only and necessarily so.

This account gives an admittedly minimalist picture of the UMM's nature. But no more is required by its function in the cosmology.[59] As XII.7 puts it, the UMM cannot be otherwise than it is and so is simple [ἁπλῶς at 1072b13 with 1015b11–12]. Thus, it must be eternal, immovable, separate from perceivable objects as well as unaffectable and unalterable. These attributes are a function of the UMM's role as final cause in the cosmological account, and as such, they demand no more than the strict reflexivity that Norman eschews. Appropriately, XII.9 contains no mention of an epistemological role for the UMM, acquisitional or otherwise, and, hence, provides no reason to move beyond the minimalist account.[60]

Let me finally turn to two advantages Norman claims for his view. One is that it alone makes sense of Aristotle's assertion in *Ethica Nicomachea* X that "the activity of the Prime Mover is the *summum bonum* of human life" (1969, 72). First, as we have seen, Aristotle says no such thing. At most we are urged to do something *like* what the UMM does. Second, the considerations advanced in support of the alleged advantage turn on his assertion that the minimalist picture gives an "air of unnecessary absurdity" to Aristotle's account, namely, that the UMM is "a sort of heavenly Narcissus, who looks around for the perfection which he [*sic*] wishes to contemplate, finds nothing to rival his own self and settles into a posture of permanent self-admiration" (63–64). Avoiding this is a further advantage claimed by Norman for his account. But there is something very wrong here. How do terms like "Narcissus," "rivaling," "settling into a posture," "self-admiration" even come to grace an account of Aristotle's UMM? It is hard to see how avoiding *this* could count in favor of any view.

Nor should we be misled by some tempting lines from *Metaphysica* I. Although neither Kahn nor Norman makes much of them (wisely, it will turn out), others have enlisted them in support of roughly the same view of productive mind (Sorabji, 1982, 306, for example). At 983a5–11, in the course of explaining that the science of "metaphysics" is the most divine and estimable [ἡ θειοτάτη καὶ τιμιωτάτη], Aristotle remarks:

And this science alone would be [ἂν εἴη] divine in two ways. For (γ) what science would most of all belong to god [μάλιστ' ἂν θεὸς

59. Here Ross was, I think, on the right track: "It is exclusively as a first mover that a God is necessary to his system" (1924, cliii), even if, as Skemp finds (1979, 231), he goes too far.

60. Without pretending to make sense of how it produces movement, one might regard the eternal circular movement of the so-called first sphere as the closest physical analogue to (imitation of?) the UMM's eternal, purely reflexive thinking.

ἔχοι] is a divine science and so would be (δ) any science that is about the divine [κἂν εἴ τις τῶν θείων εἴη]. And this science alone happens to have both, for (δ*) god is thought to be among the causes of all things and to be a sort of principle and (γ*) such a science would be had by god alone or by god most of all [μάλιστ᾽ ἂν ἔχοι θεός].

To the extent that Kahn asserts an isomorphism between the structure of divine and human *scientific* thought, this passage will be of little help. For its truths occupy higher ground. In any case, γ and, especially, its gloss γ* anticipate *Metaphysica* XII.9's discussion and so promises, if anything, the separation rather than the assimilation of human and divine νοῦς. Further-more, the passage is part of Aristotle's brief for the value of metaphysics and his usual way of indicating this is to apply the language of divinity. But, as section 1 above richly illustrates, this does not establish the sameness of human and divine νοεῖν. Accordingly, there is no hesitation in speaking of "metaphysics" as a divine science (so the indicative at 983a6–7: θεία τῶν ἐπιστημῶν ἐστί). Notice, however, that he chooses to make the present point by employing optative constructions. In effect, he characterizes his highest science counterfactually: the science that *would be* the science of god *is* the most divine and estimable science. This in no way commits Aristotle to the view that god, in fact, has or will have any such higher science—any more than 991a26–27's "ὁμοίως δὲ δῆλον ὅτι κἂν εἰ ἦν ὁ Σωκράτης ἀΐδιος" (". . . and it is clear that it would be the same even were Socrates eternal") commits Aristotle to the eternal existence of Socrates.[61] And the most the passage commits *us* to is that we are divine in the sense that we are capable, or almost capable, of something like the science that *would be* the science of god. This is hardly enough for the essential sameness of human and divine mind.

When Aristotle advocates the life of abstract or theoretical thinking, he is advocating a life characterized by the best that *we* can do. Our best is thinking in the theoretical mode, thinking of given objects, objects we become "identical" with in the thinking. Although they are the best avail-able to us, we must still think of these objects via images. Given their role in the mechanics of thought, images appear to be essential for distinguish-ing one object of thought from another.[62] Thus, *we* think ourselves only in

61. The use here of what Smyth (1920, 1786) calls the "unreal indicative" is a requirement of the reference to past time: "it would be similarly clear even if Socrates had been eternal."

62. Given *De Memoria*'s constraint that human thought cannot proceed apart from con-tinuity or time, it is worth recalling at this point that φαντασία is located, if at any one place in the soul, at the level of common sense, the very thing responsible for perception of time and continuity.

episodes of thinking and only by way of a distinct theoretical object. Although these are universals, they do not enjoy genuine ontological status and so cannot be grasped in an intellectual intuition of the "Platonic" sort. The UMM, on the other hand, directly grasps the object of its thought but the object is a particular, namely, itself. This is not, at least not obviously, theoretical thought of the human variety. What is common to both cases is that the thinking subject is a particular or particular system. The account of thinking must be conducted in terms of this constraint. For human thinking Aristotle honors this particularity not in the objects, which are universals, but in the [re]presentational devices that subserve thought of such objects. In this light the fact that the UMM's thought proceeds without images means that particularity must be located in the object of thought. Thus, *Metaphysica* XII.7, 1073a4–5, is explicit in phrasing the UMM's separation as separation from *what is perceivable* [κεχωρισμένη τῶν αἰσθητῶν] and so from what is [re]presentable by images. This is not to say that the UMM has other means of [re]presenting its object. God's thought is not [re]presentational at all; in particular it does not, like human thought, involve [re]presentation in universal judgments.

So divine thought cannot be much like human thought. Its object is a particular thought without aid of or need for [re]presentational devices. This means, in effect, that it has minimal content and this is why it is described as a νόησις νοήσεως. That human and divine thought are rather different sorts of thinking will prove problematic only to those who wish to assign the UMM more work than Aristotle thought proper for his ultimate principle.

6. THE HUMAN MIND AS A [RE]PRESENTATIONAL SYSTEM

The version of mind I have been promoting provides an alternative solution to a suppressed contradiction in Aristotle's theory of mind. The contradiction is this. On the one hand, *De Anima* is uncompromisingly committed to IM, the thesis that images are necessary for thought. Echoed elsewhere as well, at *De Memoria* 449b31–450a1, for example, IM is a well-entrenched piece of doctrine. It is also, we have suggested (chapter 1, section 3), part of Aristotle's "solution" to Brentano's problem. On the other hand, *De Anima* III.5 has been taken to imply that productive mind does not involve images because it is independent. This implies, or at least appears to imply, that images are not required for all thought. Some go so far as to urge that it enjoys a "content-free" kind of thought. So is IM false after all? The standard solution to this dilemma has been to restrict IM to thoughts of embodied entities, typically persons, and to restrict productive mind to god or some appropriate transcendent analogue. But this is a solution to a problem that arises only on the pair of assumptions that mind's independence is independence from body in a strong sense and that productive mind is in its own right the subject of acts of thinking at the intentional level. Both assumptions are questionable. As chapters 5 and 6 have urged, by independence need be indicated nothing more than the (relatively greater) independence of acts of thinking from the activity of physical structures, and by productive mind can be understood an operation that functionally subserves but is not itself a kind of thinking.

In any case, there are more straightforward grounds for doubt. First, the transcendent solution addresses a problem that need not arise at all in De Anima. In a work focusing on the individual soul it is opaque why one should discuss god's capabilities for thought unless that served the account in question.[63] But Aristotle nowhere indicates that such service is at hand, and as the last chapter argued, it is unclear how this would work in the first place. Second, IM is argued for after introduction of the distinction between receptive and productive mind. So it appears that IM is meant to cover νοῦς as a functionally structured faculty, and this runs against the transcendent solution.[64]

On just this point the merit of our interpretation emerges, for if IM is meant to apply to mind generally and if productive mind is simply that aspect of the individual mind's operation bearing on the activity but not the content of thought, then a nontranscendent solution to the alleged contradiction is achieved. What this means is that, so far as De Anima is concerned, there are no exceptions to the thesis that all thought requires images. This in turn means that all thought requires receptive as well as productive mind. Together these lower-level operations accomplish thinking, and images are central to the account.[65]

63. Brentano (1977, 183–89) adduces 430a18–22 which asserts that what acts is superior to what is affected and that in general, but not in the individual, actual knowledge is prior to potential knowledge. But this need only refer to the earlier discussed demand that faculties must be defined in terms of their function, that is, in terms of what they do. There is no need to introduce god's divine activity as the prior component of thinking.

64. Of course, friends of the transcendent solution will appeal to textual looseness in the composition of the third book of De Anima. But this should be the final rather than first court of appeal.

65. It is, perhaps, appropriate to mention Brentano's identification of receptive mind or, better, his ὁ παθητικὸς νοῦς and imagination (1977, 208). If IM holds for individual minds generally, this cannot be correct because IM implies that no thought present to such a mind—and this would include receptive mind—can be identified with the associated image. This view requires (what I argued against in chapter 3) that imagination is a kind of thought.

At this point we are brought back to Aristotle's opening discussion of the possibility that the soul exists independently, for this is registered as a possibility for νοῦς alone. *De Anima* I.1, 403a3–16, sets the terms of discussion: peculiarity, separability, and imagination. If, Aristotle says, there is something peculiar [ἴδιον] to the soul, then it may after all be separable:

1. (*a*) P is a function or affection peculiar to a soul y ⊃
   (*b*) ◊ (y exists without body)

at 403a10–11 follows because of

2. (*c*) x has a soul y & (*d*) P is a function or affection of y & (*e*) P is not a function or affection of x's body z ≡ (*f*) P is peculiar to the soul

at 403a3–5.

Where P is perception *e* is not satisfied and so it is neither peculiar to the soul nor able to exist without the body. The best candidate for separateness is, says Aristotle, thinking [τὸ νοεῖν]: it most of all seems to be peculiar [μάλιστα δ' ἔοικεν ἰδίῳ τὸ νοεῖν] (403a8). Thus, we have at 403a8–10:

3. (*g*) P is thinking & (*h*) P is a kind of imagination or P is not without imagination ⊃ (*i*) ~ ◊ (P is without body).

Several points bear mention here. First, as *i* registers, "τοῦτ'" in a9 picks up τὸ νοεῖν at a8, and thus the question is whether the function or affection of thinking involves body or not. To the extent that this is a question about episodes or operations of thinking, 6a' of chapter 4, section 5, is supported and not a weaker or acquisitional notion of dependence. Second, even were *a* satisfied for thinking, what follows, with typical circumspection, is only the *possibility* of soul's separability. Third, 3 and 2 entail that thinking is not, after all, peculiar to the soul. If we assume that Aristotle here means the human soul, one might suppose him to be claiming that thinking is not *peculiar* to the soul because god thinks as well. After all, what is ἴδιον to a thing is a property it and it alone has. But this overlooks completely the context of the argument. The point seems rather to be that because human thought always involves images, it is a sort of thinking that is peculiar to human beings. This underscores our earlier argument that human and divine thought are not activities of the same kind. That νοεῖν is peculiar to persons and not their souls reflects the non-Cartesian point that the subject of thought is a single system, a system that has a physical realization because of the demand for images.

The demand for images is in turn, I have suggested, a response to the question of how a particular (physical) system can have as objects of its cognitive attitudes what is different from it, in particular, universals. Although there are a variety of different answers to this, Aristotle, we saw, operates from the premise that the system must be capable of [re]presenting these objects.

It will be well to say something more about this notion. For one thing, the notion of [re]presentation is ambiguous, if not irresolvably cloudy. It does not, for instance, obviously require similarity between [re]-presentational device and object [re]presented. So when Aristotle says that images are *like* the objects they [re]present, he is coming down in favor of a particular style of [re]presentation. It is, in fact, one of the poles of debate within contemporary cognitive science, namely, pictorialism as opposed to descriptionalism. Roughly, descriptionalists hold that internal [re]-presentations [re]present much in the manner of ordinary symbol systems, systems such as English. What counts here is convention and interpretation. But there is nothing else, nothing intrinsic to the system of symbols that tells us what it does or could [re]present. Pictorialists, on the other hand, urge that (at least some of) our internal [re]presentations [re]present by depicting in the manner of pictures. Since it is absurd to require full depiction, a weaker notion of [re]presentation is usually countenanced. One criterion suggested recently[66] is that an internal [re]presentation [re]presents an object pictorially, only if some part of the [re]presentation [re]presents some part of the object.[67]

As formulated, the distinction is admittedly vague,[68] but it can provide some help in determining how Aristotle's φαντάσματα [re]present. We may start with the fact that 2a of the canonical text (chapter 2, section 1) requires that images be similar [ὁμοίαν] to what they [re]present. Then, at *Metaphysica* V.9, 1018a15–19, various senses of ὅμοια are parsed in terms of the various ways two things can share an attribute (or attributes). Not all attributes need be shared. Extended to the case at hand, we would appear to have the materials for an early formulation of the pictorialists' criterion. Add to this the fact that the semantic model of *De Interpretatione* (see chapter 4, section 7) distinguishes the symbolic relation holding between linguistic tokens and internal affections from the similarity holding between the latter and objects in the world (the affections are ὁμοιώτατα), and we appear to have an appreciation of the difference between pictorial and de-scriptional styles of [re]presentation—with a clear preference for pictorial-ism in the case of internal [re]presentation.

---

66. N. Block (1983, 513n13), who also mentions Kosslyn et al. (1979).
67. This, of course, leaves the nature of partial pictorial [re]presentation unexplicated.
68. See N. Block (1983) for more on this.

Admittedly, it is unclear how successfully the pictorial style applies to highly abstract theoretical thinking, say, thought of the principle of non-contradiction. But this will be a problem less with our interpretation than with Aristotle's account. In fact, it may not be a problem. Thinking of the principle of noncontradiction does require some sort of sentential [re]-presentation, internal or otherwise. One might take the further step and claim that the [re]presentation is pictorial to the extent that the logical form of the law is perspicuously displayed by the [re]presentation.[69] Thus, contemplation of something as abstract as the law of excluded middle might involve an image of a sentence formulating the law or an image of an instance of the law. Indeed, seen this way, IM turns on the claim that *purely* abstract thought is impossible. And this seems quite correct (see Nussbaum, 1978, 266, who concurs). There is nothing like thinking a pure proposition or a pure number, not even for productive mind [νοῦς ποιητικός]. To think of a proposition involves something like a sentential [re]presentation of that proposition. Indeed, if *De Anima* III. 10's calculative imagination [λογιστικὴ φαντασία] can be made to cover pictorial [re]presentations (but see chapter 4, section 7), then one kind of φάντασμα might be something like a sentence token.[70] This is not to deny intuition a role but to channel its role through [re]presentational devices. This contrasts rather dramatically with the Platonists' advocacy of direct intuition of pure forms. Such a possibility is, for Aristotle, not alive even for productive mind.

If [re]presentation requires similarity between image and object of thought, are images naturalistic pictures after all? I think it is clear from our above analysis that this is so only in certain cases and then only in a rather attenuated form (for more on this, see N. Block, 1983). More interesting is the question whether the relation between image and object of thought must be such that from inspection or mere awareness of an image a subject could know what it was an image of. Again the answer is apparently negative. Although images may be required as [re]presentational devices, we have seen that they do not in their own right have the required semantical property of aboutness. Only in the context of thinking about an object can it be meaningfully asked what the involved image is an image of. Aboutness is a feature of the complete intentional act, not of the [re]presentational structure involved in the act. So the requirement of similarity cannot have semantical force.

69. Here one is, perhaps, reminded of the sentences of the *Tractatus*, which display but do not state the form of fact that would make them true.

70. Thus, satisfying one of Field's constraints on the solution to Brentano's problem. (See chap. 1, sec. 3).

The insistence on [re]presentational devices standing in some kind of a similarity relation to objects is connected, I have suggested, with the fact that thought is an objective affair. Thus, different persons may have different images in thinking of a given object, but still each image will be similar to some objective feature of the object in question. Two geometers, each with different images, may yet think of one and the same thing. An isosceles-imaged geometer and his scalene-imaged counterpart can think and discourse on the triangle itself. And in thinking about the general properties of scalene triangles, they may both be scalene-imaged but differently so. The point is that we may ignore differences in images that are irrelevant to the [re]presentational requirements *imposed by the particular complete act in question*. This holds equally for objects such as Socrates. One person may think of Socrates in connection with an olfactory image; another may do so in connection with an auditory or visual image.[71]

But why must similarity be introduced into this story? The answer to this is that Aristotle appears to hold the theses

    A. When a subject thinks of something, that subject must be in some internal state and that state must have some relation to the object of thought

and

    B. When a subject thinks of something, that subject thinks of an actual object or of actual features of such an object.

Putting aside the compatibility of B with thought about nonexistent entities (see Wedin, 1978), it is natural for anyone holding A and B to demand that the relation between the subject's state and the object be that of similarity or partial similarity. Only if some feature of an internal state is in fact similar to the object [re]presented, does it make sense to say that the subject is in fact thinking of the object in question. Were the image involved in a thought to share nothing with the alleged object of thought, the claim to be thinking about that object would lose credibility.[72]

At least this is plausibly what Aristotle might have thought. Descriptionalism embraces an essentially symbolic style of [re]presentation. For

71. For more on the topic of this paragraph, see chap. 5, sec. 2, above.
72. While Nussbaum (1980, 364) is correct to fault Hartman for failing to connect φαντασία with the subjective feature of experince (Hartman adopts a rather straightforward classical empiricist version of φαντασία), the form of connection need not be seeing-as. For we may insist that seeing-as is still seeing [αἴσθησις] and let φαντασία function in the role of [re]presentational structure. If we need to endow αἴσθησις with explicit interpretational force, better to do so via δόξα or even νοῦς.

Aristotle that would make [re]presentation a matter of convention or shared agreement. Because the only devices we have for [re]presenting objects are internal, it would presumably follow that certain internal items are amenable to conventional agreement. But, of course, this is false. Nature, on the other hand, does nothing by convention and has fitted imagination for its role in securing intersubjectivity by arranging that it [re]presents pictorially. So, at any rate, might Aristotle have reasoned.

But this can be only part of the story. After all, nature could have gotten the same result by equipping us with descriptional [re]presentational structures. Indeed, nature might have generated either sort of structure by an evolutionary route, favoring over time those [re]presentational structures that produce the best results, that is, that subserve systems whose behavior most accurately reflects and responds to the objective features of the world. There is, in fact, some evidence in Aristotle for at least tying structure to utility. Perceptual faculties, for instance, may be functionally definable in terms of their role in discriminating certain ranges of objects in the perceptual environment and, ultimately, in terms of their role in the organism's survival. Thus, *De Sensu* 436b14–18 suggests that taste governs pursuit of the pleasant and avoidance of the unpleasant in the area of nutriment and that smell, hearing, and sight enable pursuit of food at a distance and, hence, self-preservation. Thought itself has a similar survival role, as well as a role in seeking well-being [τὸ εὖ ἕνεκα].[73] But there is no obvious reason a fitness constraint on faculties demands pictorial as opposed to descriptional [re]presentational structures. So we still need to say something more.

As a matter of fact, we can, I think, offer a plausible conjecture. Suppose Aristotle thought that crucial to any cognitive state is a certain sort of "inner" experience—that there is a certain "look" to seeing, a certain "sound" to hearing, and a certain "content" to thinking. Indeed, such features may have been deemed essential in order to explain the causal role of such states in intentional acts. It might, then, be natural to posit [re]presentations of the pictorial sort not as the inner states themselves but as the *explanation* of such states. How, if there is no pictorial aspect to our means of [re]presenting objects, can we account for this inner feature of cognitive acts? Underlying this supposed attitude might have been the intuition that without such internal states, it would be implausible to suppose that the subject is perceiving something red as something that is red or

---

73. This function of thought is, unsurprisingly, reflected in the function assigned speech: "expression [ἡ ἑρμηνεία] is for the sake of well-being [ἕνεκα τοῦ εὖ] . . . nature uses breath both to maintain internal warmth, as something necessary, and also for articulate sound [πρὸς τὴν φωνήν] so that there might be well-being [τὸ εὖ]" (420b19–22).

that the subject is perceiving that something is red rather than merely registering something red. If this is at all correct, then psychological states cannot be merely functional states for Aristotle. They are not merely internal states that bear causally on what an entity does; rather, the fact that they are causally efficacious is explained, in part, by the fact that they are pictorial [re]presentations. This is part of the point of Aristotle's maxim that a faculty in use becomes, formally at least, like its object. Perceiving, say, a red thing involves having a red [re]presentation, but there is no necessity to regard this as committing Aristotle to the claim that the subject—better, the faculty—becomes red in the sense that the object perceived is red.[74]

For contemporary cognitivists [re]presentation breeds interpretation. The task is to explain an intentional system in terms of lower-level systems, whose parts, sometimes dubbed homunculi, exchange and interpret [re]-presentations. Each such part is in turn treated as a system, subject to further lower-level analyses, until so-called primitive processors are reached. Ideally, their operations will have a purely physical explanation. It is, I think, clear that Aristotle allows room for primitive processors. The sensory organs themselves appear to be such, for they do not simply pass on uninterpreted input for interpretation higher up in the system. They are themselves cognitively significant processors. Although what is perceived is always particular, input is perceived as input of a certain type. This is part of the point of Aristotle's maxim that, although the object of perception is particular, perception is of the universal.

It is also clear that Aristotle allows room for interpretation of the requisite kind. His reminder at De Anima I.4, 408b1–18, that we should say, not that the soul thinks, but that the person thinks with or in virtue of the soul neither raises a point of style nor pleads for linguistic reform. It is a canonical remark warning us, in effect, to keep clear levels of explanation. One explains systemwide behavior by appealing to what parts of the system can do, in particular, to what the soul can do. This, in turn, is explained by appeal to operations of its parts. And here the cognitivist idiom is standard. The various senses "discriminate" determinate features of the perceptual environment; they produce reports that are generally "affirmed" by the ἀρχή of perception; sometimes something more powerful "overrides" them. These and other passages, already discussed at length, establish that Aristotle is comfortable applying cognitivistic language to functional parts of the soul and, thus, implicitly is recognizing them as lower-level interpreters.

74. See N. Block (1983, 516–18) for two ways to regard possession of "like" properties by internal [re]presentations.

The view that Aristotle incorporates into his theory of mind [re]-presentational structures that [re]present pictorially is easily construed as committing him in turn to the view that images are senselike items that [re]present in virtue of properties that we are directly aware of. Although we have uncovered little interest in this question, on Aristotle's part, we can, I suppose, still ask whether Aristotle's images are phenomenal or physical. Aristotle sometimes comes close to saying that we are aware of the image, thus giving some support to the phenomenalist reading. If images are not physiologically based, however, then thought's dependence on them could not entail its dependence on body. So they must, in some sense, be physical structures.

Aristotle is at home in both idioms, I suggest, because it simply does not matter. For certain purposes one idiom is more appropriate than the other. Problems with Leibniz's Law do not arise, first, because when we report jointly on, say, the occurrence of a certain physiological process and a certain sort of phenomenal item, there is only one thing we are reporting. In Aristotle's idiom the process and the appearance are (extensionally) the same but differ in being. One might say there is one thing variantly described, and since one description introduces an intentional context, Leibniz's Law may not apply in the first place. In the second place Leibniz's Law will not cause problems *if* Aristotle is willing to say that physiological processes do, as a matter of fact, have so-called phenomenal properties. I see no reason he would not hold this.[75]

I say this because the ontological status of entities simply is not what is most central to the cognitivist account. I am not here coming full circle and saying that there is no mind–body problem for Aristotle. There is. But it is not the post-Cartesian problem of the identity and/or difference of phenomenal and physical. Rather it is a problem concerning explanation. What is given is that "physiological" systems somehow manage to [re]present pictorially, and this cannot be explained without use of the idiom of form and likeness, an idiom that is not reducible to physiological terms— at least, we have seen, not according to Aristotle. So there will be explanatory emergence, if you will, but no ontological excess in the account of cognitive activity.

This holds equally for thinking. Here there is, of course, no obvious physiological correlate for identification with episodes of νόησις. Even the best prospect, the image, is too distant, too particular, to help. But the search for a physiological correlate is misguided in the first place and rad-

---

75. Partly for the sorts of reasons argued by Rorty (1965, 1979). *De Somno et Vigilia* I, 454a7–11, appears to reflect precisely this view in arguing that because the process of perception is not peculiar [ἴδιον] to the soul or to the body, neither is the affection [τὸ πάθος].

ically misconceives Aristotle's program. He is intent on explaining how a system must be organized, at one level, to accomplish something, thinking, at another level. Since it is mind, as a whole system, that does thinking, it is pointless to identify thinking with the activity of one of its parts. Neither productive nor receptive mind, on its own, can manage thinking. When the person thinks with his or her mind, productive mind produces or, I have suggested, retrieves from receptive mind, the place of forms, an object of thought. In so doing an image or images are inevitably involved as the means of [re]presenting the object of thought. Although the details of how this works are not made precise by Aristotle,[76] what he does say suggests that actual$_2$ possession of an object of thought cannot be reduced to occurrence of an image at a lower level of the system. Explanation, again, need not be reduction and explaining how a system thinks need not explain *what* thinking is.

Finally, perhaps, I may be permitted a speculative point about productive mind. It is, I have argued, rung in to explain, among other things, the autonomy of human thought. Recent computer-friendly cognitivists have attempted to accommodate this feature by building in something like a random-choice generator.[77] They have, in short, suggested programming a certain measure of chance into the model of thinking. I discussed above *Ethica Eudemia* VII.2's argument that the determining factor in thinking, productive mind, was something like the soul's unmoved mover, its god. But that discussion was also tailored to counter the option that the starting point of movement in the soul is merely luck and that everything thus happens by chance (ἀπὸ τύχης]. In this light, may we not suppose that Aristotle would eschew random generation as an account of mind's spontaneity, thus leaving spontaneity as an irreducible feature of the system? If so, it is no surprise to find him elevating productive mind to the level of the god within us. But so far from demanding transcendental status, this stands as his final tribute to the uniqueness of the finite system that we are. Whether or not his account of this system is ultimately correct, it is surely worthy of Aristotle.

76. Are, for instance, images the means of "storing" thoughts in receptive mind?
77. See, for instance, "On Giving Libertarians What They Say They Want," in Dennett, 1978.

POST-ARISTOTELIAN EVIDENCE
FOR THE INCOMPLETENESS THESIS

The thesis that Aristotle does not countenance imagination as a full faculty was supported in part by the observation that nowhere in the corpus do we find him mentioning φανταστά. The idea, roughly, was that faculties are defined in terms of their proper objects and that the verbal adjective is Aristotle's way of marking this. Thus, the νοητόν can be the thinkable thing as well as the thing thought, the αἰσθητόν the perceivable thing as well as the thing perceived.[1] Such a characterization gives us little that is informative about the particular objects of a given faculty. But the verbal adjective does manage to pick out the formal object of the faculty. And since formal objects in effect specify object ranges and are thus tied to faculty individuation, the effective absence of "φανταστόν" adds support to our argument that imagination is not to be identified as a faculty at all.

This line of interpretation would be enhanced considerably by the availability of texts in which the verbal adjective not only occurs but also is connected to full facultyhood for imagination. As it turns out, we have a very clear case in Proclus's commentary on the first book of Euclid's *Elements*.[2] A self-professed Platonist, Proclus offers a set of considerations in favor of regarding mathematical objects, points, lines, circles, and the like, as objects existing somehow in the imagination. Although geomtery studies universals, the practitioner of geometry cannot study them directly because they are simple and free of any sort of extension. Such items exceed, in principle, our direct comprehension and the geometer in any case treats his objects, in practice, as divisible, bisectible, and so on. Thus, in addition to sensible particulars [τὰ αἰσθητά] Proclus introduces objects that exist in the

---

1. See, for instance, Smyth (1920, sec. 472).
2. References will be to Gottfried Friedlein's edition (1873) and translations will, for the most part, follow Morrow (1970).

imagination [τὰ ἐν φαντασίᾳ τὴν ὑπόστασιν ἔχοντα]. There must be such objects, says Proclus, because sensible particulars cannot account for the clarity and exactness of our mathematical ideas. Proofs using these objects, which vary in irrelevant ways with occasion and agent of proof, provide results good for universal mathematical knowledge because they just are exemplary cases of mathematical universals. Since rough-hewn sensible particulars are not, Proclus declares in favor of two kinds of universals corresponding to the two kinds of objects. There could hardly be a clearer sign that he really does mean to talk about a different *kind* of object rather than simply a different way of regarding ordinary objects (Aristotle's adverbial theory). Notice, also, that in requiring exactness of idea to be explained by exactness of object he is adopting a fundamental Platonic assumption, again, one that Aristotle gladly relinquishes in his account of mathematical objects.

Most striking for immediate purposes, however, is Proclus's characterization of τὰ ἐν φαντασίᾳ ὑπόστασιν ἔχοντα as τὰ φανταστά (101.13). He mentions imaginal circles [τὰ φανταστὰ κύκλα at 53.9 and 23–24 and 54.24], imaginal matter [ἡ φανταστὴ ὕλη at 55.5], matter of imaginal shapes [ἡ ὕλη τῶν φανταστῶν σχημάτων at 86.12–13], and imaginal synthesis and division of figures [αἱ συνθέσεις τῶν σχημάτων καὶ αἱ διαιρέσις φαντασταί at 55.7–8]. And, speaking globally, at 285.18–22 he mentions triangles, circles, angles, lines, and all the other geometrical figures. Such objects provide not merely a distinct object range for mathematical universals; they also are the target of a distinct faculty's operations.[3] The faculty, of course, is none other than imagination itself. Had Proclus spoken merely of objects *in* the imagination there would be no call to introduce imagination as a genuine faculty. But to regard them as φανταστά is quite another matter. Moreover, the point is not just that the Proclean imagination produces φανταστά where the Aristotelian imagination produced φαντάσματα. His imagination actually operates on these alleged objects to generate knowledge.

This is clear from a variety of passages: "imagination *is moved by itself* [ἀνεγείρεται ἀφ᾽ ἑαυτῆς] to put forth what it *knows* [προβάλλει τὸ γνωστον]" (52.20–21); "because it is not outside the body. . . everything it *thinks* [ὅπερ ἂν νοῇ] is a picture or shape of its thought [τόπος καὶ μορφή]" (52.25–26); "imagination *thinks* [νοεῖ] objects as extended in virtue of the fact that it [the circle] has a sort of intelligible matter [νοητὸν ὕλην] that *is provided by* imagination itself" (52.27–53.1); "for when the imagination *knows,* it simultaneously assigns to the object of its knowledge a

---

3. See also his mention of φανταστόν in 62.11–18.

form and a limit and, in knowing, brings to an end its movement through the imaginal object;[4] it has gone through it and comprehends it" (285.7–10).

Despite the report of certain commentators, Aristotle nowhere shows signs of anticipating the Proclean view. It is simply implausible to have him similarly link φαντασία and νοεῖν. The tendency to assimilate imagination to full facultyhood is, however, completely natural for Proclus, largely because of his thoroughgoing Platonism. It is, in fact, so natural that he is able, with full confidence, to report as Aristotle's two theses the Stagirite appears never to have held. The first is that Aristotle recognizes (Proclus has "somewhere says") two kinds of matter, that of sensible particulars and that of imaginal objects. Although, as Morrow correctly points out in his note on 51.17, *Metaphysica* 1036a6–12 distinguishes between ὕλη αἰσθητή and ὕλη νοητή, glossing the latter at ὕλη φανταστῶν is, pace Morrow, not justified by *De Anima* 433a10, for that passage, we have already seen (chapter 3, section 2), does not establish that φαντασία is a form of νόησις. And, in any case, where there are no φανταστά there can be no ὕλη φανταστῶν.[5] What does justify the gloss, in Proclus's mind, is probably the fact that the *Metaphysica* indicates objects of mathematics as the ones that enjoy intelligible matter *plus* Proclus's own view that these are imaginal objects [φανταστά].

This story of how Proclus came to attribute ὕλη φανταστῶν to Aristotle is borne out by the second "suspect" thesis. As if to round out the picture of the Aristotelian imagination thinking genuine objects, he continues "for this reason [that imagination produces and knows φανταστά] a certain person has ventured to call it [the imagination] 'receptive *Nous*.'"[6] Although the reference is clearly to *De Anima* III.5, neither there nor elsewhere does Aristotle *say* any such thing. And, if Brentano's arguments for the identification are unpersuasive (see chapter 5, n. 45), Proclus does not appear even to feel the need for argument. Having raised imagination to the status of a knowing faculty, he is content to offer a rationale for Aristotle's description of it as a certain kind of νοῦς. A rationale is needed since, as a purely intellectual faculty at greatest remove from those things that are affectable, νοῦς surely would be thought impassable and immaterial. Thus,

---

4. Here Proclus has φαντάσματα! Clearly, he could not be further from Aristotle in his reading of φαντασία, then, for he regards φαντάσματα as not importantly different from φανταστά. But it is the latter that is his favorite expression precisely because it connotes the proper object of a genuine faculty.

5. Recall that, if anything, Aristotle linked matter with φαντάσματα, not φανταστά, and even then only by way of a possible mention at *De Anima* III.8, 432a9–14, that thoughts are like images but without the matter of the image.

6. Lines 52.3–4. (The parenthetical clarifications are mine.)

it is only because its activity *resembles* the highest sort of knowledge that imagination is called νοῦς and only because of its kinship [συγγένεια] with the sensory that it is called receptive—so at least Proclus (52).

Of course, if, as we have all along urged, imagination does not display activity characteristic of a genuine faculty, then the question of its having a noetic employment simply won't arise. Divergence is even more marked on the suggestion that receptive mind, because it is identified with a fully capable imagination, is itself a full faculty capable of independent exercise. We have implicitly rejected this in our insistence that receptive mind and productive mind complement each other as structures of the mind's functional organization, neither doing complete work *in its own right* but both subserving, jointly, the operation of thought at the intentional level.

To strengthen our case it may be worth noting, finally, how Proclus's practice reflects Chrysippus's preaching on the nature of the φανταστόν. Chrysippus is reported (von Arnim, 1905, II.21–22) to have distinguished between φαντασία, φανταστόν, φανταστικόν, and φάντασμα. Allowing for the trivial omission of the verbal formulation φαντάζεσθαι, Chrysippus's list parallels the ingredients of imagination retailed in chapter 2, with the important exception that he includes as a standard feature what plays no role for Aristotle, the φανταστόν. But Chrysippus also gives rather different value to the "shared" ingredients. The Chrysippean φανταστικόν (that which imagines), for example, appears to be something like a faculty of delusion and his φάντασμα (image) is defined as that which, as in the case of the melancholic or the mad, draws our delusional φανταστικόν into play. Presumably, the φάντασμα is a πάθος, or affection, in the soul but not a πάθος resulting from a φανταστόν, or object of imagination. The φαντασία, on the other hand, is a πάθος resulting from a φανταστόν. It is a state that reveals itself as well as what brings it to activity [ἡ φαντασία δείκνυσιν ἑαυτὴν καὶ τὸ πεποιηκὸς αὐτήν at II.22,1–2]. The latter is, of course, the φανταστόν. It is, Chrysippus is made to say, "that which moves the imagination [τὸ ποιοῦν τὴν φαντασίαν], for instance, the white thing and the cold thing; and anything that is able to move the soul is a φανταστόν [καὶ πᾶν ὅ τι ἂν δύνηται κινεῖν τὴν ψυχήν, τοῦτ' ἔστι φανταστόν]." When the φαντασία is active there is a φανταστόν underlying but when the φανταστικόν (that which imagines) is operative there is none [τῇ γὰρ φαντασίᾳ ὑπόκειται τι φανταστόν, τῷ δὲ φανταστικῷ οὐδέν at II.22, 8–9].

It is obvious not only that Chrysippus assigns different, non-Aristotelian, values to φαντασία, φανταστικόν, and φάντασμα but also that these do not even belong in the same list, at least not obviously. The φάντασμα stands in some causal relation to the φανταστικόν, but it is not clear that either of these has any relationship to φαντασία, certainly none that, as in

Aristotle, makes them part of an account of episodes of φαντασία. What is clear, of course, is that the φανταστόν is given an explicit and broad causal role in such an account.[7] Here there is no suggestion of φαντασία merely subserving the operation of other faculties. It is a faculty in its own right. Thus, while Chryspippus eschews Proclean Platonism in favor of more ordinary objects, the critical point is that both writers link φανταστά with full facultyhood for imagination because for both φανταστά determine an object range. As with αἰσθητά and αἴσθησις and with νοητά and νόησις so now φανταστά and φαντασία are brought together to the theoretical elevation of both.

The merits of their theories aside, Proclus and Chrysippus do appear to link full facultyhood for φαντασία to commitment to φανταστά and, thus, would appear to support our argument that absence of the latter in Aristotle's canonical theory is to be explained by his view that imagination is not itself a standard faculty but rather a general [re]presentational capability subserving the operation of such faculties.

7. See also Sextus's usage, *Adversus Mathematicos* VIII.409.

APPREHENSIVE VERSUS AUTONOMOUS THINKING

I have been urging that *De Anima* III.4 and 5 go together and that so taken they provide a (partial) functional analysis of thinking. It would not be surprising to get a rather different slant on III.4 from interpreters who read it more or less on its own. Malcolm Lowe (1983) has recently suggested that we get in the chapter an account of no less than two kinds of thinking. Lowe argues that so far from assimilating thought to sensation, what he takes to be the received view, *De Anima* III.4 aims to dissociate the two and to distinguish two kinds of thinking, apprehensive and autonomous. It should be clear that there is little disagreement on the first point, for we argued above that the analogy between thinking [νοεῖν] and perceiving [αἰ-σθάνεσθαι] is imperfect and supports only the weak claim that thinking is something like being affected. Still, it is meant to introduce that claim. Lowe, on the other hand, talks as if *no* analogy were intended. This forces him to regard what we considered distinguishing characteristics of the mind, for example, 2 and 4 of chapter 5, section 1, as merely Aristotle's objections to the then prevalent view that thinking is just a sort of sensation. While it is true that Aristotle rejects this identification, he does so at the outset of III.3 in explicitly mentioning Homer and the erring ancients. The language of III.4, however, suggests no such interest in predecessor doctrines: only Anaxagoras is named and then favorably in the course of endorsing the doctrine that mind is unmixed and has nothing in common with anything else. So it is odd to find Lowe suggesting that *De Anima* III.4 gives central place to the project of distancing sensation and thinking. That job has already seen completion and so Aristotle would seem, after all, to inaugurate discussion of thinking by taking the analogy with perceiving seriously. This need not spawn the problems Lowe, rightly, wishes to avoid so long as we bear in mind that perfect analogy falls short of

assimilation and imperfect analogy fares even worse. In any case, the disagreement here is largely a function of divergence in broader interpretive
strategies. So I want to turn to the argument that *De Anima* III.4 distinguishes two *kinds* of thinking.

Having already offered interpretation of many of the passages Lowe considers, I shall here simply indicate some problems I see in his arguments.
One concerns the way the two alleged kinds of thinking are distinguished:
autonomous thinking is that thinking whose object is a universal *or* an
absent particular and apprehensive thinking is that whose object is a perceived particular. I shall not here worry the point that this may counter the
rather popular dogma that νοῦς, at least in its proper employment, ranges
over universal truths only. Of more concern is why one would want to talk
about two *kinds* of thinking. After all, the mind, unlike other cognitive
faculties, is distinguished by the fact that its range is unrestricted. So,
initially, it might seem that there is no basis for the distinction in question.

The argument for the distinction is that Aristotle routinely distinguishes
faculties in terms of their objects and that autonomous and apprehensive
thinking have different objects. On the face of it this is an odd argument,
for one could as well argue that precisely because both *kinds* of thought
take particulars as objects, they are in fact not different in kind. Perhaps
that is why Lowe sometimes formulates the difference in terms of the means
rather than the objects of thought: the mind thinks autonomously when it
thinks via imagination and apprehensively when it thinks via sensation.
This "adverbial" formulation will not, however, generate a difference in
kind because there is no reason to suppose that the mind cannot think one
and the same object, sometimes via imagination, sometimes via perception.
What else am I doing when I daydream about a lover whom I later perceive?
Unless, that is, one were to hold that objects of autonomous thinking just
are images, whereas objects of apprehensive thinking are perceived objects.
But the manuscripts for the passage Lowe might cite in support of this
maneuver, 432a8–9, justify reading "and when one contemplates, one contemplates simultaneously with an image [φαντάσματι]"[8] as well as "and
when one contemplates, one simultaneously contemplates an image [φάν-
τασμά τι]."[9] And even were it possible to make images the objects of contemplation, perhaps following Lloyd's suggestion (1969–70) that the contemplating mind abstracts universals from images, it is not plausible for
the case of absent particulars. What would it mean to abstract an *individual,*
absent or otherwise, from an image?

---

8. So Y, as well as E, the best manuscript.
9. CLUS. SVWX have the plural φαντάσματα.

There are further reasons to resist the immediate formulation of differences in kinds of thinking. First, we have already seen that imagination is involved in the exercise of all genuine faculties, perceptual included. So the addition of imagination will not distinguish one faculty from another. Second, there is some reason to give universals a role in the account of perception itself. *Analytica Posteriora* II.19 reports that, although it is the particular that is perceived, perception is of the universal [αἰσθάνεται μὲν τὸ καθ' ἕκαστον ἡ δ' αἴσθησις τοῦ καθόλου ἐστίν]. Some commentators understandably take this remark as an embarrassment forced on Aristotle by an equally unattractive theory of concept acquisition. But *De Anima* II.12, 424a17–24, makes it fairly clear that the *Analytica Posteriora* II.19 report is of a piece with Aristotle's standard theory. The by now familiar key passage "in each case the sense [ἡ αἴσθησις] is affected by that which has color or flavor or sound, but by these not insofar as it is said to be a particular [οὐχ ᾗ ἕκαστον ἐκείνων λέγεται] but insofar as they are things of a certain kind [ᾗ τοιονδί] and in accordance with the logos," can be read as

    κ. For any faculty Φ, if F is the proper object of Φ & Φ is affected
       by F, then there is a particular x such that (i) Φ is affected by
       x qua F & (ii) Φ is not affected by x qua individual & (iii) Φ
       is affected by x qua thing of the kind F and in accordance with
       the logos governing Φing.

So in standard cases of perception one receives the form from a particular—not, however, qua particular but, rather, qua universal. Consequently, perception already involves capacity to receive universals, just what the *Analytica Posteriora* passage is urging. As κ indicates, however, this does not involve quantification over universals, and so there is still a sense in which perception is exclusively about particulars. So one might counsel that κ is a thesis issued from the outside, as it were, and has no bearing on what individuals believe they are or are not perceiving. But it at least follows that where perception involves awareness of what is perceived, universals seem required as part of the story. Otherwise, I could not believe I was perceiving, say, an orange pitcher.

Thus, thinking that involves perception, Lowe's apprehensive thinking, will also involve universals, and, hence, the two formulations of the distinction clash. To this extent also the distinction itself is suspect. This also blocks marking off universals and particulars from perceived particulars by holding that thought of an absent particular is somehow thought of a certain *kind* of object and not a particular object. Presumably, this is to be filled out by saying, rightly, that of various attitudes one can take toward objects, only perception guarantees that there will be an instance of the type in question. But now the thesis of difference in kinds of *thinking* suffers. We can, with at least equal plausibility, insist that perception involves thinking. And although this would make perception, excluding the brute animal sort, dependent on mind, mind itself would remain about universals even in perceptual contexts.

The second misgiving concerns less the distinction between autonomous and apprehensive thinking than the account of apprehensive thinking itself. It must, apparently, cover both thought about perceived particulars and learning that is based on such perception. Unfortunately, this turns out to be an unstable mixture. Begin with Lowe's claim that Aristotle approved of his predecessors' assimilation of thought to sensation for the case of apprehensive thinking. This means that apprehensive thinking fits the standard notion of being affected whereby a thing changes into its contrary by suffering destruction. Although this applies to initial learning and acquisition of knowledge (see *De Anima* II.5), it can hardly cover thought *about* perceived particulars. Here there is no question of a potential, faculty suffering destruction in the course of becoming an actual, faculty because the faculty involved in such thought is already an actual, faculty. There is simply no reason to group the exercise of an already developed faculty with the development of that faculty nor the exercise of certain knowledge with its acquisition. The one is an activity, the other a process.

The above difficulty notwithstanding, we are left with the problem that the relevant notion of learning is identical with or at least involves acquisition of concepts or universals. But we have already seen that the activity of thinking via perception—one part of the mixture that is apprehensive thinking—presupposes that universals are already on the scene. So, again, the mixture itself appears to be an unstable one.

Finally, and perhaps most important, there is neither textual warrant nor doctrinal motivation for giving so-called apprehensive thinking such a central role in *De Anima* III.4. First, the opening sentence announces as III.4's topic that part of the soul that knows and understands. This is clearly Lowe's autonomously thinking mind and the mind Aristotle means to concentrate on. This does not, of course, imply that III.4 makes no distinctions among the mind's operations. Indeed, thinking objects without matter, the business of the mind that knows, appears to be distinguished from thinking objects with matter. The latter makes an appearance in order to remove itself from and so safeguard the vital thesis that the thinking mind is the same as its object. It is, however, not clear that this distinction is equivalent to Lowe's distinction between thought via imagination and thought via perception. For thought of an object with matter does not, at least not obviously, require that the object be perceived. Surely, a geometer can think of his favorite "demonstration triangle" with, as well as apart from, its matter.

Apprehensive thinking understood as concept acquisition casts an even slenderer shadow over III.4's proceedings. Pace Lowe, 429a13's promise to investigate "how thinking comes about" is a call for a theory not of concept acquisition but of the effective cause of thought, for the first will, in any case, not be an account of how *thinking,* [νόησις] comes about but only of how the *capacity₂* for thinking comes about. And although 429b5–9 does allude to the sort of account found in *Analytica Posteriora* II.19, it does so, we have seen, only by way of focusing on the main point, namely, the nature of the activity a fully equipped thinker is capable of. Here reference is best made to *De Anima* II.5, which sorts out the various levels of faculty potentiality and actuality and makes clear that 429b5–9 and *De Anima* III.4 as a whole give pride of place to the actual exercise of the faculty of thought.

To announce, then, that the main point of *De Anima* III.4 is the distinction between autonomous thinking and apprehensive thinking is to provide a misleading characterization of what goes on in III.4. But it is the sort of thing one might expect if *De Anima* III.4 and 5 are not seen as part of a single account of thinking.[10]

10. See also Ingenkamp (1977), who splits the two chapters, finding that the νοῦς of III.4 is an objective object (*objektiver Gegenstand*) of natural science, whereas that of III.5 is an objective object available only to the introspection of inner experience.

THE RETURN OF THE
UNMOVED MOVER

In *Metaphysica* XII.6 and 7 Aristotle tells us that the UMM is (a) a substance that is activity and so (b) without matter, and it (c) exists of necessity, and (d) is the finest of things. We are also told that it is (e) without parts and (f) indivisible. The last pair of properties, along with b, appears to qualify the UMM as a candidate for the Sameness Thesis on the assumption, of course, that the UMM thinks. This assumption underlies *Metaphysica* XII.9's argument that the UMM thinks itself and that its thinking is a thinking of thinking. That argument, it will be recalled (section 5 of chapter 6), made use of the fact that an ordinary thinker's self-thinking is relative to a definite context of thought. It is not Smith but Smith's mind that thinks itself. So intuitively, one might say that ordinary thinkers are aware of their minds not directly but only by thinking of objects. This is, as it were, the closest that Smith can get to his mind. Even thought of the so-called incomposite objects must occur in the context of a combined thought—at least if chapter 4's section 5 is correct.

Aristotle appears, then, to reject the possibility of *direct* mental grasp of the self as a thinking substance. This does not mean, however, that he eschews talk of self-consciousness—so long as it submits to a propositional analysis. *Ethica Nicomachea* XII.9, 1170a29–b1, for example, appears to commit Aristotle to something like this when it asserts that we perceive that [ὅτι] we perceive and think that [ὅτι] we think. Scholarly disputes notwithstanding (see Kahn, 1966, 78), it is at least clear that the passage countenances self-consciousness for persons and that this is to be regarded as an essentially propositional notion. This is precisely the effect of the ὅτι clauses. Thus, to be aware of myself as a perceiving or thinking thing is just to be aware *that* I am perceiving or thinking.

The case of the UMM differs in several interesting ways. First, it is less something that has a mind than something that is a mind. So the Sameness Thesis may fail to apply to the UMM's thinking. Second, because the UMM is a particular, the requirement that thought be about a universal does not apply to it. Third, because it is pure activity, neither does the distinction between productive and active mind apply to the UMM. Still, there may be some temptation to regard the UMM as the limiting case of a productive mind—perhaps asserting that the UMM keeps itself eternally in existence by eternally producing itself as an object of thought. But this is a weak analogy at best.

In any case, the UMM will not think of objects that ordinary thinkers think of. In particular, the UMM does not, as Alexander and certain neo-Alexandrians hold, eternally think the objects that we episodically think. For because it is incomposite, in thinking itself it must think something incomposite. But because the UMM has no potentiality for change, it can think only one such object. Suppose it were to think two incomposites, say O_1 and O_2. Either it thinks these in combination or in separation. If the first, then it cannot be thinking itself. If the second, then the UMM would have to think two objects and so it would not be incomposite after all. Thus, Aristotle announces that its thinking must be nothing other than a thinking of thinking [νόησις νοήσεως].

The question I now want to ask is what sort of thought can we ascribe to the UMM? Well, we know that it thinks itself and that it is, among other things, the best thing, a necessarily existing thing, and a thinking thing. Thus, it might be tempting to characterize the UMM's thinking in the following terms:

A. The UMM thinks that it* is the best thing,
B. The UMM thinks that it* necessarily exists,
C. The UMM thinks that it* thinks.

But this would be mistaken. My use of the star suggests the reason. For it indicates that the pronoun "it" is being used as what Castañeda (1967 and 1968) calls a quasi-indicator. Roughly, the idea is that each of A, B, and C attributes a certain belief to the UMM. But what belief? Not, Castañeda has persuasively argued,

A'. The UMM is the best thing,

to take the first case, but rather

A*. I am the best thing.

The idea is that when "it" or, more typically, "he" or "she" is used as a quasi-indicator, it cannot be replaced by another expression that happens to designate the same thing. Thus, A is not equivalent to

A!. The UMM thinks that the UMM is the best thing

and so A′ is excluded as the proposition that A attributes to the UMM. For the UMM may have forgotten or never known that it is the UMM—perhaps because of a terminal case of cosmic amnesia. Of course, the example detracts from the point. How, some might worry, could the UMM be so fallible? Substituting something like "the author of Waverly" will make the point clearer. The author of Waverly can very well think he is the wealthiest villager around even if he has forgotten that he is the author of Waverly. Or he can believe that the author of Waverly is the wealthiest villager, perhaps because of reading a newspaper story, but yet not believe that he (himself) is this wealthiest of souls (though he in fact is). But what the author of Waverly does believe, to take the first case and to put the words into his mouth, is "I am the wealthiest villager around."

On the standard analysis the first person pronoun "I" purports to pick out a self qua self, as opposed to picking it out qua F, G, or the author of Waverly. And, when sincerely used, it cannot fail to succeed. I may be wrong in almost any belief about myself but I cannot be wrong about the fact that I believe it. Moreover, on Castañeda's account a subject is said to be self-conscious only if capable of precisely this use of the pronoun "I" (or an equivalent device). So self-consciousness is essentially connected with reflexive self-reference. For our purposes the important point is that attribution of a thought to a subject in the manner of A, B, or C, that is, by *propositions* containing quasi-indicators, amounts to attribution of self-consciousness to the subject. So if a subject lacks reflexive self-reference, such attributions will be out of order and so will attributions of self-consciousness.

If I have been right in arguing that the object of the UMM's thinking must be incomposite, then it cannot be expressed propositionally at all. In particular, it cannot be expressed in any first-person propositions. Thus, the UMM cannot think that it* is the finest of things, though surely it is; nor can it think that it* exists, though necessarily it does. And, most pleasing, the UMM cannot think that it* thinks, though it is nothing other than thinking. In short, no propositions like A* can be said to give the content of the UMM's thought. Thus, no more than productive mind can the UMM be a self-conscious thing. It may be for this reason that *Metaphysica* XII.9, 1074b33–35, eschews the use of ὅτι clauses in favor of the difficult phrase "thinking of thinking" [νόησις νοήσεως]. For the latter does not obviously introduce a propositional context.

A final word, perhaps a word of solace, to those who find this result unpleasant. Grant, for the moment, that the highest pleasure is contemplation of theoretical objects. The pleasure of such contemplation lies, I suggest, not in my thinking *that* I am thinking of a given such object but rather simply in my thinking the object. It is what, under more mystical hands, is touted as the pleasure of complete absorption or immersion in the object. By the same token, the UMM enjoys the greatest of pleasure precisely because it is eternally and necessarily immersed in the object of its thought and need not suffer even the slight distraction of thinking *that* it is thinking.

REFERENCES

Ackrill, J. L. 1972–73. "Aristotle's Definitions of *Psyche*." *Proceedings of the Aristotelian Society* 73:119–133.

———. 1965. "Aristotle's Distinction between *Energeia* and *Kinesis*." In *New Essays on Plato and Aristotle*, ed. R. Bambrough. London.

Annas, Julia. 1976. *Aristotle's Metaphysics M and N*. Oxford.

Anscombe, G. E. M. 1961. "Aristotle." In *Three Philosophers*, by Geach and Anscome. Oxford.

Aquinas, Thomas. 1951. *The Commentary on the De Anima of Aristotle*, trans. Foster and Humphries. New Haven.

Armstrong, A. H. 1957. "The Background of the Doctrine That the Intelligibles Are Not Outside the Intellect." *Les Sources de Plotin, Entretiens Hardt* 5:393–425.

Arnim, Hans von. 1905. *Stoicorum Veterum Fragmenta*. Leipzig.

Ax, Wolfram. 1978. "Ψόφος, φωνή und διάλεκτος als Grundbegriffe aristotelischer Sprachreflexion." *Glotta* 56:245–271.

———. 1971. "Zum isolierten ῥῆμα in Aristoteles' *de interpretatione* 16b19–25." *Archiv für Geschichte der Philosophie* 61:271–279.

Baeumker, Clemens. 1877. *Des Aristoteles Lehre von den äussern und innern Sinnesvermögen*. Leipzig.

Balme, D. M. 1984. "The Snub." *Ancient Philosophy* 4:1–8.

Barnes, Jonathan. 1975. *Aristotle's Posterior Analytics*. Oxford.

———. 1971–72. "Aristotle's Concept of Mind." *Proceedings of the Aristotelian Society* 72:101–114.

Beare, J. I. 1908. *Part 1, Parva Naturalia*. Oxford.

———. 1906. *Greek Theories of Elementary Cognition*. Oxford.

Benardete, Seth. 1975. "Aristotle, *De Anima* III.3–5." *Review of Metaphysics* 28:611–622.

Berti, Enrico. 1978. "The Intellection of Indivisibles." In *Aristotle on Mind and the Senses*. Proceedings of the Seventh Symposium Aristotelicum, ed. G. E. R. Lloyd and G. E. L. Owen. Cambridge.

———. 1974. "Encore à propos du prétendu dualisme d'Aristote." *Theta-Pi* 3:98–100.

————. 1973. "Aristote était-il un penseur dualiste?" *Theta-Pi* 2:73–111.

Biehl, W. 1898. *Parva Naturalia*. Leipzig.

Block, Irving. 1961. "Aristotle's Theory of Sense Perception." *Philosophical Quarterly* 11:1–9.

Block, Ned. 1983. "Mental Pictures and Cognitive Science." *Philosophical Review* 92:499–541.

Bokownew, P. 1909. "Der νοῦς παθητικός bei Aristoteles." *Archiv für Geschichte der Philosophie* 22:493–510.

Bolton, Robert. 1978. "Aristotle's Definitions of the Soul: *De Anima* II.1–3." *Phronesis* 23:258–278.

Bonitz, H. 1870. *Index Aristotelicus*. Berlin.

Brentano, Franz. 1911. *Aristoteles Lehre vom Ursprung des menschlichen Geistes*. Leipzig.

————. 1867. *Die Psychologie des Aristoteles*. Mainz. Reprint. Darmstadt, 1967. Also published as *The Psychology of Aristotle,* ed. and trans. Rolf George. Berkeley, 1977.

Bullinger, Anton. 1885. *Zu Aristoteles' Nuslehre*. Munich.

————. 1882. *Aristoteles' Nus-Lehre*. Dillingen.

Bultmann, Rudolph. 1948. "Zur Geschichte der Lichtsymbolik im Altertum." *Philologus* 97:1–36.

Burnyeat, Myles. 1981. "Aristotle on Understanding Knowledge." In *Aristotle on Science: The Posterior Analytics*. Proceedings of the Eighth Symposium Aristotelicum Padova, ed. E. Berti. Padua.

Bywater, I. 1888. "Aristotelia III." *Journal of Philology* 17:53–74.

Cartwright, Nancy, and Mendell, Henry. 1984. "What Makes Physics' Objects Abstract?" In *Science and Reality,* ed. Cushing, Delaney, and Gutting. Notre Dame.

Cashdollar, Stanford. 1973. "Aristotle's Account of Incidental Perception." *Phronesis* 18:156–175.

Cassirer, Heinrich. 1932. *Aristoteles Schrift "Von der Seele."* Tübingen. Reprint. Darmstadt, 1968.

Casteñeda, Hector Neri. 1968. "On the Logic of Attributions of Self-Knowledge to Others." *Journal of Philosophy* 65:439–456.

————. 1967. "Indicators and Quasi-Indicators." *American Philosophical Quarterly* 4:85–100.

Castoriadis, Cornélius. 1978. *La Découverte de l'imagination*. Livre 3. Paris.

Charles, David. 1984. *Aristotle's Philosophy of Action*. Ithaca.

Charlton, William. 1981. "Aristotle's Definition of Soul." *Phronesis* 26:170–186.

Clark, Stephen R. L. 1975. *Aristotle's Man*. Oxford.

Code, Alan. 1984. "The Aporematic Approach to Primary Being in *Metaphysics* Z." In *New Essays on Aristotle, Canadian Journal of Philosophy*. Suppl. vol. 10, ed. F. J. Pelletier and J. King-Farlow, 1–20.

Cooper, John M. 1975. *Reason and Human Good in Aristotle*. Cambridge.

Cope, Edward M. 1877. *The Rhetoric of Aristotle*. Cambridge. Reprint. New York, 1973.

Couloubaritsis, Lambros. 1980. "Le Problème du ΝΟΥΣ ΘΥΡΑΘΕΝ." *ΑΦΙΕ-ΡΩΜΑ ΣΤΟΝ Ε. Π. ΠΑΠΑΝΟΥΤΣΟ*. Athens.

De Groot, Jean Christensen. 1983. "Philoponus on *De Anima* II.5, *Physics* III.3 and the Propagation of Light." *Phronesis* 28:177–196.

Dennett, Daniel C. 1978a. *Brainstorms*. Montgomery.

——. 1978b. "Current Issues in the Philosophy of Mind." *American Philosophical Quarterly* 15:249–261.

Dirlmeier, Franz, trans. 1962. *Aristoteles Eudemische Ethik*. With notes. Berlin.

Driscoll, John. 1987. "The Aporias of *De Anima* Γ 4, 429b22–430a9." Paper presented at a meeting of the Society for Ancient Greek Philosophy, San Francisco, March 27.

Düring, Ingemar. 1966. *Aristoteles: Darstellung und Interpretation seines Denkens*. Heidelberg.

——. 1964. "Aristotle and the Heritage from Plato." *Eranos* 62:84–99.

——. 1961. *Aristotle's Protrepticus: An Attempt at Reconstruction*. Göteborg.

Ebert, Theodor. 1983. "Aristotle on What Is Done in Perceiving." *Zeitschrift für philosophische Forschung* 37:181–198.

Engmann, Joyce. 1976. "Imagination and Truth in Aristotle." *Journal of the History of Philosophy* 14:259–265.

Eriksen, Trond Berg. 1976. *Bios Theoretikos*. Oslo.

Ferejohn, Michael. Forthcoming. "Meno's Paradox and *De Re* Knowledge in Aristotle's Theory of Demonstration." *History of Philosophy Quarterly*.

Field, Hartry. 1978. "Mental Representation." *Erkenntnis* 13:9–61.

Fortenbaugh, William W. 1970. "On the Antecedents of Aristotle's Bipartite Psychology." *Greek, Roman, and Byzantine Studies* 11:233–250.

Freudenthal, J. 1869. "Zur Kritik und Exegese von Aristoteles' *Parva Naturalia*." *Rheinisches Museum für Philologie*, n.s. 24:81–93, 392–419.

——. 1863. *Über den Begriff des Wortes ΦΑΝΤΑΣΙΑ bei Aristoteles*. Göttingen.

Friedlein, Gottfried. 1873. *Procli Diadochi in Primium Euclidis Elementorum Librum Commentarii*. Leipzig.

Furley, David. 1978. "Self-Movers." In *Aristotle on Mind and the Senses*. Proceedings of the Seventh Symposium Aristotelicum, ed. G. E. R. Lloyd and G. E. L. Owen. Cambridge.

——. 1963. Review of *Aristotle: De Anima*, by W. D. Ross. *Classical Review*, n.s. 13:46–49.

Gosling, J. C., and White, C. C. W. 1982. *The Greeks on Pleasure*. Oxford.

Gotthelf, Allan. 1980. Review of *Aristotle's De Motu Animalium*, by Martha Nussbaum. *Journal of Philosophy* 77:365–378.

Gottschalk, H. B. 1981. Review of *Aristotle's De Motu Animalium*, by Martha Nussbaum. *American Journal of Philology* 102:84–94.

Grabmann, Martin. 1963. *Mittelalterliche Deutung und Umbildung der aristotelischen Lehre vom νοῦς ποιητικός, Sitzungsberichte der Bayerischen Akademie der Wissenschaften*. Phil. hist. Abteilung, Heft 4.

Granger, Gilles-Gaston. 1963. *La Théorie aristotélicienne de la science*. Paris.

Guthrie, W. C. K. 1981. *Aristotle: An Encounter: A History of Greek Philosophy.* Vol. 6. Cambridge.

Hamelin, Octave. 1953. *La Théorie de l'intellect d'après Aristote et ses commentateurs.* Paris.

Hamlyn, D. W. 1968. *Aristotle's De Anima, Books II, III.* Oxford.

———. 1959. "Aristotle's Account of Aesthesis in the *De Anima.*" *Classical Quarterly* 9:6–16.

Hardie, R., and Gaye, R., trans. 1930. *Physica.* Vol. 2 of *The Works of Aristotle Translated into English.* Oxford.

Hardie, W. 1976. "Concepts of Consciousness in Aristotle." *Mind* 85:388–411.

———. 1964. "Aristotle's Treatment of the Relation between the Soul and the Body." *Philosophical Quarterly* 14:53–72.

Hare, J. E. 1979. "Aristotle and the Definition of Natural Things." *Phronesis* 24:168–178.

Hartman, Edwin. 1977. *Substance, Body, and Soul.* Princeton.

Heinaman, Robert. 1982. Review of *Form and Universal in Aristotle,* by A. C. Lloyd. *Classical Review* 32:44–48.

Hett, W. S., trans. 1936. *Aristotle: On the Soul, Parva Naturalia, On Breath.* With an introduction. Cambridge and London.

Hicks, R. D. 1907. *Aristotle: De Anima.* Text with English translation and notes. Cambridge. Reprint. Amsterdam, 1965.

Hirst, R. J. 1965. "Form and Sensation." *Aristotelian Society,* Suppl. vol. 39:155–172.

Hyman, Arthur. 1982. "Aristotle's Theory of the Intellect and Its Interpretation by Averroës." In *Studies in Aristotle,* ed. Dominic J. O'Meara. Washington, D.C.

Ingenkamp, Heinz Gerd. 1977. "Introspektion in naturwissenschaftlicher Psychologie." *Rheinisches Museum für Philologie* 120:30–44.

Irwin, T. H. 1986. "Aristotelian Actions." Review of *Aristotle's Philosophy of Action,* by David Charles. *Phronesis* 31:68–89.

Jaeger, Werner. 1923. *Aristoteles: Grundlegung einer Geschichte seiner Entwicklung.* Berlin. Also published as *Aristotle: Fundamentals of the History of His Development,* trans. Richard Robinson. Oxford.

Jannone, A., and Barbotin, E. trans. 1966. *Aristote: De l'Âme.* With notes. Paris.

Joachim, H. H. 1951. *The Nicomachean Ethics: A Commentary.* Oxford.

Kahn, Charles. 1985. "On the Intended Interpretation of Aristotle's *Metaphysics.*" In *Aristoteles Werk und Wirkung.* Vol. 1, ed. J. Wiesner. Berlin.

———. 1981. "The Role of *NOUS* in the Cognition of First Principles in *Posterior Analytics* II.19." In *Aristotle on Science: The Posterior Analytics.* Proceedings of the Eighth Symposium Aristotelicum Padova, ed. E. Berti. Padua.

———. 1966. "Sensation and Consciousness in Aristotle's Psychology." *Archiv für Geschichte der Philosophie* 48:43–81.

Kenny, Anthony. 1967. "The Argument from Illusion in Aristotle's Metaphysics Γ, 1009–10." *Mind* 76:184–97.

———. 1963. *Action, Emotion, and Will.* London.

Kosslyn, S., Pinker, S., Schwartz, S., and Smith, G. 1979. "The Demystification of Mental Imagery." *Behavioral and Brain Sciences* 2:535–581.

Kraut, Richard. 1979. "The Peculiar Function of Human Beings." *Canadian Journal of Philosophy* 9:467–478.

Kufess, Hans. 1911. *Zur Geschichte der Erklärung der aristotelischen Lehre vom sogenannten ΝΟΥΣ ΠΟΙΗΤΙΚΟΣ und ΠΑΘΗΤΙΚΟΣ.* Tübingen.

Labarrière, Jean-Louis. 1984. "Imagination humaine et imagination animale chez Aristote." *Phronesis* 29:17–49.

Lear, Jonathan. 1982. "Aristotle's Philosophy of Mathematics." *Philosophical Review* 91:161–191.

Lloyd, A. C. 1981. *Form and Universal in Aristotle.* Liverpool.

———. 1976. "The Principle That the Cause Is Greater than Its Effect." *Phronesis* 21:146–156.

———. 1969–70. "Non-discursive Thought—an Enigma of Greek Philosophy." *Proceedings of the Aristotelian Society* 70:261–274.

Lloyd, G. E. R. 1968. *Aristotle: The Growth and Structure of His Thought.* Cambridge.

Lowe, Malcolm. 1983. "Aristotle on Kinds of Thinking." *Phronesis* 28:17–30.

———. 1978. "Aristotle's *De Somno* and His Theory of Causes." *Phronesis* 23:279–291.

Lycos, K. 1964. "Aristotle and Plato on 'Appearing.'" *Mind* 73:496–514.

Mansion, A. 1953. "L'Immortalité de l'âme et de l'intellect d'après Aristote." *Revue Philosophique de Louvain* 51:444–472.

Matson, Wallace. 1966. "Why Isn't the Mind-Body Problem Ancient?" In *Mind, Matter, and Method,* ed. Feyerabend and Maxwell. Minneapolis.

Merlan, Philip. 1967. "Greek Philosophy from Plato to Plotinus." Part I of *The Cambridge History of Later Greek and Early Medieval Philosophy,* ed. A. H. Armstrong. Cambridge.

Michaelis, K. G. 1888. *Zur aristotelischen Lehre vom ΝΟΥΣ.* Neu-Strelitz.

———. 1882. *Zu Aristoteles de anima III.3.* Neu-Strelitz.

Moraux, P. 1955. "A propos du *nous thurathen* chez Aristote." In *Autour d'Aristote,* ed. A. Mansion. Louvain.

Moravcsik, Julius. 1975. "Aitia as Generative Factor in Aristotle's Philosophy." *Dialogue* 14:622–638.

Morrow, Glenn R. 1970. *Proclus: A Commentary on the First Book of Euclid's Elements.* Princeton.

Mueller, Ian. 1970. "Aristotle on Geometrical Objects." *Archiv für Geschichte der Philosophie* 52:156–171.

Mugnier, René. 1953. *Aristote: Petits traités d'histoire naturelle.* Paris.

———. 1930. *La Théorie du premier moteur et l'évolution de la pensée aristotélicienne.* Paris.

Müller, Michael. 1900. "Über den Gegensatz von ἐμπειρία und τέχνη im ersten Kapitel der aristotelischen *Metaphysik*." In *Festschrift Johannes Vahlen,* ed. Wilhelm von Hartel. Berlin.

Mure, G. R. G. 1932. *Aristotle.* New York.

Nagel, Thomas. 1974. "What Is It Like to Be a Bat?" *Philosophical Review* 83:435–450.

Norman, Richard. 1969. "Aristotle's Philosopher-God." *Phronesis* 14:63–74.

Nozick, Robert. 1981. *Philosophical Explanations.* Cambridge.

Nussbaum, Martha. 1984. "Aristotelian Dualism: Reply to Howard Robinson." *Oxford Studies in Ancient Philosophy* 2:197–207.

———. 1980. Review of *Substance, Body, and Soul,* by Edwin Hartman. *Journal of Philosophy* 77:355–365.

———. 1978. *Aristotle's De Motu Animalium.* Princeton.

Owens, Joseph. 1979. "The Relation of God to the World in the *Metaphysics.*" In *Etudes sur la Métaphysique d'Aristote.* Actes du VIe Symposium aristotelicum, ed. P. Aubenque. Paris.

———. 1976. "A Note on Aristotle, *De Anima* 3.4, 429b9." *Phoenix* 30:107–118.

Patzig, Günther. 1979. "Logical Aspects of Some Arguments in Aristotle's *Metaphysics.*" In *Etudes sur la Métaphysique d'Aristote.* Actes du VIe Symposium aristotelicum, ed. P. Aubenque. Paris.

Penner, Terry. 1970. "Verbs and the Identity of Actions." In *Ryle: A Collection of Critical Essays,* ed. Oscar P. Wood and George Pitcher. Garden City, N.Y.

Pépin, Jean. 1985. "Σύμβολα, Σημεῖα, Ὁμοιώματα. A propos de *De interpretatione* 1, 16a3–8 et *Politique* VIII 5, 1340a6–39." In *Aristoteles Werk und Wirkung.* Vol. 1, ed. J. Wiesner. Berlin, 22–44.

Philip, J. A. 1962. Review of *Aristotle: De Anima,* ed. W. D. Ross. *Phoenix* 16:195–201.

Philippe, M. D. 1971. "Φαντασία in the Philosophy of Aristotle." *Thomist* 35:1–42.

Philoponus, J. 1897. *In Aristotelis de Anima Libros Commentaria,* ed. M. Hayduck. Berlin.

———. 1887. *In Aristotelis Physicorum Libros Tres Priores Commentaria,* ed. H. Vitelli. Berlin.

Putnam, Hilary. 1979. "Philosophy and Our Mental Life." In *Mind, Language and Reality.* Cambridge.

Randall, John Herman. 1960. *Aristotle.* New York.

Rees, D. A. 1971. "Aristotle's Treatment of φαντασία." In *Essays in Ancient Greek Philosophy,* ed. J. Anton and G. Kustas. Albany.

Renehan, R. 1980. "On the Greek Origins of the Concepts of Incorporeality and Immateriality." *Greek, Roman, and Byzantine Studies* 21:105–138.

Rist, John. 1966. "Notes on Aristotle *De Anima* 3, 5." *Classical Philology* 61:8–20.

Robinson, H. 1983. "Aristotelian Dualism." *Oxford Studies in Ancient Philosophy* 1:123–144.

———. 1978. "Mind and Body in Aristotle." *Classical Quarterly* 28:105–124.

Rodier, G. 1900. *Traité de l'âme.* 2 vols. Paris.

Rolfes, E. 1901. *Des Aristoteles Schrift über die Seele.* Bonn.

Rorty, Richard. 1979. *Philosophy and the Mirror of Nature.* Princeton.

———. 1965. "Mind-Body Identity, Privacy and Categories." *Review of Metaphysics* 19:24–54.

Ross, G. T. R. 1906. *Aristotle: De Sensu and De Memoria*. Cambridge. Reprint. New York, 1973.

Ross, W. D. 1961. *Aristotle: De Anima*. Oxford.

———. 1955. *Aristotle: Parva Naturalia*. Oxford.

———. 1949. *Aristotle's Prior and Posterior Analytics*. Oxford.

———. 1936. *Aristotle's Physics*. Oxford.

———. 1924. *Aristotle's Metaphysics*. 2 vols. Oxford.

———. 1923. *Aristotle*. London.

Sandbach, F. H. 1954. "A Transposition in Aristotle, Metaphysics Λ c. 9 1074b." *Mnemosyne* 7:39–43.

Schneider, Gustav. 1867. "Zu Aristoteles *de anima*." *Zeitschrift für das Gymnasialwesen* 2. Berlin.

———. 1866. "Über einige Stellen aus Aristoteles *de anima* III.3." *Rheinisches Museum für Philologie* 21:444–454.

Schofield, M. 1978. "Aristotle on the Imagination." In *Aristotle on Mind and the Senses*. Proceedings of the Seventh Symposium Aristotelicum, ed. G. E. R. Lloyd and G. E. L. Owen. Cambridge.

Sellars, Wilfrid. 1949. "Aristotelian Philosophies of Mind." In *Philosophy for the Future,* ed. Sellars, McGill, and Farber. New York.

Simplicius. 1882a. *In Aristotelis Physicorum Libros Quattuor Priores Commentaria*, ed. H. Diels. Berlin.

———. 1882b. *In Libros Aristotelis De Anima Commentaria*, ed. M. Hayduck. Berlin.

Siwek, Paul. 1965a. *Aristotelis De Anima graece et latine*. Rome.

———. 1965b. *Le De Anima d'Aristote dans les manuscrits grecs*. Rome.

———. 1963. *Aristotelis, Parva Naturalia graece et latine*. Rome.

———. 1961. *Les Manuscrits grecs des Parva Naturalia d'Aristote*. Rome.

Skemp, J. B. 1979. "The Activity of Immobility." In *Etudes sur la Métaphysique d'Aristote*. Actes du VIᵉ Symposium aristotelicum, ed. P. Aubenque. Paris.

Slakey, Thomas. 1961. "Aristotle on Sense Perception." *Philosophical Review* 70:470–484.

Smyth, H. W. 1920. *Greek Grammar*. Cambridge, Mass.

Solmsen, Friedrich. 1961. "αἴσθησις in Aristotelian and Epicurean Thought." *Mededelinger der Koninklijke Nederlandse Akademie van Wetenschappen*, AFD Letterkunde XXIV, 241–262.

———. 1957. "The Vital Heat, the Inborn Pneuma, and the Aether." *Journal of Hellenic Studies* 77:117–123.

———. 1955. "Antecedents of Aristotle's Psychology and Scale of Beings." *American Journal of Philology* 76:148–164.

Sorabji, Richard. 1982. "Myths about Non-propositional Thought." In *Language and Logos: Studies in Ancient Greek Philosophy Presented to G. E. L. Owen,* ed. M. Schofield and M. Nussbaum. Cambridge.

———. 1974. "Body and Soul in Aristotle." *Philosophy* 49:63–89.

———. 1972. *Aristotle on Memory*. Providence.

Steinthal, H. 1890. *Geschichte der Sprachwissenschaft bei den Griechen und Römern*. 2 vols. Berlin.

Theiler, Willy. 1966. *Aristoteles: Über die Seele*. Berlin.

Tiles, J. E. 1983. "Why the Triangle Has Two Right Angles Kath' Hauto." *Phronesis* 28:1–16.

Todd, Robert. 1981. "Themistius and the Traditional Interpretation of Aristotle's Theory of *PHANTASIA*." *Acta Classica* 24:49–59.

———. 1980. Review of *Aristotle's De Motu Animalium*, by Martha Nussbaum. *Phoenix* 34:352–355.

Torstrik, Adolfus. 1862. *Aristotelis De Anima Libri III*. Berlin. Reprint. Hildesheim, 1970.

Tracy, Theodore. 1982. "The Soul/Boatman Analogy in Aristotle's *De Anima*." *Classical Philology* 77:97–112.

Trendelenburg, F. A. 1877. *Aristotelis De Anima Libri Tres*. Berlin. Reprint, Graz, 1957.

Tricot, J. 1951. *Parva Naturalia*. Paris.

———. 1947. *Aristote: De L'âme*. Paris.

Verdenius, W. J. 1971. "Human Reason and God in the *Eudemian Ethics*." In *Untersuchungen zur Eudemischen Ethik*. Akten des 5. Symposium Aristotelicum, ed. P. Moraux and D. Harfinger. Berlin.

de Vogel, C. J. 1973. "Quelques Problèmes à propos de l'exposé de M. Berti." *Theta-Pi* 2:111–113.

Wallace, Edwin. 1882. *Aristotle's Psychology*. Cambridge.

Warnock, Mary. 1976. *Imagination*. Berkeley.

Waterlow, Sara. 1982. *Nature, Change, and Agency*. Oxford.

Watson, G. 1982. "ΦΑΝΤΑΣΙΑ in Aristotle. *De Anima* 3.3." *Classical Quarterly* 32:100–113.

———. 1966. *The Stoic Theory of Knowledge*. Belfast.

Webb, Philip. 1982. "Bodily Structure and Psychic Faculties in Aristotle's Theory of Perception." *Hermes* 110:25–50.

Wedin, Michael V. 1988. "Aristotle on the Mechanics of Thought." *Society for Ancient Greek Philosophy*. Portland, Oreg.

———. 1986. "Tracking Aristotle's ΝΟΥΣ." In *Human Nature and Natural Knowledge: Essays Presented to Marjorie Grene on the Occasion of Her Seventy-Fifth Birthday*, ed. A. Donagan, A. N. Perovich, and M. V. Wedin. Dordrecht.

———. 1984. "Singular Statements and Essentialism in Aristotle." In *New Essays on Aristotle, Canadian Journal of Philosophy*. Supp. vol. 10, ed. F. J. Pelletier and J. King-Farlow.

———. 1978. "Aristotle on the Existential Import of Singular Sentences." *Phronesis* 23:179–196.

———. 1973. "A Remark on *Per Se* Accidents and Properties." *Archiv für Geschichte der Philosophie* 55:30–35.

Whittaker, John. *God Time Being, Two Studies in the Transcendental Tradition in Greek Philosophy*. *Symbolae Osloenses*. Supp. vol. 23. Oslo.

Wieland, Wolfgang. 1967. *Die aristotelische Physik*. Göttingen.

Wiesner. Jürgen. 1985. "Gedächtnis und Denkobjekte—Beobachtungen zu *Mem*. 1, 449b30–450a14." In *Aristoteles Werk und Wirkung*. Vol. 1, ed. J. Wiesner. Berlin.

Wijsenbeek-Wijler, Henriette. 1976. *Aristotle's Concept of Soul, Sleep, and Dreams*. Amsterdam.

Wilkes, Kathleen. 1978. *Physicalism*. London.

Williams, C. J. F. 1965. "Form and Sensation." *Aristotelian Society*. Supp. vol. 39:139–154.

Wittgenstein, Ludwig. 1961. *Tractatus Logico-Philosophicus*. Trans. Pears and McGuinness. London.

Wolfson, H. A. 1947. "The Knowability and Describability of God in Plato and Aristotle." *Harvard Studies in Classical Philology* 56–57:233–249.

Woodger, J. H. 1952. *Biology and Language*. Cambridge.

Woods, M. J. 1982. *Aristotle's Eudemian Ethics, Books I, II, and VII*. Oxford.

GENERAL INDEX

Action: purposive requires image, 41, 112; agent reflexively self-aware, 172; elements of, 216

Activity [ἐνέργεια]: distinguished from movement, 32; light activity of the transparent, 178; productive mind essentially this, 183

Actualization [ἐντελέχεια]: kinds distinguished, 14–15; faculties as (first) actualizations of initial capacities, 15; exercise of faculty a second actualization, 15–17

Affection [πάθος]: peculiar to soul, 7, 247; common to body and soul, 7; considered dialectically, 7; not reducible to physical processes, 7–9; mental-physical dichotomy not appropriate, 39n; accompanied by pleasure or pain, 112; similar to object, 150, 151; not reducible to functional state, 251–52. See also Image; Perceptual state; Thought

Albinus, 228n

Alexander, 187n, 241n; productive mind as god, 225, 228n

Anachronism, ix, 18–19, 221

Anaxagoras, 196, 260

Annas, Julia, on mathematical objects, 4n, 5n

Anscombe, G. E. M., 240

Aquinas, Thomas: on canonical text, 25, 29n; on productive mind, 176n, 192

Armstrong, A. H., 228n

Articulate sound [φωνή]: link with intelligence, 147; subject to molding, 153–55; some beasts have it, 153. See Semantical model

Assertion: Hicks's simple naming variety, 110–11; likened to pursuit, 111; different from imagination, 122; combines thoughts, 124

Averroës, 173n

Avicenna, 173n

Ax, Wolfram, 151n; on avian speech, 153

Barbotin, E., 144n

Barnes, Jonathan, 86n, 206n, 212; on induction, 156; receptive mind involved in concept acquisition, 176

Beare, J. I., 23n, 61n, 73, 77n; on how images represent, 139–40; on object of thought, 139

INDEX OF PASSAGES